Shakespeare, Italy, and intertextuality

Manchester University Press

Shakespeare, Italy, and intertextuality

edited by
MICHELE MARRAPODI

Manchester University Press
Manchester and New York
distributed exclusively in the USA by Palgrave

Copyright © Manchester University Press 2004

While copyright in the volume as a whole is vested in Manchester University Press, copyright in individual chapters belongs to their respective authors, and no chapter may be reproduced wholly or in part without the express permission in writing of both author and publisher.

Published by Manchester University Press
Oxford Road, Manchester M13 9NR, UK
and Room 400, 175 Fifth Avenue, New York, NY 10010, USA
www.manchesteruniversitypress.co.uk

Distributed in the United States exclusively by
Palgrave Macmillan, 175 Fifth Avenue,
New York, NY 10010, USA

Distributed in Canada exclusively by
UBC Press, University of British Columbia, 2029 West Mall,
Vancouver, BC, Canada V6T 1Z2

British Library Cataloguing-in-Publication Data is available

Library of Congress Cataloging-in-Publication Data is available

ISBN 978 0 7190 6667 2 paperback

First published by Manchester University Press in hardback 2004

This paperback edition first published 2014

The publisher has no responsibility for the persistence or accuracy of URLs for any external or third-party internet websites referred to in this book, and does not guarantee that any content on such websites is, or will remain, accurate or appropriate.

Printed by Lightning Source

Contents

List of illustrations		*page* vii
Notes on contributors		ix
Acknowledgements		x

1 Introduction: intertextualizing Shakespeare's text   1
Michele Marrapodi

Part I Theory and practice

2 Seven types of intertextuality   13
Robert S. Miola

3 English bodies in Italian habits   26
Keir Elam

4 Shakespeare and Plutarch: intertextuality in action   45
Alessandro Serpieri

5 'Voilà la belle mort': the crisis of the aristocracy in *Troilus and Cressida*   59
Mario Domenichelli

Part II Culture and tradition

6 Beyond the Reformation: Italian intertexts of the ransom plot in *Measure for Measure*   73
Michele Marrapodi

7 'The story is extant, and writ in very choice Italian': Shakespeare's dramatizations of Cinthio   91
Jason Lawrence

8 Intertextual transformations: the *novella* as mediator between Italian and English Renaissance drama   107
Charlotte Pressler

9 Shakespeare's Italian intertexts: *The Taming of the/a Shrew* 118
Fernando Cioni

Part III Text and ideology

10 'What news on the Rialto': luxury, sodomy, and miscegenation in *The Merchant of Venice* 131
Anthony G. Barthelemy

11 *Othello* italicized: xenophobia and the erosion of tragedy 145
Pamela Allen Brown

12 The politics of plot: *Measure for Measure* and the Italianate disguised duke play 158
Michael J. Redmond

13 'The three-fold world divided': *Julius Caesar* in the light of *Theologia Platonica* 176
Claudia Corti

Part IV Stage and spectacle

14 Cleopatra's barge and Antony's body: Italian sources and English theatre 197
J. R. Mulryne

15 Intertextuality and the chess motif: Shakespeare, Middleton, Greenaway 216
Jeffrey A. Netto

16 'Rare Italian master(s)': Roman art in *Romeo and Juliet*, *Antony and Cleopatra*, and *The Winter's Tale* 227
François Laroque

17 Shakespeare in the *bottega:* art works, apocrypha, and the stage 239
Giorgio Melchiori

18 Afterword: Italy as intertext 253
Keir Elam

Select bibliography of recent publications 259
Index 269

List of illustrations

3.1 The naked Englishman. (By courtesy of the British Library)	page 28
3.2 From *Vincentio Saviolo his Practise*. (By courtesy of the British Library)	40
17.1 *Cristo Redentore*, in the Church of San Vincenzo Martire at Bassano Romano, Viterbo	245
17.2 *Cristo Risorto*, by Michelangelo Buonarroti in the Church of Santa Maria sopra Minerva, Rome	246
17.3 Detail of the *Cristo Redentore* (Foto Vasari)	248
17.4 The third of the three pages known as Addition in Hand D (probably Shakespeare's) in the manuscript *Booke of Sir Thomas Moore*. (By courtesy of the British Library)	249
17.5 Detail of the left hand of the *Cristo Redentore*. (Foto Vasari)	250
17.6 A hand drawing a hand, attributed to Michelangelo Buonarroti. (Foto Vasari; by courtesy of Silvia Danesi Squarzina)	250

Notes on contributors

Anthony G. Barthelemy is Associate Professor of English Literature at the University of Miami. He is the author of *Black Face Maligned Face* (1987) and other essays on Renaissance drama. He has edited a collection of critical essays on *Othello* (1994).

Pamela Allen Brown is Assistant Professor at University of Connecticut, Stamford. She has published articles on Shakespeare's Venetian plays, on *The Taming of the Shrew*, and Ben Jonson. Her book *Better a Shrew than a Sheep: Women, Drama, and the Culture of Jest in Early Modern England* is forthcoming from Cornell University Press.

Fernando Cioni is a research scholar at the University of Florence. He has written several studies on Shakespeare and a book on contemporary English dramatists. He is editor of the New Variorum edition of *The Taming of the Shrew*.

Claudia Corti is Professor of English at the University of Florence. She is Co-Editor of *Rivista di Letterature Moderne e Comparate* and of the series 'Studi di Letteraure moderne e comparate'. Her most recent books include *Macbeth: la parola e l'immagine* (1983), *Shakespeare illustrato* (1996), and *Silenos: Erasmus in Elizabethan Literature* (1988). She has edited *I contesti culturali della letteratura inglese: il Rinascimento* (1994).

Mario Domenichelli is Professor of English at the University of Florence. He is the author of *Il limite dell'ombra* (1994) and other books on Shakespeare, Renaissance drama, and modern English literature.

Keir Elam is Professor of English Drama at the University of Bologna. His books include *The Semiotics of Theatre and Drama* (1980) and *Shakespeare's Universe of Discourse* (1984). His edited volumes include *Shakespeare's Today* (1984) and *La grande festa del linguaggio* (1986). He is currently completing a volume on the languages of contemporary drama and is editing *Twelfth Night* for Arden 3.

François Laroque is Professor of English at the Sorbonne Nouvelle-Paris III. He is editor of *Cahiers Elisabéthains*. He has written extensively on Shakespeare and early modern drama. His works include *Shakespeare's Festive World* (1991), a number of collections of essays, and editions of Renaissance plays.

Jason Lawrence is a Lecturer in English at the University of Hull. He completed his PhD at Oxford. He has published on Samuel Daniel, Italian lyric drama, and Shakespeare. He is currently working on a book about Tasso's affinities in European literature, art, and opera.

Notes on contributors

Michele Marrapodi is Professor of English Literature at the University of Palermo. He is Associate Editor of *Cahiers Elisabéthains*, Co-Editor of *Shakespeare Yearbook*, Associate Editor of *Seventeenth-Century News*, and Italian Correspondent of *Shakespeare Quarterly*. His books include *'The Great Image'* (1984), *La Sicilia nella drammaturgia giacomiana e carolina* (1989), and *L'odissea di Pericles* (1999). His edited volumes include *Shakespeare's Italy* (1993), *The Italian World of English Renaissance Drama* (1998), *Italian Studies in Shakespeare and His Contemporaries* (1999), and *Shakespeare and Intertextuality* (2000).

Giorgio Melchiori, CBE, FBA, is Professor Emeritus of English, University 'Rome Three'. He is Life-Trustee Shakespeare Birthplace Trust, and Honorary Trustee International James Joyce Foundation. He has edited many plays by Shakespeare and his fellow dramatists and published books on Shakespeare, Yeats, and Joyce. His most recent works include *Shakespeare's Garter Plays* (1994), *Shakespeare: Genesi e struttura delle opere* (1994), the New Cambridge edition of *Edward III*, and *The Merry Wives of Windsor* for Arden 3.

Robert S. Miola is Gerard Manley Hopkins Professor of English at Loyola College, Baltimore. His books include *Shakespeare's Rome* (1983), *Shakespeare and Classical Tragedy* (1992), *Shakespeare and Classical Comedy* (1994), *Shakespeare's Reading* (2000). He has edited *Every Man in His Humour* (2000) and a collection of critical essays on *The Comedy of Errors* (1997).

J. R. Mulryne is Professor of English at the University of Warwick. He has edited a number of Renaissance plays and published several works on Shakespeare and Elizabethan drama. His edited volumes include, among many others, *War, Literature and the Arts in Sixteenth-Century Europe* (1989), *Theatre of the English and Italian Renaissance* (1991), *Theatre and Government under the Early Stuarts* (1993), and *Making Space for Theatre* (1995)

Jeffrey A. Netto teaches English at Modesto College, California. He has written on Shakespeare, Renaissance drama, and eighteenth- and nineteenth-century English literature.

Charlotte Pressler is a Lecturer at South Florida Community College. She recently received her PhD in Renaissance Literature from the University of Buffalo and is revising her doctorial dissertation for publication.

Michael J. Redmond is a Lecturer in English at the University of Palermo and a former Commonwealth Scholar at the University of Sussex, England. He has published several articles on Shakespeare and Renaissance drama. He is completing a book on the political functions of Italian culture in the drama of Shakespeare and his contemporaries.

Alessandro Serpieri is Professor of English Literature at the University of Florence. He has written extensively on Shakespeare, Romantic and modern poetry, and contemporary drama. His books include *John Webster* (1966), *T. S. Eliot: Le strutture profonde* (1973), *I sonetti dell'immortalità* (1975), *Othello: l'eros negato* (1978), and *Retorica e immaginario* (1986). He has edited *Shakespeare's Sonnets* (1991), *The Texts of Hamlet* (1997), and *Shakespeare's Late Plays* (2001).

Acknowledgements

A rather different version of this volume appeared in Italy under the title *Shakespeare and Intertextuality: The Transition of Cultures between Italy and England in the Early Modern Period*, Rome, Bulzoni Editore, 2000. The present collection differs in many respects in both content and focus. As regards content, the volume provides new contributions, replacing some chapters and adding new ones by other scholars; as to focus, the chapters retained have been totally revised and updated.

In reshaping this book, the editor gratefully acknowledges his indebtedness to a number of scholars and friends who have been generous with patience, expertise, and advice. Among many others, I would like to mention Giorgio Melchiori, Alessandro Serpieri, Keir Elam, Robert S. Miola, Peter Dawson, and especially Michael J. Redmond. Matthew Frost, Head of Editorial at Manchester University Press, was the real mentor of the project, having encouraged the idea of the volume from the outset.

As ever, my fullest debt is to my wife Maria, and especially to my daughters Lavinia and Virginia, for having constantly been a real source of faith, hope, and encouragement.

Formal thanks are due to the various organisations and institutions which granted permission for the reproduction of the drawings and pictures.

Michele Marrapodi
Palermo

1

Introduction: intertextualizing Shakespeare's text

MICHELE MARRAPODI

Recent contributions to the understanding of the narrative and dramatic construction of the plays of Shakespeare and his fellow dramatists have profited from a comparative approach which has examined the theatrical ancestry of the plays outside positivistic source studies and determined their most direct literary and non-literary legacies.[1] The structure and functionality of Shakespeare's dramaturgy have proved to be embedded in a manifold corpus of intertexts stretching from classical Greek and Latin New Comedy to early modern culture, via the mediation of novelistic literature, Italian cinquecento theatre, educational tracts, and Renaissance dramatic theory.

One reason for this successful flourishing of intertextual analysis of early modern English drama is, of course, the Renaissance practice of poetic imitation, which established as a common rule the principle of creative intertextuality introduced by the early humanists. *Imitatio* thus became the aesthetic principle of literary production. Among the most influential theorists, Francesco Robortello, Lodovico Castelvetro, and Angelo Piccolomini associated it, in varying degrees, with Aristotle's precept of *emulatio*. Ariosto referred to it, more or less explicitly, in his prologues to *Cassaria* (1508), *Suppositi* (1509), and *La Lena* (1529).[2] Giraldi Cinthio's *Discorso Intorno al Comporre delle Commedie e delle Tragedie* (1543) related *imitatio* to the didactic concept of moral catharsis.[3] In his *Compendio della Poesia Tragicomica* (1601), Giambattista Guarini takes it as the basis of human experience and a necessary component of every art. In Guarini's own words, 'imitation is almost a production of something new', the natural aim of poetry itself, and therefore apt to justify the birth of tragicomedy as a mixed dramatic genre, harmoniously representing the variety of life for the benefit of the spectators.[4]

As a consequence, the classical tradition was ransacked in the theatre through a variety of forms and with different perspectives by way of the related concept of *contaminatio*, involving the refashioning of plots and motifs taken from both Greek and Latin New Comedy, as well as the mediation of narrative sources, such as the tales of Boccaccio and other novelistic literature. Hence, as customarily mentioned in the prologues to cinquecento comedy, several playwrights modelled their plays' dialogues and narrative construction on a well-balanced combination of diverse theatrical antecedents or theatregrams, usually taken from Plautus and Terence, and sometimes seasoned with Boccaccian narremes. Alongside this reinvention of new plot material, the principle of *contaminatio* was supplemented by that of *complicatio*, the use of multiple subplots, characters, and situations. As I have mentioned elsewhere, this was the case with Ariosto's comedic experiments in the rehandling of *commedia nova* and of Giraldi Cinthio's corresponding theory of *nova tragedia*.[5]

In order to disentangle the most consistent line of textual transmission among such a convoluted network of possible echoes and derivations, the dynamic of intertextuality has emphasised the distinction between two main areas of retrievable sources, influences, and repetitions: the category of textual heritage, a dissemination of *topoi*, motifs, and theatregrams, even when unconsciously encoded in the diachronic process of a long-established written tradition; and the migration of ideas, a circulation of non-literary discourses and cultural transactions embedded in the synchronic process of cultural exchange between countries belonging to the same culture, episteme, or epoch.[6] This second category of socio-cultural-anthropological transmission, broadly defined in such specific terms as 'dialogism', 'polyphony', and 'interdiscursivity' by Mikhail Bakhtin, Alessandro Serpieri, and Cesare Segre, respectively, as well as, more recently, in such concepts as 'circulation of social energy' and 'paralogue' by Stephen Greenblatt and Robert S. Miola, has opened up a new horizon of intertextual research where linguistic and non-linguistic cultural forces are absorbed and reproduced through the explicit mediation of a written text.[7]

Drawing from the rich encounter of different perspectives arising from the intense critical debate of recent years, this volume seeks to provide a general survey of current approaches to intertextual discourse in Shakespeare's drama. The chapters are grouped into four parts, corresponding to the four main critical contributions to the complex subject of Shakespearean intertextuality: 'Theory and Practice', 'Culture and Tradition', 'Text and Ideology', and 'Stage and Spectacle'. Without any claim to providing an exhaustive classification, this introduction summarizes the themes covered in each part, while Keir Elam's Afterword on 'Italy as Intertext' rounds off the present collection and orients its aims and contents towards lines of future developments. In taking further productive fields of research and concern succinctly into consideration, Elam indicates the still fruitful, as yet largely unexplored, ideological potential inherent in the idea of Italy as a treasure trove of intertextual, and indeed interdiscursive, confrontation between texts and cultures.

Theory and practice

As this volume shows, contemporary intertextual studies of Shakespeare are taking account of a wider range of literary and cultural fields than ever before, moving beyond the traditional investigation of direct sources. In considering the vast range of influences that may have affected the London stage, we must have a clear idea of the possible relations between texts, authors, and conventions at the time Shakespeare was writing. Robert S. Miola's contribution, outlining the types of intertextual transactions in early modern literature, offers the basis for a theoretical model of the processes of mediation through which ideas, styles, themes, and interpretive strategies passed across national divides. He defines three broad categories of intertextual circulation: the direct process of authorial reading, wider literary traditions, and cultural modes of reading and interpretation. While direct analogues are marked by clear verbal echoes, as with the borrowing of lines from *The Spanish Tragedy* during the period, recent scholars are increasingly addressing the more subtle dispersal of socio-literary discourses and audience expectations, 'paralogues', that highlight intellectual and political meanings in the period as a whole. However, in codifying the abundance of possible textual interfaces, Miola is careful to warn against the perils of studies that offer anecdotes in place of rigorous and extensive research.

One of the commonest themes of early modern accounts of Anglo-Italian relations was the figure of the English ape, the Englishman who adopts the clothing and habits of foreign nations without regard to his own. By focusing on Shakespearean representations of English culture, where foreign characters discuss England in plays set abroad, Keir Elam looks at how bodily and behavioural codes were transmitted through texts. The intertextuality of the body and, as Elam terms it, the 'look-at-them-looking-at-us' trope come to the fore in the striking scene in *The Merchant of Venice* where Portia surveys the manners and physical attributes of her international cast of suitors. The satirical ethnography, picking up on established stereotypes of the nations involved, culminates in the portrait of the Englishman who buys his clothes and behaviour from Europeans. The passage symptomizes English fears about the absence of domestic cultural self-confidence. By discussing in detail the circulation of the Italian fashion of duelling, Elam suggests that fear of imitation informs Shakespeare's treatment of the body in the duelling episodes in *Hamlet* and *Twelfth Night*.

The way in which Shakespeare transformed and adapted his sources to suit the political agenda of his drama is still an object of dispute and an area of fruitful investigation. Alessandro Serpieri offers the results of his analysis and those of a research group that he directed to study the dramatist's process of transcodification from Plutarch's *Lives* to the Roman plays. To explain the dramatist's shift from his established sources, this body of work has been attentively scrutinized and classified according to a typology of different procedures, each indicating a particular strategy of attenuating and amplifying effects, involving reduction and amplification of focus, rhetoric, style, and discourse. Each of these elements is capable of interfering considerably with ideology, plot construction, and individual characterization, producing significant changes from the original stories.

The practice of revision, adapting previous works, was the commonest form of intertextuality used by Shakespeare. In *Troilus and Cressida*, Mario Domenichelli asserts that the crisis of the aristocracy at the end of the sixteenth century made untenable the chivalric values epitomized by the grief that Achilles feels for his slain opponent in the *Iliad*. In Shakespeare's version, the powerful myth of a 'handsome death' is radically challenged, replaced by scenes emphasizing the dishonourable tactics of Achilles. For although it was a powerful tenet of chivalry, used in recording the last moments of Renaissance men such as Sir Philip Sidney, the play concentrates on the violence, dishonour, and deceit of war. Domenichelli suggests that for Shakespeare the *topos* of a *bella morte* was untenable in the face of the upheavals brought about by a changing literary and political scene.

Culture and tradition

Despite the long-established concern with direct sources, focusing on clear verbal and thematic relations between specific texts, the nature of Shakespeare's use of Italian works continues to be a source of debate. While it is accepted that plays such as *Measure for Measure*, *Othello*, and *The Taming of the Shrew* are informed by Italian analogues, the processes and implications of mediation have been less clear. The influence of Italian literature and drama throughout Europe ensured that early modern English writers and audiences could compare the variations on these sources produced in Germany and France. The main plot of *Measure for Measure*, as Michele Marrapodi suggests, needs to be seen in terms of the dispersal of Italian texts and ideas in the period. The monstrous ransom story, recounting the sexual exploitation of a female kinswoman of a captive facing death by a dishonest judge, circulated in *novelle*, religious tracts, comedies, and tragedies throughout the continent. As taken up by Martin Luther, who recounts the execution of the judge by a wise ruler, the story celebrates retributive punishment and the power of secular law. Later versions mitigated the tale of exploitation by furnishing a happy ending. Marrapodi places Shakespeare's contribution to this discourse within a trajectory of cultural transactions. By following the variants established in Giraldi Cinthio's Counter-Reformation versions and reducing the responsibility of the crime drawing from Boccaccio, Shakespeare was able to provide a humanist treatment of weakness and forgiveness.

With the number of different versions of the same story circulating in Europe, critics need to entertain the possibility that Shakespeare may have used simultaneously more than one source, in more than one language. Jason Lawrence's account of the verbal parallels between *Othello* and *Orlando Furioso*, consolidating the threads of earlier source studies, suggests that the dramatist may have used Robert Greene's adaptation of Ariosto as a supplement to his consideration of Italian originals. For although the question of Shakespeare's knowledge of Italian is fundamental to intertextual study, it does not follow that he had to have a perfect facility in the language. He may have thus read an Italian text alongside more accessible versions in his native language. Lawrence posits a network of relations between Shakespeare, Ariosto, and the variations on Ariosto in the works of Greene and Giraldi Cinthio, tracing how *Othello* incorporates elements that are unique to each of the sources.

With the limited contacts between the Italian and English theatres during the early modern period, a function of the obstacle represented by the barrier of language, the process of the intertextual exchanges between specific English and Italian dramatic works is especially complex. With the radical obstacles to direct borrowing created by language, access, and diverse theatrical practices, as Charlotte Pressler proposes, the *novella* served as an essential mediator, transforming obscure dramatic texts into elements of large collections that provided a fund of good stories for English playwrights. Through a reading of the parallel sources of *Twelfth Night*, considering English and Italian prose versions of the learned comedy *Gl'Ingannati*, she measures the transactions through which the Italian *commedia erudita* arrived in early modern England. With the circular negotiations between theatre and prose, across cultural and linguistic boundaries, the fixed rhetorical structures of Italian comedy are supplanted by the unlocalised perspectives of Shakespeare's theatre.

The theatrical practices of the early modern stage were marked by the recycling of established narratives, genres, and dramatic forms. Each Shakespearean text can be sited within a matrix of intertexts, revealing traces of authorial selection, transformation, and transcodification of previous material. Fernando Cioni shows that, alongside the obvious relationship with the anonymous 1594 quarto *The Taming of a Shrew*, the dreaming man induction of *The Taming of the Shrew* involves a complex amalgam of prose sources, dramatic motifs, and the adaptation of classical comedy on the Italian Renaissance stage. The play reveals evidence, he claims, of a double process of borrowing, shedding light on the content of the jest played on the drunken man and its incorporation within the theatrical convention of the induction. In so far as the text is a product of a series of quotations and revisions, however, the pleasure of the audience comes from its familiarity or, for the cognoscenti, from its opportunity for intertextual interpretation.

Text and ideology

While traditional studies of references to Italy in the early modern theatre have concentrated on questions of accuracy, with scholars evaluating Shakespeare's knowledge of its geography and society, recent work has paid more attention to the manner in which cautionary Italian stereotypes formed an essential part of English political discourses. For although English dramatists and translators eagerly quoted from the country's literary sources, as Michael J. Redmond has noted in an important recent study, their attitude towards these sources continually 'marks the tension between the reverence for Italian culture fostered by an educational regime based on Latin and the demonization of contemporary Italian religious and social practices'.[8] The contributions in this section address the negative vision of Italy in Shakespeare, showing how its would-be vices served as a pretext for discussing complex domestic issues.

The sexual and political vision that Shakespeare provides of Venice continues to challenge intertextual scholars. In *The Merchant of Venice*, Anthony Barthelemy argues, the ethnocentric intolerance of the English myth of the city informs the homosocial elements of the treatment of the story of the merchant and his bachelor friend. From the influential warnings of Roger Ascham onwards, sexual problems were central to English accounts of Venetian *mores*. By locating his treatment of Antonio's forbidden desire outside England, taking advantage of these established negative images, the playwright contains the dangerous implications of his theme. In so far as Antonio's fear of discovery enables Bassanio to pursue a mercenary marriage and a financially successful career in shipping, Barthelemy notes that Shakespeare's dislocation of sexual themes is reflected in the very content of the plot.

In both *The Merchant of Venice* and *Othello*, Shakespeare employs Venice as a site of racial conflict. For Pamela Allen Brown, the extent to which the play's vision of the city reveals traces of early modern racism precludes definition of it as tragedy. She claims that, through the use of dramatic forms drawn from the *commedia dell'arte*, *Othello* caters to contemporary domestic prejudice, transforming tragedy into satire with the choice of what would have been seen as a farcical parody of a tragic hero. In the context of anti-foreigner riots and the expulsion of people of African origin from England by Queen Elizabeth, Brown contends that the London theatre audience would have responded to Othello in comic terms of colour-based racism. Italian stereotypes allow the Bard to explore all the ugly elements of the English psyche.

The importance of Italy as the home of political thought, where early modern English courtiers eagerly displayed their knowledge of the nation's theories and history, tends to be set apart from studies of anti-Italian discourses. In his stimulating account of the intertextual synergies of the disguised duke plot in *Measure for Measure*, drawing on generic conventions established in plays by Shakespeare's contemporaries, Michael J. Redmond demonstrates that the Jacobean theatre's treatment of statecraft was a function of the cultural fixation upon Italian politics and vice. Indeed, for Machiavelli and Guicciardini themselves, early modern Italian political theory was marked by the moral and political failures of the Italian city states, offering negative models of bad government. The development of the disguised duke subgenre, staging the changing economy of power in the Renaissance, reflects the strains between an admiration of Italian thought and horror of the nation's continual crises. Through an in-depth reading of contemporary political plays, with a significant account of the parody of the subgenre in Edward Sharpham's *The Fleire*, Redmond shows that the ending of *Measure for Measure*, with Isabella's unsettling silence in the light of the Duke's marriage proposal, betrays the tensions within Shakespeare's unstable bonding of the traditional ransom story, the disguised duke theatregram, and New Comedy.

The assessment of Marsilio Ficino in Renaissance England is the starting point for Claudia Corti's reading of the movements of unity in *Julius Caesar*. The philosophy of Ficino, with its threefold division of human nature, combined the Platonic and Christian traditions, creating a composite scheme of the universe. Ficino's teaching was introduced in England by John Colet, Dean of St Paul's Cathedral, and its influence spread throughout the Renaissance. The leading characters in Shakespeare's *Julius Caesar* reflect the Ficinian vision of three states of being: the Angelic world of the mind, the soul, and the corporeal body of the world. This framework gave the dramatist a basis for expressing what he already knew in clear philosophical terms, establishing a coherent vision of political activity inside and outside his Roman play's stage-world.

Stage and spectacle

Alongside the influence of printed sources upon Shakespeare, current intertextual studies are beginning to look at the plays in the light of other areas of discourse. The influence of Italy in every area of cultural production, from art to acting styles, is inevitably reflected in the Shakespearean text. The celebrations of the Elizabethan court, as J. R. Mulryne notes in his discussion of *Antony and Cleopatra*, drew on the conventions and practices established in Venice and Florence. The fundamental figure in this transition of cultures was Inigo Jones, who imported the pageantry of Italian state entertainment for his royal audiences. Mulryne trenchantly shows that the treatment of Cleopatra's barge, usually linked by editors to written works, is rooted in the performance world of the English court. The importance of pageantry, where masques were written and performed together with the dramatic works of the players, provides an important entry into the society's vision of the elite.

The discursive patterns established in early modern painting and sculpture are another important area of intertextual study. Jeffrey Netto's reading of *The Tempest* addresses the aesthetic context of the brief moment where Prospero discovers Ferdinand and Miranda playing chess. He suggests that the chess motif in Renaissance portraiture, a conventional rendering of erotic love play, informs Shakespeare's treatment of the growing desire linking the two lovers. Indeed, upon seeing the game in progress, Prospero intervenes and warns Ferdinand to rein in his dalliance. The transfer of aesthetic tropes to the dramatic text, with some intriguing references to Middleton and modern aesthetic interpretations in parallel fields such as Greenaway's cinematic rendering, underlines the self-reflexivity of Shakespeare's late plays, where the cultural traditions of Europe seem to be consciously cited and included.

The issues opened up by Netto, in his treatment of ekphrastic intertextuality in Renaissance portraiture and the parallel arts, find fertile ground in François Laroque's vision of Roman art motifs and the influence of Mannerism in *Romeo and Juliet*, *Antony and Cleopatra*, and *The Winter's Tale*, where we experience a subtle intertextual confrontation, enriched with word games and metatheatrical effects, with the Italian tropes of Renaissance art and paintings. While *Romeo and Juliet* posits a natural 'Roman' background in intricate word games, involving the power itself of naming the characters and their world of images, *Antony and Cleopatra* provides a link with Italian erotica in both literature and painting in the visionary fantasies at work in the lovers' language. In *The Winter's Tale* direct and indirect references to Italian Renaissance artists are self-reflexively exploited in the statue scene in such a way that both imagery and diction combine visual with acoustic anamorphosis, reconciling the play's binary oppositions between nature and art, criss-crossing localities, and pagan and Christian ideals in renewed humanist coherence.

The aesthetics of intertextuality finds a suitable hunting ground in the dramaturgy of Shakespeare and in the wider corpus of Renaissance drama as a whole, especially in the idea of its theatrical ancestry and the legacy of the polyvalent process of the composition of a play. The influence of Renaissance art and its problems of authenticity, regarding the question of the original hand or imitative artefact, provide an ideal context for Giorgio Melchiori's fruitful considerations of the case of the theatrical text. The presence in Renaissance Italy of an indefinite group of minor young artists working in the master's *bottega*, often gaining their apprenticeship by contributing to their leader's work, if not replacing his hand with their own, may be equated with the writing conditions of dramatists in early modern England. Hence the question of authorship must take into account the idea of a collaborative dramatic corpus, where individual contribution is often overshadowed by the common theatrical practice at the time. In his brilliant 'An excursus on hands', Melchiori illustrates the problem of attribution in his editions of the apocryphal plays by Shakespeare and Marston.

Intertextualizing Shakespeare's text 9

The multiplicity of views and critical strategies in the present collection offer a deliberate attempt to assess the fundamental aspects of intertextuality in some of the major cultural fields involved in the compositional genetics of early modern dramatic production, a subject in which methodological premises and disciplinary confines are far from being univocally established in current trends in the study of the Renaissance stage.

Notes

1 Among the most recent comparative investigations into the field of early modern drama see in particular Louise George Clubb, *Italian Drama in Shakespeare's Time* (New Haven, Yale University Press, 1989); Robert S. Miola, *Shakespeare and Classical Tragedy: The Influence of Seneca* (Oxford, Clarendon Press, 1992), and, by the same, *Shakespeare and Classical Comedy: The Influence of Plautus and Terence* (Oxford, Clarendon Press, 1994); Keir Elam, 'The Fertile Eunuch: *Twelfth Night*, Early Modern Intercourse and the Fruits of Castration', *Shakespeare Quarterly*, 47:1 (spring 1996), 1–36; Robert Henke, *Pastoral Transformations: Italian Tragicomedy and Shakespeare's Late Plays* (Newark, University of Delaware Press, 1997); and M. Marrapodi, ed., *The Italian World of English Renaissance Drama: Cultural Exchange and Intertextuality*, (Newark, University of Delaware Press, 1998).
2 See, for instance, Ariosto's prologue to *I Suppositi* where he admits his indebtedness to Plautus's *Captivi* and Terence's *Eunuchus*, pointing out, however, 'sì modestamente però che Terenzio e Plauto medesimi, risapendolo, non l'arebbono a male, e di poetica imitazione (*poetic imitation*), più presto che di furto, li darebbono nome'. L. Ariosto, *Tutte le opere*, ed. Cesare Segre, 5 vols (Milan, Mondatori, 1974), vol. 4, p. 198.
3 See G. B. Giraldi, *Discorso Intorno al Comporre delle Commedie e delle Tragedie*, in *G. B. Giraldi Cinzio: Scritti critici*, ed. C. Guerrieri Crocetti (Milan, Marzorati, 1973), pp. 223–4 and ff.
4 Giambattista Guarini, *Il Pastor Fido e il Compendio della poesia tragicomica*, ed. Gioachino Brognoligo (Bari, Gius. Laterza & Figli, 1914), pp. 221: 'l'imitare è quasi un produrre alcuna cosa di nuovo, la quale operazione è per se stessa carissima alla natura, che se ne serve a conservar se medesima nelle spezie, riparando di tutte quello che tuttodì se ne perde. Or la poetica, fra tutte quelle arti che nell'imitazione spendono il lor talento, riesce maravigliosa, non solo perché imiti gli atti umani, nella quale opera non è sola, ma perciocché imita colla favella, nella quale è unica imitatrice, conciosiacosaché tutte l'altre con altri mezzi e istrumenti esercitino l'imitazione, ma niuna con la favella, ch'è propria della poetica.'
5 See 'Prologue' and 'Retaliation as an Italian Vice in English Renaissance Drama: Narrative and Theatrical Exchanges', in M. Marrapodi (ed.), *The Italian World of English Renaissance Drama: Cultural Exchange and Intertextuality*, pp. 9–19 and 190–207.
6 Cf. Paola Pugliatti, 'Intertextuality, Interdiscursivity, Dialogism', in T. Pugliatti, G. Barbera and C. Zappia, eds, *Studi in onore di Alessandro Marabottini* (Rome, De Luca Editore, 1997), pp. 389–93.

7 On the theory of intertextuality and its terminology see in particular M. Bakhtin, 'Discourse in the Novel', in *The Dialogic Imagination: Four Essays*, ed. Michael Holquist, trans. Caryl Emerson and M. Holquist (Austin, University of Texas Press, 1981); Roland Barthes, *S/Z* (Paris, Seuil, 1970); J. Kristeva, *The Kristeva Reader*, ed. Toril Moi (Oxford, Basil Blackwell, 1986); C. Segre, 'Intertestuale/interdiscorsivo: Appunti per una fenomenologia delle fonti', in Costanzo Di Girolamo and Ivano Paccagnella, eds, *La parola ritrovata: Fonti e analisi letteraria* (Palermo, Sellerio Editore, 1982), and, by the same, *Teatro e romanzo: Due tipi di comunicazione letteraria* (Turin, Einaudi, 1984); Alessandro Serpieri, 'Polifonia shakespeariana', in *Retorica e immaginario* (Parma, Pratiche Editrice, 1986); Judith Still and Michael Worton, 'Introduction', in M. Worton and J. Still, eds, *Intertextuality: Theories and Practices* (Manchester, Manchester University Press, 1990); Heinrich F. Plett, 'Intertextualities', in H. F. Plett, ed., *Intertextuality* (Berlin, Walter de Gruyter, 1991); Stephen Greenblatt, *Shakespearean Negotiations: The Circulation of Social Energy in Renaissance England* (Oxford, Clarendon Press, 1988); Louise George Clubb, 'Intertextualities: Some Questions', in Marrapodi, ed., *The Italian World of English Renaissance Drama: Cultural Exchange and Intertextuality*, pp. 179–89; and, by the same editor, *Shakespeare and Intertextuality: The Transition of Cultures Between Italy and England in the Early Modern Period* (Rome, Bulzoni Editore, 2000); Graham Allen, *Intertextuality* (London, Routledge, 2000); Robert S. Miola, *Shakespeare's Reading* (Oxford, Oxford University Press, 2000); and Louise George Clubb, 'Italian Stories on the Stage', in A. Leggatt, ed., *The Cambridge Companion to Shakespearean Comedy* (Cambridge, Cambridge University Press, 2002), pp. 32–46.

8 Michael J. Redmond, '"I have read them all": Jonson's *Volpone* and the Discourse of the Italianate Englishman', in Marrapodi, ed., *The Italian World of English Renaissance Drama*, p. 123.

Part I
Theory and practice

2

Seven types of intertextuality

ROBERT S. MIOLA

This chapter is an attempt to map out some complex territory – namely, the range of intertextual transactions evident in early modern literature, especially Shakespeare. Here the term 'intertextuality' encompasses the widest possible range of textual interactions including those of sources and influences. The focus is on distinct and separate texts interacting, rather than on collaborations, different voices in the same text, or purely linguistic expressions, such as puns, homophones, foreign words and phrases, phonemes, and etymological play. Heinrich Plett distinguishes between this broad understanding of intertextuality and the highly specialized usage of Kristeva, Barthes, and Derrida that excludes varieties of conscious and unconscious imitation from consideration.[1] Based on assumptions about language and meaning that seem increasingly untenable, the post-structuralist approach fails to address the most prevalent intertextual relationships in the period. These relationships occupy this preliminary exercise in distinction.

We may distinguish among seven types of intertextuality, though this number is open to reduction or addition. These seven types divide into three categories. Unequally present in the types and categories are three variables: first, the degree to which the trace of an earlier text is tagged by verbal echo; second, the degree to which its effect relies on audience recognition; third, the degree to which the appropriation is eristic. The distinctions between types and those between categories are not absolute and exclusive; rather these divisions all appear on a continuum with various shadings and overlappings. The continuum moves from closest approximations to ever freer adumbrations, from conscious, positivistic, and author-directed imitations, through more distant and subtle evocations, to, finally, intertextualities that exist in discourses created by the reader, rather than the writer.

14   *Theory and practice*

Category I

This category comprises specific books or texts mediated directly through the author. Revision, translation, quotation, allusion, sources, conventionally understood, an author's earlier work – all belong here. Largely the dynamic consists of authorial reading and remembering, though performances count too (as a kind of reading) and the memory may be subconscious rather than conscious and purposeful. Emrys Jones, for example, well demonstrated the shaping influence of Mystery Play cycles on Shakespeare's histories and tragedies.[2] The evidence for textual transactions in Category I has largely been the identification of verbal iteration or echo (those endless and often disappointing lists of parallel passages) though there are verbal possibilities in matching concatenations as well, in lexical or imagistic patterns.[3] There is also non-verbal evidence available in scenic form, rhetorical and stylistic figuration, and thematic articulation.

Type 1: Revision

This type of intertextuality features a close relationship between anterior and posterior texts, wherein the latter takes identity from the former, even as it departs from it. The process occurs under the guiding and explicitly comparative eye of the revising author. The revision may be prompted by external circumstance – censorship, or theatrical, legal, or material exigencies. Alternatively, the revision may simply reflect an author's subsequent wishes. The reviser who is not the author presents another scenario and an entirely different set of problems and considerations. In all cases, however, the transaction is linear, conscious, and specific, marked by evidence of the reviser's preference and intentionality.

  Modern editors disagree about the legitimacy of revision prompted by external circumstance. The editors of the Oxford Shakespeare, for example, noted that Shakespeare changed the name of Oldcastle to Falstaff in response to protests from Oldcastle's descendants; they restored the name Oldcastle in *1 Henry IV*, rejecting a change that resulted from 'unsolicited censorship' and which did not reflect original authorial intention or initial stage practice.[4] Editors who define the text more as a product of cultural and social factors than as individual property necessarily place less emphasis on authorial intention as a criterion of textual authenticity. They tend to view external factors as legitimate co-creators of the historical artefact that comes down to us as text. For them, Falstaff will always be Falstaff.

  Editors have by and large approved authorial revision that appears to be unconstrained by external factors, that presumably reflects subsequent intentions. Normally, readers respect an author's right to second thoughts. But this sort of revision has also become vexed and problematic. For one thing, audiences several hundred years distant can never be sure that second thoughts have come freely bidden by the promptings of the Muse, untinged by circumstance, exigency, or accident. Printed texts in the period differ from each other for all sorts of reasons. Early modern plays, for example, arise from various kinds of copytexts, sometimes marked by collaborating authors, actors, scribes, and bookkeepers, always produced by compositors, printers, and proofreaders. Folio *King Lear* (1623) cuts some three hundred lines from the earlier Quarto version (1608) and adds one hundred new ones. The later version probably represents a theatrical revision but no one can be sure that Shakespeare alone was the reviser and that no external factors prompted the changes. Ben Jonson's revision of *Every Man in His Humour* provides another interesting case: the Quarto (1601) features a Florentine setting and characters with Italian names; the Folio (1616) features a London setting and English character names, along with many additions and deletions. Editors and critics have been nearly unanimous in approving the revision, and consequently it has dominated critical and theatrical history. They have assumed that the author controls the text and that revision brings it to ontological and aesthetic completion. But this assumption falsifies literary history. The Quarto represents the version staged by the Lord Chamberlain's Men for 1598 audiences at The Curtain; its Italian setting, satire on duelling, tobacco, and sonnetteering, and abiding concern with the art of poesy perfectly fitted its original moment at the end of the century. The Folio version takes advantage of later developments in city comedy and inaugurates Jonson's monumental construction of himself and his career in a collection of works. Each text appeared in specific form at a specific time for specific reasons. Furthermore, one scholar has recently argued that certain Folio alterations in the play, namely the cuts in the fifth act, resulted from material circumstances: Jonson and the printer had set aside six quires for the play and simply ran out of room.[5] The intertextual relationship between a text and a revised version is always more complex than the regnant critical assumptions allow.

Revision of a work by another represents a very different scenario. Readers tend to view this sort of revision as illegitimate interference. (Witness the disrepute of the allied terms – piracy, plagiarism, disintegrationism.) So too authors, sometimes with very good reason. Robert Persons, SJ, for example, was shocked to find his devotional book *The First Book of the Christian Exercise* (1582), 'Perused' and republished by a Yorkshire minister, Edmund Bunny. Bunny kept the title and most of the text but excised Catholic materials and altered the language to fit Protestant orthodoxy. In 1584 and in subsequent editions, Persons responded in a 'Preface' which listed Bunny's 'shifts, and fallacies, and other abuses' (*The Christian Directory*, 1607, sig. *3). The problem is not merely one man's dishonesty, Persons, explained, but heresy, and its general tendency to corrupt books of devotion. Persons cites similar injuries to the works of Thomas à Kempis, St Augustine, St Bernard, and, of course, the corruptions and falsifications of Holy Scripture perpetrated by Luther, Zwingli, Calvin, and others.

In the less exalted precincts of the theatre, Elizabethans frequently collaborated in various ways. And though publication was a secondary concern at best, many today still cherish the ideal of the single, unified author(ity) who produces a text. Critical favour has now shifted toward the A-text of Christopher Marlowe's *Doctor Faustus*, now thought to be closer to Marlowe's original manuscript, and away from the B-text, which represents a mix of authorial and theatrical provenances, and which contains additions by several later playwrights. If the chronological distance between the texts is great, then the second text takes life as an adaptation. Adaptations are literary progeny that bear direct and immediate descent from originary texts and that exist in a very conscious counterpoise of tribute and criticism. Shakespeare's plays have sustained adaptations by many, including Dryden, Garrick, Cibber, and Tate, as well as the recent radical revisions of Kurosawa and Marowitz. In these transactions the reviser appropriates the authority of the author, and assumes control of the text. If an author's revision of his or her own work asserts his or her power and domination, then the reviser of another's work enacts a rebellion and usurpation.

Type 2: Translation

Translation transfers, 'carries across', a text into a different language, recreates it anew. The later text explicitly claims the identity of the original, its chief project an etiological journey to itself, or to a version of itself. Translations are generally grouped according to source language, and judged by standards of 'fidelity', i. e., the closeness of the rendering to the original and the success of the translator in representing the original's literary quality and effects.

But the usual distinctions among translation verbatim, paraphrase, and metaphrase, deflect attention from the real difficulty inherent in this type of intertextuality – namely the unbridgeable cultural and linguistic spaces between languages and cultures. Translations from Greek or Latin best illustrate this difficulty, where it has been called the problem of belatedness. The consequent varieties of estrangement, linguistic and cultural, Thomas M. Greene has helpfully gathered together under the rubric 'Historical Solitude', 'the disquiet stemming from the historicity of the signifier', the sense of pathos and irrecoverable loss in confrontation with classical antiquity.[6] Chapman's *Iliad* provides an interesting example here, especially as the translator repeatedly claims (in commentary and prefatory materials) to have caught the true sense and spirit of Homer (even reporting later on in *Euthymiae Raptus* a Homeric bardophany). The change from Homeric biology and religion to humoural anatomy and Reformation belief effects pervasive reimagining:

untranslatable terms such as *phrenes*, *thumos*, and *Hades* become, for example, 'wits', 'heart', and 'hell', respectively, each betokening different values in a different physical and moral universe.

Despite its claims, every line of Chapman's great work, informed by linguistic and cultural change, transforms the original Greek.[7] Homer, for example, uses the same Greek verse for the important deaths of Patroclus and Hector; the *psuchê* of each flies from the body, *hon potmon gooosa, lipous' androtêta kai hêbên*, 'lamenting its fate, leaving behind manhood and youth' (8.857, 22.363). Homer's *psuchê*, perhaps deriving from a word for breath, sometimes vanishing like smoke sometimes appearing with wings, begins its own lament; the participle deriving from *goân*, expresses private sorrow and communal grief. The *psuchê* mourns *potmon*, one's fate, what befalls people, one of those huge abstractions that negate human life; the lament asserts the value of those who belong to generations that go to the earth like so many leaves. Chapman portrays a different drama, the soul of Patroclus, 'sorrowing / For his sad fate, to leave him young and in his ablest age'; that of Hector, 'mourning his destinies, / To part so with his youth and strength'. *Psuchê* changes to 'soul', a word freighted with Biblical overtones and two millennia of intense discussion. The infinitive constructions and personal possessive pronouns present the drama of individual deaths, not the sad fate of all mortals. To varying extents all translations exhibit this kind of intertextual impossibility.

Type 3: Quotation

Quotation literally reproduces the anterior text (whole or part) in a later text. (For general purposes of description, we may view textual allusions as a types of quotation, in effect, quotation without verbal iteration, quotation as reference not re-enactment.) Quotations may be variously marked for reader recognition, by typographical signals, by a switch in language, for example, or by the actual identification of the original author or text: Holofernes remembers a school text, Mantuan's *Eclogues*: '*Fauste, precor gelida quando pecus omne sub umbra ruminat*, and so forth. Ah, good old Mantuan!' (*LLL* 4.2.91–3). Sometimes authors simply weave quotations into the new context: Hamlet's 'Come, the croaking raven doth bellow for revenge' (3.2.251–2) combines two lines from *The True Tragedy of Richard III* (1594). Readers might analyse quotations in early modern texts grammatically, according to quantity, quality, distribution, frequency, interference, and markers, and pragmatically according to sender, receiver, code, place, time, medium, and function. Critics might also assess the degrees to which audience recognition is assumed or necessary (though this is often difficult). 'Who ever loved that loved not at first sight?' (*AYL* 3.5.82), for example, seems consciously designed to evoke a popular text, perhaps, or poet, Christopher Marlowe. Pistol's 'Have we not Hiren here?' (*2H4* 2.4.159) replays a tag line bandied about in the drama. An interesting problem arises with such lines and very familiar phrases. If audience recognition is clearly indicated, as with Pistol's verse here or, for that matter, any parody, then our assumptions about familiarity with the main text may begin paradoxically to reverse themselves. The reputation of certain lines and fragments (this one from Pistol or 'O eyes, no eyes, but fountains frought with tears' from *The Spanish Tragedy* 3.2.1) took on a life of their own separate from original contexts. They may be merely stock jokes rather than fragments of well-known texts. Proverbs, verses from ballads and songs, isolated lines, then, often merely trade in common linguistic currency. In our day, for example, recitation of the catch-phrase 'To be or not to be' does not necessarily indicate familiarity with the original context or play.

Whatever categories one employs, criticism might well consider a quotation's evocative value in context. Titus quotes Ovid, *Terras Astraea reliquit* (4.3.4), 'Astraea has left the earth', in a play replete with Ovidian allusion, one which features the *Metamorphoses* as an important prop on stage, which replays in sophisticated fashion the myths of Philomel, Procne, and Tereus, as well as the myth of the world's Four Ages.[8] The quotation consciously evokes classical myth to portray the absence of divine order and justice in the corrupt world. Sometimes the power of the evocation becomes clear only in association with other quotations. Quotations from Seneca *tragicus* gradually yield to quotations from his philosophical essays in Chapman's *Bussy D'Ambois* thus marking a shift in standards of judgement.

Quotations often appear as text fragments in later texts that are themselves whole. Other kinds of poetical works in the Renaissance consist almost wholly of quotations, the various centos, chrestomathies, commonplace books, and florilegia so popular in the period. An author like Mirandula (*Illustrium poetarum flores*, Lyons, 1566), for example, arranges quotations from various authors under moral categories such as Anger, Patience, Despair. That anthology of anecdote and wise saying, William Baldwin's *A Treatise of Moral Philosophy* (1547) enjoyed many reprints and expansion throughout the period. In such works the quotations entirely comprise the new text; they are completely decontextualized and exist now in a new dialogue with each other, the boundaries of which have been determined by the compiler. Erasmus's great *Adagia* presents a sophisticated and interesting variation on this kind of quotation intertextuality; this collection glosses Greek and Latin proverbs with thousands of ancient references and quotations.

The name of Erasmus provides transport into the regions of scholarly rather than literary intertextualities. The great scholars and editors of the early modern period applied immense learning to the elucidation of texts. This application often took the form of quotation and allusion in commentary, marginalia, or notes. Sometimes an editor makes explicit what is implicit in a text; a great Renaissance edition of Virgil (*Opera*, Venice, 1544, for example), provides illustrative passages from Homer and other Greek as well as Latin writers. Sometimes the commentary more actively shapes interpretation; the German Jesuit Spanmüller (Jacobus Pontanus) published a Virgil bedecked with detailed moral, allegorical, and symbolic commentary, *Symbolarum libri XVII Vergilii* (Augsburg, 1599). The scholarly practice of parallel citation, reference, and glossing, so important to quotation intertextuality in the period, sometimes carried back over into original compositions. Early modern authors used these practices to create their texts: Spenser published the glosses of 'E. K'. on *The Shepherd's Calendar*, for example; Jonson supplied explanatory and erudite notes to *The Masque of Queens*. These complex polyphonies represent an important subdivision of quotation intertextuality.

Type 4: Sources

Source texts provide plot, character, idea, language, or style to later texts. The author's reading and remembering directs the transaction, which may include complicated strategies of *imitatio*. The source text in various ways shapes the later text, its content, or its rhetorical style and form. There are at least three subdivisions possible here.

The source coincident. Here the earlier text exists as a whole in dynamic tension with the later one, a part of its identity. The later one may simply respond to an earlier one: Ralegh writes a famous reply to Marlowe's Passionate Shepherd, for example. Gabriel Harvey and Thomas Nashe engage in a pamphlet war. The serious literature of controversy, political and religious, employs extensive quotation and reference so that the originating text and present response take on a new identity. Thomas More's *The Confutation of Tyndale's Answer*, for example, quotes Tyndale in block before offering a point-by-point refutation. Additionally, a later text may complete an earlier one. Both George Chapman and Henry Petowe published continuations of Marlowe's *Hero and Leander* in 1598. In all cases of this sort, knowledge of the earlier is necessary for understanding of the later; the relationship is based on parity and recognition as the two assume a kind of corporate identity.

The source proximate. This is the most familiar and frequently studied kind of intertextuality, that of sources and texts. The source functions as the book-on-the-desk; the author honors, reshapes, steals, ransacks, and plunders. The dynamics include copying, paraphrase, compression, conflation, expansion, omission, innovation, transference, and contradiction.

Shakespeare's use of North's Plutarch in *Julius Caesar* provides a good example of a proximate source. There are numerous verbal and non-verbal markers identifying the primary source of the play, though no stage moment requires this identification for effect. Earlier critics such as Nicholas Rowe and Samuel Johnson thought Shakespeare's reliance on the source excessive and detrimental to the action. Later generations, perhaps spurred by MacCallum, focus on

Shakespeare's creative departures from Plutarch, his aggressive reworking of historical narrative into tragic drama.[9] These include innovation (Casca, the quarrel scene, the character of Lucius), omission (most of Caesar's early career), transference – the switching of characters and reattribution of personal traits: Plutarch's Caesar suspects both Brutus and Cassius, not just Cassius; the conflict about leading the right wing actually occurs between Brutus and Cassius, not Antony and Octavius (5.1.16–20), where it foreshadows future discord and Antony's eventual fall. And Shakespeare contradicts the source outright: Plutarch's Brutus visits Caius Ligarius, whereas Shakespeare's receives him; Plutarch's Caesar is a powerful swimmer whereas Cassius's Caesar in the play almost drowns; Plutarch's Caesar cannot read Artemidorus' warning because of the crowd; Shakespeare's, in a significantly self-conscious gesture of largesse, refuses to consider it: 'What touches us ourself shall be last served' (3.1.8). Even in a closely followed source, there appears an interesting range of intertextual dynamics.

The source remote. This last term includes all sources and influences that are not clearly marked, or that do not coincide with the book-on-the-desk model. The field of possibilities here widens to include all that an author previously knew or read: grammar-school texts, classical stories and authors, the Bible, evident in allusions, turns of phrase, or reappropriated motifs. The dynamic still consists of reading and remembering, even if the process of recollection and rearticulation occurs in the subconscious mind of the author. Remote sources often include the work of particularly original, earlier playwrights: Thomas Kyd, for example, who readapted Senecan conventions to the Elizabethan stage; Christopher Marlowe, who served as *agent provocateur* for early Shakespeare, as Nicholas Brooke put it;[10] John Lyly who created brilliant English comedies of rhetorical wit and love. Ovid, and Virgil appear as remote sources everywhere. Obviously, the calibration of intertextual distance must be to some degree subjective, depending on one's knowledge of a playwright and sense of his working habits and creative processes.

Category II

Category II contains traditions. An originary text radiates its presence through numberless intermediaries and indirect routes – through commentaries, adaptations, translations, and reifications in other works. It exists in combination with other originary texts, largely as a set of inherited expectations, reflexes, and strategies. The source remote does not lie far off from the traditions of Category II. But there is a real distinction between the direct influence of, say, a sixth-form Virgil passage, half-remembered many years later, and the indirect influence of traditions, *in which the originary text may never have ever been read by the author at all.*

Type 5: Conventions and configurations

Poets constantly appropriated and adapted numerous conventions from classical, medieval, and continental literatures, formal and rhetorical. Senecan conventions in tragedy, the chorus, messenger, domina-nutrix dialogue, stichomythia, and soliloquy, for example, have all attracted due attention.[11] So have Plautine and Terentian conventions in comedy: eavesdropping, disguise, lockouts, stock characters like the witty slave, bragging soldier, blocking *senex*, and so on.[12] Configurations of classical character and situation also appear importantly in the drama: Shakespeare adapts the New Comedic triangle consisting of importunate *adulescens*, blocking *senex*, and nubile *virgo* into marvellous, varied, and expressive tensions throughout his career. *A Midsummer Night's Dream* presents a relatively simple adaptation: Egeus blocks Hermia's love for Lysander and commands her to marry Demetrius; the lovers flee into the enchanted forest and the daughter eventually triumphs over her father. More complicated variations appear in the triads of Lear–Cordelia–Burgundy and France, Polonius–Ophelia–Hamlet, Prospero–Miranda–Ferdinand. No single Plautine or Terentian play acts as the 'source' (proximate or remote); instead Shakespeare, like most Elizabethans, reworks inherited traditions, creating various combinations of character, action, and genre. The very stuff and substance of his work ultimately derives, by whatever indirect route, from classical origins, from discrete texts that have now become pervasive presences.

The marvellous outpouring of Italian drama in the cinquecento, itself rooted in classical tragedy, history, romance, and epic, also supplied conventions and configurations, while altering dramatic horizons of expectation and possibility. Louise George Clubb has elegantly and persuasively demonstrated the power and flexibility of theatregrams, the interchangeable 'units, figures, relationships, actions, *topoi*, and framing *patterns* ... that were at once streamlined structures for svelte play making and elements of high specific density, weighty with significance from previous incarnations'.[13] Once Ariosto, Bibbiena, Machiavelli, and others had written, cross dressings, garrulous nurses, and witty, wondrous women passed permanently into the vocabulary of European theatre. Shakespeare may have read none of these dramatists in Italian or in translation yet he could no more have escaped them in the practice of his craft than moderns can escape Freud or Marx, though only a relatively small percentage of people have actually had direct contact with those seminal thinkers.

Type 6: Genres

Category II intertextuality also includes the wide range of linkings implicit and explicit in generic choices. These may appear in individual signifiers (e.g., the play-within-the-play of revenge tragedy, the singing shepherds in pastoral), which function much like conventions, or range to broader and less discrete forms. On the far end of the spectrum often a sophistication and smoothness of adaptation makes difficult positive identification of origins: Spenser's *The Faerie Queene* absorbs classical, medieval, and contemporary works into a new creation; Milton yokes and challenges epical and Biblical traditions in *Paradise Lost*. Italian pastoral (and not just *Aminta* and *Il Pastor Fido*) as well as Italian tragicomedy inspire and inflect Renaissance poetry in England and on the continent.[14] Often genres commingle surprisingly.

One Shakespearean example may demonstrate the subtlety and evocative power of generic intertextuality. No one has ever successfully proved that Shakespeare ever read a single line of Petrarch's *Canzoniere*. Yet any reader of Shakespeare's sonnet sequence or *Love's Labour's Lost* recognizes an intimate familiarity with the conventions and genre that Petrarch (along with Dante and others) originated. These conventions and assumptions, in turn, Shakespeare further adapts in *Romeo and Juliet*, where Petrarch is appropriately invoked by Mercutio (2.4.38–40). Romeo in love with Rosaline seems to be conventional Petrarchan lover, full of fanciful and literary paradoxes:

> Why, then, O brawling love! O loving hate,
> O anything of nothing first create,
> O heavy lightness, serious vanity,
> Misshapen chaos of well-seeming forms,
> Feather of lead, bright smoke, cold fire, sick health,
> Still-waking sleep, that is not what it is!
>
> (1.1.176–81)

And Romeo, in love with Juliet, appears to outgrow all this. Yet, in the last act we find various Petrarchan images and *topoi* assembling themselves into new paradoxes; in different senses we witness on stage the misshapen chaos of well-seeming forms, the still-waking sleep, that is not what it is. One of the most famous Petrarchan images is the lover as a ship at sea; we recall Petrarch's 189 and Sir Thomas Wyatt's celebrated translation: *Passa la nave mia colma d'oblio / per aspro mare, a mezza notte, il verno*, 'My galley charged with forgetfulness / Thorough sharp seas in winter nights doth pass'; the poem concludes starkly: *Morta fra l'onde e la ragion e l'arte: Tal ch'i' incomincio a disperar del porto*, 'Drowned is the reason that should me comfort, / And I remain despairing of the port.'[15] Romeo uses the same imagery:

> Come, bitter conduct, come, unsavory guide,
> Thou desperate pilot, now at once run on
> The dashing rocks thy sea-sick weary bark!
>
> (5.3.116–18)

Instead of the lover desiring a safe port from the seas of unrequited love and suffering, Romeo wants shipwreck. Shakespeare does not transform by some unknown intermediary a specific Petrarchan text or image; rather, here and throughout the last scene, where the lovers unite in death, he transforms the lyric genre of the *dolce stil novo*, giving it a new shape and name, harnessing Petrarchan energies in service of drama. Overgoing the Petrarchan lover, Romeo is absolute unto death. The lyric becomes subsumed in tragedy.

Category III

In the age of intertextual *écriture*, this last category consists of what any audience brings to a text rather than what the author put in. The focus moves from texts and traditions to the circulation of cultural discourses. Cesare Segre has called this kind of intertextuality, 'interdiscursivity', which he defines as 'i rapporti che ogni testo, orale e scritto, intrattiene con tutti gli enunciati (o discorsi) registrati nella corrispondente cultura e ordinati ideologicamente, oltre che per registri e livelli',[16] 'the relationships that each text, oral and written, holds with all other utterances (or discourses) recorded in a corresponding culture and organized ideologically, according to registers and levels'. This means in practice whatever the literary critic perceives as revelatory of cultural poetics; he or she, not the author, brings the text to the table.

Type 7: Paralogues

Paralogues are texts that illuminate the intellectual, social, theological, or political meanings in other texts. Unlike texts or even traditions, paralogues move horizontally and analogically in discourses rather than in vertical lineation through the author's mind or intention. Today, critics can adduce any contemporary text in conjunction with another, without bothering at all about verbal echo, or even imprecise lines of filiation. In some ways the discussion of paralogues departs from past critical practices, bringing new freedom; but, of course, new perils threaten: rampant and irresponsible association, facile cultural generalization, and anecdotal, impressionistic historicizing. Though some would not care to admit it, the practice of adducing paralogues is not new. E. M. W. Tillyard's citations to Richard Hooker's *Laws of Ecclesiastical Polity* and Dionysius the Areopagite's treatise on celestial hierarchies function intertextually as do post-structuralist citations of the *hic mulier* pamphlets as background to the gender play of early modern literature. The same holds true for modern uses of *The Return of Martin Guerre*, the rhetoric of Elizabeth or James I, or the documents of colonial discourse, though now moderns tend to see literary texts as contested sites, rather than as self-contained, discursively significant wholes.

This chapter does not propose an inclusive system but attempts to make some sense of a joyful abundance. The new millennium will doubtless disclose new types of intertextuality to add to this preliminary listing. Some already clamor for attention. *Onomastic intertextuality*, for example, may include the range of allusion, reference, and significance evoked simply by a name,

Theseus, for example, or Helen.[17] *Printing intertextuality* can signify the accidental inclusion of one text in another during the printing process. Randall McCleod, for example, notes an advertisement for Peacham's soap transferred accidentally to a George Herbert text (private correspondence). *Reception intertextuality* may reverse the chronological axes entirely so that later texts can influence the reading and printing of earlier ones. Woodcuts to Italian editions of Virgil, especially Book 6, for example, show the enormous influence of Dante's *Commedia* on conception and understanding of the ancient poet. And, finally, we may consider *forgery*, as a kind of ghostly intertextuality, wherein an anterior text pretends to be an original. Forgery occupies a large role in the literary and cultural history of this period. John Wolfe faked Italian imprints to boost the sale of his books; for the same reason, William Jaggard published in *The Passionate Pilgrim* under the name of William Shakespeare, though the collection included some twenty poems by other poets. Lorenzo Valla momentously exposed as a fake the *Donation of Constantine*, which gave temporal power to the Church. Antony Grafton, moreover, reminds us of extensive forgeries in Gratian's *Decretum*, in the *Corpus* of Latin inscriptions, and even in Erasmus's work.[18] In forgery there is a complete assumption of identity that denies ontological difference. The text makes an etiological journey to itself, perhaps, in the case of the forgery of a known text at least, the *terminus ab quo*, of Category I, though many other distinctions are possible.

Notes

1 Heinrich, F. Plett, ed., *Intertextuality* (Berlin, Walter de Gruyter, 1991), pp. 3–4. See also Michael Riffaterre, 'Syllepsis', *Critical Inquiry*, 6 (1980), 625–38; 'Intertextual Representation: On Mimesis as Interpretive Discourse', *Critical Inquiry*, 11 (1984), 141–62. For a critique of post-structuralist assumptions see Brian Vickers, *Appropriating Shakespeare* (New Haven, Yale University Press, 1993).

2 Emrys Jones, *The Origins of Shakespeare* (Oxford, Oxford University Press, 1977), pp. 31–84. Quotations from Shakespeare below are cited from *The Complete Works*, ed. David Bevington, updated 4th edn (New York, 1997).

3 See, for instance Caroline F. E. Spurgeon, *Shakespeare's Imagery and What It Tells Us* (Cambridge, Cambridge University Press, 1935); John W. Velz, 'Sir Thomas More and the Shakespeare Canon: Two Approaches', in T. H. Howard-Hill, ed., *Shakespeare and 'Sir Thomas More'* (Cambridge, Cambridge University Press, 1989), pp. 171–95.

4 Stanley Wells, Gary Taylor, *et al.*, *William Shakespeare: A Textual Companion* (Oxford, Oxford University Press, 1987; New York, 1997), p. 330.

5 James A. Riddell, 'Jonson and Stansby and the Revisions of *Every Man in His Humour*', *Medieval and Renaissance Drama in England*, 9 (1997), 81–91.

6 Thomas M. Greene, *The Light in Troy: Imitation and Discovery in Renaissance Poetry* (New Haven, Yale University Press, 1982), pp. 4–27 (p. 8).

7 See Robert S. Miola, 'On Death and Dying in Chapman's *Iliad*: Translation as Forgery', *International Journal of the Classical Tradition*, 3 (1996), 48–64.
8 Jonathan Bate, *Shakespeare and Ovid* (Oxford, Oxford University Press, 1993), pp. 101–17.
9 M. W. MacCallum, *Shakespeare's Roman Plays and Their Background* (London, 1910).
10 Nicholas Brooke, 'Marlowe as Provocative Agent in Shakespeare's Early Comedies', *Shakespeare Survey*, 14 (1961), 34–44; cf. Maurice Charney, 'The Voice of Marlowe's Tamburlaine in Early Shakespeare', *Comparative Drama*, 31 (1997–8), 213–21.
11 Gordon Braden, *Renaissance Tragedy and the Senecan Tradition: Anger's Privilege* (New Haven, Yale University Press, 1985); Robert S. Miola, *Shakespeare and Classical Tragedy: The Influence of Seneca* (Oxford, Clarendon Press, 1992).
12 Daniel C. Boughner, *The Braggart in Renaissance Comedy* (Minneapolis, Minnesota University Press, 1954); Leo Salingar, *Shakespeare and the Traditions of Comedy* (Cambridge, Cambridge University Press, 1974); Robert S. Miola, *Shakespeare and Classical Comedy: The Influence of Plautus and Terence* (Oxford, Clarendon Press, 1994).
13 Louise George Clubb, *Italian Drama in Shakespeare's Time* (New Haven, Yale University Press, 1989), p. 6.
14 See Clubb, *Italian Drama*; Robert Henke, *Pastoral Transformations: Italian Tragicomedy and Shakespeare's Late Plays* (Newark, University of Delaware Press, 1997).
15 Francesco Petrarca, *The Canzoniere*, trans. Mark Musa (Bloomington, Indiana University Press, 1996); Sir Thomas Wyatt, *Collected Poems*, ed. Joost Daalder (London, Oxford University Press, 1975), p. 25.
16 Cesare Segre, *Teatro e romanzo: due tipi di comunicazione letteraria* (Turin, Einaudi, 1984), p. 111.
17 See Peter Holland, 'Theseus' Shadows in *A Midsummer Night's Dream*', *Shakespeare Survey*, 47 (1994), 139–51.
18 Anthony Grafton, *Forgers and Critics: Creativity and Duplicity in Western Scholarship* (Princeton, Princeton University Press, 1990).

3

English bodies in Italian habits

KEIR ELAM

Cucullus non facit monachum : habit and habitus

Towards the end of the sixteenth century a number of publications appeared describing contemporary English society as it were from without, i.e. from a 'foreign' perspective, although they were in fact written by Englishmen. The most renowned of these 'from without' sociological or ethnographical surveys are William Harrison's *Description of England* (first published Holinshed in 1577, and again in 1587) with its mapping of English institutions, the English class system and English customs, and John Stow's *Survey of London* (1598), which restricts the focus of national panoramas such as Harrison's by zooming in on the capital. Together with the maps of London and England of the same period, such as John Norden's 1600 pictorial survey or the *Civitatis Londini* panorama (also 1600), these descriptions betray both the desire to affirm national identity and a certain anxiety regarding the perception of England and the English in a period of greatly increased contact with Europe and beyond (testified to by the simultaneous outbreak of travel literature, bilingual dictionaries, etc.). The French sociologist Pierre Bourdieu's remarks on the 'space of life-styles' seem pertinent to such self-scrutiny: 'the question of this [social] space', in Bourdieu's words, 'is raised within the space itself … the agents have points of view on this objective space which depend on their position within it and in which their will to transform it is often expressed'.[1]

In their attempt to define their social space and perhaps defend their cultural boundaries, Harrison and his colleagues inevitably enter into the comparative mode: us versus them. And the strategy they adopt is what we might term the 'look-at-them-looking-at-us' trope. A vivid example of such a foreigner's-eye-view strategy is found in Harrison's chapter 'Of their apparel and attire', in which the author inveighs against his compatriots for abandoning their traditional native garb in favour of a mish-mash of continental fashions: 'for which I say most nations do not unjustly deride us, as also for that we do seem to imitate all nations round about us, wherein we be like to the *polypus* or chameleon'.² Harrison produces a paradoxical optical twist by pretending to look at the English from the derisive viewpoint of the very foreign nations they strive to imitate. There is a double-loop projection at work here, going outwards and back again, boomerang fashion: other nations mock us because, in mimicking them, we camouflage and so betray our own natures.

Harrison's lament, therefore, is that of the unenglishing of the body of England, across all of its social classes, through the promiscuous and indiscriminate mixing of alien national modes. The result is a corporeal hybridization or *contaminatio* that fails to produce a distinctive and recognizably English style of dress:

> the phantastical folly of our nation (even from the courtier to the carter) is such that no form of apparel liketh us longer than the first garment is in the wearing, if it continue so long, and be not laid aside to receive some other trinket newly devised by the fickle-headed tailors, who covet to have several tricks in cutting, thereby to draw fond customers to more expense of money. For my part, I can tell better how to inveigh against this enormity than describe any certainty in our attire; sithence such is our mutability that to-day there is none to the Spanish guise, to-morrow the French toys are most fine and delectable, ere long no apparel as that which is after the high Almaine fashion, by-and-by the Turkish manner is generally best liked of, otherwise the Morisco gowns, the Barbarian fleeces ... and the short French breeches make such a comely vesture that, except it were a dog in a doublet, you shall not see any so disguised as are my countrymen of England.³

The unenglishing of the English body, moreover, is synonymous with its unmanning, a collective loss of the traditional distinguishing marks of gender: 'I will say nothing of our heads, which sometimes are polled, sometimes curled, or suffered to grow at length like woman's locks.' This effeminization process is mirrored, vice versa, in the virilization of women who

> 'do now exceed the lightness of our men ... What should I say of their doublets with pendant codpieces on the breast, ... their galligascons to bear out their bums and make their attire to fit plum round (as they term it) about them ... their bodies are rather deformed than commended? I have met with some of these trulls in London so disguised, that it hath passed my skill to discern whether they were men or women.⁴

Harrison's chapter on their/our apparel and attire begins with an illustrated anecdote on the difficulty of the Tudor physician and writer Andrew Boorde in representing the dressed English body:

> An Englishman, endeavouring sometime to write of our attire ... when he saw what a difficult piece of work he had taken he gave over his travel, and only drew the picture of a naked man, unto whom he gave a pair of shears in the one hand

and a piece of cloth in the other. To the end he should shape his apparel after such fashion as himself liked, sith he could find no kind of garment that could please him any while together.

Boorde's representational problems are such that in the end he is forced to figure the Englishman naked (figure 3.1), complete with threatening scissors ready for the cut; Harrison reprints Boorde's woodcut in his account:

3.1 The naked Englishman (from William Harrison, *Description of England*, in *Holinshed's Chronicles*, ed. Lothrop Withington, London: Camelot Classics, 1989).

The illustration is accompanied by Boorde's poem on the same theme:

> I am an English man and naked as I stand here,
> Musing in my mind what raiment I shall wear;
> For now I will wear this, and now I will wear that;
> Now I will wear I cannot tell what.
> All new fashions be pleasant to me;
> I will have them, whether I thrive or thee.[5]

The anecdote suggests that Harrison's charge of un-English activities, and particularly the accusation regarding the mimetic syndrome or imitation compulsion, is itself an English rhetorical *topos*. This is further confirmed by the authoritative support it receives in the *Homily against Excess of Apparel* that Elizabeth I commanded to be preached in the churches. The homily rehearses the theme of denationalization as denaturalization, and the topic of unenglishing as unmanning, and it likewise plays the look-at-them-looking-at-us game by pretending to adopt the point of view of a foreigner in order to accuse Elizabeth's subjects of excessive foreignness, an act of perception that is narrated as a sort of emperor's-new-clothes fable, as if the Englishman were seen for the first time by a child or alien who perceives only naked folly:

Yea many men are become so effeminate, that they care not what they spend in disguising themselues, euer desiring new toyes, and inuenting new fashions. Therefore a certaine man that would picture euery countreyman in his accustomed apparell, when hee had painted other nations, he pictured the English man all naked, and gaue him cloth vnder his arme, and bade him make it himselfe as hee thought best, for hee changed his fashion so often, that he knew not how to make it. Thus with our phantasticall deuises, wee make our selues laughing stockes to other nations.[6]

Here, then, is another paradox: the Englishman is so excessively overdressed that he can only be represented naked. By adopting new and foreign fashions, the English strip themselves of their 'accustomed apparel' and are left physically and morally defenceless. Behind this nudity trope lies its opposite, namely the notion that the innate habit of the English is plainness in dress and in behaviour, that *nuda veritas* or plain truthfulness that became a successful puritan slogan. By negative inference, therefore, we get a stereotype picture of the true Englishman as a simple, natural, plain-dressing and straight-talking ingénue, unfit for sophisticated finery. By aping alien habits, he has merely exchanged one form of nakedness for another.

Harrison's sociological look-at-them-looking-at-us strategy reappears in Shakespearean drama in the form of a recurrent 'alienation' device that consists in having characters from supposedly foreign settings – 'them' – talk directly about the early modern English, 'us' in the audience. The most famous example of this device is probably the gravedigger's 'Danish' sarcasm about all the English being mad, in *Hamlet* 5.1. A more elaborate instance is Portia's survey of her suitors in *The Merchant of Venice* 1.2. In anatomizing the bodies and manners of the pretenders to her hand, Portia provides her own essay in comparative ethnography, a satirical anatomy of, respectively, Italian (specifically Neapolitan), French, German, Scottish and English behavioural traits. Thus she gives us a Neapolitan prince mono-maniacally obsessed with horses; a County Palatine morbidly fixated on melancholy; a French lord who is master of all the arts, which, however, add up to nothing ('He is every man in no man', l. 50); a German whose only distinctive feature is that of being perennially drunk; and a Scotsman who has no national or cultural identity at all if not as victim of his bully neighbour the Englishman. But it is the latter, the young English baron Falconbridge, who not surprisingly earns the most detailed portrait:

> NERISSA What say you then to Falconbridge, the young baron of England?
> PORTIA You know I say nothing to him, for he understands not me, nor I him: he hath neither Latin, French, nor Italian, and you will come into the court and swear that I have a poor pennyworth in the English: he is a proper man's picture, but alas! who can converse with a dumb-show? How oddly he is suited! I think he bought his doublet in Italy, his round hose in France, his bonnet in Germany, and his behaviour everywhere. (1.2.63-73)[7]

Portia's 'united nations' panorama of her suitors bears a certain resemblance to William Harrison's, mocking, among others, the same nationalities referred to in Harrison's survey: the Moors, Germans, French, and, of course, the English, whose chief distinguishing trait, as in Harrison, is their unique ability to combine the styles of all the other countries put together. Portia comes as close here as any Shakespearean character to looking straight into the auditorium: her gaze is directed mercilessly at the contemporary end-of-century Englishman, present in the historical here and now of 1590s London within the upper echelons of The Theatre. Portia's caricature of the archetypal Englishman is pitched in explicit opposition to all the other portraits combined, for the simple reason that the English baron endeavours to be the others combined. Not a potpourri of the arts like the Frenchman, the Englishman is none the less a behavioural and costumic mélange, a semiotic 'mingle-mangle', to use Puttenham's term. He is 'oddly suited', i.e. bizarrely dressed because badly matched. What emerges from Portia's cameo portrait, apart from the passing and polite compliment to supposed English good looks ('a proper man's picture'), is a patchwork identity constructed awkwardly and uncertainly from the imitation of alien modes, a miscellany of alterity that betrays a woeful lack of cultural self-confidence: 'he bought ... his behaviour everywhere'.

The verb 'bought' here is significant, within the context of a play whose discourse, even the language of Belmont, is so contaminated by the lexical currency of commerce. The English baron has purchased his behaviour, like his clothes, implying that he has acquired his somewhat dubious social status, and probably his title, on the upward mobility market, and is therefore identifiable as a bourgeois *arriviste* in unconvincing aristocratic drag. Falconbridge joins the ranks of the excluded outsiders – ethnic Others like the Jew and the Moor – and not only because of his nationality but also and above all because of his social class. It is therefore appropriate that he should be decked out as a sort of icon of cultural otherness.

This points to the fact that Portia looks at 'us', at the late sixteenth-century English middle classes eager to get on and up in the world (and possibly to take over the world) with the condescending graciousness of class and national privilege, from her position as an aristocratic lady 'richly left' within the Venetian city state, which represented par excellence not only ancient commercial splendour but also cultural refinement: in a word, civility. Portia radiates effortless civilized *savoir faire*; Falconbridge exudes instead eager-to-please primitive gaucherie. They speak different languages, not only because Portia knows no English (she is supposedly speaking Italian) while Falconbridge suffers from proverbial English monolingualism. The real problem is that he does not 'speak' any of the body languages (dress code, etiquette, comportment) that to her are innate and that he frantically imitates but fails hopelessly to assimilate. Portia's cameo of Englishness represents the rather masochistic *mise-en-scène* of a collective sense of cultural inferiority.

In the terms of Pierre Bourdieu, the difference between Portia and her suitor is one of 'taste', defined as 'a class culture turned into nature, that is *embodied*'. As Bourdieu suggests – and as Portia demonstrates with consummate ease – 'the body is the most indisputable materialization of class taste',[8] while the exchange of uncomprehending looks between the Italian lady and the English baron perfectly exemplifies what Bourdieu characterizes as 'the dichotomy between the "aesthetic gaze" and the "naive gaze"'.[9] Portia's sense of aesthetic superiority towards the naive and bungled attempts by the Englishman to continentalize his body and his 'behaviour', as she terms it, is of course somewhat ironical since she is supposedly looking and speaking from the hated continent. It is also ironical that Portia should confirm Harrison's anti-continental ideology, since she herself, or at least the actor who plays her, is the perfect epitome of the effeminizing Italianate transvestism that the English author so detests. And she will go on to worsen the situation by further cross-dressing as Balthazar, taking on 'such staring attire as in time past was supposed meet for none but light hussies only, is now become an habit for chaste and sober matrons', as Harrison puts it in his virulent attack on female cross-dressing.[10]

Harrison produces in his anti-transvestite tirade an interesting if perhaps unintentional pun on the word 'habit'. The unnatural continental *habit* – *habitus*: apparel or habiliments – has become by a process of contagion an English vice or bad *habit*: *habitudo* or habitude. Outward appearance not only expresses an individual state of mind, it becomes, with familiarity, a collective convention and thus threatens the very constitution of English society. We encounter the same *habitus/habitudo* pun in Shakespeare, for example in Malvolio's musings on becoming a prominent gentleman 'in the habit [dress/ mode of behaviour] of some sir of note' (*Twelfth Night* 3.4.73). And given its sociological implications, one might further extend Harrison's 'habit' to include Pierre Bourdieu's definition of the 'habitus' as the meaning-producing interiorization of social constraints, of the very kind that the conservative Harrison endeavours to resist: 'The habitus', writes Bourdieu, 'is necessity internalized and converted into a disposition that generates meaningful practices and meaning-giving perceptions; it is a general, transposable disposition which carries out a systematic, universal application':[11] in other words, the habitus is the whole set of introjected class, national and indeed gender dispositions that produces what Portia calls 'behaviour': 'The habitus', Bourdieu explains, 'is a system of durable, transposable dispositions which functions as the generative basis of structured, objectively unified practices.'[12] And in particular, the habitus generates our most characteristic and unconscious modes of behaviour such as style of body movement: 'Orienting practices practically, they [the schemes of the habitus] embed what some would mistakenly call values in the most automatic gestures or the apparently most insignificant techniques of the body – ways of walking or blowing one's nose, ways of eating or talking.'[13]

The question is, in the context of early modern cultural relations, to what extent the habitus, as opposed to the mere habit or apparel, is really, to use Bourdieu's term, 'transposable' across cultures. It is the habitus, not the habit, that makes the man; or as Feste says, again in *Twelfth Night* (as if in answer to Malvolio) '*cucullus non facit monachum*: that's as much to say, as I wear not motley in my brain.' (1.5.53–5):[14] the habit (cucullus) does not determine the mental disposition or habitus of the subject. If Portia speaks and moves with the effortless class and national habitus of a Renaissance Italian lady, poor Falconbridge can only mimic the appearance, not the bodily and behavioural disposition of continental gentry.

For Harrison, instead, continental modes of behaviour, as opposed to mere apparel – habitus rather than habit – may indeed be learned, and specifically in Portia's Italy. In his much-quoted chapter 'Of degrees of people in the commonwealth of England', Harrison attacks what he calls 'these Italianates and their demeanour', laying the blame on English cultural tourism in Italy itself: 'This gay booty got these gentlemen by going into Italy; and hereby a man may see what fruit is afterward to be looked for where such blossoms do appear … for they have learned in Italy to go up and down also in England with pages at their heels finely apparelled, whose face and countenance shall be such as sheweth the master not to be blind in his choice.' The fact that even servants have learned to prance up and down *all'italiana*, transgressing not only against Englishness but against strict class boundaries, is the sign of a behavioural epidemic that threatens the national identity at large.

Osric his practise

The areas of behaviour particularly associated with Italy were the courtly disciplines or arts of the body, such as genteel modes of walking (Harrison's 'going up and down'), curtseying, dancing, and fencing. This latter art, in its newer and more ornate forms, had been so strongly influenced by the Italian school as to prompt George Silver to issue a Harrison-like defence of English fencing style in his *Paradoxes of Defence*, printed in 1599 by Edward Blount (future publisher of Shakespeare's First Folio) and dedicated to Robert Devereux, second Earl of Essex. In his dedicatory Epistle to the Earl Silver likens fencing to other forms of bodily behaviour, subject to influence and vogues: 'Fencing (Right honorable) in this new fangled age, is like our fashions, euerie daye a change, resembling the Cameleon, who altereth himselfe into all colours saue white: so fencing changeth into all wards [i.e. defensive movements] saue the right' (A3v). And immediately afterwards, in his 'Admonition to the noble, ancient, victorious, valiant, and most brave nation of Englishmen', in attacking what he calls 'these Italianated, weake, fantasticall, and most divellish and imperfect fights', Silver rehearses the naked Englishman trope that we find in Harrison and others; in his version Italian fencing modes denude (and so emasculate) the English fighter by robbing him of his natural style of combat:

> If that man were now aliue, which beat the maisters for the scholars fault, because he had no better instructed him, these Italian fencers could not escape his censure, who teach us Offense, not Defence, and to fight, as Diogenes scholers were taught to daunce, to bring their liues to an end by Art. Was Ajax a coward because he fought with a seuen foulded Buckler, or are we mad to go naked into the field to trie our fortunes, not our vertues.[15]

Silver's protest extends to the weapons themselves: he complains of the excessive length of the Italian sword and rapier which renders them ineffective in practical defence (one might suspect a form of poniard envy here). His comparative stance, however, like Harrison's, is primarily ideological and indeed ethical, a stand in favour of reliable English naturalness against fancy but untrustworthy Italian artfulness:

> And if I should chuse a valiant man for seruice of the Prince, or to take part with me or anie friend of mine in a good quarrell, I would choose the unskilful man, because unencombred with false fights, because such a man standeth free in his valour with strength and agilitie of bodie, freely taketh the benefit of nature, fights most braue, by loosing no opportunity, either soundly to hurt his enemie, or defend himselfe, but the other standing for his Defence, upon cunning Italian wardes, *Pointa reuersa*, the *Imbrocata*, *Stocata*, and being fast tyed unto these false fightes, standeth troubled in his wits.[16]

Silver's contempt is aimed principally against the most fashionable contemporary Anglo-Italian fencing manual of the day, *Vincentio Saviolo His Practise*, published four years earlier, in 1595. Saviolo's patron, not by chance, was the same Earl of Essex to whom Silver dedicates his volume, so that there have been may be a real conflict of interests in act between the rival fencers, although Saviolo had died in the meantime. Silver supports his denigration of Vincentio's ineffectual artfulness with two possibly apocryphal stories involving the Italian master, one involving his humiliation by the English master of defence Bartholomew Bramble, the other concerning a challenge from Silver himself and his brother Toby to Saviolo and his colleague and compatriot Jeronimo, for having placed in doubt the skill of English swordsmen; despite placarding London, Southwark, and Westminster with their challenges, they find no trace of their cowardly opponents:

> These two *Italian* fencers, especially *Vincentio*, said Englishmen were strong men, but had no cunning, and they would go backe too much in their fight, which was great disgrace unto them. Upon these words of disgrace against Englishmen, my brother

Toby Silver and myself, made challenge against them both ... Do the gentlemen what they could, these gallants would not come to the place of triall. I verily thinke their cowardly feare to answere this chalenge, had utterly shamed them indeed.[17]

Inevitably the combat between the two writers and fighters descends into the territory of words as well as wards, and of the rival claims of the Italian and English languages to be the *lingua franca* of fencing. Saviolo, a first-generation Italian immigrant from Padua, apologizes for his poor command of English, while making some claim to Englishness himself by paying a conventional tribute in his conclusion to 'this most glorious Elizabeth our gracious Queene' (Mm3v). He leaves all the technical terms, however, in Italian, and, despite Silver's attempts to anglicize the sport, they remained Italian ever after, much to his chagrin, prompting the English fencer to produce his own logorrhoeic cascade of Italian jargon by way of resentful satire:

> Now, o you Italian teachers of Defence, where are your *Stocatas, Imbrocatas, Mandritas, Puntas,* & *Puynta Reversas, Stramisons, Passatas, Carricados, Amazzas,* & *Incartatas,* & playing with your bodies, remouing with your feet a litle aside, circle wise winding of your bodies, making of three times with your feet together, marking with one eye the motion of the aduersary, & with the other eye the aduantage of thrusting?[18]

For that matter, even Saviolo has his scholar protest somewhat (self-)ironically, 'But I pray you why doo use so many stoccataes and imbroccataes?'[19]

In any event, this clamorous linguistic and corporeal combat finds, I believe, a direct echo in a play performed shortly after Silver's paradoxical defence of English fence, namely *Hamlet*. In the final scene of the play – especially in the Q2 text – the discursive and behavioural politics of cultural attrition are again on display. Hamlet's encounter with the courtier Osric presents a satirical cameo on the perils of continentalization of the English (officially Danes). Excessively decked out in apparel, in behaviour and in speech, Osric is the perfect epitome of the fears of Harrison and Silver (affectation, effeminacy, etc.). The episode begins with Osric's eulogy to Laertes as the perfect gentleman and master of the courtly continental arts:

> OSRIC Sir, here is newly come to court Laertes – believe me, an absolute gentleman, full of most excellent differences, of very soft society and great showing. Indeed, to speak feelingly of him, he is the card or calendar of gentry; for you shall find in him the continent of what part a gentleman would see.
> (5.2.106–11)[20]

Osric's verbal as well as vestiary finery provoke Hamlet to produce the 'habit' pun mentioned earlier: he comments sarcastically that 'only got the tune of the time and outward habit of encounter', i.e. he has assimilated only the fashionable phraseology and apparel or conventions of civil conversation ('encounter'), not civility as such, the habit not the habitus.

English bodies in Italian habits

The particular verbal-corporeal code that allows Osric to show off his mastery of the polite arts is the language of fencing, not surprisingly since the official topic of the dialogue is Hamlet's duel with Laertes.[21] Indeed, not only do they discuss the art of armed combat, they act it out, as it were, in advance, in the sense that the exchange itself mimics the moves of a fencing bout, with Hamlet and his second Horatio on the attack in mocking Osric's linguistic affectations, and the courtier endeavouring uncertainly to parry the blows:

> HAMLET The concernancy, sir? Why do we wrap the gentleman in our more rawer breath?
> OSRIC Sir?
> HORATIO Is't not possible to understand in another tongue? You will to't, sir, really...
> HAMLET What's his weapon?
> OSRIC Rapier and dagger.
> HAMLET That's two of his weapons. But well.
>
> (5.2.122–43)

Hamlet expresses an apparently Silver-like conservatism in his resistance to Osric's linguistic contaminations. That the Anglo-Italian fencing debate may indeed lie behind this exchange finds confirmation in Osric's earnest allusion – immediately mocked by Hamlet – to 'Rapier and dagger' (l. 142), which probably echoes Saviolo's *Practise*, whose title continues: *in two bookes: the first intreating of the use of the Rapier and Dagger, the second of Honour and Honourable Quarrels*. Saviolo's first book on 'the rapier and dagger' is the technical part of his manual, which gives copious and minutely detailed instructions on exotically named parts of the weapons and on the secrets of the *stoccata*, the *punta reversa*, and the *imbroccata*. It is this technical language – particularly the naming of parts – with its supposed cultural kudos that Osric goes on to deploy in the vain attempt to impress the Prince, even if the terms he employs are more French than Italian:

> The King, sir, hath wagered with him six Barbary horses, against the which he has impawned, as I take it, six French rapiers and poniards, with their assigns, as girdle, hanger, and so. Three of the carriages, in faith, are very dear to fancy, very responsive to the hilts, most delicate carriages, and of very liberal conceit.
> (5.2.144–50)

Fencing talk was a relatively recent and still glamorous discourse genre in England, and the social status of fencing itself was still uncertain. In Italy, the strict rules of the *duello* originally represented an institutionalization of the street brawl, which was 'civilized' through the imposition not only of technique but also of a powerful code of honour. The tensions between these two spheres, the Italian street fight and the codified 'art', are dramatized in the less than courteous fight scene in *Romeo and Juliet*, where the dying Mercutio disparages his opponent Tybalt, who has just '*thrust[ed] Mercutio in*', '*under Romeo's arm*' (stage direction in Q1), as one 'that fights by the book of arithmetic', i.e. according to the fencing manual, rather than the laws of honest combat (3.1.103-4). In any event, the result of this civilizing effort was that Italian fencing guides were hybrid texts, in part how-to handbooks (teach yourself vendetta), in part conduct books based on the chivalric code of honour. Hence Saviolo's two books, one on rapier and dagger, one on the rules 'Of Honour and Honorable Quarrels'.

In England, the sociological connotations of the rapier were quite different. Duelling was officially banned, but the fact that Saviolo was able to make his living by teaching 'his practice' in London suggests the extent to which the art was cultivated among the gentry and, perhaps more to the point, among aspiring candidates to gentrification. In 1591 John Florio alludes to Saviolo's fencing school 'in the little street where the well is … at the sign of the red Lyon'.[22] And it flourished above all in one particular domain of social interaction: namely, the London stage. One of the points to the verbal skirmish between Hamlet and Osric is that the actor Richard Burbage (as Hamlet) and at least one other actor in the company (as Laertes) had to be genuinely skilled in fencing. This was far from unusual: we know that the great clown Richard Tarlton, for example, was a qualified Master of Fencing.[23] Burbage and his colleague had actually gone through the kind of training prescribed by Saviolo, if not directly at his hands,[24] and indeed they had to put their practical know-how on display later in the same scene. In this sense fencing was unique in bringing together dramatic action, a specific performance skill and a highly developed 'foreign' cultural code.

At the same time, and still on stage, 'fence' was an easy object of social and stylistic satire precisely because of its elitist and 'alien' status. Book I of Saviolo's *Practice* had already been travestied in Ben Jonson's *Every Man in His Humour* (1598) in which Shakespeare acted (but did not fence). Bobadilla's lesson to Matheo on how to avenge the insult of Signor Giuliano, who has threatened to fetch Matheo a bastinado, mimics Saviolo's 'platonic' dialogue between master and pupil: 'come hither, you shall challenge him: I'll shew you a trick or two, you shall kill him at pleasure, the first *stoccado* if you will, by this air'.[25] This seems to come straight out of Saviolo: 'when a man knoweth himselfe to haue rightly receiued the lye, by and by to auoide the proofe, he seeketh to giue the bastonado'.[26] Bobadilla goes into precise detail on moves and body posture, acting them out on stage, with more than a hint of homoerotic potential in the engagement of thrusting male bodies: 'So, sir, come on, oh, twine your body more about, that you may come to a more gentleman-like guard … Why thus, sir: make a thrust at me; come in upon my time; control your point, and make a full career at the body: the best-practis'd gentlemen of the time term it the *passado*, a most desperate thrust, believe it.'[27]

The lesson survives in the London version, where it is more clearly a farcical spoof on the Italianate affectation rife in the capital.

Meanwhile, Book 2 of Saviolo's treatise – 'Of Honour and Honorable quarrels' – had already been parodied by Shakespeare in the final scene of *As You Like It*, in Touchstone's virtuoso disquisition on the 'degrees of the lie' in conducting a quarrel.

> JAQUES Can you nominate in order now the degrees of the lie?
> TOUCHSTONE O sir, we quarrel in print, by the book, as you have books for good manners. I will name you the degrees. The first, the Retort Courteous; the second, the Quip Modest; the third, the Reply Churlish; the fourth, the Reproof Valiant; the fifth, the Countercheck Quarrelsome; the sixth, the Lie with Circumstance; the seventh, the Lie Direct. All these you may avoid but the Lie Direct; and you may avoid that, too, with an 'IF'. (5.4.87–97)

Here we have the fool Touchstone in the role of the 'maister' V[incentio] (perhaps with a glance back towards his predecessor and authentic master of fencing Tarlton), and Jaques in the role of his suitably admiring pupil. Saviolo dedicates an ample section of his guide to 'the giuing and receiuing of the Lie, whereupon the Duello & the Combats in diuers sortes doth insue'.[28] Saviolo's typology distinguishes between three species of lie: lies certain (or affirmative), lies conditional (beginning with 'if': compare Touchstone's 'with an If', l. 97) and lies vain or foolish. Touchstone inflates this taxonomy into seven. The 'lie' in this context is not a falsehood but, on the contrary, the accusation of falsehood: 'hee unto whome the lie is wrongfullie giuen', explains Saviolo in his discussion 'Of the manner and diuersitie of Lies', 'ought to challenge him that offereth that dishonour, and by the swoorde to proue himselfe no lyer.' (Book 2, R4v). This is the underlying scenario of the Italian duel: the fight is a defence not only of one's rights but of one's being right, the active rebuttal an unjust charge. Saviolo sets up a brief narrative enactment of his scenario: 'Example, Caius sayth to Seius that hee is a traitor: unto which Seius aunswereth by giuing the lie: whereupon ensueth, that the charge of the Cobat falleth on Caius, because hee is to maintaine what hee sayd, and therefore to challenge Seius.'[29]

The *duello* thus becomes a trial by combat whose result sanctions the moral supremacy of the Caius or Seius. Or indeed of Hamlet or Laertes. If Shakespeare makes fun, through Osric, of the technical jargon of fencing and the ceremonial pompousness of its preparatory rituals, the duel itself is an altogether more serious piece of dramatic and stage business. *Hamlet* in fact respects the deep structure of the giving-the-lie scenario: (1) Laertes accuses Hamlet of a 'wicked deed', namely causing Ophelia's death (5.1.241); (2) Hamlet gives Laertes the lie, claiming that his love for Ophelia was greater than that of 'Forty thousand brothers' (5.1.264) and challenges Laertes to a duel ('Why, I will fight with him upon this theme' (261); (3) Laertes, encouraged by Claudius, accepts the challenge. So far, so orthodox. The combat, moreover, is not to the death, and not for revenge – Saviolo insists that 'Combat was ordayned for iustifieing of a truth, and not to laye open a waie for one man to reuenge him of another' (Book 2, Z4v) – since Laertes declares himself 'satisfied in nature, / Whose motives in this case should stir me most / To my revenge' (5.2.181-3), and fights, like Hamlet, 'to proue himselfe no lyer' (Book 2, R4v).

The duel in *Hamlet* goes wrong because it reverses Mercutio's dying complaint about excessive formality. Formally it is impeccable, as Osric's presiding presence guarantees. Where it deviates from the rule books is in the non-technical and, in theory, marginal goings on, particularly in the question of third-party intervention. Saviolo is at pains to spell out the code of behaviour for 'padrini', or accompanying persons, who are to act as mediators or 'as it were proctors, for the iniuries, the lyes, the cartels, and challenges ... for the better conseruation of the right use of chiualry' (Book 2, Aa4r). This is not precisely the role that the *padrino* (or *padrone*) Claudius takes upon himself, and it is of course his interference that causes the duel to degenerate into a bloodbath.

Unhatched rapiers in Illyria

Many of the issues I have been addressing here – seeing ourselves from without, defining Englishness, culture clashes, the attempted assimilation of imported codes and languages, and specifically the rituals of duelling – come together in a different and in some ways definitive fashion in another beginning of century play, *Twelfth Night*, in which the presence of two Englishmen – Sir Toby Belch and Sir Andrew Aguecheek – in the supposedly exotic and in some ways Italianate space of Illyria allows Shakespeare to create the comic spectacle of English bodies endeavouring to adapt to a continental habitus. The main locus of the comedy's farcical staging of Englishness is Act 3, and is again centred on the physical and discursive practice of fencing. Sir Toby, for his own amusement, persuades Sir Andrew to challenge his supposed rival in love, Viola–Cesario, to a duel, knowing full well that no such event is likely to come about owing to the unpromising human material at his disposal (it is tempting to hear an echo here of Silver's story of his and his brother Toby's challenge to Vincentio, which comes to nothing owing to cowardice).

As part of his strategy for mortifying the foolish Sir Andrew, the self-elected fencing master Sir Toby, like Claudius, knowingly makes a mockery of the rules regarding third-party intervention in quarrels. Saviolo exhorts the *padrini* or seconds to employ their diplomatic wisdom in order to avoid unjustified duels: 'such gentlemen as doe counsel or accompany a man, ought to be judges of the quarrel, for unto them it belongs chiefly to know if the quarrel deserve trial by arms or no' (Book 2, Aa3v). In the case of Sir Andrew not only does the quarrel not deserve a trial by arms, but there is no quarrel at all, apart from the one invented by his *padrino*. This is Toby's comic masterpiece: to set up all the ritual paraphernalia of the *duello* without cause and (given the absolute incompetence of the supposed duellers) without outcome, at least until the arrival of Sebastian, who spoils the fun by giving Andrew, Toby, and all the bastinado.

The main focus of Sir Toby's mystification of his gull, however, concerns the crucial question of the 'lie'. 'Lie' in fencing parlance is an abbreviated form of 'give the lie', which as we have seen is the mainspring of duelling rites. Toby, instead, equivocates, reducing the business of lie-giving to the simple telling of lies: 'as many lies as will lie in thy sheet of paper, although the sheet were big enough for the bed of Ware in England, set 'em down' (3.2.44–6). This is the hole at the centre of the quarrel in *Twelfth Night*: since Sir Andrew cannot legitimately defend his honour because Cesario has not given him the lie, and therefore has nothing to fight about, all he can do is invent, or tell 'lies'.

Regarding the style of the challenge, Toby's advice looks suspiciously like an outright parody of the Anglo-Italian fencing master, who devotes a substantial part of his manual to the discourse genre of 'Cartels, or Letters of Defiance', an essential part of the *duello*. Saviolo's prime rule is that of succinctness: 'When Cartels are to be made, they must be written with the greatest brevity that may be possible, framing the quarrell with certaine, proper, and simple woordes' (Book 2, X1r). Here is Toby's version of what appears to be the same sound advice: 'Go, write it in a martial hand, be curst and brief. It is no matter how witty, so it be eloquent and full of invention' (3.2.40–2). In effect, however, Toby's counsel manages to say the opposite of what it seems to be saying, by way of a rhetorical paradox. Sir Andrew's letter of challenge should achieve invention (rhetorical *inventio* or substance) and eloquence (rhetorical *elocutio* or style) without being 'witty', i.e. intelligent. This is an open invitation, promptly accepted by Aguecheek, to fill his 'cartel' with long-winded and dim-witted vituperation ('be curst'). The resulting composition is a small masterpiece of bad-tempered non sequitur and pompous self-contradiction:

> Youth, whatsoever thou art, thou art but a scurvy fellow. Wonder not, nor admire not in thy mind, why I do call thee so, for I will show thee no reason for 't. Thou comest to the Lady Olivia, and in my sight she uses thee kindly: but thou liest in thy throat; that is not the matter I challenge thee for. (3.4.149–58)

There is a further twist here regarding the intertextual exchange between the comedy and the fencing manual. Saviolo, evidently aware of the comic potential of his scenario, produces his own burlesque of the incompetent 'cartel' in his chapter dedicated, significantly, to 'foolish Lyes': 'And hereupon it cometh', he warns, 'that every day there riseth from the common sort of new and strange foolishnesses, as he who will give the lie ere the other speak, saying: if they say that I am not an honest man, thou liest in thy throat' (Book 2, T2v). This is not only a perfect description of Aguecheek's behaviour, but is also verbatim what he actually writes in his epistle ('thou liest in thy throat'). At the heart of both epistolary disasters is a misinterpretation of the significance and timing of lie-giving. Sir Andrew first gives the lie in advance – 'ere the other speak', as Saviolo puts it – and then goes on immediately to belie his own lie-giving by denying that it is in any case the cause of the quarrel ('that is not the matter …'), thereby undoing his accusation in the very act of making it.

Later in the same scene, in his second duelling dialogue with Sir Andrew, Sir Toby shifts discursive territory and moves back to Book I of Saviolo's *Practice*, 'Of the use of the rapier and dagger'. Describing the supposedly diabolical skills of Aguecheek's opponent, Belch succeeds in terrifying his 'scholar' even further through a barrage of technical terms:

> Why, man, he's a very devil, I have not seen such a firago. I had a pass with him, rapier, scabbard, and all: and he gives me the stuck in with such a mortal motion that it is inevitable; and on the answer, he pays you as surely as your feet hits the ground they step on. They say he has been fencer to the Sophy. (3.4.278–92)

Rhetorically, Sir Toby's hyperbolic eulogy of Cesario is parallel to Osric's praise of Laertes in *Hamlet* 5.2 (see above), with the small difference that Belch is giving the lie here to Viola's actual duelling incompetence. In constructing his elaborate lie, Toby marshals a strategic mélange of anglicized *termini tecnici*: 'pass' (the *passata*), 'scabbard' (l. 280) is the sheath protecting the sword: 'rapier, scabbard and all' incongruously implies that Cesario's sword remained unsheathed during their putative 'pass', but the bewildered Aguecheek fails to pick up the irony; 'stuck in' (from *stoccata*); even the apparently non-technical and ominous 'mortal motion' (i.e. deadly movement, l. 281) comes from the manual, 'motion' being a highly disciplined and regulated stepping movement or ward.

3.2 The *stoccata* (from *Vincentio Saviolo his Practise*, 1595)

As with his previous advice to his scholar, Sir Toby bends the rules of Saviolo's Italian art to his own ends. Vincentio exhorts his trainee fencer always to defend himself when attacked in a 'stuck' by warding off the blow and responding with a countermove: 'break the stoccata with his left hand, and answer him again with the other' (Book 1, 17r; see figure 3.2).

Toby, on the contrary, warns his scholar that 'on the answer, he pays you' – i.e. if you attempt to return his thrust, he puts paid to you – virtually inviting Sir Andrew to offer himself during the duel as an unmoving and passive target for Cesario's mortal motion (just as he is of Toby's verbal moves against him). Andrew's sublime innocence of both the bodily and the discursive languages of fence gives the lie to his outburst in Act 1, when, to justify his ignorance of foreign tongues and of the intellectual humanistic arts in general, he laments 'I would I had bestowed that time in the tongues that I have in fencing, dancing and bear-baiting. O had I but followed the arts!' (1.3.90–3). He is as monolingual as Portia's Falconbridge, and the time he has supposedly dedicated to the bodily arts has been ill invested.

Toby most precious – and, for Andrew, incomprehensible – lexical gem, however, is the non-technical but exotically recherché 'firago' (l. 279), a variant of 'virago', literally man-like woman. Sir Toby's striking choice of epithet not only introduces the topic of androgyny explicitly into the comedy, it also seems to imply that he has seen through Cesario's mask. The term could be applied in early modern English to a ferocious *male* warrior (*OED* 2b) – in this sense unwittingly predicting the arrival, in the following scene, of the male 'virago' or fierce fighter Sebastian – but the connotations of femininity were prevalent, so much so that in the Vulgate version of Genesis 2:23, 'Virago' is Adam's name for Eve, and thus for woman *tout court*. Belch's depiction of Cesario as a ferocious Amazon-like woman recalls the gallery of man-like woman combatants – from the Amazons themselves to Joan of Arc – presented by Saviolo, who unlike Harrison expresses admiration for such mannish fighters. Of particular interest in the context of *Twelfth Night* are Saviolo's accounts of cross-dressed female warriors such as 'a Portingall gentlewoman that for religions sake about 4. yeeres now past, lefte of the apparell of her sexe, and went as a souldier into Barberie, where she behaued her selfe so resolutely, that she was in short time after made a Captaine' (Book 2, Mm1r). The most evident irony here is that while Sir Toby's description of the firago Cesario matches Saviolo's, Viola's own behaviour fails conspicuously to correspond to either.

As for the exotic firago him/herself, Cesario is another victim of fencing discourse as a mode of rhetorical terrorism. In a doubly sadistic mirror game, Sir Toby exercises the same brand of mystification he used with Andrew in order to convince Cesario of his antagonist's expertise and ferocity:

> SIR TOBY Dismount thy tuck, be yare in thy preparation, for thy assailant is quick, skilful, and deadly … Therefore, if you hold your life at any price,

betake you to your guard; for your opposite hath in him what youth, strength, skill, and wrath can furnish man withal.

VIOLA I pray you, sir, what is he?

SIR TOBY He is knight, dubbed with unhatched rapier and on carpet consideration, but he is a devil in private brawl ... Therefore on, or strip your sword stark naked: for meddle you must, that's certain, or forswear to wear iron about you.

(3.4.222–56)

Again the 'technical' jargon here involves both the weaponry and the tactical moves of the duel. A 'tuck' (l. 225) was a small rapier (from Italian *stocco*), the very weapon that Cesario, according to Sir Toby at l. 280, keeps safe in its scabbard.[30] Toby gives Cesario an analogous hint regarding Sir Andrew's weapon, i.e. that he never uses it: not only is the rapier used to knight him 'unhatched' – i.e. unhacked, used not for combat but for ceremonial purposes (l. 237) – but his own sword, as we discover, is likewise unmarked (with attendant allusions to Sir Andrew's oft-hinted impotence). Indeed, Belch goes perilously far here in satirizing not only his crony's prowess but even his very knighthood, which he has received 'on carpet consideration' (l. 238), i.e. he was knighted at court rather than on the battlefield. Sir Andrew, like Portia's Baron Falconbridge, has probably purchased his title: there is a likely pun here on 'consideration' in the sense of sum of money. Francis Markham in his *Book of Honour* reserves special contempt for this social category: 'these [knights] of the vulgar or common sort are called *Carpet-Knights*, because (for the most part) they receive their honours from the King's hand in the court, and upon Carpets, and such like Ornaments belonging to the King's State and Greatness.'[31] Sir Toby has in effect given the game away regarding Aguecheek's standing as armed knight, but all is one to Viola who, like her 'opposite', fails to take the hint, presumably terrified by Sir Toby's warning to take up a correct defensive position ('betake you to your guard' (ll. 232–3): another fencing expression) and by his peremptory injunction to 'meddle' (fight).

The exit line of Belch's dire warning revisits the topic of the androgynous firago: 'forswear to wear iron' (ll. 255-6), i.e. give up wearing a sword, and thereby admit to cowardice, or symbolically (and in Cesario's case materially) to castration.[32] It is indeed the phallic prospect of fighting a duel that threatens to blow Viola's gender cover. When Belch returns to the attack by insisting that he intends – against all the rules of fencing etiquette – to fight without a 'quarrel' 'for the supportance of his vow' (i.e. merely to justify his challenge), the terrified Viola is prompted to confide her weapon-less state to the audience: 'Pray God defend me! A little thing would make me tell them how much I lack of a man' (3.4.307–9). Viola lacks not only a long sword but even a more modest weapon or 'little thing', such as a rapier.

The exchange is perfectly mirrored in Belch's claim to Aguecheek that it is Cesario who insists on fighting without cause:

SIR TOBY Come, Sir Andrew, there's no remedy, the gentleman will for his honour's sake have one bout with you; he cannot by the duello avoid it, but he has promised me, as he is a gentleman and a soldier, he will not hurt you. Come on, to't.
SIR ANDREW Pray God he keep his oath!

(3.4.312–17)

Cesario's supposed self-justification 'by the duello', i.e. by the rules governing the code of duelling, is – like Aguecheek's putative desire to combat 'for the supportance of his vow' – ideological nonsense, since all the duelling books, starting from Muzio's seminal *Il duello*, go out of their way to denounce fighting without a just quarrel.[33]

The antagonists are united in error, or at least in Toby's lies. Just as they are united in terror: Viola's rapier-less condition is matched by Andrew's unwillingness to draw or use his weapon, with the implication that Cesario is not the only unmanned male on stage. The histrionic spectacle that *Twelfth Night* offers us is the exact opposite to the duel scene in *Hamlet*: here we have two actors, one of them doubly cross-dressed, pretending not to be able to do what in fact they have been trained to do. The resulting farce may not have pleased either the artful Vincentio or the earnest George Silver (or indeed his brother Toby), but is an example of what can happen when naked English bodies try on refined Italian habits.

Notes

1 Pierre Bourdieu, *Distinction: A Social Critique of the Judgment of Taste*, trans. Richard Nice (Cambridge, Mass., Harvard University Press, 1984), p. 169. On this topic see also Bourdieu's 'Social Space and Symbolic Space', in *Practical Reason: On the Theory of Action* (Cambridge, Polity Press, 1998), pp. 1–14.
2 William Harrison, *Description of England*, ed. L. Whitington (as *Elizabethan England*) (London, Walter Scott, 1899), p. 181.
3 Harrison, *Description*, pp. 107–8.
4 Harrison, *Description*, pp. 110–11.
5 Harrison takes both the poem and the illustration from Andrew Boorde, *The Fyrst Boke of the Introduction of Knowledge* (London, William Copland, 1550), p. 6.
6 *Homily against Excess of Apparel*, ed. Ian Lancashire, Renaissance Electronic Texts, 1.2, University of Toronto, 1997, II.6.1-145-153.
7 William Shakespeare, *The Merchant of Venice*, ed. John Russell Brown, Arden Shakespeare, second edition (London, Methuen, 1955).
8 Bourdieu, *Distinction*, p. 190. On Bourdieu's concept of the *habitus* see also Bridget Fowler, *Pierre Bourdieu and Cultural Theory: Critical Investigations* (London, Sage Publications, 1997); Derek Robbins, *The Work of Pierre Bourdieu: Recognizing Society* (Boulder, Westview Press, 1991); Richard Harker, Cheleen Mahar and Chris Wilkes, eds, *An Introduction to the Work of Pierre Bourdieu: The Practice of Theory*

(Houndmills, Macmillan, 1990).
9 Bourdieu, *Distinction*, pp. 250–1; see also Fowler, *Pierre Bourdieu and Cultural Theory*, p. 46.
10 Harrison, *Description*, p. 111.
11 Bourdieu, *Distinction*, p. 170.
12 Pierre Bourdieu, *Outline of a Theory of Practice*, trans. Richard Nice (Cambridge, Cambridge University Press, 1979), p. vii.
13 Bourdieu, *Distinction*, p. 466.
14 William Shakespeare, *Twelfth Night*, ed. J. M. Lothian and T. W. Craik, Arden Shakespeare, 2nd edn (London, Methuen, 1975).
15 George Silver, *Paradoxes of Defence* (London, Edward Blount, 1599), A5v.
16 Ibid., p. 71.
17 Ibid., p. 67.
18 Ibid., p. 55.
19 Saviolo, Book 1, p. 17r.
20 This is the Q2 text as collated in the Arden Shakespeare *Hamlet*, 2nd edn, ed. Harold Jenkins (London, Methuen, 1982).
21 On fencing in *Hamlet* see James L. Jackson, '"They Catch One Another's Rapiers": The Exchange of Weapons in *Hamlet*', *Shakespeare Quarterly*, 41:3 (fall 1990), 281–98. On fencing and early modern English drama in general see Robert E. Morsberger, *Swordplay and the Elizabethan and Jacobean Stage*, Jacobean Drama Studies 37 (Salzburg, Universität Salzburg, 1974).
22 John Florio, *Florios second frutes* (London, 1591).
23 See Andrew Gurr, *The Shakespearean Stage 1574-1642* (Cambridge, Cambridge University Press, 1992), p. 86.
24 The Italian maestro was teaching in the capital in the 1590s (he is reported dead by George Silver in 1599). On the fencing–theatre connection see Linda Carlyle McCollum, 'The Fencing School in Blackfriars', *Blackfriars' Journal*, 1:1 (1998).
25 Ben Jonson, *Every Man in His Humour*, 1.3, in *The Complete Plays* (London, Dent, 1910), pp. 10-11.
26 *Vincentio Saviolo's Practise in two bookes: the first intreating of the use of the Rapier and Dagger, the second of Honour and Honourable Quarrels* (London, 1595), Book 2, Z4r–Aa1v.
27 Ben Jonson, *Every Man in His Humour*, 1.3, pp. 10–11.
28 Saviolo, Book 2, sig. S2r.
29 Saviolo, Book 2, sigs R3r–R4v.
30 In *Hamlet* Osric pretentiously calls the straps attaching the sword to the belt 'carriages' (5.2.148); Sir Toby's 'dismount' seems to play on the same metaphor.
31 Francis Markham, *Book of Honour* (London, 1625), p. 71.
32 Compare Sir Andrew's self-undoing threat to Maria at 1.3.62–3: 'And you part so, mistress, I would I might never draw sword again.'
33 The *OED* gives this as the first recorded use of 'duello' in English, but it is anticipated by Don Armado's complaint in *Love's Labour's Lost*, 1.2.171–2: 'The *passado* he respects not; the *duello* he regards not.' *Love's Labour's Lost*, ed. H. R. Woudhuysen, 3rd edn (London, The Arden Shakespeare, 1998).

4

Shakespeare and Plutarch: intertextuality in action[1]

ALESSANDRO SERPIERI

When Shakespeare started to work on Plutarch at the end of the 1590s he had already produced all his English history plays, with the exception of the late *Henry VIII*, and had therefore refined his dramaturgical ability in selecting, transforming, and adapting for the stage the historical events drawn from his sources. However, Plutarch now offered him new angles of perception for the dramatization of history. The biographical account of great personages of the past radically distinguished the Greek historian from the annalistic and sequential exposition of the English *Chronicles* he had dealt with up to that point. Plutarch's *Lives* aimed at narrating events through the motivations and 'demonic' aspirations of complex personalities which shaped the course of history: it is not by accident that the parallel lives of the two characters he always accounted for (one Greek, one Latin) were followed, in almost all cases, by a sort of final balance in which virtues and vices, merits and faults, of the two were compared. Moreover, the political aspect was always explored together with the ethical, the temperamental and the heroic.

And that is not all. The style of Plutarch's narration affected – no less than his character-centred account of history – Shakespeare's dramatic style. In Plutarch he found a vivid, often stage-like, rhythm, supported by a skilful use of various points of view which added both to the suspense and to the theatricality of the events narrated. All these qualities of Plutarch's prose encountered the keen interest of a playwright who, in staging history, must have felt only too grateful if he was offered highly scenic episodes which he might select and arrange in the rapid, essential economy of a play.

First of all, however, he had to filter his abundant source material. This had to be done at the level of the fabula. In order to create the stage story, he selected both events and characters, according to his semantic and ideological intentions. Such selection entailed, on one side, the omission, integration, and dislocation of events, and, on the other, a preliminary actantial adaptation, which consisted in the choice of the active forces to be opposed in the dramatic *agon* and in the actors–characters who had to represent those forces.[2] The very choice and reshaping of the fabula was, arguably, the first massive intervention by Shakespeare; he had somehow to reshape, to transform, the narrative material in order to transcodify it from narration to drama. But transformation and transcodification are, in a way, inseparable and strictly interdependent – the first being not necessarily a preliminary choice at all points of the developing action, since temporal or spatial constraints of the stage might have required, as an afterthought, a reshaping of the narrative fabula.

Let us, however, follow a logical progression. In transforming the source story and creating his own, at least in its main outlines, he adopted the sequences of the story he was interested in, omitted more or less large portions of it, and, at the same time, invented events or situations which would fit into his own dramatic fabula. Confronted with the task of putting the whole action on stage, he had then to transcodify the adopted narrative sequences into dramatic and theatrical scenes. We are here at the level of plot, which is of paramount importance, involving the ordering of the material – which had been selected to form the fabula of the play, with the addition of new invented events – and its distribution into episodes and scenes, which could hardly follow the order of the narrative source.

I must go back here for a moment to the procedure followed by the whole research group in the study of the histories and of the Roman plays in relation to their sources. In order to carry out a thorough analysis of the construction of the plot in relation to the source, and to investigate the process of transformation and transcodification from one genre into another, we found it necessary to juxtapose, in the first place, the two series of texts and compare them in order to point out the correspondences and non-correspondences between them. This could be done only by segmenting them both at the level of actions and/or topics. It was then possible to set up a tabulation in which the corresponding sequences, and sub-sequences, of the two texts (source and play) could be shown on the same page, or were related one with another through cross-references. This makes at once evident, by the presence of full or empty spaces on one side or the other, the omissions, the additions, and even more complex procedures such as meshing, embedding, or dislocation of units.

After carrying out such an analytical tabulation of each play together with its main source, each researcher went on to comment on all the types of transformation and transcodification procedures employed – scene by scene – in the construction of the dramatic text and their rate of functionality within the scope of the whole play. And it was at this stage that we were able to get at least a glimpse of the playwright at work in his workshop.

The plot of the play thus emerged as a complex reshaping of the narrative source. We had to distinguish the morphology from the syntax of Shakespeare's transformation and transcodification.

The morphology regards the relationship between the dramatic units, or sequences, and the narrative ones: a kind of equivalence occurs when these sequences are of an analogous importance and extension in the two texts; expansion is of course a dilatation of the dramatic sequence when compared with the narrative one, compression being the opposite (and a very frequent one, owing to the peculiar economy of drama in respect of the more abundant pace of narration).

The syntax, on the other hand, regards the way in which the chosen unit-sequences (conceived morphologically according to equivalence, expansion or compression) were distributed, cut up, meshed, embedded, and dislocated in the play's sequential order. The main syntactical operations followed by Shakespeare appear to be the following: (*a*) dislocation, a very frequent mode of dramatic rearrangement of the sequences or sub-sequences of the source plot; (*b*) subdivision, which occurs when a unit of the source, let's call it *X*, composed of two sub-units – *ab* – is presented in the play in two non consecutive units: *Xa* and *Xb*; (*c*) meshing, an operation opposite to the preceding, which occurs when two non-consecutive but related units of the source – let's call them *X1* and *X2* – converge into a single *X1–2* unit of the play; (*d*) embedding, which is an extremely important dramatic procedure through which separate sequences of the source, *X* and *Y*, are employed in the following way: *X* becomes the main frame within which *Y* is inserted.

The construction of the plot constituted the very first step of the research. Other transcodification procedures had then to be taken into account, regarding the dramatic exploitation of time, space, point of view, and finally discourse. But there is not enough space here to give a satisfactory report of such complex semiotic operations. I will therefore offer just a few examples of intertextual procedures in the construction of *Julius Caesar*.

Historical dislocation on the level of fabula: embedding and duplication of space

When the narrative events in *Julius Caesar*, in Act 1, scene 1, are compared with the historical fabula which Shakespeare found in Plutarch, two main procedures of historical dislocation are evident: displacement and redistribution. The triumph celebrated by Caesar in October 45 BC for his victory over Pompey's sons at Munda, Spain (17 March 45) is displaced to the Feast of the Lupercalia of 15 February 44, only a fortnight before the Ides of March when Caesar was killed by the conspirators led by Brutus and Cassius. Dramatic time contracts historical events in order to create rhythm and suspense, and to link one situation with another, one scene with the next. The subsequent scene in the play (1.2) takes place on the same day, the Feast of the Lupercalia, when Caesar was offered a diadem by Antony and refused it several times, thus obtaining shouts of joy from the crowd which was reluctant to grant the status of king, symbolized by the crown, to the man who in any case had already achieved the rank of supreme leader of Rome and had gained an absolute power over its empire. In Plutarch's *Life of Caesar* we read:

> At that time, the feast Lupercalia was celebrated, the which in olde time men say was the feast of sheapheard or heard men, and is much like unto the feast of the Lycaeans in Arcadia. But howsoever it is, that day there are divers noble mens sonnes, young men … which run naked through the citie, striking in sport them they meete in their way, with leather thongs, haire and all on, to make them give place. And many noble women and gentle women also, goe of purpose to stand in their way, and doe put forth their handes to be striken … perswading themselves that being with childe, they shall have good deliverie, and also being barren, that it will make them to conceive with childe. *Caesar* sate to beholde that sport upon the pulpit for orations, in a chaire of golde, apparelled in triumphing manner. *Antonius* who was Consull at that time, was one of them that ranne this holy course. So when he came into the market place … came to *Caesar*, and presented him a Diadeame wreathed about with laurell. Whereupon there rose a certaine cry of rejoycing, not very great, done onely by a few, appointed for the purpose. But when *Caesar* refused the Diadeam, then all the people together made an outcry of joy … *Caesar* having made this proofe, found that the people did not like of it, and thereupon rose out of his chaire, and commanded the crowne to be caried unto *Iupiter* in the Capitoll. After that, there were set up images of *Caesar* in the city with Diadems upon their heades, like kings. Those, the two Tribunes, *Flavius* and *Marullus*, went and pulled downe: and furthermore, meeting with them that first saluted Caesar as king, they committed them to prison.[3] (pp. 786–7)

Shakespeare had spotted this event in Plutarch as the one that could best convey the historical point at stake, namely the possible transformation of the republican state into a monarchy: a transformation that was sought after by Caesar, and his ally Antony, and was opposed by public opinion in general and by the rising republican conspiracy in particular. This event was therefore the most suitable to establish the actantial forces in the field and create the dramatic momentum of the play. Shakespeare chose this sequence of *The Life of Caesar* as the main situation on which to build the first strategic phase of his plot. Within it he embedded the sequence following soon afterwards in the same *Life*, dealing with the formation of the republican conspiracy, and the parallel sequences of *The Life of Brutus* concerning the part that Cassius played in encouraging the popular discontent against Caesar because of his private hatred for him, and his temptation of Brutus.

Shakespeare was certainly attracted by the scenic rhythm of Cassius' temptation of Brutus in *The Life of Brutus*, as he always was when drawing on sources, such as Plutarch, which offered narrative 'scenes' with direct or indirect dialogues. He must have read it very carefully because not only did he reproduce its internal articulation, at the same time operating a remarkable expansion, but very likely he also exploited some of its verbal traces in the actual construction of the preceding first scene of the play. There he dramatized the contrast between the mob, which flows through the streets of Rome to grant Caesar the triumph for his victory, and the tribunes who rail at them because that triumph was undeserved or inappropriate. The battle of Munda had, indeed, been fought and won not against foreigners but against Pompey's sons, who were Romans just as they were. Let us read some lines of the temptation sequence of *The Life of Brutus*, where Cassius says to Brutus: 'Thinkest thou that they be cobblers, tapsters, or such like base mechanicall people, that write these billes and scrowles which are found daily in thy Praetors chaire, and not the noblest men and best citizen that do it?' (p. 1057).

Compare this with 1.1.2–5: 'What, know you not, / (Being *mechanical*) you ought not walk / Upon a labouring day without the sign / Of your profession?', and with the figure of the Cobbler who soon intervenes.[4] We find two words, *cobblers* and *mechanical*, which appear only once and four times respectively in Shakespeare's canon (the verb *to cobble* having one occurrence in the same scene, and, as a past participle, another one curiously enough in *Coriolanus*, another Roman play). We may therefore infer that he was struck by these verbal elements in the temptation sequence of *The Life of Brutus* and built the beginning of his first scene on them, probably being attracted by the punning possibilities offered by the word *cobbler* (both 'shoemaker', as is his trade in the play, and 'patcher', as he delights to appear with his equivocations in ll. 9–31 when he alone wittily replies to the tribunes' reproach).

Let us now move on to see how skilfully Shakespeare constructed the second scene, drawing on both his sources. A lesser playwright would probably have followed the narrative progression of his sources, dramatizing, first, the offering of the crown to Caesar during the 'holy course' of the Lupercalia, and then Cassius' temptation of Brutus in order to involve him in the conspiracy against Caesar (according to that order of cause and effect which emerges from two consecutive sequences of *The Life of Caesar*), or vice versa. But Shakespeare preferred to present the two facts in the same place and at the same time, thus achieving formidable effects of the reciprocal focalization of their ideological and political significance. He embeds Cassius' temptation within Caesar's celebration of the feast and of the display of his great power. To do so, that is to achieve a contemporaneousness between the two events, he had to invent a particular use of the stage space. He transferred offstage the public event of the 'holy course', and of Antony's offering of the crown to Caesar, while onstage he presented the private scene of Cassius and Brutus.

But what happens offstage is in fact simultaneously present onstage, through the flourishes and shouts which reach the two republicans during their dialogue on the possibility and lawfulness of an insurrection against Caesar.

The two – Brutus in particular – interpret these signals, the shouts of the crowd, in the wrong way: the crowd is in fact applauding Caesar's refusal of the crown, but Brutus takes this applause as an acclamation for kingship: see Brutus at ll. 79–80: 'What means this shouting? I do fear the people / Choose Caesar for their king.' We may suppose that Brutus is persuaded to join and lead the conspiracy more by this false construing of the meaning of what is going on offstage than by Cassius' temptation. This is the way great drama works, when compared with its narrative sources: it combines, by displacement and/or embedding, what is sequential in narrative, and thus exploits the possibilities of stage space and stage time to the utmost. Here the effect is that all of Caesar's story, in its imminent apotheosis, resounds in the ears of the two republicans and convinces them that their insurrection is justifiable.

Expansion at the level of plot

The most impressive instance of expansion in *Julius Caesar*, when compared with Plutarch, lies in Antony's famous oration in 3.2. In *The Life of Caesar* there is no mention of this oration, while in that of Brutus we find the following account:

> Afterwards when *Caesars* body was brought into the market place, *Antonius* making his funerall oration in prayse of the dead, according to the auncient custome of Rome, and perceiving that his wordes moved the common people to compassion: he framed his eloquence to make their harts yerne the more, and taking *Caesars* gowne all bloudy in his hand, he layed it open to the sight of them all, shewing what a number of cuts and holes it had upon it. (p. 1062)

We witness in this passage, beyond Antony's oratorical mode, the emergence of his propositional attitude and, most of all, of his perlocutionary verbal and gestural action. It is probable that Shakespeare found the main cues for his expanded elaboration of Antony's speech here. But even more important is the corresponding passage in *The Life of Antony*, which he certainly consulted at least from this moment on:

> And therefore when *Caesars* body was brought to the place where it should be buried, he made a funerall oration in commendation of *Caesar*, according to the auncient custome of praising noble men at their funerals. When he saw that the people were very glad and desirous also to heare *Caesar* spoken of, and his praises uttered: he mingled his oration with lamentable words, and by amplifying of matters did greatle move their hearts and affections unto pity and compassion. In fine, to conclude his oration, he unfolded before the whole assembly the blouddy garments of the dead, thrust through in many places with their swords, and called the malefactors, cruell and cursed murtherers. With these words he put the people into suche a fury. (p. 975)

The elements are much the same as those found in the passage from *The Life of Brutus*, but there are more details and, above all, Antony's oratorical and rhetorical mode is clearly signalled: 'by *amplifying* of matters'. Furthermore, Antony's showing of Caesar's mantle, which is so effective in the scene, is here narrated in more detail. In the play, Antony's oration is just one great rhetorical amplification, aimed to transform the initial statement 'The noble Brutus / Hath told you Caesar was ambitious' (3.2.78–9) into the opposite indirect statement, implicit in the text, 'Since Caesar was not ambitious, his killing has not been noble or honourable but ignoble, and dishonourable'. Shakespeare would also have been able to find a very precise indication of Antony's oratorical or stylistic mode at the beginning of *The Life of Antony*: 'He used a manner of phrase in his speech, called Asiaticke, which caried the best grace and estimation at that time, and was much like to his manners and life: for it was full of ostentation, foolish braverie, and vaine ambition' (p. 969).

It is possible that, as has been argued, Shakespeare drew also from Appian's historical account of the facts, but he found in Plutarch's *Lives* the essential elements for the articulation of this famous scene.

Subdivision at the level of plot

We will examine two examples of this dramatic procedure. In a sequence of *The Life of Caesar* Plutarch recounts the signs, prodigies, and oracles which preceded, and announced, Caesar's death. Among them, he mentions the prophecy of a Soothsayer:

> Furthermore, there was a certaine Soothsayer that *had given* Caesar warning long time afore, to take heede of the day of the Ides of March, (which is the fifteenth of the moneth) for on that day he should be in great danger. That day being come, Caesar going unto the Senate house, and speaking merily unto the Soothsayer, *tolde* him, the Ides of March be come: so be they, softly *aunswered* the Soothsayer, but yet are they not past. (p. 787, my italics)

Plutarch narrates this episode in a single sequence on two different temporal planes: past perfect ('had given') and perfect ('tolde', 'aunswered'). The episode was rich in meaning, conveying the paradigm of foreboding, superstition (and the dismissal thereof), and, most of all, fatality, which is so central to this play (as it is to Plutarch's *Life of Caesar*). Shakespeare, therefore, could not avoid dramatizing it. But to do so, he had to transpose it from the logic of narrative presentation to that of drama. He thus had to subdivide it into two different stage sequences, in order to transcodify the two different temporal planes that narration can deal with in a single sequence by simply making use of two different tenses (here, as we have seen, past perfect and perfect), which unite events occurring at a temporal distance from each other.

The playwright cannot present, in *the same stage time*, the narrative past perfect and perfect. Therefore he must anticipate the past perfect somewhere in his play and only later will he be able to utilize the perfect tense in the continuous present of drama. Shakespeare used the past perfect part of the episode at the beginning of 1.2, soon after Caesar's first entrance on stage. The first eleven lines of that scene present a dialogue between Caesar, Calphurnia, and Antony regarding the superstition attached to the holy course or chase of the Lupercalia, according to which barren women, if touched in the chase, would 'Shake off their sterile curse'. Caesar asks Antony to touch Calphurnia, and he thus reveals both his desire for a son and his deep-rooted superstition. Soon afterwards the Soothsayer calls him by name and warns him to beware of the Ides of March. Caesar dismisses him as a 'dreamer'. Even if he is superstitious on the private level, he cannot be so on the public one. Used here, the first part of Plutarch's episode fulfils the task of outlining the contradictory character of Caesar. The second part of the episode will be used at the beginning of Act 3, when Caesar is just about to be assassinated.

The second example refers to 2.3, a very short scene based on a sequence of *The Life of Caesar* which deals with another warning:

> And one Artemidorus …, a Doctor of Rethoricke in the Greeke tongue, who by meanes of his profession was very familiar with certaine of Brutus confederates, and therefore knew the most part of all their practices against Caesar: came and brought him a little bill written with his owne hand, of all that he ment to tell him. He marking how Caesar received all the supplications that were offered him, and that hee gave them straight to his men that were about him, pressed nearer to him, and sayed: Caesar, reade this memoriall to your selfe, and that quickly, for they be matters of great waight and touch you nearely. Caesar tooke it of him, but could never read it, though he many times attempted it, for the number of people that did salute him. (p. 788)

Shakespeare subdivided this episode too, even though at first sight it seems that a montage of different temporal levels is not employed here. The temporal logic is very similar to that of the Soothsayer episode: Artemidorus *brought* Caesar a message which he had previously written (the past participle *written* assumes here the same function as the past perfect). Moreover, this past participle refers to an act of writing, and not to a speech act or to an action. In this case, the narrative form permits the writer (Plutarch) to inform the reader about the *contents* of that act, whereas dramatic form cannot do so. Shakespeare solves the problem by making Artemidorus read his own message in a short scene (2.3), thus informing the audience about its contents. Later, at the beginning of Act 3, soon after the short dialogue between Caesar and the Soothsayer, the second part of the episode is utilized and transformed.

Perspective and judgement of the narrator and of the playwright: the different constraints of prose and drama

In the third act of the play the course of Roman history changes radically. When it seems that, with the death of Caesar, the republican regime is safe and Brutus will become the new democratic leader of the state, Antony's oration reverses the situation by stirring up the mob against the conspirators it had previously applauded. Riots go wild in the city and the poor poet Cinna is lynched only because of his homonymy with Cinna the conspirator. The scene puts an end to the whole act. Act 4 opens on a completely different scenario. Time has passed. We are now in a private place, where the new leaders of the empire – Antony, Lepidus, and Octavius – are engaged, even before discussing state affairs, in unleashing their vengeance on all their adversaries. Now Shakespeare has abandoned *The Life of Caesar* and follows *The Life of Brutus*, but at the same time glances at *The Life of Antony* which may offer him some important details on the events which he is going to dramatize. One passage, in particular, concerning the lists of proscription which was arranged by the new leaders, must have attracted his attention. This is how it goes in *The Life of Antony*:

> But yet they could hardly agree whom they would put to death: for every one of them would kill their enemies, and save their kinsmen and friends. Yet at length, giving place to their greedy desire to be revenged of their enemies, they spurned all reverence of bloud, and holines of friendship at their feete. For Caesar left *Cicero* to *Antonius wil, Antonius* also forsooke Lucius *Caesar*, who was his Uncle by his mother: and both of them together suffered *Lepidus* to kill his owne brother Paulus. Yet some writers affirme, that *Caesar* and *Antonius* requested Paulus might be slaine, and that *Lepidus* was contented with it. (p. 977)

And here is how the fourth act of the play opens:

> ANTONY These many, then, shall die; their names are pricked.
> OCTAVIUS Your brother too must die; consent you, Lepidus?
> LEPIDUS I do consent.
> OCTAVIUS   Prick him down, Antony.
> LEPIDUS Upon condition Publius shall not live,
>   Who is your sister's son, Mark Antony.
> ANTONY He shall not live. Look, with a spot I damn him.
>
>   (4.1.1–6)

Shakespeare does not take into account the scruples mentioned at the beginning of Plutarch's passage, and therefore confers even more cruelty to the meeting. As for the exchange of victims that the new leaders allow each other in the 'hit' lists, he substantially follows his source. Cicero's name is not mentioned among those whom Antony condemns to death (but it will be referred to later in the third scene, 4.3.176–9). One might presume that his name is omitted here because the play has cut out all the historical events following Caesar's death, events related to the alliance between Octavius and Cicero against Antony and to the ensuing war: Cicero had stirred Octavius against Antony, who therefore now seeks his revenge, but, owing to the omission of all this in the play, his motivation would not have been understood by the audience. Another detail to be noted is that Antony's uncle, Lucius Caesar, is transformed by Shakespeare into his nephew Publius, historically non-existent. At first sight there seems to be no reason for such a substitution, except, perhaps, that of rendering the condemnation of a young nephew more ruthless than that of an old uncle. The name chosen for him, Publius, reflects another peculiar Shakespearean elaboration of his sources. At this point of the play, having abandoned the historical sequence of events, he gathered scattered information from all of them. He was now following very closely *The Life of Brutus* and certainly looked at the passage of the lists of proscription there too, and not only in *The Life of Antony*. He might have been attracted by a few lines, immediately preceding this passage, in which mention is made of the lawsuit started in absentia by Octavius against Brutus and the other conspirators. All of them were condemned, and both the people and many nobles were dismayed at such cruel action: 'Among them', Plutarch writes, 'the teares fell from Publius Silicius eyes who shortly after, was one of the proscripts or outlawes appointed to be slaine.' That name probably impressed Shakespeare and was associated with a very sensitive and just person. Anyway, this is the name he chose to identify Antony's nephew, who appeared in the place of his uncle Lucius Caesar mentioned in *The Life of Antony*, whose name might have confused the audience: the great Caesar had died and no other should receive that name at least for a while. Note that Octavius himself will be called only Octavius till 5.1 when he receives both the name of Octavius and that of Caesar, the *new* Caesar he is going to become.

But what is more important to note is the mercilessness of this exchange which opens Act 4 with the new developments of history in Rome: the exchange is made of only six brief and brutal lines, in which quite a few men are sentenced to death in a total disregard for kinship and affection. On this cruelty Plutarch expressed a very clear and negative judgement in a passage of *The Life of Antony* immediately following the one quoted above:

> In my opinion there was never a more horrible, unnaturall, and crueller change then this was. For thus chaunging murther for murther, they did aswel kil those whom they did forsake and leave unto others, as those also which others left unto them to kill: but so much more was their wickednesse and cruelty great unto their friends, for that they put them to death being innocents, and having no cause to hate them. (p. 977)

Unlike the narrator, the playwright cannot express any judgement with his own voice. He may attribute it to one of his characters, but then it will be perceived by the audience as a disputable opinion depending on the role of that character in the action. The only way of conveying in drama a judgement on what the characters are doing relies on the form in which their action is presented. From that form the audience may gather both the meaning and the assessment of the action. What Shakespeare wants to communicate here is immediately evident: he opens the scene without any introductory remarks which might explain or justify the decisions which are abruptly taken. He uses peremptory phrases whose bureaucratic performativity – 'their names are prick'd', 'Prick him down', 'with a spot I damn him' – sounds like a violent representation of the ensuing physical suppression of the people involved. And no emotion is revealed by any of the three characters asking or suffering the death of their kindred. The merciless logic of power displays a terrific anticlimax in relation to the great outbreak of passions which has just taken place in the third act: it is not by accident that the first sharp and gelid speech is given to Antony, the great actor and provoker of passions in the previous scenes. This is how Plutarch's harsh judgement gets transcodified on stage.

Equivalence at the level of plot, but also involving discourse

I shall finally give here one example of equivalence, a procedure in which the source sequence and the play sequence turn out to be of relatively analogous mode and extent in the two texts. Instances of equivalence usually occur when the source passage is narrated in a scenic manner.

Still with reference to *Julius Caesar*, we can see already, in 2.1.233–309, how closely Shakespeare follows Plutarch in his dramatization of the dialogue between Brutus and Portia which is rendered 'scenically' by Plutarch himself. But another, more impressive, example is to be found in the dramatization of Plutarch's account of Brutus being visited by the ghost of Caesar before the battle of Philippi. Let us examine the two passages very closely by segmenting them into comparable units marked by the same progressive alphabetical letters:

The Life of Brutus (p. 1069):

> (A) one night very late (when all the campe tooke quiet rest) as hee was in his tent with a litle light, thinking of weighty matters: / (B) he thought he heard one come in to him, / (C) and casting his eye towards the dore of his tent, that he saw a wonderfull straunge and monstruous shape of a body / (D) comming towards him, / (E) and sayd never a word. / (F) So *Brutus* boldly asked what he was, a god or a man, and what cause brought him thither. / (G) The spirit aunswered him, I am thy evill spirit, *Brutus*: / (H) and thou shalt see me by the city of Philippes. / (I) *Brutus* being no otherwise afraied, replied againe unto it: well, then I shall see thee againe. / (L) The spirite presently vanished away …

56   *Theory and practice*

Julius Caesar 4.3.273–85:

                         Enter the Ghost of Caesar
BRUTUS (A) How ill this taper burns! / (B) Ha! who comes here?
    (C) I think it is the weakness of mine eyes
    That shapes this monstrous apparition.
    (D) It comes upon me: / (E) / (F) art thou any thing?
    Art thou some god, some angel, or some devil,
    That mak'st my blood cold, and my hair to stare?
    Speak to me what thou art.
GHOST (G) Thy evil spirit, Brutus.
BRUTUS   (H) Why com'st thou?
GHOST To tell thee thou shalt see me at Philippi
BRUTUS (I) Well: then I shall see thee again?
GHOST Ay, at Philippi
BRUTUS Why, I will see thee at Philippi then: (L)   [Exit Ghost.]
    Now I have taken heart thou vanishest.

Let us see now how the narrative segments are transcodified in the play:

(A) Shakespeare transcodifies the temporal ('one night very late') and spatial ('in his tent') information provided by the narrator into an economical speech-act by Brutus, in which the deictic indication of the candle sets the scene at night and at the same time calls the attention to something ominous about to happen ('how *ill*').

(B) The source transmits an impression which Brutus must verify ('He thought he heard'). The playwright renders it by an exclamation followed by a question, at the same time revealing the emotional attitude of Brutus.

(C) The dramatic enunciation ('I think') makes explicit, in a direct form, the indirect propositional attitude of the source ('he thought … that he saw') and emphasizes the emotional attitude of Brutus' refusal to grant the status of reality to the 'monstrous' apparition, which is immediately linked to the speaker by the deictic 'this'.

(D) Here too the deictic 'me', which transcodifies Plutarch's anaphoric 'him', renders the spatial indication of the source in terms of proxemic and kinetic relationship (the Ghost is approaching the 'I' who speaks on the stage). Dramatic speech always interacts with non-linguistic actions which come to be linguistically registered and presented.

(E) The narrative phrase which indicates the silence of the Ghost seems to be transcodified in an ellipsis in the middle of l. 276: the onstage silence of the Ghost seems in fact to prompt the following question by Brutus: 'Art thou any thing?', which significantly closes with a direct invitation to speak: 'Speak to me what thou art.'

(F) The narrative sentence implies an illocutionary act (asking in order to get information) which is conveyed by indirect speech. In the play, this becomes a direct illocution through a series of questions. It should also be noticed that through the adverb *boldly* Plutarch indicates the emotional attitude of Brutus in his questioning of the Ghost: namely, his courage in spite of his fear of the supernatural apparition. The playwright transmits this attitude both by making Brutus *express* his fear ('That mak'st my blood cold, and my hair to stare') and at the same time by making him courageously question the Ghost. The effect of the enunciation is therefore something like: 'you frighten me, but I still challenge you to tell me who you are'.

(G) The narrative sentence conveys a direct speech-act governed by a verb of saying: 'aunswered'. The playwright reproduces that speech-act exactly, eliminating the governing verb, which is incompatible with theatrical mimesis.

(H) The second part of the Ghost's answer is dramatized by a dialogue of question and answer.

(I) Same procedure.

(L) The narrative sentence registers a non-linguistic act, which Shakespeare transcodifies first by a stage direction and then by Brutus' verbal indication of the same act ('Now ... thou vanishest'). It should also be noticed that the phrases 'I have taken heart' and 'I would hold more talk with thee' transcodify the emotional attitude of Brutus pointed out in segment I of the source ('being no otherwise afraied').

This microanalysis shows most of the procedures of transcodification which take place in a faithful dramatic reproduction of a narrative 'scene'. Since the narrative voice is absent in drama, the characters assume or perform both the *énoncés* and the *énunciations* transmitted by the narrative text. They express their propositional or emotional attitudes and directly perform the illocutionary or perloctionary acts which in a narrative text are always governed by the narrator. In drama, the passions undergo no mediation, that is why the stage-world imitates life.

Notes

1 This article draws on the findings of a much larger research group dedicated to a semiotic analysis of Shakespeare's use of source material in the construction of plot and discourse in the English and Roman history plays. I directed the overall project which saw the vital participation of the following scholars: Anna Bernini, Aldo Celli, Serena Cenni, Claudia Corti, Keir Elam, Giovanna Mochi, Susan Payne, and Marcella Quadri (and, for a time, Loretta Innocenti). The outcome was a four-volume publication: *Nel laboratorio di Shakespeare: Dalle fonti ai drammi* (Parma, Pratiche Editrice, 1988). The first volume dealt with *The Theoretical Framework*, which was both the premise and the result of the studies carried out by the individual researchers on individual plays; the second volume addressed *The First Tetralogy*; the third concerned *The Second Tetralogy*; the fourth and last focused on

The Roman Plays. This final volume includes my detailed analysis of *Julius Caesar* in relation to Plutarch's *Lives* of Caesar, Brutus, and Antony. Together with a very sketchy account of some of the main operations observed in the theoretical framework, the present chapter offers a brief selection of what resulted from my study of the play's dramatic construction.

2 For the concept and use of the 'actantial model' in drama see Keir Elam, *The Semiotics of Theatre and Drama* (London, Methuen, 1980), pp. 126–34.

3 Quotations are drawn from North's translation of the *Lives* (1595 edn), the one which Shakespeare presumably consulted.

4 Line references are from *Julius Caesar*, The Arden Shakespeare, third series, ed. David Daniell (Walton-on-Thames, Nelson, 1988).

5

'Voilà la belle mort': the crisis of the aristocracy in *Troilus and Cressida*

MARIO DOMENICHELLI

Voltaire did not like Shakespeare. Certainly, as he wrote in his *Lettre sur les Anglais*, the English Bard was a 'vigorous genius, a fecund, a natural, a sublime genius', however, unfortunately, he had 'no notion of good taste, no knowledge of rules'.[1] As Voltaire wrote to D'Alembert in 1776, 'cet abominable Shakespeare … n'est en verité qu'un Gilles de village, … qui n'a pas écrit deux lignes honnêtes'.[2] The fact is that in that same year Pierre Letourneur had published the first two volumes of his translation of Shakespeare. Voltaire took the publishing event as a kind of personal outrage. He became very unreasonably enraged and began campaigning against that horrible translation, also dismissing the English Bard as a 'vilain singe'.[3] In any case the French *maître* read that translation as the sign that the realm of Reason and good taste was over, and that France was sinking back into barbaric times. In order to defend France from that danger, as Voltaire triumphantly announced to D'Argental,[4] he had written a letter to the French Academy. The letter was publicly read on 25 August 1776. Not content with this, Voltaire wrote a second letter to the Academy in which he exposed the theatrical malpractices in the English staging of Shakespeare's works. Voltaire's second letter closed with an account of *Troilus and Cressida*. What was really sickening to Voltaire was the utter unconventional vulgarity of what he insisted on defining as a tragedy. The *pièce* was the most perfect illustration of Shakespeare's lack of taste, so that no doubt could remain about Corneille's, Racine's, and Molière's superiority over that English 'saltimbanque', that 'Gilles couvert de lambeaux'.[5] But what is most meaningful from our point of view is that the scene epitomizing theatrical abomination in Voltaire's eyes was the scene of Hector's death.[6] In Voltaire's classicistic unitarian logic of decorum, Hector's indecent, unheroic, and therefore unlikely death marked the broadest possible fracture between two opposing ideas of theatre, and of the world in a crisis of transition from an old to a new *Weltanschauung*.

The duel between Achilles and Hector in the *Iliad*, as one may remember, is the very focus of the whole action, and the very terminal point of attraction of the whole poem, which may even be described as an account of the war of Troy told through the story of the challenge between the two major heroes. All considered, Shakespeare's curt treatment of Hector's death poses a problem. In *Troilus and Cressida* there is no insistence on Achilles' grief for Patroclus's death at the hands of Hector. Thus Hector's death is almost unjustified, or justified only as an act of violence through which Achilles falsely asserts his own individual superiority as a warrior, with the result that the sequence of Hector's death becomes a sort of tragical-grotesque parody of the 'knightly encounters' of the classical and Italian epic tradition. What is being deconstructed is the epic chivalric *topos* of the so-called *bella morte*, the chivalric ideal of 'handsome death'. One may remember that in Tolstoy's *War and Peace*, written in the 1860s, at a certain point, after the battle of Austerlitz, Napoleon visits the battlefield covered with the bodies of the fallen. Among them there lies the noble and of course very distinguished body of Prince Andréy Bolkonsky who still holds in his hand the regimental banner. On seeing this the Emperor says: 'Voilà la belle mort.' Indeed, the idea of *la belle mort* and 'heroic defeat' is one the most powerful and most persistent icons in what Curtius called the system of chivalric virtues,[7] and in the aristocratic system of values.

Troilus and Cressida generally deals with the crisis of the aristocracy at the Renaissance crux of the end of the sixteenth century, and more particularly with the defeat of the aristocratic faction and ideology at the close of the Elizabethan age.[8] *La belle mort* is a well known commonplace in what we might call chivalric hagiographies. Let us consider three of these briefly. In 1524, le Chevalier Bayard died at Romagnano, struck by an unknown musketeer; in 1527 it was Giovanni dalle Bande Nere's turn, with his right leg bone broken by some springald shot; some sixty years later Sidney too was wounded in the thigh by an unknown firearm and had, as he said, 'la cuisse rompue' which killed him in the end. The same story of unvanquished valour in the face of death seems to be told in Le Loyal Serviteur's *Joyeuse histoire* of Le Chevalier Bayard, and in Fulke Greville's *Life of Sidney*. Both le Chevalier Bayard and Sir Philip Sidney[9] were 'chevaliers sans peur et sans reproche', and the very flowers of Renaissance chivalry and martial gentility. In his famous letter relating Giovanni de' Medici's last hours, Pietro Aretino described another such perfect gentleman and gallant soldier's perfect death.[10] We may also recall the episode in which Essex, after a quarrel with Ralegh for the Queen's favour, decided to leave the court for the Dutch war, and wrote: 'If I return I will be welcomed home; if not, *una bella morire* is better than a disquiet life.'[11]

During the Trojan council in Act 2, scene 2 of *Troilus and Cressida*, Troilus says that Helen cannot be given back, as she is 'a theme of honour and renown'[12] and the very embodiment of the Trojan chivalric value-system. As a matter of fact the Trojan prince is affirming the extreme value of what is to be obtained through Helen, that is a perfect knight's ideal 'handsome death' as the final perspective point from which the worth (in honour and renown) of a whole life-itinerary is to be judged.

Of course the figure of *la bella morte* is a commonplace feature in Renaissance chivalry romances and epic poems. Let us consider the martial deaths in Ariosto and Tasso, and the destiny of characters such as Agramante or Soliman. In Tasso's *Liberata* – Fairfax's translation *Jerusalem Delivered* was published in 1600 – the *topos* of *la bella morte* is clearly embodied in Clorinda's tragic death in Canto XII. Clorinda is the woman-warrior killed by Tancred who is tragically in love with his *bella inimica* (beautiful enemy). Clorinda's beauty in *extremo spiritu* is not only the embodiment of the knight's *Todesliebe*, it is the very semi-allegorical icon, and the very emblem of the Renaissance chivalric ideal of *il bel morire*:

> D'un bel pallor ha il bianco volto asperso,
> come a' gigli sarian miste viole,
> e gli occhi al cielo affisa, e in lei converso
> sembra per la pietate il cielo e 'l sole;
> e la man nuda e fredda alzando verso
> il cavaliero in vece di parole
> gli dà segno di pace. In questa forma
> passa la bella donna, e par che dorma.
>
> (Stanza 69)[13]

In Shakespeare this handsome death *topos* is frequent. Hotspur and Richard III are extreme examples of the antagonist's *obduratio*: Hotspur represents aristocratic pride as an eccess of *magnanimitas* and Richard III embodies in his warrior's death the satanic perversion of *fortitudo*. Weak Richard II too is given *la belle mort*, and dies while defending his life with valour. Even a scoundrel like Edmund is granted a chivalric death after the knightly encounter with Edgar in *King Lear*. It is in *Hamlet*, of course, that the whole problem is dealt with in a problematic key. What seems to be in question in *Hamlet* is not handsome death but the choice between a 'good' or 'bad' death. Hamlet's father was killed in the full bloom of his sins, and had no time for repentance. Hamlet has his chance to kill Claudius after the representation of the *Tragedy of Gonzago*. Claudius, however, is praying in the chapel, and Hamlet does not kill him, considering that, killed while repenting, Claudius would not receive eternal punishment. Hamlet himself, at the end of the play, is decreed martial honours by Fortinbras, as if the pale prince were a soldier fallen in the battlefield, which in a way he certainly is. Of course Hamlet is a gentleman, 'a courtier, a scholar, and a soldier' who has fought an obviously losing battle against mutability, to reassert his identity broken, indeed shattered by his father's murder and by the terrible italianate knowledge Hamlet has acquired of the world as a theatre. The world appears to be a huge lie, unveiling murder and lust, will to endless acquisition, and unlimited greed in a series of figures which can well be summed up by the universal Wolf of Ulysses' prophecy in *Troilus and Cressida* (1.3.119–24).

Troilus and Cressida, written one or two years after *Hamlet*, deals with the same problem of the loss of identity, and indeed of the loss of the world of the aristocracy in the face of the fortunes quickly made by a new class of self-made *homines novi*. It deals with Essex's last attempt to win back the aristocracy's traditional role, and the right to the interpretation and perception of reality according to the aristocracy's existential poetics, in contrast with the vulgarity of what in Italian were called 'la gente nova' (new people). Shakespeare's play may be defined as a cynical (philosophically so) and hopeless comment on the Elizabethan chivalric revival brought to a sudden end by Essex's failed revolt and consequent execution in 1601.[14]

Troilus and Cressida was no remake of Homer's *Iliad* (however, Chapman's *Seven Books* had a great importance for Shakespeare's play), but of Chaucer's *Troilus and Creseyde* (1385–86), even if Shakespeare was also much influenced by William Fiston's 1596 rewriting of Caxton's 1474 translation of Raoul Lefèvre's *Recueil*. This, in its turn, was a rewriting of Guido delle Colonne's *Historia destructionis Troiae* (1287) which was a Latin version of Benoît de Sainte-Maure's long epic poem *Le Roman de Troye* (1170–80). In all versions of the two lovers' story drawn from the much longer tale originally told by Benoît (Boccaccio's *Filostrato*, Chaucer's *Troilus and Creseyde*, also Greene's almost forgotten *Euphues, His Censure to Philautus*, 1587),[15] Hector's death either is not mentioned at all (and the only one who gets very ungentlemanly killed by Achilles is Troilus) or is as briefly mentioned as in Shakespeare. In Chaucer, Hector's death takes four lines describing Achilles' felony :

> For as he drough a king by thaventayle,
> Unwar of this, Achilles through the Mayle
> And through the body gan him for to ryve;
> And thus this worthy knight was brought of lyve.[16]

Benoît de Saint-Maure, dealing with the same subject matter, after telling the story of the long challenge between the two champions, had long before already described Hector's death as death by felony:

> Li cri i sont grant e li hu,
> Qu'Ector ot un rei abatu,
> Prendre le vout et retenir,
> At as lor par force tolir:
> Par la ventaille le teneit,
> Fors de la presse le traeit,

> De son escu ert descoverz,
> E quant l'aparceit li coilverz,
> C'est Achillès, qui le haeit,
> Cele part est alez tot dreit.
> Dreit a lui broche le destrier,
> Nel pot guarir l'auberc doblier
> Que tout le feie et le poumon
> Ne li espande sor l'arçon.
> Molt le trebuche toz envers
> E poi d'ore est pale e pers.
> Ha! Las, com pesant aventure!
> Tant par est pesme e tant est dure
> Com dolorose destinee![17]

Guido delle Colonne in his *Historia destructionis Troiae* tells the same story, and closes laconically enough: 'Achilles accepta quadam lancea valde forti non advertente Hectore, in ipsum irruit et letaliter vulneravit in ventre si quod eum mortuum deiecit ab equo.'[18] In Benoît, in Guido, in Lefèvre, and in Caxton, Troilus too is killed by Achilles. After Hector's death, Troilus becomes Troy's defensor and champion. In the nineteenth battle Troilus, after leading a raid in the Greek camp, must face Achilles, whom he has very gentlemanly already granted truce. Achilles gathers his Myrmidons and orders them to look for Troilus and kill him. Troilus is surrounded by Achilles' Myrmidons, and gallantly fights against an overwhelming mass of enemies until his horse is killed. Achilles does not give quarter, and comes to murder Troilus who is trapped under his fallen horse and is already almost dead ('Grant crualté – writes Benoît – grant felonie', l. 21444).[19] Guido comments on Troilus' death by saying that Homer was wrong in describing Achilles as a hero, while it is clear that he was a coward and a felon. In Boccaccio's *Filostrato*, Hector's death is not told, and Troilus is the only one who gets killed by Achilles; but the episode takes up little space. Prince Troiolo, deceived by Criseida, rages throughout the battlefield in search of revenge. He inconclusively fights many times against Diomedes, then he dies at Achilles' hands:

> L'ira di Troiolo in tempi diversi
> a' Greci nocque molto sanza fallo,
> tanto che pochi ne gli usciono avversi
> che non cacciasse morti dal cavallo,
> sol che ei l'attendesser si perversi
> colpi donava; e dopo lungo stallo,
> avendone già morti più di mille
> miseramente un di l'uccise Achille.
>
> (VIII.27)[20]

Or, in Chaucer's rephrasing of Boccaccio's lines:

> The wratthe, as I began yow for to seye,
> Of Troilus, the Grekes boughten dere;
> For tousandes his hondes maden deye,
> As he that was with-outen any pere,
> Save Ector, in his tyme, as I can here.
> But weylaway, save only goddes wille,
> Dispiteously him slough the fiers Achille.[21]

Shakespeare's brief sequence comes from a long-established tradition in which it is clear enough that Hector (and/or Troilus) is the magnanimous knight, and Achilles the felon, the traitorous knight, or he is at least unloyal, even though everything is to be understood within the boundaries of the chivalric system and knightly codification. The brief brutality, or even pathetic irony through which Troilus' and Hector's deaths are told in Boccaccio and Chaucer must be essentially due to the necessity of keeping close to, and swerving as little as possible from the main theme thread of Cressida's lack of faith, and betrayal. Be that as it may, that 'miserable death', Boccaccio's 'misera morte', or Chaucer's 'despituous death' ('cruel, pitiless death'), does not seem to take any really noticeable ideological space: and it must be remembered that the version of Troilus' death in Benoît definitely folllows all the traits of Rolland's handsome chivalric death at Roncevaux. This is why the importance of Hector's indeed miserable death in *Troilus and Cressida* must not be undervalued as it entails a reversal of the whole value-system of chivalry and what we might call the 'subtraction', Shakespeare's removal of Troilus' traditional *belle mort*, must be considered in the same light.

It is clear that Shakespeare's treatment of Hector's death is no *hapax*. Yet it assumes relevance to become in its brutality the true and main figure of the complex problem dealt with in Shakespeare's revisitation of the *Troy Book* tradition. In *Troilus and Cressida* the paradigmatic trait of Achilles' felony is even more enhanced through a different, somewhat expanded articulation of the elements inherited from the tradition. In Act 5, scene 8, Hector has just killed an enemy clad in a rich armour. Hector comments on his cowardly opponent's ugly death by saying: 'Most putrefied core so fair without'. Hector's 'day's work' is over and he disarms himself. 'Enter Achilles' with his Myrmidons. In a previous scene, Hector had surprised Achilles with his arms 'out of use' and had granted him a truce according to the rules of chivalry (5.6). Now Achilles shows his intention to take advantage of the situation. Hector asks for a truce: 'I Am unarmed, forego this vantage, Greek.' Achilles shouts to his men: 'Strike, fellows, strike! This is the man I seek.' Hector is slain in a sort of Mafia settlement of accounts, or as in one of those London streetfights which were quite common among the Elizabethan aristocracy. Achilles then explains the meaning of Hector's death: 'So, Ilion, fall thou next! Come, Troy sink down; / Here lies thy heart, thy sinews, and thy bone.' Then he adds, multiplying felony with lies: 'On, Myrmidons, and cry you all amain / "Achilles hath the mighty Hector slain"'. Then he orders the body of Hector to be tied to his horse's tail to drag it up and down the battlefield. Of course, no mention is made of the story of Priam's request to have his dead son's body back. There is no hint at any funerary pyre in the dawn (which is exactly how *The Iliad* ends), or to any honour reserved to the dead hero.

Shakespeare's laconicism in the treatment of Hector's death makes some important overtones resound very distinctly. There is no heroic death of any kind in *Troilus and Cressida*. During the representation of the battle in the last act, there is only one other direct reference to a warrior fallen in action. It is true that the audience is reminded of Patroclus' death, which, however, is very quickly announced as a matter of no importance. The only other death almost represented on stage is the death of the fairly armed and clad cowardly warrior who gets killed by Hector. Thus we must conclude that the only one directly accompanying Hector to the land of the dead is that warrior defined as a 'most putrefied core so fair without'.

I do not know of any other similar example of what we might call a rhetorically contrived 'subtraction' of *la bella morte*. Shakespeare's perspective on the decline of chivalry must be therefore extremely radical and hopeless. In the aristocratic, chivalric mentality death counts more than life, since it is mainly through a handsome death that a knight can acquire honour and renown and *la belle mort* is the climatic moment in which all the worth of a life is judged according to the aristocracy's only correct political perspective. The absence, or indeed the subtraction, of *la belle mort* decrees the end of what Huizinga once defined the chivalric dream of the heroic and loving life.

I said I do not know of any other example of willful removal of *la belle mort*. This is not completely true. In a recent article of mine[22] I tried to underline a partial similarity of perspective between Shakespeare's *Troilus and Cressida* and Pietro Aretino's epic *fragmenta*, *L'Orlandino* (1536–47, prob. 1542), which was well-known during the sixteenth century[23] and the less fortunate *L'Astolfeide*.[24] While Thersites seems to be translating almost literally into English Aretino's 'frankly speaking manner', Ulysses represents the very ideological core and soul of what we might call a sound Renaissance interpretation of Machiavelli in the Protestant line of such Italian *fuoriusciti* as Petruccio Ubaldini, and Jacopo Castelvetro (one of these wrote the Preface to the 1584 Italian edition of Machiavelli's *Il Principe*, published by John Wolfe in London). On the whole, Aretino's approach to epic and chivalric romance is quite close, in its protolibertine, cynical key, to Shakespeare's remake of the Trojan war in which all the aristocratic myths of heroism, of love and honour, including *la bella morte* as the key figure of the system of chivalric virtues, are given for 'dead and gonne'.

Knights, as they have always been fabled – writes Aretino – never existed. They were no knights errant but a bunch of 'arrant knaves': 'Ruggiero, a most fair youth, / was both Agramante's and Charles' fag, / Gradasso and Mandricardo both stallions / who never left the tavern, / Rinaldo a beastly man, with no brain, / knight errant from tavern to brothel' (I.4). As regards the ladies: 'Of Angelica, Marfisa, Bradamante, / Of Fiordiligi, of Morgana and Alcina' – says Aretino – 'I won't sing; anyone who is not unlearned can guess their loving life, / I shall compare it to the whore–errant's, Antea, Origilla and Fallerina. / Ancroia too was errant and a whore / And Gabrina was of the whole bunch the very bawd' (I.8) The whole chivalric tradition of love seems to take place in a brothel, or in a key of *Venus vaga*, or venereal errantry, in the sense of street prostitution. And, of course 'This is the very truth! Only my own Aretino never tells fables / like Sir Pulci, the Count, and Ariosto' (I.9). Shakespeare's Thersites, talking about Ajax, calls him 'an ass' (2.1.42–3), Menelaus is 'the primitive statue and oblique memorial of cuckolds' (5.1.53); Achilles has no brain, (2.1.96–9), Patroclus is Achilles' bitch (2.1.111), and the whole war, considering that 'all the argument is a whore and a cuckold' (2.3.69–72) seems a kind of brothel fight. Diomedes, talking to Paris about Helen, calls her a whore, and Paris a lecher, while Menelaus is a cuckold, but *ça va sans dire*. Thus that terrible cormorant war swallowing money and friends is sheer nonsense (5.1.533–76). Both Thersites and Diomedes are in the same Aretinesque philosophical line developing Renaissance cynicism into libertine thought.

It is true that in Aretino's epic *fragmenta* nobody dies. This is easily understandable since death is a serious thing; while in Aretino's perspective chivalric romances are only a huge heap of lies that must be exposed through mock-epic. However, a kind of multiple comic subtraction of the *topos* in question here is to be found in *L'Orlandino*, which is to be considered not as a mere *divertissement* but as a part of a much wider genealogy, and as it were, a deconstruction of morals which include *I Ragionamenti d'Amore* and *I Ragionamenti delle Corti* as a sort of satyric analysis of Castiglione's ideal courtier, and Bembo's neoplatonism. Also, one must remember that Chaucer's *Troilus and Creseyde* was for the English court what Petrarch's *Canzoniere* was for Italian courts, and Italian *cortegiani*; Chaucer's poem, like Petrarch in Bembo's linguistic theory and practice, defined an English high-mimetic linguistic model of *lingua cortigiana* (courtier's language), and a way of perceiving one's own emotions, therefore structuring the self-perception of one's own mind, of one's own soul, or psyche.[25] This must be understood if one wants to see the whole scope of ideological implications in *Troilus and Cressida* and the reasons for its satirical, parodic, and tragical-grotesque strategy.

In *L'Orlandino*, Canto II (and the last), Astolfo, the English knight, fights against Cardus. 'Mirror of Prudence' as he is (meaning that is a coward), Astolfo gets soon unhorsed and surrenders immediately: 'Do not unsheath thy sword, for pity's sake / My lord, please, Miserere mei! / Cardus laughed and said: meeseems / thou must go back to thy lord as an armless footman' (II.6).

In short, the defeated knight does not get killed. Being a coward he has no right to death, not to mention *la bella morte*; he has only the right to lose his status of knight, and to be reduced to an unarmed footman. In *L'Astolfeide* the same question is posed in even clearer terms . The 'heroes' (a bunch of drunkards, boasters, rakes and brothelgoers) must face the terrible Arcifanfano, a giant. The first knight sent to fight against Arcifanfano is Berlinghieri who 'taken by shame and fear at the same time / goes into the field forcing his own coward nature'. Berlinghieri tries his best, but he gets unhorsed by his terrible opponent after a very brief and grotesque fight, and flees to Paris. Berlinghieri too becomes an unarmed footman and loses his aristocratic status. Astolfo then is sent against the terrible giant and finds himself soon with his bum on the ground. Then, the 'heroes' decide to send Ugieri the Dane, who is a stout fellow. Ugieri dismounts the giant and takes him prisoner. Arcifanfano is not killed. Once the 'heroes' have him in their hands, they very cowardly decide to calm him down in the way this is usually done with bulls, and the whole sequence that follows is described as a bull's castration. Death has no right of residence in Aretino's mock heroic realm and is comically replaced by figures of *degradatio* and uncrowning and, on top of it all, by the grotesque figure of castration.

Shakespeare's play that had begun with an armed Prologue preparing the audience to a 'tragical historie', closes on Troilus *furioso* seeking revenge on Diomedes in the battlefield. The play ends on the wilful removal of all tragical catharsis. Troilus is as dead as Hector at this point. He has lost his own chivalric identity and the world of values on which it was grounded. Troilus is utterly lost and does not seem to belong to anywhere any longer since: 'Hector is dead: there is no more to say' (5.11.22). Troilus' experience of the new world seems to be shaped as an example *au contraire* of the traditional ideological and self-fashioning itinerary of the young knight (such as Ruggiero, Tancredi, and Rinaldo) finding his path *ad perfectionem virtutis* through love and war: 'l'armi e gli amori' of the chivalry romance tradition. It is true that Troilus becomes as *furioso* as Ariosto's Orlando, and for a very similar reason; Mars has gone mad because of Venus' tantalizing flight away from him, with inconstant Cressida taking Angelica's place. Yet, through love, because of love, Troilus suffers the most terrible and remediless *desengaño*, to use the Spanish topically baroque word. The world for him has lost the only meaning it used to have of 'glory and renown', now the meaning of the world is nothing but 'ignomigny and shame' which are Troilus' last words addressed to Pandarus. The character of Pandarus, a Trojan nobleman in all the previous versions of the *Troy Book*, in Shakespeare becomes a pimp tainted by Neapolitan bone-ache which will take him to his grave in two months' time (5.11.50-3).

The play that had begun with the armed Prologue under the sign of Mars closes under the sign of a debased Venus with Pandarus' epilogue and the threat to spread contagion throughout the whole world and, of course, among the audience in first place. The contagion being threatened is of a metaphorical and ideological kind; it is a syphilis of the mind, a philosophical disease opening holes and flaws in the axiological system, in what Greenblatt might perhaps call 'master fiction' or Lyotard and Foucault would once define as 'récit du pouvoir'. The very last word of the play is 'diseases', sealing a love and honour story under the traditional sign of Mars and Venus, touched by the new world leprosy. That contagion, those 'diseases', are Mutability's time-markers and they represent an ideological space which is exactly the opposite of the ideological space covered by the chivalrous figure of *la bella morte*. Death is not handsome in Pandarus' epilogue; it is disfigured, instead, together with love, into some grotesque emblem of putrefaction and disorder belonging to Ulysses's dark wolvish world. That emblem is also the mark through which *Troilus and Cressida* undefines itself in the conventional terms of comedy or tragedy, being of course neither; being, as it were, an impossible tragedy, and an unlikely comedy.[26] A hindered tragedy, or a tragedy *manquée* we might say, the mark of hindrance, or of the *manque*, being, as Voltaire justly indicated, the absence of the heroic climax, and of the knight's *bella morte*.

Voltaire was right, after all, and after his own fashion. Hector's death in *Troilus and Cressida* powerfully symbolizes not only the end of Troy, and of the chivalric world identified with the Trojan warriors' *Weltanschauung*. Hector's death had also come to symbolize, for aught Voltaire might see, the end of the heroic world, and therefore, indeed, the end of the high-mimetic world of tragedy denied through the grotesque and the total disorder and confusion in genre. It came to symbolize the end of Voltaire's theatrical world of rules, too. By drawing the shape of some minor ideological apocalypse at the beginning of the seventeenth century, Shakespeare's generically undefinable play also came to portray perfectly the senescence of the *ancien régime* through the senescence of its poetics of the Aristotelian rules, and of *les bienséances*. Voltaire had grown too old to bear all that.

Notes

1 Lettre VIII in *Oeuvres complètes* de Voltaire avec des notes et une notice historique sur la vie de Voltaire par Jean Antoine Nicolas de Caritat Marquis de Condorcet, 13 vols (Paris, Furne, 1835–42), vol. 5, p. 30.
2 Voltaire, *Oeuvres*, vol. 13, p. 381, lettre to D'Alembert, 3 September 1776.
3 Voltaire, *Oeuvres*, vol. 13, p. 572, lettre to De la Harpe, 15 August 1776.
4 Voltaire, *Oeuvres*, vol. 13, p. 370, 30 July 1776.
5 Voltaire, *Oeuvres*, vol. 9, p. 307.
6 Voltaire, *Oeuvres*, vol. 9, p. 307. See Voltaire's two letters to the Académie on the occasion of the publication of the first two volumes of Shakespeare's *Oeuvres* in Pierre Letourneur's translation, *Shakespeare traduit de l'anglois*, 20 vols, Paris,

1776–82, éd. corrigée par F. Guizot et A. Pichot (Paris, Ladvocat, 1821).
7 Ernst Robert Curtius, *Europäische Literatur und lateinisches Mittelalter* (Bern, A. Francke AG Verlag, 1948); English trans. *European Literature and the Latin Middle Ages* (New York and Evanston, Harper and Row Publishers, 1963). See chapter XVIII.
8 See my '"The courtier's, soldier's, scholar's eye, tongue, sword": Italianate Cynicism, Knowledge of the World, and the Collapse of Chivalry in *Troilus and Cressida*', *Shakespeare Yearbook*, 10 (1999), 427–59.
9 *La très joyeuse, plaisante et récréative histoire, composée par le Loyal Serviteur* (1527), ed. Louis Moland (Paris, Garnier, 1882), containing also extracts from other biographies of Bayard, including Guillaume du Bellay's *Les mémoires*, see pp. 426–7; Fulke Greville, *Life of the Renowned Sir Philip Sidney* (publ. 1652), ed. Nicholas Smith (Oxford, Oxford University Press, 1907); Mark Caldwell has also edited *The Life* in *The Prose of Fulke Greville Lord Brooke*, The Renaissance Imagination, no. 26 (New York and London, Garland, 1987), p. 82.
10 Pietro Aretino, *Lettere*, ed. Paolo Procaccioli (Rome, Salerno Editrice, 1997), tomo I, Libro I, pp. 54–9.
11 Lytton Strachey, *Elizabeth and Essex* (London, The Curtis Publishing Company, 1928), p. 33.
12 *Troilus and Cressida*, in *The Oxford Shakespeare*, ed. Stanley Wells and Gary Taylor (Oxford, Oxford University Press, 1988), 3.2.199. All quotations are taken from this edition.
13 I give my own translation, since Fairfax's version is somehow misleading: 'A beautiful pallor is spread on her white visage, / and it is as if the color of the lilies were intermingled with violets; / her eyes are cast to heaven; / and both sky and sun seem to be moved downward to her by pity. / Her naked cold hand she raises / to the knight, instead of words / as a sign of peace. And in this shape / the beautiful woman passes away as if she were falling asleep.' See Fairfax's translation, *Jerusalem Delivered*, 1600, ed. Henry Morley (New York and London, The Cooperative Publishing Society, 1901), p. 255.
14 See Bevington's 'Introduction' to his Arden edition of *Troilus and Cressida* (Walton-on-Thames, Nelson and Sons, 1998); see also Eric Mallin, 'Emulous Factions and the Collapse of Chivalry', *Representations*, 29 (1990); repr. in E. Mallin, *Inscribing the Time: Shakespeare and the End of Elizabethan England* (Berkeley, University of California Press, 1995); James E. Savage, '*Troilus and Cressida* and Elizabethan Court Factions', *University of Mississippi Studies in English*, 5 (1964), 43–66; see also Paul N. Siegel, 'Shakespeare and the New Chivalry Cult of Honour', *Centennial Review*, 86 (1964), 9–70; Elaine Eldridge, 'Moral Order in Shakespeare's *Troilus and Cressida:* The Case of the Trojans', *Anglia*, 104 (1986), 33–44.
15 Much has been written on this subject: see Carl Young, *The Origin and Development of the Story of Troilus and Cressida* (London, Chaucer Society, 1908); Piero Boitani, ed., *The European Tragedy of Troilus* (Oxford, Oxford Univeristy Press, 1989); see also Montague Summers's introduction and notes to Dryden's *Troilus and Cressida*, in John Dryden, *The Dramatic Works*, 6 vols (London, The

Nonesuch Press, 1930); Robert K. Presson, *Shakespeare's 'Troilus and Cressida' and the Legends of Troy* (Madison, Madison University Press, 1953). On Hector's death in particular see Oskar Sommers, *The Recueyll of the Histories of Troy written in French by Raoul Lefevre*, trans. and printed by William Caxton (London, Nutt, 1894); see also Bevington, 'Introduction', pp. 33–7; Stephen J. Lynch, 'Hector and the Theme of Honour', *Upstart Crow*, 7 (1987), 68–79; Curtis Brown Watson, *Shakespeare and the Renaissance Concept of Honour* (Princeton, Princeton University Press, 1960); Alice Shalvi, 'Honour in *Troilus and Cressida*', *Studies in English Literature*, 5 (1965), 292 ff. As regards Greene and Shakespeare see James Herford's *Greene Romances and Shakespeare* (London, New Shakespeare Society, 1888).

16 *The Works of Geoffrey Chaucer* from the text of W. W. Skeat (Oxford, Oxford University Press, 1930); *Troilus and Creseyde* is in vol. II: Book V, stanza 223.

17 *Le roman de Troye par Benoît de Sainte-Maure*, d'après tous les manuscrits connus, par Léopold Constans (Paris, Firmin Didot, 1904), ll. 16215–33: 'There are great clamour and cry as Hector has unhorsed a king; and wants to seize and hold him, and pulls him by the sallet, and takes him out of the *melée*, and does not cover himself with his shield. Villain Achilles, who hates him, when he sees him uncovered spurs his horse against him. The double coat of mail cannot save Hector, whose liver and lungs are shed on the saddle. Hector is unhorsed, and falls dead to the ground. He becomes pale and livid. Helas! What a terrible adventure! How hard and bad it is. What a sorry destiny!'

18 Guido de Columnis, *Historia destructionis Troiae*, ed. N. E. Griffin (Cambridge, Mass., Medieval Academy of America, 1936), p. 175.

19 See Benoît, ll. 21370–450; Guido, *Historia*, pp. 203–5; Caxton, *Recueyll*, pp. 638–40.

20 My translation: 'Troilus's fury many times / never failed to inflict much damage on the Greeks, / And few faced him who were not unhorsed and killed, / If they stayed to fight / so wickedly did he strike, and after a long while / when he had killed more than thousand Greeks / One day he was miserably killed by Achilles.'

21 Skeat, *The Poetical Works of Geoffrey Chaucer*, Book V, stanza 258 (p. 240).

22 See my '"The courtier's, soldier's, scholar" eye, tongue, sword', *Shakespeare Yearbook*, 10 (1999).

23 *The Orlandino* went through a series of editions and pirate prints before 1600. One of these is in the British Library Catalogue under the title of *Le valorose prove degli arcibravi paladini* printed by Baleni in Florence between 1570 and 1580.

24 Both *L'Orlandino* and *L'Astolfeide* are contained in Danilo Romei's edition, of Pietro Aretino's *Poemi cavallereschi* (Rome, Salerno, 1995). My translation.

25 See H. A. Mason, *Humanism and Poetry in the Early Tudor Court* (London, Routledge and Kegan Paul, 1959), p. 143 ff.

26 On the problem of genre classification of Shakespeare's play see Bevington's 'Introduction', pp. 1–6.

Part II
Culture and tradition

6

Beyond the Reformation: Italian intertexts of the ransom plot in *Measure for Measure*

MICHELE MARRAPODI

In his intent to separate the authority of secular rulers from any interference with the realm of the Church, Martin Luther concludes his Reformist pamphlet, entitled *Von Weltlicher Oberkeit* (*On Secular Authority*), by reporting a story about Duke Charles of Burgundy as an example of good judgement not found in law-books and learned doctrine but taken from free good sense and unfettered reason, in the true spirit of love and natural law:

> A nobleman captured his enemy. The wife of the captive came to ransom him. The nobleman said he would give the man back to her if she slept with him. The woman was virtuous, but wanted her husband released, and so she went and asked her husband whether she should do it to get him freed. The man wanted to be free and to save his life, and permitted it. But the day after the nobleman had slept with the woman, he had her husband beheaded, and gave him to her dead. The woman complained of this to Duke Charles who summoned the nobleman and ordered him to take the woman as his wife. After the wedding day, he had the man beheaded, placed the woman in possession of his goods and restored her honour.[1]

The striking similarity with the main plot of *Measure for Measure* cannot be ignored; less evident may appear the fact that Luther published his pamphlet in March 1523, twenty-four years before the story's earliest account, the so-called 'Letter' written in 1547 by a Hungarian student; thirty-three years before Claude Rouillet's Latin tragedy *Philanira* (1556); and at least forty-two and fifty-five years, respectively, before the appearance of Shakespeare's most direct sources, the narratives and plays of Giraldi Cinthio – the fifth *novella* of the eighth day of the *Hecatommithi* (1565), posthumously dramatized as *Epitia* in 1583 – and George Whetstone's two-part play *Promos and Cassandra* (1578), transformed into a prose version in *Heptameron of Civill Discourses* in 1582.

Luther himself mentions as a precedent for his anecdote the tale narrated by

St Augustine in *De sermone Domini in monte*, reported by Geoffrey Bullough in the second volume of his *Narrative and Dramatic Sources of Shakespeare*. Here, a man is confined to prison and threatened to death if he does not pay a pound of gold by a fixed date. The poor wretch is desperate since he has no gold – he is however married to a very beautiful wife. A wealthy man, infatuated with this woman, offers to pay the debt in exchange for a sexual assignation. The woman obtains her husband's consent, and agrees to yield in order to save his life. However, in the end, she only gets a purse of earth. When she protests to the governor, he frees her husband from the debt, adding also 'that the woman should be installed as the mistress of the piece of land whence she had received earth in place of gold'.[2]

What is particularly interesting for the construction of Shakespeare's play is the fact that Luther's predicament endorses the idea of a retributive justice underlying the tale's subtext with a providential design which equally distributes reward and punishment through the hands of the inspired duke. For the Reformist Luther, this anecdote is a 'truly princely punishment on wickedness', offering 'so just a judgement that everyone is bound to approve it and find written in his heart that it is right'.[3]

The major subsequent early modern versions of what Mary Lascelles has called 'the story of the monstrous ransom' tend to soften the severity of the duke's punishment through the intercession of the widow's pleading, or to turn the tale into a happy ending by the final revelation that the man sentenced to death, in these accounts the woman's brother, is alive.[4] This last twist, adopted by Whetstone's *Promos and Cassandra* and Giraldi Cinthio's post-humous play *Epitia*, is taken up by Shakespeare. In order to understand the dramatist's own variations of a well-worn story and established tradition, it would be useful to look anew at some neglected English and Italian intertexts which may help to define a more comprehensive trajectory of cultural trans-actions than positivistic source studies.

The issues of misused justice and abuse of authority were widespread in novelistic literature and offered material for diverse uses and reuses stretching over the history of drama through frequent adaptations from Boccaccio's Plautine and *fabliau*-like derivations and other writers' *novelle*.[5] The *Decameron*, which was ransacked as a sort of prose theatre for the making of plot structures in early modern drama, proving in Borsellino's terms that 'the origins of modern comedy are inseparable from its narrative components',[6] presents a number of tales which, though they cannot be taken as analogues, do provide some links with the topic of justice in *Measure for Measure*.

In the sixth tale of the fourth day, a young man suddenly dies in his lover's arms during a secret encounter. The unhappy lady, Andreana, decides to carry his body outside her property with the help of her *fantesca* but she is caught by the Podestà who, although he soon realises that Andreana bears no responsibility, threatens her, saying that she will be freed only on condition that she yields to him. The girl rejects the indecent proposal, which is followed by an attempted rape, and, once her innocence is finally established, she enters a convent. Here are the words of the tale in the 1620 Tudor translation:

> The Potestate hearing this, and perceiving that Andreana was little or nothing at all faulty in the matter, her beauty and good carriage kindled a villainous and lustful desire in him towards her, provoking him to the immodest motion, that upon granting his request, he would release her. But when he saw, that all his persuasions were to no purpose, hee sought to compasse his will by violence; which like a vertuous and valiant Virago, shee worthily withstood, defending her honour Nobly, and reproving him with many injurious speeches, such as a lustfull Letcher justlie deserved.[7]

The moral ethic of an egalitarian justice is at work in the fourth tale of the first day, where a monk is punished by his abbot for sleeping with a country wench but is cunning enough to let the abbot lie with the same woman. Once the abbot is accused of the same fault, he is obliged to pardon the monk. The tale's narrative emphasizes that 'A Monke having committed an offence, deserving to be very grievously punished, freed himselfe from the paine to be inflicted on him, by wittily reprehending his Abbot, with the very same fault'.[8] As is common in Boccaccio, who seeks to equate male vices and virtues with those of women, this story is balanced by a proto-feminist version, which occurs in the second tale of the ninth day. Here, a nun, named Isabella, takes the place of the monk and is severely reprehended by her sisters and the abbess for her incontinency, but she is freed from any chastisement since the abbess has committed the same sin. The moral of the story, related by Madam Eliza, is 'that whosoever is desirous to reprehend sinne in other men, should first examine himselfe, that he be not guiltie of the same crime'.[9] It may not be a fortunate coincidence that Shakespeare's heroine is called Isabella and is, in fact, a sister, in the double sense as kin to Claudio and a votaress. A common feature in all these narratives, however, is the invitation to question oneself before castigating the vices of others, a moral which also arises from the subtext of *Measure for Measure*.

An early depiction of a corrupt judge in English drama is provided by the interlude *Apius and Virginia* (c. 1567), a 'Tragicall Comedie' in Senecan fashion which opposes a ruler's corruption to a maid's chastity. We find the climax of the play in the words of Virginius to his daughter:

> Oh hearken, deare daughter, attend thou my sounde.
> Iudge Apius, prickt forth with filthy desire,
> Thy person as lemmon doth greatly require,
> And no kinde of intreatie, no feare nor no shame,

> Will he heare aledge defending the same.
> And straight without staying, in paine of my death,
> I must bring thee thither; wherfore stop my breath,
> O Sisters; I search, I seeke and I crave
> No more at your handes but death for to have,
> Rather then see my daughter deflourde,
> Or els in ill sorte so vildely devoured.
>
> (Scene vii, 786–9)[10]

The story of Appius and Virginia, related by Livy and other Latin historians, was included in Giovanni Fiorentino's *Il Pecorone* (X, 2, 1558) and William Painter's *Palace of Pleasure* (1566), and was later translated by Philemon Holland in 1600. In John Webster's adaptation, dated by some scholars as early as 1603–4, Virginius kills his daughter to avoid the lecherous abuse of Appius who is pretending to judge the false imputation, plotted by himself and his counsellor, that Virginia is a slave in order to enjoy her. Shakespeare refers to the myth of Virginia in *Titus Andronicus*, also in the title hero's stabbing of his mutilated daughter to cleanse her offended honour, whereas another play of violated chastity, Heywood's *Rape of Lucrece* (c. 1607), draws in turn from Shakespeare's early narrative poem. This latter's association with the same family group is made clear from the words of Virginius at the close of Webster's tragedy:

> Two Ladies fair, but most infortunate,
> Have in their ruins rais'd declining *Rome* –
> *Lucretia* and *Virginia*, both renown'd
> For chastity.
>
> (5.2.192–5)[11]

For although Tyndale's opinion of the Lucrece myth sustains the search for martyrdom in her sacrifice of a pagan chastity, Webster's and Heywood's plays are remarkable examples of a dramaturgy deeply concerned with the corrupting influence of power, a motif frequently rehearsed in Shakespearean tragedy and a recurring *topos* in both English and Italian early modern drama.[12]

In her volume, now a reference point for intertextual and comparative research in the field of Italian and English drama, Louise George Clubb maintains that Shakespeare's handling of new comedic elements from both classical and early modern theatre

> is another demonstration of his working on the principles of nova comedia, not by borrowing plots from sources but by *contaminatio* of structures, recombining in novel ways theatergrams that had become part of a large common repertory, discarding those that were not to the purpose of the highly individual structure of each of his plays.[13]

However, Clubb pays less attention to the case of *Measure for Measure*, a play which she cursorily deals with in her discussion of the woman-as-wonder trope, whereas further investigation into the theatregrams of classical and Italian comedies, both learned and serious, as well as novelistic literature, may prove extremely interesting. One of the earliest learned prose comedies, Ugolino Pisani's *Philogenia* (c. 1435), dramatizes the sexual harassment of a virgin by a reckless young man who, after his abuse, bribes an unscrupulous priest to marry her to a peasant. Related examples of misused authority at women's expense can be found in *commedia erudita* plot structures, which adapted the New Comedic models of Plautus and Terence. They can also be found in *commedia grave* experiments, which refashioned materials taken from a *contaminatio* of Italian *novelle*, histories, and romances, replacing the classical *topos* of fate and whorish fortune with the Counter-Reformation belief in the intervention of Providence. Frequent moral-political issues such as the exercise of power, the conflict between a public '*ragion di Stato*' and private passions, and the disquieting relationships between politics and ethic, rigour and mercy are at the heart of the most popular themes exploited by the Reformation and Counter-Reformation traditions in both Italian and Italianate English drama.[14]

A deeply ideological sequence in *Measure for Measure* comes out at the opening of Act 2 in the dispute between the inflexible Deputy and his counsellor Escalus about the nature of secular authority. On the one hand, we have in Angelo's contention of an inexorable justice and apparently untouched behaviour – ''Tis one thing to be tempted, Escalus, / Another thing to fall' (2.1.17–18) – the merciless proposition of a Draconian ruler, whose absolute power is exalted, as in the case of the medieval king, by the strict execution of the law. On the other hand, Escalus' position holds the Renaissance, Counter-Reformation view based on mercy and humane understanding of the faults of others, a principle which extols, not weakens, the very nature of authority and kingly power.[15] This scene looks ahead to the central dialogue between Angelo and Isabella on the weighed use of punishment and forgiveness in the public task of administering justice (2.2), suggesting the presence of a political level, nourished by conflicting Reformist and Counter-Reformist attitudes, which delineates the difference between a pitiless tyrant driven by strictness and rigour and a perfect judge guided by moderation and equity:

> ISABELLA No ceremony that to great ones longs,
>   Not the king's crown, nor the deputed sword,
>   The marshal's truncheon, nor the judge's robe,
>   Become them with one half so good a grace
>   As mercy does ...
> ANGELO Your brother is a forfeit of the law,
>   And you but waste your words.

ISABELLA Why, all the souls that were, were forfeit once,
And He that might the vantage best have took
Found out the remedy. How would you be
If He, which is the top of judgement, should
But judge you as you are?

(2.2.59–77)[16]

Considered in its religious terms, the dialogue reflects the theological conflict of the early Renaissance between the Protestant vision of a punitive God who dispenses retributive justice according to human faults and merits, based on Old Testament doctrine, and the Roman Catholic conception. As sustained by the Counter-Reformation, the Catholic ideal was that of the forgiving God of the New Testament, a prompter of love and grace and an example of virtues for all Christians through the embodiment of human experience. In *The Merchant of Venice*, Portia holds the same enlightened vision as the wise ruler, aiming at the affirmation of secular authority through Christian mercy in the legal dispute with Shylock's claim for rigour and strict justice, demonstrating how religious doctrine combines ideologically on the stage with the exercise and ethic of power:

The quality of mercy is not strain'd,
It droppeth as the gentle rain from heaven
Upon the place beneath: it is twice blest,
It blesseth him that gives, and him that takes,
'Tis mightiest in the mightiest, it becomes
The throned monarch better than his crown.
His sceptre shows the force of temporal power,
The attribute to awe and majesty,
Wherein doth sit the dread and fear of kings:
But mercy is above this sceptred sway,
It is enthroned in the hearts of kings,
It is an attribute to God himself;
And earthly power doth then show likest God's
When mercy seasons justice.

(4.1.180–93)[17]

Portia's plea for godlike mercy, which exalts the great image of secular authority as a divine attribution, appears stronger than Isabella's because it sounds more like an affirmation of kingly virtues than a moral appeal. Although she needs to be prompted by Lucio, Isabella follows a similar strategy in the attempt to cure Angelo's perverse reasoning, which leads him to hide the idea of pity by reversing the sense of the law itself:

ANGELO The law hath not been dead, though it hath slept;
Those many had not dar'd to do that evil
If the first that did th'edict infringe

Had answer'd for his deed. Now 'tis awake,
Takes note of what is done, and like a prophet
Looks in a glass that shows what future evils,
Either new, or by remissness new conceiv'd,
And so in progress to be hatch'd and born,
Are now to have no successive degrees,
But ere they live, to end.
ISABELLA   Yet show some pity.
ANGELO I show it most of all when I show justice;
For then I pity those I do not show,
Which a dismiss'd offence would after gall,
And do him right that, answering one foul wrong,
Lives not to act another.

(2.2.91–105)

The contrast between the two opponents is therefore replete with religious premises and debated in clearly political terms. The only fault in Isabella's own reasoning, albeit imbued as it is with the Christian ethic, is that she idealizes too much the virginity of her body over her soul, rejecting any possibility whatsoever of negotiating Claudio's acquittal with Angelo. In this she proves to be too extreme and absolute in her assumptions insomuch as she will be subjected, as it were, to a process of spiritual growth over the course of the play. This last issue invites thoughts on how these principles arose in the moral and political thinking of the early modern period, questioning also what social and ideological forces were involved in the debate on equity in the administration of justice. The contention of this chapter is that the wave of Counter-Reformist ideals, responsible for a rethinking of the royal prerogative of secular authority, combined with principles of moral equity founded on Christian virtues, is compatible and indeed explicable in critical terms with the dramatist's use, directly or indirectly via the mediation of other sources, of Italian intertexts, and specifically of Giraldi Cinthio's *novelle*, imbued with the spirit of the Counter-Reformation.

In her pleading to the Emperor for Iuriste's life, even though the deputy has sentenced her brother to death, the heroine of Giraldi Cinthio's story, Epitia, observes:

> Non è sacratissimo Imperatore, punto minor loda, a chi tiene il governo del mondo … l'usare la clemenza, che la giustizia: che ove questa mostra che i vizii gli sono in odio, e perciò dan lor gastigo, quella lo fa simigliantissimo agli Iddii immortali.[18]

> (It is no less praise, most holy Emperor, for him who holds the government of the world … to practise clemency than to practise justice. For whereas justice shows that vices are hated, and gives them their punishment, clemency makes a ruler most like to the immortal gods.)[19]

Giraldi Cinthio's entire oeuvre and the *Hecatommithi* in particular are nurtured by the new principles that guided the Roman Church towards the Tridentine Council. The principles affected the Church's influence, however contradictory that may seem, in the clash between a public '*ragion di Stato*' and utopian perspectives, not only on moral and religious issues but also on all cultural and literary aspects of the late Italian cinquecento. In the theatrical field, the new moral ethic arising from the event was responsible for the rapid shift of theatrical practices, inspiring the definition of *commedia grave*, the theorization of *tragedia nova*, and the creation of the new genre of tragi-comedy.[20]

Besides his experiments with *Orbecche* (1541), offered as a model for a new tragedy, and theorized in his *Discorso Intorno al Comporre delle Commedie e delle Tragedie* (1543) as a means to cleanse the passions by the crude exposure of *scelus*, Giraldi Cinthio's Senecan depictions of lustful tyrants are also amongst the commonest characterisations of the newly conceived Italian genre, *tragedia di fin lieto*, more responsive to the Counter-Reformation ideals, and its novelistic variations in the *Hecatommithi* as well as other early modern collections. In the *Proemio*, Giraldi overtly expresses an anti-Reformist attitude from the outset, as shown by the reference to the 1527 Sack of Rome (which provided the occasion for the storytelling) by 'a very big and powerful German army, stained by the pestiferous heresy of Luther and his followers', with the intent of destroying Rome and assassinating the Pope and his holy prelates.[21] As has been pointed out, the new didacticism brought about in the *Hecatommithi* is evident in Giraldi's inclusion in the first edition of his earlier *Dialoghi della Vita Civile*, aiming at the formation of the ideal citizen of a perfect society, as well as in the presence of various dedicatory letters, each introducing every group of *novelle*, by which 'the author could supply the reader with an important and authoritative key, focusing on the fundamental concepts and issues of each day and indicating the most important points of strength and contact'.[22]

The new Counter-Reformist spirit, exalting the values of love and marriage, the workings out of Providence, and the rewarding outcomes of a divine justice, informs the ideological structure of the *Hecatommithi* as a whole and finds its completed theoretical application as a new dramatic subgenre in Giovan Battista Guarini's *Compendio della Poesia Tragicomica* (1601).[23] As Guarini refers in his *Compendio*,

> se sarà domandato che fine è quello della poesia tragicomica, dirò ch'egli sia d'imitare con apparato scenico un'azione finta e mista di tutte quelle parti tragiche e comiche, che verisimilmente e con decoro possano stare insieme, corrette sotto una sola forma drammatica, per fine di purgar con diletto la mestizia degli ascoltanti.[24]

(if asked what is the aim of tragicomic poetry, I will say that it is to imitate with theatrical means a false and mixed action of all those tragic and comic parts, that realistically and with decorum can stay together, ruled by only one dramatic form, in order to cleanse with delight the sadness of the listeners.)

In defence of the construction of *Il Pastor Fido*, Guarini explains the five acts of the play, justifies its very structure, and describes the main subject in terms of 'an unhappy lover by means of his faith wonderfully made happy'.[25]

A fundamental theme in the conception of tragicomedy is the favourable resolution of a potentially tragic situation by the rewarding power of the lovers' faith. The concept of divine 'Providence', a keyword in the favourable resolution *topos*, serves the theatrical purpose of redressing a situation which would otherwise be impossible to manage in this new direction in order to reward virtue and create a happy ending. It is worth pointing out that, of the six uses of the term 'Providence' in the Shakespearean canon, the most significant occur twice each in *Hamlet* and *The Tempest*, namely in well-known passages closely related to explicit ethical and religious issues by the majority of critics.[26] The two remaining uses, in *Troilus and Cressida* (3.3.196) and *Julius Caesar* (5.1.106), carry lesser religious connotations but they all occur in plays dated after the Counter-Reformist works of Giraldi Cinthio, whereas Guarini's *Compendio* was printed together with *Il Pastor Fido* in 1602 and translated into English in the same year. The most effective passage, though, in relation to the sudden reversal of events following the strategy of suspense and expectation of the new dramaturgy, is to be found in 4.3 of *Measure for Measure*, in the episode of the death by fever of the pirate Ragozine, whose head, sent to Angelo in substitution for Claudio's, sets right a baffling situation, follows the comedic mood of Barnardine's unwillingness to die, rejects inappropriate violence, and establishes a thematic link between the trick of the substituted bedmate and that of the substituted corpse:

> PROVOST Here in the prison, father,
>   There died this morning of a cruel fever
>   One Ragozine, a most notorious pirate,
>   A man of Claudio's years; his beard and head
>   Just of his colour …
> DUKE O, 'tis an accident that heaven provides.
>   Dispatch it presently; the hour draws on
>   Prefix'd by Angelo.
>
>   (4.3.68–78)

In his rewarding investigation of the plots of *Epitia* and *Measure for Measure*, Richard Proudfoot epitomizes the affinities and contrasts between the two plays to conclude that Shakespeare 'reveals his manipulation of events by building the manipulator into his action', that is by making the Duke capable of directing, as in the lines quoted, improbable and even unforeseeable events towards their right conclusion.[27] The implication of a providential design providing an important twist for the play's ideological construction is not taken into account. The reason for this uncertainty in the interpretation of the Duke's role lies in the objective ambiguities of his characterization caused by the complex legacy of the play's intertextual history and its intricate religious context. In contrast with traditional, Reformist and Pre-Reformist, renderings of the ransom story, Shakespeare's *Measure for Measure* falls somewhat apart in that it combines three distinct narrative lines, all pertaining or referring to Italian *novelle*, but propelling them in a thoroughly novel direction.[28] Shakespeare's own handling, dramatizing Counter-Reformation attitudes, aims at a more humane understanding of the frailties of man, transforming a specifically individual vice into a general evil. In such a dramatic perspective, Isabella does not yield to Angelo: Mariana, a new character drawing like Elena in *All's Well that Ends Well* from Boccaccio's *Decameron*, must take her place. In order to follow the traces of Shakespeare's shift from conventional issues for a possible explanation of the play's unexpected resolution, we must go back to the narrative tradition and examine its moral content more closely.[29]

The theatregram of the lewd magistrate is embedded in the wider agenda of justice and its representation in novelistic literature. In a recent article, Ullrich Langher has highlighted examples of what she calls distributive, reciprocal, and commutative justice in Boccaccio's tales and other early modern writers.[30] In most cases, the dispensation of distributive justice, administered by a higher or kingly authority, is underlined by the *novella*'s symmetrical construction to symbolize equal compensation of reward and punishment. Among early modern writers of *novelle*, Giraldi Cinthio has proved to be obsessed with the political theme of justice. To 'the monstrous ransom' motif he devoted not one but three tales and a *tragedia mista* or *di fin lieto*. While the fifth *novella* of the eighth day and its dramatization, *Epitia*, more directly relevant to *Measure for Measure*, have received in-depth analysis, the other two *novelle* (the second and the sixth of the fifth day) have been almost entirely neglected.

In the second *novella* of the fifth day, the Baron Viaste is infatuated with Locrino's wife, Dorothea, and asks to enjoy her as a lover. Locrino explains the cause of his sadness to Dorothea, who invites him to comply though she firmly rejects the Baron's proposition. Unable to have her, even with Locrino's consent, Viaste accuses Locrino of theft and condemns him to death. The King transforms the sentence into life imprisonment. With the aid of the jailer, who knows that he is innocent, Locrino escapes from prison and lives in exile with his wife. In the meantime, Viaste falls seriously ill and before dying confesses his crimes. The King summons the innocent couple to court and restores their rights. Locrino's reputation is saved, Dorothea's honesty is celebrated, and Viaste's riches are given to the couple.

The sixth *novella* of the fifth day is more relevant to the specific issues of Shakespeare's play, deserving close attention for its unconventional treatment of retributive justice. Here, a tailor is sentenced to death for robbery. The Potestate promises the wife, named Gratiosa, that he will annul the death sentence in exchange for a sexual encounter. The woman appeals to the ruler of the land, who frees the tailor and condemns the Potestate to death. The departure from traditional versions of this *topos* lies in the narrator's overt intention to provide some justification for the Potestate's crime through the vivid account of the woman's exceptional beauty. The narrator offers her sensuality as an object of pleasure for the male gaze, implicating the reader in the Potestate's desire:

> Era costei di età di diciotto anni, o in quell torno, & di aspetto gratiosissimo, & soave, con gli occhi viuaci, ma modesti: & pareano le sue guancie vermiglie rose, & bianchi gigli, che fossero dalla natura, con maestra mano, insieme congiunti: alle quali aggiungeano marauigliosa bellezza due labbra, che pareano di corallo; Et, per non andare ogni minuta parte raccontando, tale ella si offriua a chi la miraua, che, per quello, che di fuori si vedeva, di leggieri si potea comprendere, ch'ella fosse in ogni sua parte bellissima. (p. 453)

> (She was eighteen years old, or around that age, and of appearance so sweet and beautiful, with vivid but modest eyes, and her cheeks seemed red roses, and white lilies, as if nature, with crafty hand, had fused them together: to which two coral-like lips were added to make a wondrous beauty; and, not to indulge in details, she thus offered herself to the sight of men that for what was visibile outside, one could easily perceive, how she was in every part very beautiful alike.)

Struck by such a source of eroticism, the Potestate tries first to persuade her that her husband does not deserve such a beauty, that she should be pitied for her destiny, and that she will now have the opportunity to be freed, become a widow, and marry a better man. But this strategy is unsuccessful. The woman keeps pleading desperately for her husband's life. The Potestate offers to free him and give her gold enough to live happily with her husband on condition that she yields to him. The woman refers everything to the Duke, who thus decides the whole business:

> faccio gratia della vita al tuo Marito, & voglio, ch'egli habbia tanto di quel di costui, quanto basti a pagare le robbe imbolate: & voglio, oltre ciò, che dimane, in vece del tuo Marito, egli sia per la gola impiccato. (p. 456)

> (I free your husband from his death sentence and I order that he will receive from the Potestate money to reimburse his robbery, and I also order that tomorrow, instead of your husband, the other will be hanged.)

The friends of the Potestate try to plead for the judge's life, pointing out his youth and the woman's exceptional beauty, but to no avail. Among the courtiers, there is a cunning young gallant who, turning to the Duke, says ironically:

> Signore, questi Diauoli bianchi portano con esso loro, troppo gran tentationi, da poterui resistere, & ne rimangon vinti spesse volte i più saggi, & i più vecchi, non che i giouani, come è il Podestà: però egli è degno di scusa, se a così fiero assalto, qual gli hà dato la costei beltà, è rimasto vinto. Forse anco se vostra Eccellenza non fosse in ira, come ella è, non se ne sarebbe difesa. (p. 457)
>
> (Sir, these white devils bring with them too many temptations that it's hard to resist and often the wisest, oldest, and the youngest men are won as happened to the Potestate, but he is worthy to be pardoned if, because of her beauty, he has violently assaulted the woman. Perhaps if your highness were not so angry as you are, even you would not have defended yourself.)

Everybody laughs at the gentleman's words and even the Duke, though worried, is unable to stop smiling. The friends of the Potestate then begin to plead for his life, urging the Duke that the Potestate should lose his office and pay for the tailor's theft. The tailor is freed from the death sentence and, with the money received from the Potestate, lives honestly from his profession, enjoying the faithfulness of his beautiful wife.

This particular shift in the narrative of the story, mitigating its dramatic content through a blend of tragic and comic elements, is taken up by Shakespeare. As he disrupts his initial extremes of rigour, Angelo pursues the same direction as the scrupulous judge driven to folly by sexual attraction in Giraldi Cinthio. Escalus first refers to this underlying issue:

> the resolute acting of your blood
> Could have attain'd th'effect of your own purpose,
> Whether you had not sometime in your life
> Err'd in this point, which now you censure him,
> And pull'd the law upon you.
>
> (2.1.12–16)

In her pleading for Claudio, Isabella follows the same reasoning on two subsequent occasions:

> If he had been as you, and you as he,
> You would have slipp'd like him, but he like you
> Would not have been so stern.
>
> (2.2.64–6)

And, more persuasively,

> Go to your bosom,
> Knock there, and ask your heart what it doth know

> That's like my brother's fault. If it confess
> A natural guiltiness, such as is his,
> Let it not sound a thought upon your tongue
> Against my brother's life.
>
> (2.2.137–42)

Angelo's reaction is expressed in the same oxymoronic language and seems to follow the same rhetoric as that used by the young courtier's reference to 'white devils' in Giraldi Cinthio's *novella*, with the addition of a further element of eroticism aroused by the girl's devotion to her order. His doubts and faults, however, make him appear more human and real than Isabella's obstinate resolution. For a moment, her cunning request to look at his own heart to see whether he may feel the same desire as Claudio did for Juliet sounds to him like an invitation to sin. The dramatist emphasizes this underlying motif in the deputy's self-tormenting soliloquy:

> What's this? What's this? Is this her fault, or mine?
> The tempter, or the tempted, who sins most, ha?
> Not she; nor doth she tempt; but it is I
> That, lying by the violet in the sun,
> Do as the carrion does, not as the flower,
> Corrupt with virtuous season. Can it be
> That modesty may more betray our sense
> Than woman's lightness? Having waste ground enough,
> Shall we desire to raze the sanctuary
> And pitch our devils there?
>
> (2.2.163–72)

He returns to the same issue in a subsequent scene, while awaiting his second encounter with Isabella, this time also playing with his own name:

> Let's write good angel on the devil's horn –
> 'Tis not the devil's crest.
>
> (2.4.16–17)

Angelo's vacillation leads him to question human nature and to the conclusion that 'we are all frail' (2.4.121). Subtly, he tries to persuade Isabella to yield since 'women are frail too' (l. 123). Her nature is made to be conquered by man and therefore her refusal to surrender may appear an act of cruelty like the death sentence she is criticising. In Act 3, this is a move that even Claudio attempts to pursue in order to soften Isabella's strict morality:

> What sin you do to save a brother's life,
> Nature dispenses with the deed so far
> That it becomes a virtue.
>
> (3.1.133–5)

But Isabella does not accept compromise, as Epitia, the heroine of Giraldi Cinthio's most direct source, does, in choosing to save her brother's life by surrendering to Iuriste's sexual blackmail with the promise of marriage. In so doing, Shakespeare's Isabella proves to be too absolute, pursuing an idea of unconditional physical chastity which confuses her Christian ethic with pride and honour. Thus she even coldly retorts to her brother:

> Thy sin's not accidental, but a trade,
> Mercy to thee would prove itself a bawd;
> 'Tis best that thou diest quickly.
>
> (3.1.148–50)

In order to depart from this world of extremes, Isabella is re-educated in the function of virtue by the Duke's direction, culminating in the reconciliation scene. If she was first ready to accept her brother's death without stirring, just to keep her virginity aloof, untouched by the world's corruption ('More than our brother is our chastity', 2.4.184), she can now kneel with Mariana to plead for Angelo's life, undertaking a process of spiritual growth prompted by the oblique manoeuvres of the inspired Duke; a process that also operates on the guilty conscience of Angelo, who invokes a deadly punishment on his head, transforming him from 'a cruel oppressor into a repentant sinner'.[31]

The idea of equity underlying the final words of Vincentio, whose sudden reappearance in Vienna works for both a moral and a political recovery of a corrupt stage-world, may thus refer not only to the biblical law of an eye for an eye and a tooth for a tooth but also to the possibility that Shakespeare wanted to embody the frailties of human nature in his dramatic design, since all the main characters, in one way or another, are involved in the same temptation. By repeating the same motif of sexual union in three different couples – Claudio–Juliet, Angelo–Mariana, and Lucio–'wronged woman' – the play's symmetrical construction endorses the predicament of the New Testament: 'Whoever is without sin, throw the first stone.'[32] The 'fantastical Duke of dark corners' is not only, therefore, the metonymic expression of his disguise and attempt to spy and scrutinize the human soul; he is also the symbolic embodiment of man's darkest corners, his fragile nature and his infinite miseries, acting, sometimes through imperfect and even comical improvisations, as the 'frailer spy' of a general evil.[33] Hence his invitation to Isabella appears the natural conclusion of a personal quest for a better understanding of human nature exposed to the temptation of power and, at the same time, evidence of the Duke's own learning through the pseudo-omnipotent authority of his spying into the hearts of the people. As for Isabella's, there is no need of an answer. Despite the uneasiness of a number of critics, Isabella's silence fits adequately into the convoluted rush of the finale, where mutual reconciliation and multiple marriage theatregrams emerge from the play's symmetrical structure as a natural closure. To speculate about Isabella's silent attitude is to betray the self-contained dimension of the theatrical text, filling in its stage conclusion with our ideological demands. For although Isabella's renewed characterization in the final part of the play may seem to lead towards a positive response to the Duke's proposal, the real question is that she must remain speechless because the reconciliation scene requires no comment, whatever it may be. Of all the silent women in Shakespeare, Isabella is the most eloquent because her reconciled role melts into the anthropocentric vision of Shakespeare's religion, mitigated by the spirit of Counter-Reformation of its orthodox Christian rules.[34]

In contrast with Martin Luther's predicament of an egalitarian justice and other early Tudor versions condemning human frailties to retributive punishment, Shakespeare deconstructs the monstrous ransom story, endorsing more closely than has been noticed Giraldi Cinthio's Counter-Reformation variants which, drawing on Boccaccio's radical *novelle*, aim at a more humane treatment of human weakness. As in one of his celebrated sonnets, extraordinarily representing the didacticism of the same religious questioning ('No, I am that I am, and they that level / At my abuses reckon up their own'), Shakespeare's portrayal of Angelo's guilty conscience may thus appear a minor fault if seen in the light of a general evil which maintains that 'All men are bad and in their badness reign';[35] a vice with which the Duke himself, in his final proposition to Isabella, seems to be primarily concerned, implicating all the characters in the common destiny of the imperfect and fragile condition of humanity.

Notes

1 M. Luther, *On Secular Authority: How far does the Obedience owed to it extend?* (*Von Weltlicher Oberkeit*, Worms, 1523). I quote from the modern English version, edited and translated by Harro Hoepfl, *Luther and Calvin on Secular Authority* (Cambridge, Cambridge University Press, 1991), pp. 42–3. See also this reference in N. W. Bawcutt's edition of the play (Oxford, Oxford University Press, 1991), p. 14.

2 G. Bullough, *Narrative and Dramatic Sources of Shakespeare*, vol. II (London, Routledge and Kegan Paul, 1958), pp. 418–19.

3 Luther, *On Secular Authority*, p. 43.

4 Mary Lascelles, *Shakespeare's* Measure for Measure (London, The Athlone Press, 1953), pp. 6–28.

5 See, in this regard, A. C. Lee, *The Decameron: Its Sources and Analogues* (London, David Nutt, 1909).

6 Nino Borsellino, '*Decameron* come teatro' in *Rozzi e intronati: esperienze e forme di teatro dal 'Decameron' al 'Candelaio'* (Rome, Bulzoni Editore, 1974), p. 16.

7 *The Decameron*, 'The Tudor Translations', ed. W. E. Henley with an Introduction by E. Hutton, vol. II (London, David Nutt, 1909), p. 203.

8 *The Decameron*, ed. Henley, vol. I, p. 61.
9 *The Decameron*, ed. Henley, vol. IV, p. 136.
10 R. B., *Apius and Virginia*, in *Tudor Interludes*, ed. Peter Happé (Harmondsworth, Penguin Books, 1972).
11 J. Webster, *Appius and Virginia*, in *The Complete Works of John Webster*, ed. F. L. Lucas, vol. III (London, Chatto & Windus, 1927).
12 See William Tyndale, *The Obedyence of a Chrysten Man* (ed. 1561): 'She sought her owne glory in her chastite and not gods'; quoted in J. W. Lever's Arden edition of *Measure for Measure* (London, Methuen, 1965), pp. lxxx–lxxxi.
13 Louise George Clubb, *Italian Drama in Shakespeare's Time* (New Haven and London, Yale University Press, 1989), p. 11.
14 As regards the influence of Counter-Reformation in Italy on either field of prose and drama see, among other studies, Bruno Porcelli, *La novella del Cinquecento* (Rome and Bari, Laterza, 1973); Nicola Badaloni, Renato Barilli, and Walter Moretti, *Cultura e vita civile tra Riforma e Controriforma* (Rome and Bari, Laterza, 1973); Alberto Asor Rosa, *La cultura della Controriforma* (Rome and Bari, Laterza, 1974).
15 See my treatment of Giraldi Cinthio's 'political' tragedy *Orbecche* in relation to the retaliation *topos* in early modern drama, 'Retaliation as an Italian Vice in English Renaissance Drama: Narrative and Theatrical Exchanges', in M. Marrapodi, ed., *The Italian World of English Renaissance Drama: Cultural Exchange and Intertextuality* (Newark, University of Delaware Press, 1998), pp. 190–207.
16 J. W. Lever, ed., *Measure for Measure* (London, Methuen, 1965). Line references refer to this edition.
17 J. R. Brown, ed., *The Merchant of Venice* (London, Methuen, 1966).
18 G. B. Giraldi Cinthio, *De Gli Hecatommithi* (Vinegia, MDLXVI), II, p. 429.
19 This and all other English translations are mine.
20 Cf. Porcelli, *La novella del Cinquecento*, pp. 86–94; Badaloni, Barilli and Moretti, *Cultura e vita civile tra Riforma e Controriforma*, pp. 147–75, and, for the social and political aspects, Asor Rosa, *La cultura della controriforma*, pp. 51–68.
21 G. B. Giraldi Cinthio, *Gli Ecatommiti* (Turin, Cugini Pomba and Comp., 1853), *Proemio*: 'un grossissimo e potentissimo esercito di gente alamana, macchiata della pestifera eresia di Lutero, e dei suoi seguaci' (p. 9).
22 Susanna Villari, *Per l'edizione critica degli Ecatommiti* (Messina, Sicania, 1988), p. 31.
23 On Cinthio's and Guarini's contribution and the origin of tragicomedy in England see Marvin T. Herrick, *Tragicomedy: Its Origin and Development in Italy, France, and England* (Urbana, University of Illinois Press, 1955), pp. 63–92.
24 Giambattista Guarini, *Il Pastor Fido e il Compendio della poesia tragicomica*, ed. Gioachino Brognoligo (Bari, Gius. Laterza & Figli, 1914), p. 246.
25 Guarini, *Il Pastor Fido*, p. 276: 'Dico pertanto che, non essendo altro il principal soggetto di questo dramma che un amante infelice per mezzo della sua fede maravigliosamente fatto felice.'
26 On the Renaissance religious controversy over the intervention of Providence in human affairs see especially H. H. Adams, *English Domestic or Homiletic Tragedy, 1575 to 1642* (New York, B. Blom, 1943), p. 18; W. R. Elton, *King Lear and the Gods* (San Marino, Ca., Huntington Library, 1966), pp. 9–33; R. G. Hunter, *Shakespeare*

and the Mystery of God's Judgements (Athens, Georgia University Press, 1976), pp. 101–26; and Alan Sinfield, 'Hamlet's Special Providence', *Shakespeare Survey* 33 (1980), 89–97.
27 Richard Proudfoot, '"It is an accident that heaven provides": Shakespeare's Providence in *Measure for Measure*', in Sergio Rossi and Dianella Savoia, eds, *Italy and the English Renaissance* (Milan, Unicopli, 1989), p. 165.
28 In his edition of *Measure for Measure*, James Lever describes the play's plot structure as falling into three dramatic patterns or, as I prefer to call them, theatregrams: the corrupt magistrate, the disguised ruler, and the substituted bedmate. From each of these three thematic developments we may trace back a distinct narrative tradition, which often intertwines with other recurring themes.
   It is noteworthy to indicate the corresponding prose variations of Whetstone's tale of *Promos and Cassandra*, concerning the self-revelation of Andrugio who, guided by divine Providence, discovers himself and pleads for the cause of his sister: '"I humbly thank Your Majesty," quoth Andrugio, and discovering himself, showed the providence of God and the means of his escape and, tendering his sister's comfort above his own safety, he prostrated himself at His Majesty's feet humbly to obey the sentence of his pleasure.' In *Elizabethan Tales*, ed. Edward J. O'Brien (London, G. Allen & Unwin Ltd, 1937), p. 165.
29 For a study of the bed-trick in early modern drama see Marliss C. Desens's *The Bed-Trick in English Renaissance Drama: Explorations in Gender, Sexuality, and Power* (Newark, University of Delaware Press, 1994). Desens points out the utility that in *Measure for Measure* the bed-trick and its sexual implications provide for both women: 'For Isabella, it allows her to save her brother's life and to avoid Angelo's intended rape. For Mariana, it allows her to regain the reputation and social status that Angelo's rejection has lost her. However, ... the two women are acting out the fantasy of sexual entrapment that patriarchal societies ascribe to women and that those societies fear' (p. 83).
30 U. Langher, 'The Renaissance Novella as Justice', *Renaissance Quarterly*, LII (summer 1999), 311–41.
31 See Gerald M. Pinciss, '*Measure for Measure*: Saints' Lives and "Heavenly Comforts"', in *Forbidden Matter: Religion in the Drama of Shakespeare and His Contemporaries* (Newark, University of Delaware Press, 2000), p. 44. On Isabella's characterization, Pinciss writes: 'Isabella seems to undergo a remarkable change when she joins Mariana in pleading for Angelo's life. Her new understanding, her change in attitude, suggests how much more complex the basic story material has become when it is transformed into post-Reformation drama' (p. 47). The critic's vision of the play, however, leads him to consider the heroine's self-representation in line with 'the saint's life play', a motif derived from Renaissance religious conflicts between Papists and Puritans. On the religious controversies of early modern England see in particular R. M. Frye, *Shakespeare and Christian Doctrine* (Princeton, Princeton University Press, 1963), pp. 63–110.
32 See my essay 'From Narrative to Drama: The Erotic Tale and the Theater', in *The Italian World of English Renaissance Drama: Cultural Exchange and Intertextuality*, p. 54. On the biblical language of the play see N. Shaheen, *Biblical References in*

Shakespeare's Comedies (Newark, University of Delaware Press, 1993), pp. 185–202; and particularly S. Marx, 'True Lies and False Truths: *Measure for Measure* and the Gospel', in *Shakespeare and the Bible* (Oxford, Oxford University Press, 2000), pp. 79–102. According to Marx, 'The Duke's political goal, like the New Testament God's, is to re-establish lost authority over a community that has strayed from itself–that is, to achieve a reformation. Reformation entails repudiation of existing statutes, both ecclesiastical and secular, in order to strengthen government with the "spirit" of voluntary compliance ... Vincentio is modelled upon the New Testament pacifist leader who maintains his subjects' allegiance with surveillance, intimate appeals to conscience, and miraculous spectacles of punishment and forgiveness' (p. 100).

33 See L. Schleiner, 'Providential Improvisation in *Measure for Measure*', *PMLA*, 97 (March 1982), 227–36. See also, in this regard, R. Kirkpatrick, *English and Italian Literature from Dante to Shakespeare: A Study of Source, Analogue, and Divergence* (London, Longman, 1995), pp. 288–93.

34 On Shakespeare's religion see Giorgio Melchiori's *Shakespeare's Dramatic Meditations: An Experiment in Criticism* (Oxford, Clarendon Press, 1976). Comparing the use of religion in the poetry of Donne and Shakespeare, Melchiori concludes: 'Donne, though placing Man always right in the middle of the picture, expresses a hard-won orthodox Christian view of his relation to God, helped out by theological doctrines; Shakespeare's religion, by comparison, is not theological – it is, I would say, anthropological, or rather anthropocentrical' (p. 193).

35 Sonnet 121, in Katherine Duncan Jones, ed., *Shakespeare's Sonnets* (London, Thomson, 1997). This sonnet displays a suggestive similarity in both iconic and thematic concerns. The metaphors of 'frailties' and 'spies', among others, also recall the discussion of justice in the play.

7

'The story is extant, and writ in very choice Italian': Shakespeare's dramatizations of Cinthio

JASON LAWRENCE

The extent of Shakespeare's knowledge of Italian has been a vexed critical issue ever since Richard Farmer first questioned the playwright's linguistic abilities in the late eighteenth century.[1] Despite repeated attempts throughout the twentieth century to demonstrate that Shakespeare read at least some of his many Italian sources in the original language,[2] there has persisted a marked reluctance to accept the possibility. This has led to what Smart describes as a 'craze for translation-hunting',[3] by which Shakespeare's knowledge of Italian materials must always be mediated through either English or, if they do not exist, through French versions: 'one meets with difficulty in the study of his sources because where the original of a drama or comedy is clearly an Italian *novella*, Shakespeare seems often to have had access to it through an earlier English play or poem, or through a French or English translation'.[4]

However, if Shakespeare studied modern languages in the manner of many of his contemporaries, he is much more likely to have approached the source stories and their translations as parallel texts, in the manner encouraged by John Florio and his contemporary language teachers. Simonini argues that 'it would seem that Shakespeare read a number of French and Italian dialogue manuals and dictionaries, and perhaps even studied languages in that manner', citing several instances of Shakespeare's indebtedness, in plays from the early 1590s, to passages in both *Florios First Frutes* (1578) and his *Second Frutes* (1591).[5] Shakespeare's familiarity with Florio's dialogue manuals suggests, at the very least, a keen interest in learning Italian, which problematizes the argument of those who would still question his ability to acquire even a reading knowledge of the language.[6]

It is hard to comprehend why the range of Shakespeare's mental activity should thus be restricted and why there should be such eagerness to explain away his knowledge of any language but his own. By this process we create a Janus-headed Shakespeare – a man of two personalities. He was both very clever and very stupid – so clever that he could write the dramas, and so stupid that he could not learn a foreign language – a feat performed every year by many thousands of less gifted minds – or could not understand that it was worth learning.[7]

In the following consideration of Shakespeare's use of Italian materials, focusing on the dramatization of the works of Giambattista Cinthio in both *Measure for Measure* and *Othello*, this chapter will highlight the importance of the playwright's collation of various sources, and the mediation of an original through different versions of it, including translations, in the process of composition. The synthesis of sources is a characteristic of all Shakespeare's dramatic work, as Bullough's eight-volume compendium has ably demonstrated,[8] but it is admitted only reluctantly, if at all, in the case of Italian materials. Lothian, for example, in discussing the narrative sources for *Twelfth Night*, focuses on Barnabe Riche's tale of Apolonius and Silla from *Riche his Farewell to Militarie Profession* (1581), and concludes that 'no clear indebtedness either to Bandello or to Belleforest can be established', despite citing plausible verbal parallels from the Italian and French versions, which are not in Riche's story.[9] Yet this reductive pattern, whereby knowledge of a translation or adaptation necessarily precludes a knowledge of the original work, denies Shakespeare the ability to garner details from *both* foreign and native versions of a source.

The aspect of Cinthio's own literary practice most relevant to Shakespeare's dramaturgy in these plays is the Italian's adaptation of prose sources for dramatic purposes; of the nine plays printed in the posthumous 1583 edition of *Le Tragedie di M. Gio. Battista Giraldi Cinthio*, seven share their plots with tales from Cinthio's own prose collection, *Gli Hecatommithi*, first printed in 1565. It is not always clear whether the *novelle* predate the dramatic versions;[10] however, given the respective dates of the two editions, Shakespeare is likely to have approached the plays as dramatizations from an earlier prose source.

This does, of course, raise the question of *how*, and when, Shakespeare came to be acquainted with Cinthio's works, and how extensive his knowledge of them was. Patey suggests that 'if Shakespeare was not directly familiar with Giraldi's critical works, he knew, and this is plain axiomatic fact, his tragedies and "novelle"', although the evidence is certainly not as uncontested as this would imply.[11] The problem arises with identifying the precise Italian sources for *Measure for Measure*, where Cinthio's tale exists in both a prose version (*Hecatommithi*, VIII, 5) and a dramatic version (*Epitia*); Shakespeare's play does have many points of contact with the alterations made to the ending of the story for Cinthio's final *tragedia di fin lieto*, although Lascelles still questions whether he could have had access to a play that was printed in a solitary Italian edition.[12] There is no such uncertainty in the case of Cinthio's *novelle*: stories from his prose collection start to find their way into English anthologies almost immediately after their first printing.[13] Amongst the earliest renditions from Cinthio into English prose are the three tales in *Riche his Farewell to Militarie Profession*, printed in 1581,[14] and it may have been by means of this collection that Shakespeare first came to read Cinthio's stories. Shakespeare was reading Riche alongside Bandello, or possibly Belleforest, at the start of the seventeenth century as a source for *Twelfth Night*. Muir claims that 'Shakespeare was presumably scanning Cinthio's book in his search for plots in the early years of the seventeenth century',[15] which suggests that he turned directly to the Italian collection, which would provide him with the raw materials for *Othello* and *Measure for Measure*, soon after encountering Cinthio's 'Italian Histories' through Riche's adaptations.

In considering the final scene of *Measure for Measure*, it is important to demonstrate how Shakespeare's innovations reveal the rich interplay of the various foreign and native versions of the source story in his play. In this long scene Shakespeare concentrates variously on the anxieties of Isabella, Angelo, Mariana, and Lucio, which take the play beyond both versions of Cinthio's original tale. At the conclusion of the Italian *novella* the focus is exclusively on the reactions of Epitia and Iuriste, who correspond to Isabella and Angelo respectively, whilst in *Epitia* there is the additional figure of Angela, who intercedes on her brother Iuriste's behalf and who, according to Ball, may have suggested the character of Mariana to Shakespeare.[16] The revelation that Epitia's brother Vico has, in fact, been preserved comes only in the dramatic version, where it provides the final *peripeteia* in the concluding scene. Shakespeare adds an onstage recognition to this reversal by having the muffled Claudio actually appear in *Measure for Measure*, albeit silently. The sense of wonder onstage is, however, held in constant check by the levels of discomfort to which the characters are subjected in the denouement. Shakespeare's decision to withhold knowledge of her brother's survival from Isabella until his belated appearance leads to a significant change of emphasis at the end of the play:[17] in *Epitia* it is only when the heroine learns that Vico is still alive that she will speak out for Iuriste, whereas Shakespeare requires Isabella, at Mariana's behest, to speak in defence of Angelo *before* Claudio's reappearance. The sense of genuine emotional and moral turmoil that permeates the final scene of *Measure for Measure* prevents any easy acceptance of the comic pattern that the multiple marriages may ultimately suggest.

The precedent for the brother's survival in Cinthio's own dramatization of his story seems to be the decisive factor in assessing Shakespeare's indebtedness to *Epitia*; as with Cinthio's play, the denouement in *Measure for Measure* builds up to this revelation at the climax of the play. There is, however, a similar precedent in a native source, also existing in both a prose and a dramatic version, which further complicates the issue. Both versions of George Whetstone's adaptation of Cinthio's story predate the printing of *Epitia*, and yet they too contain the unexpected reappearance of the heroine's brother, in this case Andrugio, who returns disguised as a friar at the story's conclusion.[18] Lever has demonstrated Shakespeare's knowledge of Whetstone's two-part play *The Right Excellent and Famous Historye of Promos and Cassandra*, printed in 1578,[19] but there is some strong evidence to suggest that he had also read the prose version contained in *A Heptameron of Ciuill Discourses*, printed in 1582. The collection contains stories adapted from Cinthio, Bandello, and Boccaccio, and the tale of Promos and Cassandra is part of the fourth day, where it is related by a Madam Isabella. It is immediately preceded by 'the aduenture of Fryer *Inganno*', constructed loosely from two *novelle* in the *Decameron*,[20] in which the foolish country girl Farina is duped by the friar into believing that the spirit of St Fraunces is in love with her, in order to facilitate his own seduction of her. Farina is informed of Inganno's real intentions by the 'parrishe prieste', who sends an ugly maid, Leayda, in her place to the assignation with the friar. The priest's switching of the two women in Whetstone's story is highly suggestive for the exchange of Mariana and Isabella, proposed by Duke Vincentio in his disguise as a friar, for the liaison with Angelo in *Measure for Measure*, which has no precedent in any of the direct sources.

The evidence points to the conclusion that Shakespeare is familiar with *both* the foreign and native versions of his source, and also that he knows them in both their narrative *and* dramatic forms. This apparent synthesis of all the available versions allows Shakespeare to explore fully the dramatic potential of the original Italian story. It demonstrates both the breadth of Shakespeare's reading in assimilating aspects of the plot from a disparate set of sources and his ability to fashion this material into a coherent dramatic whole, experimenting with Cinthio's own model for *tragedia di fin lieto*.

Shakespeare returns to Cinthio's work in this period for the construction of *Othello*, based on the tale of the Moor and Disdemona from the third decade of *Gli Hecatommithi* (III, 7). There is no prior Cinthian dramatic version for the tragedy in this case, yet Shakespeare still approaches the prose story by means of other Italian and native literary sources in his dramatization of it. In an essay considering Ariosto's *Orlando Furioso* as an analogue for *Othello*, Maristella Lorch argues that it is important to look beyond the direct source in Cinthio.

If we choose to read *Othello* in the light of an Italian source, we should allow ourselves the freedom of looking outside the recognized direct source, in this case the *Hecatommithi*, and try to consider as worthy of Shakespeare some powerful expressions of Italian Renaissance thought.[21]

She is not the first critic to posit a connection between the play and Ariosto's poem, although previously the focus has been on fairly minute verbal correspondences, in an attempt to demonstrate that Shakespeare did know the poem in Italian, as well as possibly in Harington's translation. Thus, Smart has suggested that Othello's first account of the origin of the handkerchief that he has given to Desdemona, which has no equivalent in Cinthio's story, derives from Ariosto's description of the two-thousand-year-old pavilion embroidered by Cassandra, which Melissa transports to Paris for the wedding of Ruggiero and Bradamante in the final canto of the poem:

> Una donzella de la terra d'Ilia,
> ch'avea il furor profetico congiunto,
> con studio di gran tempo e con vigilia
> lo fece di sua man di tutto punto.
>
> (XLVI, lxxx, 3–6)[22]

Smart points out that 'in Harington's translation there is no mention of prophetic fury', and so any allusion in Shakespeare's lines is directly to the Italian original.[23]

More recently, Cairncross has detected verbal parallels between the play and another episode from Ariosto's poem, a connection which he implies was triggered initially by a phrase in Cinthio's story, which occurs in an identical narrative situation in *Orlando Furioso*. Muir quotes the Moor's warning to his Ensign from the *novella* as the source for Othello's demand of 'ocular proofe' (3.5.363) from Iago of Desdemona's infidelity, to demonstrate that Shakespeare had read the original Italian version, rather than, or possibly together with, Chappuys's French translation:[24] 'Se non mi fai, disse, vedere cogl'occhi quello che detto mi hai, viviti sicuro, che ti farò conoscere, che meglio per te sarebbe, che tu fossi nato mutolo'. Cairncross notes that the same phrase is found in exactly this situation in the fifth canto of Ariosto's poem, when Ariodante demands similar proof of Ginevra's infidelity from the scheming Polinesso:

> ma ch'io tel voglia creder, non far stima,
> s'io non lo veggio con questi occhi prima.
>
> (V, xli, 7–8)[25]

Shakespeare has, of course, already used Ariosto's tale as the source of the Claudio and Hero plot in *Much Ado About Nothing*, and his verbal association of it with another Italian tale of the wrongful and malicious accusation of female infidelity is immediately striking. Indeed, Cairncross cites another verbal parallel between *Othello* and Ariosto's Italian, which confirms the correlation and suggests retrospectively that Shakespeare's knowledge of the episode was direct, and not mediated solely through later versions by Bandello, Spenser, or Harington, when he first made use of this material in the final years of the sixteenth century.[26]

Cairncross's model for Shakespeare's association, and then conflation, of different Italian sources into one play offers an interesting means of approaching *Othello*, although his particular example elucidates only one episode of the plot. The rest of this chapter will trace a similar, but more detailed, pattern for Shakespeare's use of Italian materials in the play, which will concur with Lorch, and will demonstrate a greater correspondence between *Othello* and the primary narrative sequence of *Orlando Furioso* than has previously been appreciated.

Shakespeare seems to be alluding playfully to Ariosto's poem in the central scene of *As You Like It*, where a character named Orlando inscribes the name of his beloved in the bark of the trees in the forest of Ardenne:[27] in the twenty-third canto of the Italian poem the discovery of the beloved's name, alongside that of Medoro, similarly carved on the trees of a French forest, is the first step in the eponymous hero's descent into madness, as he comes to understand that Angelica is in love with another soldier. It is one of the most instantly recognizable motifs of the *Orlando Furioso*, and, as such, is given a key role in the plot of Robert Greene's loose adaptation for the stage of the central canto of Ariosto's poem, *The Historie of Orlando Furioso, One of the twelue Pieres of France*, performed in 1592, and printed in 1594. Shackford has suggested that Shakespeare borrows the motif from Greene's play, rather than from Ariosto directly, for his pastoral play.[28]

The idea that Greene's play may be, for Shakespeare, an intermediary between an Italian source and his own work opens up a range of interesting possibilities, which will allow a reconsideration of the relationship between the two playwrights, most evident in Shakespeare's extensive use of Greene's prose romance, *Pandosto, or the Triumph of Time* (1588), in *The Winter's Tale* (1611). From a series of semi-autobiographical pamphlets printed in the early 1590s one can deduce that Greene travelled to the continent, probably in the middle of the 1580s, where he spent time in both Spain and Italy. The connection with Italy is of particular interest, as half of the surviving plays that are attributed solely to him are significantly indebted to Italian sources. The mere title of *The Historie of Orlando Furioso* advertises its Italian origin, although Greene is very free with his treatment of Ariosto's narrative in shaping his plot; in contrast, *The Scottish Historie of Iames the Fourth, slaine at Flodden*, printed posthumously in 1598, follows the outline of its Italian prose source quite closely. This source is the first story in the third decade of *Gli Hecatommithi*, which of course also provides the story of the Moor and Disdemona.[29]

Greene's play is, after Whetstone's *Promos and Cassandra*, the earliest example of an adaptation for the English stage from Cinthio's *novelle*, and, as such, it provides an important precedent for Shakespeare, who utilizes the Italian prose collection for both *Othello* and *Measure for Measure*. The chronological proximity of the two Shakespeare plays suggests that they form a twin response to a recently discovered source.[30] Thus, some ten years after Greene's experiment in dramatizing one of Cinthio's tales, Shakespeare attempts a similar process in two distinct plays. Is the precedent merely coincidental, or does the later playwright become aware of what his predecessor had been doing, as his own familiarity with the Italian's work develops? Cinthio's tale of Astatio and Arrenopia, the basis of Greene's play, is part of the same decade as his tale of the Moor, and they share the already familiar theme of the wrongful accusation of infidelity, aimed at the central female character. It is, however, Shakespeare's knowledge of *both* the narrative and the dramatic sources in Cinthio for *Measure for Measure* that is most telling, as the situation is identical in the case of Greene's play; the tale of Astatio and the queen whom he deserts and tries to have killed, which already ends in restoration and reconciliation in the prose version, is dramatized in *Arrenopia*, also printed in the edition of 1583. I am suggesting not that Greene himself was necessarily aware of the story in both of its forms,[31] but rather that Shakespeare *was* in a position to detect the features of these narratives that were suitable for dramatic treatment, through the prior examples of both Greene and Cinthio himself.

This triangular connection between Shakespeare, Greene, and Cinthio leads back to the original contention that Greene's version of *Orlando Furioso* works as an intermediary between Shakespeare's drama, and an Italian source. If Shakespeare's reading of Cinthio for *Measure for Measure* illuminates Greene's method of using Cinthio for *James IV*, then Shakespeare's reading of the Italian story for *Othello* seems to have called to mind Greene's treatment of Ariosto in another of his dramatic works. As the freedom with which Greene treats Ariosto's narrative shows, Shakespeare's alterations align the plot with the story of the Moor in the Italian *novella*. Once again, the dominant theme becomes the unfounded accusation of female infidelity.

The source for Greene's play is nominally the twenty-third canto of *Orlando Furioso*, or more particularly the final forty stanzas of it, in which the narrator details Orlando's incipient madness as he realizes that the scornful Angelica has given herself to the pagan soldier Medoro, and is thus finally beyond his attainment. Greene's play also deals with the madness of its central character, but it is motivated in a vastly different way. In *The Historie of Orlando Furioso* Angelica is in love with, and faithful to, the paladin Orlando, whom she has chosen in preference to the pagan kings gathered at the court of the Emperor Marsilius. One of the disappointed rivals, the County Sacrepant, seeks to undermine their relationship by spreading the false suggestion that Angelica is unfaithful to Orlando with her servant Medor. He attempts this by carving their names on the trees, and hanging love poems in the wood where Orlando walks, the means of discovery taken directly from Ariosto:

> And on those trees that border in those walkes,
> Ile slily haue engravn on everie barke
> The names of Medor and Angelica.

> Hard by Ile haue some roundelayes hung vp,
> Wherein shalbe some posies of their loues,
> Fraughted so full of fierie passions,
> As that the Countie shall perceiue by proofe,
> Medor hath won his faire Angelica.
>
> (547–55)[32]

His plan swiftly achieves its aim, and Greene's hero is reduced to a series of incoherent mutterings, which remind Honigmann of Othello in his Iago-prompted descent into madness: 'Woods, trees, leaues; leaues, trees, woods: tria sequuntur tria. Ho Minerua, salve, God morrow how doo you to day? Tell me sweet Goddesse, will Ioue send Mercury to Calipso to let me goe. Will he? why then hees a Gentleman euerie haire a the head on him' (843–8).[33]

The general outline of the plots, and, in particular, the correspondence in the central characters' insanity induced by their suspicions of cuckoldry hint at a connection between Greene's play and *Othello*, which can be confirmed by some verbal parallels in the opening scenes. Shakespeare consciously recalls Greene's characterization of Orlando at the start of the play, as he arrives at the African court in his suit for Angelica, in his conception of Othello in Venice. In their first speeches, each character feels compelled to stress his lineage to counter the suggestion that he is unworthy of the affections of the beloved, Angelica and Desdemona respectively:

> Lords of the South, & Princes of esteeme,
> Viceroyes vnto the State of Affrica:
> I am no King, yet am I princely borne,
> Descended from the royall house of France,
> And nephew to the mightie Charlemaine,
> Surnamde Orlando the Countie Palatine.
>
> (99–104)

>   'Tis yet to know –
> Which, when I know that boasting is an honour,
> I shall promulgate – I fetch my life and being
> From men of royal siege, and my demerits
> May speak unbonneted to as proud a fortune
> As this that I have reached.
>
> (1.2.19–24)[34]

Equally, both characters are eager to stress the unusual dangers that they have encountered in their military lives, and the recurrence of one particular word in *Othello* makes the link explicit. The *OED* cites Shakespeare's play for the first recorded use of 'anthropophagi' in English, but, in fact, Greene has used the word over ten years earlier in Orlando's account of his arrival at the African court:

> The Seas by Neptune hoysed to the heauens,
> Whose dangerous flawes might well haue kept me backe;
> The sauage Mores & Anthropagei
> Whose lands I past might well haue kept me backe;
>
> (117–20)

Shakespeare's usage occurs in Othello's explanation to the Venetian Senate of how he has successfully wooed Desdemona with tales of his military exploits:

> Wherein of antres vast and deserts idle,
> Rough quarries, rocks and hills whose heads touch heaven
> It was my hint to speak – such was my process –
> And of the cannibals that each other eat,
> The Anthropophagi, and men whose heads
> Do grow beneath their shoulders.
>
> (1.3.141–6)[35]

Othello's conclusion ('She loved me for the dangers I had passed / And I loved her that she did pity them', 168–9) demonstrates the impact of his storytelling, and has a strong precedent in epic for the effect that it has on the auditor. Burrow argues that Ariosto conceives of the relationship between Angelica and Medoro as a reworking of that between Dido and Aeneas in *The Aeneid*, and he highlights the shared quality of pity felt by the female characters, inspired in each case by the autobiographical stories related by their future lovers:[36]

> insolita pietade in mezzo al petto
> si sentí entrar per disusate porte,
> che le fe' il duro cor tenero e molle,
> e piú, quando il suo caso egli narrolle.
>
> (XIX, xx, 5–8)

Shakespeare, then, offers an epic dimension to Othello's self-conception of his relationship with Desdemona, although there is a conscious irony inherent in this Ariostan precedent. It is, of course, Angelica's and Medoro's relationship that leads directly to Orlando's love-driven madness, a disease to which Othello himself is soon to fall prey, through Iago's promptings, in Cyprus.

In demonstrating how Shakespeare makes use of Greene's version of Ariosto's narrative, it is also important to suggest that he turns directly to the *Orlando Furioso* in the process of composing *Othello*. Both Greene and Shakespeare emphasize the importance of storytelling as a theme in their plays, but each garners details independently from the Italian poem. Thus, Greene recasts the shepherd's true tale from Ariosto (XXIII, cxviii–cxx), which confirms to Orlando the love of Angelica and Medoro, by means of disguising Sacrepant's servant as a shepherd to misinform Orlando about Angelica and Medor ('And when he heares a shepheards simple tale, / He will not thinke tis faind', 563–4). Shakespeare also understands the importance of the pastor's story in Ariosto, but chooses to emphasize a different aspect of it. When the shepherd has concluded the account of the lovers' sojourn in his farmhouse, he produces a token from Angelica, left as a mark of her gratitude. This is a precious bracelet that Orlando had given to his beloved, and its appearance in another's possession has devastating consequences:

> All'ultimo l'istoria si ridusse,
> che 'l pastor fe' portar la gemma inante,
> ch' alla sua dipartenza, per mercede
> del buono albergo, Angelica gli diede.
> Queste conclusion fu la secure
> che 'l capo a un colpo gli levò dal collo.
>
> (XXIII, cxx–cxxi)[37]

Earlier in the narrative Ariosto has implied that the bracelet has magical qualities, having originally been in the possession of the sorceress Morgana (XIX, xxxviii), and it is the significance, and effect, of the bracelet in the Italian poem which suggests to Shakespeare the importance of the love-token in *Othello*, which has far greater weight than the handkerchief in Cinthio's story. This is conveyed predominantly through the elaborate history of the handkerchief that Othello describes to Desdemona when he first suspects that she has given it away.[38] This account contains an allusion to another part of Ariosto's poem, the description of the marriage pavilion in the final canto. Shakespeare uses Ariosto to imbue Othello's handkerchief with the associations of enchantment of both the bracelet and the pavilion. Equally striking, of course, is the effect on the two central characters when confronted with evidence of the exchange of their love-tokens.

Iago has some precedent in Greene's Sacrepant, but in his adroit manipulation of Othello, especially with regard to the General's attachment to the handkerchief, his role also corresponds to that of the narrator in Ariosto's poem, whose timely production of the bracelet, the 'ocular proofe' of Angelica's love, finally overthrows Orlando's mental stability. Iago re-introduces the theme of the lost handkerchief at the start of the fourth act to similarly grave effect, with Othello referring to it obsessively as his epilepsy begins:

> Handkerchief! confessions! handkerchief! – To confess, and be hanged for his labour! First to be hanged, and then to confess: I tremble at it. Nature would not invest herself in such shadowing passion without some instruction. Is it not words that shakes me thus. Pish! Noses, ears, and lips. Is't possible? Confess! handkerchief! O devil! (4.1.37–43)[39]

Shakespeare follows Ariosto rather than Greene in delineating carefully the steps of Othello's mental collapse,[40] and the trance that precedes his 'savage madness' recalls Orlando prostrate on the ground for three entire days, before the outbreak of his 'gran furor':

Afflitto e stanco al fin cade ne l'erba,
e ficca gli occhi al cielo, e non fa motto.
Senza cibo e dormir cosí si serba,
che 'l sole esce tre volte e torna sotto.
Di crescer non cessò la pena acerba,
che fuor del senno al fin l'ebbe condotto.

(XXIII, cxxxii, 1–6)[41]

Despite the different courses of the two protagonists' destructive insanity, Lorch claims that she 'cannot help sensing in this dramatic degradation of his great hero ... the influence on Shakespeare of Ariosto's creation of a *folle* Orlando'. She supports this by suggesting that some of Othello's expressions in his madness 'are directly traceable to passages of the *Furioso*',[42] although the only verbal parallel that is actually cited is from the final scene of the play, where Othello, in response to Lodovico's enquiry, echoes the conclusion of Orlando's great monologue on the verge of his breakdown:

That's he that was Othello: here I am.

(5.2.281)

Non son, non sono io quel che paio in viso:
quel ch'era Orlando è morto et è sotterra;
la sua donna ingratissima l'ha ucciso.

(XXIII, cxxviii, 1–3)[43]

If Orlando's declaration of his loss of identity is paralleled in Othello's confession, then the opening line of Ariosto's stanza is equally resonant in *Othello*, where the constant tension between seeming and being adds a dramatic dimension to the motivation for the action beyond anything found in Cinthio's story. The line is echoed in Desdemona's stunned reaction to Othello's insistence that she produce the apparently lost handkerchief ('My lord is not my lord, nor should I know him / Were he in favour as in humour altered', 3.4.125–6), in the debate between Othello and Iago on the nature of Cassio's honesty ('Certain, men should be what they seem', 3.3.131), and, most strikingly, in Iago's declaration to Roderigo in the opening scene:

For when my outward action doth demonstrate
The native act and figure of my heart
In complement extern, 'tis not long after
But I will wear my heart upon my sleeve
For daws to peck at: I am not what I am.

(1.1.60–4)[44]

The switching of this line from Ariosto's epic protagonist to the play's arch manipulator is typical of the transformations of expectation that Shakespeare employs in *Othello*. The schematic reversal of the implied qualities of black and white in honest Othello and dishonest Iago is repeated in his adjustment to the central relationship of Ariosto's poem. There, the Christian knight Orlando is in love with the pagan princess Angelica, where Shakespeare, in following Cinthio, has the Moorish soldier in love with a Christian woman.

Despite this reversal of situation, the *Orlando Furioso* clearly provides Shakespeare with an epic precedent for the doomed relationship, in which the hero is distracted from his habitual military life with tragic consequences, because of an unaccustomed romantic infatuation. Many of the alterations that Shakespeare makes to Cinthio's original *novella* reflect his desire to lend to the play a heroic quality, and to raise the status of his story above that of the prose source. The Italian word '*novella*' can convey the meaning of 'news' in a modern sense,[45] and there is an almost sensationalist aspect to the sordid conclusion in Cinthio, where the Moor and his ensign attempt to cover up their brutal murder of Disdemona. Shakespeare rejects this ending outright, and not merely because of the difficult stage business of having the roof collapse on the already murdered wife. His conception of the status and character of Othello would not allow for such a denouement, even if a trace of it is permitted in Othello's gleeful appearance, as Iago wounds Cassio in the final act. This change of status is conveyed not simply by making the Moor a General instead of a Captain, as in Cinthio, but rather by investing him with a fragile military nobility, for which Shakespeare finds a literary model in the figure of Orlando in both Ariosto's epic poem, and Robert Greene's play.

The presence of the *Orlando Furioso* behind Shakespeare's treatment of Cinthio's story may help to account for his most significant addition to the material derived from the *novella*. The Turkish threat to Venetian Cyprus, which leads to Othello's urgent posting there as governor, is entirely Shakespeare's invention. With reference to Richard Knolles's *Generall Historie of the Turkes*, printed in 1603, Jones offers a plausible date for the historical setting of the action of *Othello*, and argues that this historical specificity is intended to appeal directly to King James, whose interest in the ongoing European conflict with the Turks had been registered in his poem *Lepanto*.[46] The addition also provides an epic dimension to the background of the play by highlighting the conflict between Christian and pagan powers, a theme central to the two great Italian epics of the sixteenth century, *Orlando Furioso* and Tasso's *Gerusalemme Liberata*.[47] Ironically, of course, it is the fortunate destruction of the Turkish fleet in the storm off Cyprus which removes the military necessity of Othello's posting, and leaves him instead in the unfamiliar private sphere of personal relationships. For a play based on a simple and sordid Italian prose tale of jealousy and murder, and which has been described as 'so embarrassingly domestic' in its frequent comparisons to the contemporary English domestic tragedy,[48] it is striking that Shakespeare's central action in *Othello* should also deliberately recall the most celebrated portrayal of an epic hero, dislocated from his military context to the point of insanity, through the intense power of his affections:

> Farewell the neighing steed and the shrill trump,
> The spirit-stirring drum, th'ear-piercing fife,
> The royal banner, and all quality,
> Pride, pomp and circumstance of glorious war!
> And, O you mortal engines whose rude throats
> Th'immortal Jove's dread clamours counterfeit,
> Farewell: Othello's occupation's gone.
>
> (3.3.354–60)

Notes

1 Richard Farmer, *An Essay on the Learning of Shakespeare* (Cambridge, 1767).
2 See, for example, Ball's conclusion on the playwright's use of Cinthio's play, *Epitia*: 'it is clearer than ever that Shakespeare read Italian sufficiently well not only to encompass the general structure of a narrative but to be able to catch up a phrase here, a bit of business there, of which he might make effective use'. Robert H. Ball, 'Cinthio's *Epitia* and *Measure for Measure*', in E. J. West, ed., *Elizabethan Studies and Other Essays in Honor of George F. Reynolds* (Boulder, University of Colorado Series, 1945), pp. 132–46 (p. 146).
3 John S. Smart, *Shakespeare: Truth and Tradition* (London, Edward Arnold and Co., 1928), p.183.
4 Arthur Lytton Sells, *The Italian Influence in English Poetry: From Chaucer to Southwell* (London, Allen and Unwin, 1955), p. 204.
5 Rinaldo C. Simonini, *Italian Scholarship in Renaissance England* (Chapel Hill, University of North Carolina, 1952), p. 103; he cites passages from *The Taming of the Shrew* and *Love's Labour's Lost*. Further examples of Shakespeare's borrowings from Florio are given by Mario Praz, 'Shakespeare's Italy' in *The Flaming Heart* (New York, Doubleday, 1958), pp. 164–7, and Naseeb Shaheen, 'Shakespeare's Knowledge of Italian', *Shakespeare Survey*, 47 (1994), 161–9 (pp. 162–3).
6 'One is not sure that he knew very much Italian': Sells, *Italian Influence*, p. 200.
7 Smart, *Shakespeare*, p. 184.
8 Geoffrey Bullough, *Narrative and Dramatic Sources of Shakespeare* (London, Routledge, 1957–75), 8 volumes.
9 J. M. Lothian and T. W. Craik, eds, *Twelfth Night* (London, Routledge, 1975), pp. xlii–xliii.
10 See P. R. Horne, *The Tragedies of Giambattista Cinthio Giraldi* (London, Oxford University Press, 1962), pp. 15–22, for the problems of dating Cinthio's plays.
11 Caroline Patey, 'Beyond Aristotle: Giraldi Cinzio and Shakespeare', in S. Rossi and D. Savoia, eds, *Italy and the English Renaissance* (Milan, Unicopli, 1989), pp. 167–85 (p. 169).
12 Mary Lascelles, *Shakespeare's Measure for Measure* (London, Athlone Press, 1953), pp. 12–13. For details of Shakespeare's indebtedness to *Epitia* see the following

source studies: Louis Albrecht, *Neue Untersuchungen zu Shakespeares Maß für Maß* (Berlin, 1914); Frederick E. Budd, 'Material for a Study of the Sources of Shakespeare's *Measure for Measure*', *Revue de Littérature Comparée*, 11 (1931), 711–36; Ball, 'Cinthio's *Epitia*', pp. 132–46; Madeleine Doran, *Endeavors of Art: A Study of Form in Elizabethan Drama* (Madison, University of Wisconsin Press, 1954), pp. 385–9.

13 Two tales in the second tome of William Painter's *Palace of Pleasure*, printed in 1567, are based on *Gli Hecatommithi*.
14 Riche's story *Of Nicander and Lucilla* is based on the third tale of the sixth decade in Cinthio (VI, 3), that *Of Fineo and Fiamma* on II, 6, and that *Of Gonsales and his vertuous wife Agatha* on III, 5.
15 Kenneth Muir, *The Sources of Shakespeare's Plays* (London, Methuen, 1977), p. 182.
16 Ball, 'Cinthio's *Epitia*', pp. 133–4.
17 'But I will keep her ignorant of her good, / To make her heavenly comforts of despair / When it is least expected' (4.3.108–10). *Measure for Measure*, ed. James Lever (London, Methuen, 1965), p. 116.
18 Lascelles comments on the improbability of Whetstone knowing Cinthio's play: Lascelles, *Measure*, p. 18.
19 Lever, *Measure*, pp. xli–xliii.
20 Boccaccio's stories are IV, 2, and VIII, 4. See Herbert G. Wright, *Boccaccio in England from Chaucer to Tennyson* (London, Athlone Press, 1957), pp. 166–7.
21 Maristella de Panizza Lorch, 'Honest Iago and the Lusty Moor: the Humanistic Drama of *Honestas/Voluptas* in a Shakespearean Context', in J. R. Mulryne and Margaret Shewring, eds, *Theatre of the English and Italian Renaissance* (Basingstoke, Macmillan, 1991), pp. 204–20 (p. 219).
22 *Orlando Furioso*, ed. Lanfranco Caretti (Turin, Einaudi, 1966), p. 1404. 'A Trojan damsel with a prophetic gift, named Cassandra, had devoted long vigils to making it all with her own hand' (translation by Guido Waldman, *Orlando Furioso*, Oxford, Oxford University Press, 1983, p. 566).
23 ''Tis true, there's magic in the web of it. / A sibyl that had numbered in the world / The sun to course two hundred compasses, / In her prophetic fury sewed the work' (3.4.71–4). *Othello*, ed. E. A. J. Honigmann (Walton-on Thames, Nelson, 1997), p. 245; Smart, *Shakespeare*, p. 183.
24 Muir, *Sources*, p. 183. 'If you do not make me see with my own eyes what you have told me, be assured, I shall make you realize that it would have been better for you had you been born dumb' (translation by Geoffrey Bullough, *Narrative and Dramatic Sources of Shakespeare*, London, Routledge, 1973, vol. 7, p. 246).
25 Andrew S. Cairncross, 'Shakespeare and Ariosto: *Much Ado About Nothing, King Lear,* and *Othello*', *Renaissance Quarterly*, 29 (1976), 178–82 (p. 181). Caretti, *Orlando*, p. 107; 'But don't imagine I'll believe what you said unless first I see it with my own eyes' (Waldman, *Orlando*, pp. 43–4).
26 Othello's outraged response to Iago's suggestion that he has discovered Desdemona and Cassio in bed together innocently ('Naked in bed, Iago, and not mean harm?', 4.1.5) recalls the phrasing of Polinesso's plan to entrap Ariodante's beloved in a compromising situation by means of her servant Dalinda, 'quando allora Ginevra si ritrouva /nuda nel letto' (V, xxiv, 6–7).

27 'Run, run, Orlando; carve on every tree / The fair, the chaste, and unexpressive she' (3.2.9–10). *As You Like It*, ed. Allan Brissenden (Oxford, Oxford University Press, 1994), p. 155.
28 M. Hale Shackford, 'Shakespeare and Greene's *Orlando Furioso*', *Modern Language Notes*, 39 (1924), 54–6.
29 Greene's source was identified by P. A. Daniel in *Athenaeum* (October 1881), p. 465.
30 The earliest recorded performances of both plays are as part of the first Jacobean court season in 1604: *Othello* is performed at Whitehall on 1 November, and *Measure for Measure* on 26 December. Muir suggests that the latter play 'was written about the same time as *Othello*'; Muir, *Sources*, p. 182. Owing to the closure of the theatres in London between May 1603 and April 1604, there is the attractive possibility that Shakespeare is working on both plays simultaneously during this period of enforced inactivity.
31 Sanders, in a modern edition of *James IV*, claims that 'I have been unable to find any verbal echoes to indicate that ... he [Greene] used Cinthio's own dramatic adaptation of the story, the neo-classical *Arrenopia*', which contains only the material found in the fifth act of Greene's play. See Norman Sanders, ed., *The Scottish History of James the Fourth* (London, Methuen, 1970), p. xxx.
32 *The History of Orlando Furioso, 1594*, ed. W. W. Greg (Oxford, Oxford University Press, 1907).
33 Honigmann suggests that 'Othello's fit in some ways resembles ... the raging of the hero in Greene's *Orlando Furioso*': Honigmann, *Othello*, p. 256.
34 Honigmann, *Othello*, p. 129.
35 Honigmann, *Othello*, p. 144.
36 Colin Burrow, *Epic Romance: Homer to Milton* (Oxford, Clarendon Press, 1993), pp. 66–7. Caretti, *Orlando*, p. 539. 'An unaccustomed sense of pity stole into her breast by some unused door, softening her hard heart, the more so when he related his story to her' (Waldman, *Orlando*, pp. 218–19). Ariosto makes the connection between the two sets of lovers directly by means of the cave, where Angelica and Medoro's romantic liaisons take place: 'nel mezzo giorno un antro li copriva, / forse non men di quel commodo e grato, / ch'ebber, fuggendo l'acque, Enea e Dido, / de' lor secreto testimonio fido' (XIX, xxxv, 5–8).
37 Caretti, *Orlando*, p. 693. 'The herdsman ended his story by having the bracelet brought in – the one Angelica had given him on her departure as a token of thanks for his hospitality. This evidence shown in conclusion proved to be the axe which took his head off his shoulders at one stroke' (Waldman, *Orlando*, p. 280).
38 'That handkerchief / Did an Egyptian to my mother give, / She was a charmer and could almost read / The thoughts of people. She told her, while she kept it / 'Twould make her amiable and subdue my father / Entirely to her love; but if she lost it / Or made a gift of it, my father's eye / Should hold her loathed and his spirits should hunt / After new fancies' (*Othello*, 3.4.57–65).
39 Honigmann, *Othello*, p. 256. Lorch says of Othello that 'he acts out his madness in a language which seems to parallel Canto XXIII of the *Furioso*. In Shakespeare's play, however, the situation is quite different, since Iago is in perfect charge of

Othello, replacing what in the *Furioso* I would define as the role of the poet Ariosto'; Lorch, 'Honest Iago', p. 217.

40 Alfonso Sammut, in *La Fortuna dell'Ariosto nell'Inghilterra Elisabettiana* (Milan, Vita e Pensiero, 1971), criticizes Greene's handling of Orlando's madness in comparison to the subtlety of Ariosto's original: 'Nella delineazione della pazzia del protagonista, ad esempio, ammiratissima in tutti i secoli per il meraviglioso crescendo, il Greene dimostra una completa carenza della psicologia dell'insanità mentale' (p. 113).

41 Caretti, *Orlando*, p. 696. 'Weary and heart-stricken, he dropped onto the grass and gazed mutely up at the sky. Thus he remained, without food or sleep while the sun three times rose and set. His bitter agony grew and grew until it drove him out of his mind' (Waldman, *Orlando*, pp. 281–2).

42 Lorch, 'Honest Iago', p. 216. There are no precise references to Ariosto's poem given for the phrases that she suggests Shakespeare took from it.

43 Honigmann, *Othello*, p. 326; Caretti, *Orlando*, p. 695. 'I am not who my face proclaims me; the man who was Orlando is dead and buried, slain by his most thankless lady' (Waldman, *Orlando*, p. 281).

44 Honigmann, *Othello*, pp. 119–20.

45 See *Italian Renaissance Tales*, ed. Janet L. Smarr (Rochester, Solaris Press, 1983), pp. xvii–xxxiii, and *Barnabe Rich His Farewell to Military Profession*, ed. Donald Beecher (Ottawa, Dovehouse, 1992), pp. 30–1.

46 Emrys Jones, '*Othello*, Lepanto, and the Cyprus Wars', *Shakespeare Survey*, 21 (1968), 47–52.

47 Tasso draws a parallel between the First Crusade and the modern European conflict with the Turks, when he suggests, in a dedication written before the battle of Lepanto in 1571, that Alfonso II may become a second Godfrey: 'È ben ragion, s'egli averrà in pace / il buon popol di Cristo unqua di veda, / e con navi e cavalli al fero Trace / cerchi ritòr la grande ingiusta preda, / ch'a te lo scettro in terra o, se ti piace, / l'alto imperio de' mari a te conceda' (I, v, 1–6). *Gerusalemme Liberata*, ed. Lanfranco Caretti (Turin, Einaudi, 1971), pp. 14–15.

48 Dympna Callaghan, *Woman and Gender in Renaissance Tragedy: A Study of King Lear, Othello, The Duchess of Malfi and The White Devil* (Hemel Hempstead, Harvester, 1989), p. 35. See also David Farley-Hills, *Shakespeare and the Rival Playwrights, 1600–1606* (London, Routledge, 1990), pp. 104–35.

8

Intertextual transformations: the *Novella* as mediator between Italian and English renaissance drama

CHARLOTTE PRESSLER

The new structuralist approaches to Renaissance drama of Louise George Clubb and others focus on the stock characters and plot elements common to both Italian and English drama. Among them are the familiar scenes and characters of New Comedy: the bawdy nurse, the clever manservant, the parasite, the miser, the impotent old man, the superannuated virgin (and so on). These are used by Renaissance playwrights to generate 'new' plays as recombinant versions of old.[1] Yet such evidence as there is for direct contact between Italian and English theatres before 1600 is sparse and fragmentary. Certainly, some sort of contact must have occurred. In Italy, the rediscovery of Plautus' comedies by humanist scholars of the early fifteenth century had led to what has been called a movement for an 'experimental' theatre in the sixteenth.[2] Gentleman amateurs of the theatre grouped together in 'academies' or societies, whose aim was to reinterpret the norms of classical theatre in plays responding to the social and political situations of their own times: this was the *commedia erudita* of the Italian cinquecento. One such play, *Gl'Ingannati* ('The Deceived'),[3] a reworking of Plautus' *Menaechmi* which makes the look-alike twins brother and sister, has long been recognized as a source of *Twelfth Night*. Attempts to trace the precise relationships between the plays, however, have produced instead a tangled web of resemblances among what has been called the '*Ingannati* family',[4] in which the genre of prose fiction known as the *novella* served as an essential mediator between Italian and English stages.

The differences between *Twelfth Night* and *Gl'Ingannati* are apparent. *Gl'Ingannati* has a contemporary setting: the realistically rendered city of Modena, familiar to its audience. *Twelfth Night* is set in 'Illyria', a generalized place on the Adriatic coast, remote from its English audience. The time of *Twelfth Night* is non-specific and its topical references are few. The time of *Gl'Ingannati* is contemporary with its production, and the play is deeply topical, for it is one character's attempt to repair the damage his family had suffered during the 1527 Sack of Rome that sets the plot in motion.

All but one of the principal characters of *Gl'Ingannati* are hard-headed members of the merchant classes; they and their servants enact the 'realistic depictions of contemporary urban Italian life' that Robert Henke has found typical of early cinquecento Italian comedy.[5] *Twelfth Night*'s characters, on the other hand, are almost entirely drawn from the nobility and gentry, and a gentry of a leisured and rather fantastical sort.

In what psychoanalytic criticism might read as the most significant change, the *vecchi* of *Gl'Ingannati*, the fathers with comically inappropriate marriage plans whose consent is required for the comic resolution do not appear as characters in *Twelfth Night*. Yet the old family servants, male and female, whose supporting roles as helpers, mediators, tricksters, and bawdy critics of the pretensions of the upper classes are crucial in Plautine comedy, are also missing from *Twelfth Night*.

In sum, the young lovers of *Gl'Ingannati* seek with the help of their servants to reintegrate themselves into, and in the process repair, the damaged social order of contemporary Italy; to this, their fathers, as the social order's representatives, must give their consent. The young lovers of *Twelfth Night* are on their own, in an indeterminate place and time where authority is personated by the pompous steward Malvolio and the older generation by the drunken, swaggering Sir Toby Belch. Without parents, servants, nurses or tutors, they must start fresh and improvise the order they wish to achieve.

As Jack D'Amico has observed in a recent article,[6] these are differences grounded in the staging practices characteristic of Italian and English theatre. For D'Amico, there is an 'essential continuity between the theatrical representation of the place where the action unfolds and the felt quality of that place' (265). The fixed set characteristic of the Italian theatre, a realistically rendered cityscape against which the comedy is performed, offers an 'idealised image of the city as structure' (267). Ultimately a place of rational control, the city is 'perturbed but not dissolved' by the 'fluid, metamorphosing power of erotic love' (267). The 'harmonious blending of structures employed in the *prospettiva* of Italian comedy', D'Amico writes, 'provides a visual frame for the action of a comedy as it moves temporally to its happy ending' (266), while 'the disguises and shifting identities … complicate but never transcend the city as the measure of human life' (282).

On the other hand, the 'marvellous fluidity' (278) of the unlocalized English stage set mirrors the fluidity of desire in *Twelfth Night*, its 'ability to create strange experiences' (283) which 'reward those who have been willing to give up a fixed image of the self and to follow those elusive echoes which lead toward some as yet unseen perspective' (281). The power of language in Shakespearean comedy, D'Amico writes, is the power to 'project images, to create fluid perspectives that dissolve obstructions and reshape the urban world of comedy' in the space opened up by the unlocalized, indeterminate English stage (266).

Despite their similarities, then, *Gl'Ingannati* and *Twelfth Night* inhabit fundamentally different theatrical worlds, realized in fundamentally different plays. Both strive to effect the reintegration of their characters into their worlds, but the English characters must, and the Italian characters may not, reshape the worlds into which they will reintegrate themselves. Each comedy is conditioned by, and differentiated through, the staging practices of the theatres in which it was performed.

The differences between the theatrical practices of Italian and English theatre companies would have made direct interchange between the two very difficult in practice. A comedy designed for the 'world' of the fixed Italian stage is not easy to adapt to the shifting perspectives and fluid projections of the unlocalized English stage. It has to forgo the fixed cityscape of the Italian theatre, the frame which asserts the ultimate control of reason. In so doing it abandons the Italian comedic *telos*: reintegration into the visible frame of the city, the measure of human life. More: on an unlocalized stage using few props and, at most, minimal backdrops, the setting is not presented visually to the audience but given through the characters' speeches:

VIOLA What country, friends, is this?
CAPTAIN This is Illyria, lady.[7]

On such a stage, the city is there if and only if a character says that it is, and it is only what a character has said that it is. Now characters who strive with all their might to integrate themselves into a structure which they believe to be fixed, durable, and visible to all, but which in fact exists only in their own verbal projections, may be fit subjects for comic ridicule, but they will not be comic heroes.

In emphasizing the protean character of time and space experienced in the English public theatre, I am dissenting from David Bevington's analysis in *Action Is Eloquence*.[8] For Bevington, the English stage is not unlocalized, since 'the significant element [of the English stage] is not scenic verisimilitude but spatial relationship'.[9] Actions grouped *above, below, before, within* the 'imposing structures' of its stage façade visually define 'hierarchical social patterns' according to a 'well-understood language of theatrical space'. The English state, like the Italian, then, 'seem[s] to offer [the audience] reassurance both of reliably perceived meaning in the theatre and of a larger fixity in the social and moral order'.[10]

Yet, Bevington finds, Shakespeare uses the language of this hierarchical visual space to create visual ironies, to frame 'a world of illusion, escape, and rebellion against authority'.[11] In *Twelfth Night*, Shakespeare refrains from any but the most ironic uses of visual hierarchies.

Perhaps, however, this sort of irony is not a Shakespearean invention. The ironic use of spatial relationships to undercut expected hierarchies is common in early English drama.[12] Thus, in John Skelton's *Magnificence* (1520–23), the title character, haughty and proud, is sued to by the Vices he knows as Pleasure and Sober Sadness, but whom the audience knows to be Courtly Abusion and Cloaked Collusion. The ironic contrast is between the spatial language of courtly hierarchy used to order the stage grouping, and the abusive intentions of the Vices towards the man to whom they bow. The general argument here is that the spatial 'language' of the English stage early included destabilization and irony, facilitated by the use of the generalized architecture of halls for backdrops, which required the verbal projection of location by the actors.

To return, then: though Italian and English Renaissance comedies had a common repertoire of plot and character elements, theatre historians make it clear that considerable divergences existed between Italian and English theatre practices, hampering interchange.

Genetic criticism establishes, however, that the proximate source of *Twelfth Night* is not a play but Barnabe Riche's *novella Of Apolonius and Silla*.[13] Here I will sketch the generic/genetic history of the *Ingannati novelle* as the successive transformations of the tale that mediated its passage from *commedia erudita* to Shakespearean comedy.

The earliest known collection of Italian *novelle*, the *Novellino*,[14] already has the variety of subject matter, the didactic purpose, and the flexible ethical attitudes characteristic of the genre. In these tales, Fortune rules much of human life, but intelligent men and women can adjust their plans to variable circumstances. Maintaining the *appearance* of family honour is all-important to the protagonists; but their real goal is to satisfy as much as possible of their own desires while keeping their own and others' reputations intact. As in the *commedia erudita*, the characters' desires inhabit but do not rupture the over-arching, conventional civic order that frames these early tales.

The sixteenth-century collections of Matteo Bandello (*Novelle*, 1554)[15] and Giraldi Cinthio (*Hecatommithi*, 1565) mark a change in the conventions of the genre. Now the focus is not on the clever tricks and stratagems with which characters achieve their goals. Instead, the tales are concerned with the accidents to which human affairs are subjected. Bandello and Giraldi Cinthio offer a disconnected succession of random happenings against a background of political and economic disorders, preferring to write about extreme situations, and valuing the 'marvellous', whatever its ethical kind. They stress the pathos of their protagonists' situations, subjected to their own and others' violent passions and the equally violent forces of war. Such tales offer survival tools in the collapsing world of early sixteenth-century Italy. As Robin Kirkpatrick has written, they 'mirror a cultural situation in which there is no stable viewpoint'.[16]

The sixteenth-century Italian *novella* thus extends the genre's characteristic relativism to the social order itself. The order of their world, if it has one, is mysterious and providential, not intelligible and rational; for the order of reason is ruptured by actions reason cannot comprehend. As Francesco Bondini had written in one of the few contemporary theorizations of the *novella*, his 1574 *Lezioni sopra il Comporre delle Novelle*:

> much more amazing [than the wonders of the natural world] is the human intellect especially in its moments of perversity: love can lead us to destroy the object of love, as Deianara destroyed Hercules; in Oedipus we can see a trust in reason lead to its own overthrow; amazingly, it is as if in the human intellect there were a living force that destroyed the rationality of that intellect and the arguments that rationality might employ so as not to fall into such error.[17]

Matteo Bandello, who converted the *Ingannati* plot into one of his *Novelle* (II: 36), sets most of his action against the familiar backdrop of the *commedia*; his characters pop in and out of each other's houses in a way that asks the reader to imagine a fixed Serlian *prospettiva* standing behind the narrative. The rational order presupposed by the main action of the tale, however, is problematized by Bandello's introduction, a meditation on the excessive force of love joined with a lamentation over the outrages perpetrated at the Sack of Rome.

Love in *Gl'Ingannati* had not been given an excessive character. There, love was a means by which the social order might be repaired. The lovers' stratagems ended by restoring the fortunes of their families, disrupted and damaged by the Sack of Rome. Love in Bandello, however, is capable of subordinating even cosmic reason to its ends. Love makes lovers do marvellous and excessive things (*cose ... meravigliose e strabocchevoli*); incredible deeds become at once credible if we are told that they were done by lovers. As the Greek fables tell us, even the gods themselves behave madly and shamefully when in love. When juxtaposed with his account of the 'incests, sacrileges, rapes, and murders' perpetrated at the Sack of Rome by the 'enemies of the faith of Christ', the German and Spanish soldiers he calls 'worse than Turks', love becomes by implication the one power excessive enough to be contraposed to such outrageous impieties.[18] Bandello's lovers, then, no longer inhabit the fixed, rational order of the *Ingannati* city. This order was destroyed for good by the Sack of Rome, and now love (and violence) range without limit. In Bandello's tale, framed by the ruined order of reason and the limitlessness of love, the movement toward the fluid perspectives of a *Twelfth Night* has begun.

English versions of Italian *novelle* begin to appear in the 1560s. These are not translations but adaptations of the Italian tales; and their writers, perhaps in an attempt at self-legitimation, associate them with the humanist genre of the *exemplum*. Thus William Painter, in his preface to the *Palace of Pleasure*, tells his readers that he is about to set before them 'the vglye shapes of insolencye and pride, the deforme figures of incontinencie and rape, the cruell aspectes of spoyle, breach of order, treason, ill lucke and ouerthrowe of States and other persons' so that they may imitate the actions of the virtuous characters in the tales and abhor and shun those of the vicious:

> And although by the first face and view, some of these may seeme to intreat of vnlawfull Loue, and the foule practices of the same, yet being throughly reade and well considered, both old and yonge may learne how to auoyde the ruine, ouerthrow, inconuenience and displeasure, that lasciuious desire and wanton wil doth bring to their suters and pursuers. All which maye render good examples, the best to be followed, and the worst to be auoyded: for which intent and purpose be all things good and bad recited in histories, Chronicles and monumentes, by the first authors and elucubrators of the same.[19]

But the characters in English *novelle* not only are *exempla*; they also present themselves through *exempla*, in elaborate speeches responding to plot situations and deliberating over their actions, offered to the readers as models of verbal expression.

To further their didactic purposes, *novella* writers enrich their material with 'copious' ornamentation. In Renaissance rhetorical theory, ornament adds 'vividness' to an *exemplum*. The more vivid the *exemplum*, the greater impression it will make on the reader's memory and the better it will serve its didactic function – or so the theory goes. In practice, 'vividness' in the presentation of vice may instead sweep the reader away with wonder, even admiration, compromising any 'moral', and perhaps the reader's own morals also. Between the rhetorical value of 'vividness' and the didactic goals of the moralized text, then, there is a profound and difficult gap. English *novella* writers respond to their critics by defensively padding their tales with thick layers of moralization, supplied by a strong narrator and imposed *ad hoc*. Robin Kirkpatrick has justly called the resulting style both 'extreme and uncertain'.[20]

One of the more important rhetorical techniques *novella* writers use to moralize their tales is the strategic deployment of adages or 'sentences'. This 'sub-literary small form', as Rosalie Colie once called it,[21] has been the subject of an extensive theoretical literature, beginning with Aristotle's *Rhetoric* and extended in the Renaissance by Giraldi Cinthio and Minturno.

Though the 'sentence' is a 'small form', its uses are multiple. At the beginning of a *novella*, the 'sentence' functions as a prologue, announcing the *topos* to be handled in the narrative. Within the narrative, as Geoffrey Bennington has written, it appears 'in the form of maxims, aphorisms, and generalising assertions, ... sentences which *lay* down the law'.[22] Renaissance literary theorists, who, like Bennington, base their analyses on Aristotle, Cicero, and Quintilian, offer similar theorizations of the 'sentence'. As Minturno writes in his 1564 *L'Arte Poetica*, the sentence is 'something which is uttered as appertaining universally to life and morals'.[23] Giraldi Cinthio, in his 1554 *Discorso intorno al Comporre dei Romanzi*, comments that 'as soon as sentences are reduced to the particular, they lose the name and fall short of being sentences'.[24] Sentences, however, are also used, according to Minturno, to present 'characters and habits ... the disposition and tendency of the mind, and the qualities and appetite of the man who speaks'.[25]

To summarize: a sentence, in Renaissance practice, may present either a consensus opinion, one which is presumed to be shared by both the writer and the readers; or it may be used for 'characterization', in which case neither the writer nor the readers need accept – indeed, may vigorously reject – the character's morality. However, as Minturno is careful to point out, sentences in a 'poetic' work ought always to be introduced by particular characters: 'Remember', he writes, 'you are not a teacher of manners nor of learning, but one who is narrating; you should introduce them in the action and the words of someone else'.[26]

Three forms of sententious authority, then, compete in Renaissance theorizations: that of the *topos*, the theme handled in a particular tale; that of the universalizing propositions of consensus morality; and that of the claim of any particular character to act or speak in line with consensus morality. It is the last of these three that is most important here. For the action of a *novella* frequently pauses so that characters may give, explicate, and defend in set speeches the maxims that establish 'plausibility structures' for their actions. These speeches avail themselves of 'the fact that a given narrative proposition can be subsumed under different and contradictory sententious propositions'.[27] That is, characters choose just those 'sentences' that allow favourable constructions of their actions, building up speeches of justification the reader is expected to judge as partial and specious. However, since the rhetorical ideal of 'vividness' applies to the characters' speeches as well as to the narrator's descriptions of their actions, these speeches may be so vivid as to overwhelm and disarm the reader's critical judgement, nullifying their usefulness as *exempla*.

To prevent this, the narrator of an English *novella* frequently intrudes into the narrative, hoping to correct the overwhelming impression his characters' 'false' rhetoric might be making on his readers. Attempting to moralize each successive, presentationally vivid incident in the narrative, he is pulled in multiple and inconsistent directions. His own rhetoric, which should ground the tale in consensus morality, becomes haphazard and situational. In short, it begins to resemble the rhetoric of his characters.[28] The narrator's own claim to moral authority is severely undermined, as he becomes one more idiosyncratic rhetorician deploying 'sentences which have lost the name of sentences'. The result is an ever more destabilized, ungrounded narrative.

Thus in Barnabe Riche's *Of Apolonius and Silla*, as Yvonne Rodax once commented,[29] the characters are neither controlled by the narrator nor in full control of their narrative destinies. Their attempts to understand and moralize their own positions are undercut by an ironizing narrator who refuses to accept their set speeches at face value. In *Twelfth Night*, that improvisational, situational nature of the characters' understandings is still more marked; moreover, the ironizing narrative voice has survived the transition from narrative to play, having been assumed by Feste the Fool.

It may be noted, in this context, that most of the characteristics differentiating *Twelfth Night* from *Gl'Ingannati* also distinguish Riche's *novella Of Apolonius and Silla* from Bandello's. Riche's tale, like *Twelfth Night*, takes place at an indeterminate time and in a generalized exotic setting: the eastern regions of Cyprus and Constantinople at a time then some 150 years in the past. The journalistic concern displayed by Bandello, who gives the source for each story he tells, and locates each within a particularised historical setting, gives way to an indeterminacy that perhaps reflects the English narrative's status as a relatively timeless *exemplum*, rather than, as in the Italian tale, an account of events within a particular social context.

The merchant and servant characters of *Gl'Ingannati* persist in Bandello's *novella*, though the role of the *vecchi* is given less prominence, the number of servants has been reduced, and the raucous and often bawdy action of the subplots involving servant characters has been dropped. Riche's characters, on the other hand, are, like Shakespeare's, somewhat exoticized aristocrats. Silla, who corresponds to *Gl'Ingannati*'s Lelia, Bandello's Nicuola, and *Twelfth Night*'s Viola, is the daughter of the governor of Cyprus, 'an ancient duke' (182). Catella in Bandello, like Isabella in *Gl'Ingannati*, is the unmarried daughter of one of the merchant *vecchi*, but Julina in Riche is 'a noble dame, a widow, whose husband … was one of the noblest men that were in the parts of Greece' (187), and the head of an independent household, as Olivia in *Twelfth Night* will be.

Julina's newly independent status, however, lessens the role of the other *vecchio*, Lelia/Nicuola/Silla's father, to that of a mere accessory. Riche's *novella*, then, seems to be preparing the way for the absent fathers of *Twelfth Night*. One might ask why, in the English versions of the *Ingannati* plot, the *vecchi* start to disappear. The answer might be that they are no longer the privileged utterers of 'sentences' in the narrative. Renaissance literary theory considered it the task of old men to enunciate the consensus morality that is the verbal analogue of the fixed cityscape, the order of conventional reason framing an Italian comedy. The characters of English *novelle*, however, begin to negotiate the plausibility structures of the narrative among themselves; the authoritative narrator becomes one more participant, and an anxious one, in this play. The resulting destabilization of authority makes grave old men obsolete.

Though the motivations of Riche's characters tend to be as situational as those of their Italian analogues, his women characters present themselves through moralized reflections which take seriously the conventional views of love, chastity, and women's honour, offering elaborate examinations of their emotions and motives. Riche's Julina, while more governed by her desires than Silla, and so answering in some respects to the appetitive young widow of the Italian versions of the tale, has an exquisite sense of honour and shame missing from her Italian analogues. While they seem to exist principally as the free-floating female sexual desire through which the families of the two merchant fathers will eventually be joined, Julina is torn by desires she struggles to understand from others' perspectives as well as her own.

Well able to act in her own behalf, as indeed her Italian counterparts had been, she also offers 'sentences' constructing plausibility structures for her own and others' actions. Julina has become able to set forth and defend rhetorically, and perhaps even imaginatively project, the order in which she locates her own desires. Her half-articulate Italian counterparts are legitimated not by their own but by others' speech; that is, by their fathers' consent to their marriages, set against and upheld by the rational order of the city.

Finally, Riche's narrative voice is distinguished by its ironic and distanced tone, as in the following address to his women readers: 'Gentlewomen, according to my promise, I will here for brevity's sake omit to make repetition of the long and dolorous discourse recorded by Silla for this sudden departure of her Apolonius, knowing you to be as tender-hearted as Silla herself, whereby you may the better conjecture the fury of her fever' (183). He has, as it were, given up the attempt to control his characters with his superior moralizations, and contents himself with aloof, occasionally mocking asides to the reader.

In *Twelfth Night*, the situationally ironized 'sentences' of the *novella* become quibbles tossed so rapidly from one character's mouth to another's that the authority the enunciation of a sentence should confer begins to circulate at dizzying speed. In a play that makes Sir Toby Belch the chief enunciator of maxims and sentences, both kinds of authority are at risk. This is the man who can take a maxim from William Lily's Latin grammar: *Diliculo surgere saluberrimum est* ('It is most healthful to rise early'), and turn it into a jesting affirmation of the moral worthiness of drunkards: 'Approach, Sir Andrew. Not to be abed after midnight is to be up betimes; and "Deliculo surgere", thou know'st' (2.3.1–3). But as Feste observes: 'A sentence is but a chev'ril glove to a good wit. How quickly the wrong side may be turned outward!' (3.1.11–13).

The characters of *Twelfth Night* are not attempting to align their actions with consensus morality. Rather, they use maxims and quibbles as starting points for the improvisation of their irreducible 'singularities', none of which sum up to a 'common place'. If *Gl'Ingannati* represents free-floating physical desire finding its place within the rational order of the city, *Twelfth Night* lets language float free, elaborating the paradoxes of desire within an improvised social order. Personal identity is confounded in twinship, no desire has a constant object or place, and Viola's cry 'Prove true, imagination, O prove true' (3.4.375) may be the only sentence commanding universal assent.

It was, however, the mediating genre of the *novella* that, in transmitting the conventions of Italian *commedia erudita* to English audiences, began to relativize the fixed structures of order and reason which framed Italian comedy. The English *novella*, by problematizing the rhetorical structures that constructed its narrative authority, opened up its narrations, if not entirely willingly, to the de-universalized, individuated perspectives that would be explored on the English stage. When a *novella* is turned into a play, whatever remaining authority its narrator provides will be dropped, along with the narrator. If the de-universalized perspectives of the English *novella* are then played out on the shifting, unlocalized English stage, something very much like *Twelfth Night* may be the result.

Notes

1 See Louise George Clubb, *Italian Drama in Shakespeare's Time* (New Haven, Yale University Press, 1989).
2 See Ronald W. Vince, *Renaissance Theatre: A Historiographical Handbook* (Greenwood, 1984), pp. 4–5.
3 Accademia degli Intronati di Siena, *La Commedia degli Ingannati* (Florence, Leo S. Olschki, 1953). An English translation by Bruce Penman, with the title of *The Deceived*, may be found in *Five Italian Renaissance Comedies*, ed. Bruce Penman (Harmondsworth, Penguin, 1978).
4 Geoffrey Bullough's *Narrative and Dramatic Sources of Shakespeare: Volume II, The Comedies, 1597–1603* (London, Routledge and Kegan Paul, 1958) is the standard account of *Twelfth Night*'s sources. The genetic problem is discussed by Keir Elam in 'The Fertile Eunuch: *Twelfth Night*, Early Modern Intercourse, and the Fruits of Castration', *Shakespeare Quarterly*, 47: 1 (1996), 1–36.
5 See Robert Henke, *Pastoral Transformations: Italian Tragicomedy and Shakespeare's Late Plays* (Newark, University of Delaware Press, 1997), p. 19.
6 Jack D'Amico, 'Example of *Gl'Ingannati* and *Twelfth Night*', *Comparative Drama*, 23:3 (1989), 265–83.
7 William Shakespeare, *Twelfth Night*, ed. Stephen Greenblatt, Walter Cohen, Jean E. Howard, and Katharine Eisaman Maus (London, Norton, 1997). All subsequent quotations are taken from this edition.
8 See David Bevington, *Action Is Eloquence: Shakespeare's Language of Gesture* (Cambridge, Mass., Harvard University Press, 1984), especially chapter 4, 'The Language of Theatrical Space'.
9 Bevington, *Action*, pp. 108 and ff.

10 Bevington, *Action*, pp. 99–100.
11 Bevington, *Action*, pp. 108.
12 See Bevington, *Action*, chapter 1, 'Visual Interpretation: Text and Context', pp. 12–14.
13 Barnabe Rich or Riche, *Barnabe Riche his Farewell to Military Profession* [1581], ed. Donald Beecher, Medieval & Renaissance Texts & Studies, Binghamton, 1992. All subsequent quotations from Riche are taken from this edition.
14 *The Novellino or One Hundred Ancient Tales*, ed. Joseph P. Consoli (New York, Garland, 1997). See also in this context Janet Levarie Smarr, *Italian Renaissance Tales* (Rochester, Solaris, 1983).
15 Matteo Bandello, *Novelle*, a cura di Gioachino Brognoligo, 3 vols (Bari, Gius. Laterza & Figli, 1931).
16 Robin Kirkpatrick, *English and Italian Literature from Dante to Shakespeare: A Study of Source, Analogue and Divergence* (London, Longman, 1995), p. 237.
17 Quoted in Kirkpatrick, *English and Italian Literature*, p. 232.
18 See Bandello, *Novelle*, vol. 3, novella XXXVI, pp. 252–3.
19 William Painter, *The Palace of Pleasure*, ed. Joseph Jacobs [1567, 1575] (London, David Nutt, 1890; rpt New York, Dover, 1966), p. 5.
20 Kirkpatrick, *English and Italian Literature*, p. 250. Striking examples can be found in Geffraie Fenton's adaptations of Bandello's *novelle*, *Certain Tragical Discourses of Bandello* (London, David Nutt, 1898; rpt. AMS, 1967).
21 Rosalie Colie, *The Resources of Kind* (Berkeley, University of California Press, 1973), pp. 32–6. I am indebted also to Mary Thomas Crane, *Framing Authority: Sayings, Self, and Society in Sixteenth-Century England* (Princeton, Princeton University Press, 1993), and Ann Moss, *Printed Common-place Books and the Structuring of Renaissance Thought* (Oxford, Clarendon Press, 1996).
22 See Geoffrey Bennington, *Sententiousness and the Novel: Laying down the Law in Eighteenth-Century French Fiction* (Cambridge, Cambridge University Press, 1985), p. xi; italics in original.
23 Antonio Minturno, *L'Arte Poetica*, trans. Allan H. Gilbert, in Gilbert (ed.), *Literary Criticism: Plato to Dryden* [1564] (Detroit, Wayne State University Press, 1962), p. 299.
24 Giovanni Battista Giraldi Cinthio, *Discorso intorno al Comporre dei Romanzi*, trans. as *On romances* by Henry L. Snuggs [1554] (Lexington, University of Kentucky Press, 1968), p. 151.
25 Minturno, *L'Arte Poetica*, p. 299.
26 Minturno, *L'Arte Poetica*, p. 300.
27 Bennington, *Sententiousness*, p. 121.
28 On this point see René Pruvost, *Matteo Bandello and Elizabethan Fiction*, Paris, Bibliothèque de la Revue de Litterature Comparée, 1937, though Pruvost's evaluation differs from mine.
29 Yvonne Rodax, *The Real and the Ideal in the Novella of Italy, France and England* (Chapel Hill, University of North Carolina Press, 1968), p. 190.

9

Shakespeare's Italian intertexts: *The Taming of the/a Shrew*

FERNANDO CIONI

The study of the intertexts of *The Taming of the Shrew* is complicated by its relationship with the anonymous 1594 quarto *The Taming of a Shrew*.[1] As is well known, the quarto has been considered a source, an adaptation, and a piratical version of *The Shrew*. If we accept the so-called revision theory, the analysis of the intertexts underlying *A Shrew* and *The Shrew* will throw light on the process of the theatrical construction of Shakespeare's play, showing us how the 'original' Shakespearean text could have been at a certain point of its dramatic and theatrical history. This chapter, moving from some theoretical remarks on intertextuality in theatre and drama, will focus on the intertexts of two of the three plots of the play(s): the Induction (Christopher Sly's plot) and the Wooing plot (with particular reference to the Plautine intertext).

Studies on intertextuality lead us to take a different approach to the question of sources: no longer as mere comparative criticism but as a semiotic scrutiny of the modes of selection, transformation, and transcodification of the source texts.[2] In the case of the dramatic text the study of the sources should take also into account the passage from narrative plot to dramatic plot, the passing from 'told story' (*histoire racontée*) to 'telling story' (*histoire racontant*), and the mode of transcodification from narrative form to dramatic form. This is true also when the source text is a dramatic text, being in the process of composition a mere fictional text, unless it is treated as a 'theatrical' text.

The dramatic intertext may affect directly or indirectly a dramatic text. Plutarch is a direct intertext for the composition of *Julius Caesar, Antony and Cleopatra*, and *Coriolanus*; Plautus is an indirect source when filtered through the Italian Renaissance plays (see, for instance, the Plautus filtered through the use of Gascoigne's translation of Ariosto's *Supposes*). As far as the theatrical intertext is concerned, this is a particular kind of text, which, as Keir Elam puts it, 'cannot but bear the traces of other performances at every level, ... the scenery (which will "quote" its pictorial or proxemic influences), the actor (whose performance refers back, for the cognoscenti, to other displays), directorial style, and so on'.[3] If it is true that such a practice is easily traceable in modern and contemporary theatre where promptbooks, souvenir editions, reviews, and audio and video recordings provide us material for a reconstruction of the performance, it is also true that such research concerning theatre conventions can be also carried out for the Renaissance theatre. Elizabethan introductory scenes such as prologues, inductions, and choruses can be studied in relation to the extensive use of prologues, monological and dialogical, in the Italian theatre of the sixteenth century.[4]

The role of the dreaming man, as employed in the two Shrew plays, draws on a common figure in literature from the Middle Ages to the Renaissance. The most ancient version is that of *The Arabian Nights*, whose tales go back to the ninth and tenth centuries. The tales had their origin from different cultural and literary traditions, the Indo-Persian, the Egyptian, that of Baghdad. Variations on the theme circulated in Europe since the early Renaissance, starting from the various versions of Marco Polo's journeys. The earliest known printed version of the 1320 Latin translation by the Dominican monk Francesco Pepoli or Pipino is that published in about 1484–85.[5] Pipino's version contains the reference to the 'dreaming man'. The work is divided into three books, but the division could not be due to Pipino. Pipino's version, which appears to have been executed in the later years of Marco Polo's life, is the most widespread of the Polo texts. There are fifteen manuscripts containing Pipino's version, plus seven in the vernacular. A number of printed editions is linked with this version. The Latin version published by Simone Grynaeus (but edited by Giovanni Huttich) in the *Novus orbis* (Basle, 1532) is different from Pipino's. It is a retranslation into Latin from some versions.

The first English printed edition[6] of Marco Polo was a translation from the Spanish version[7] of Rodrigo (Fernandez) de Santa Ella (or Santella) published in 1503. The English version by John Frampton was published in 1579. The Spanish text – and the English one – do not come from the Latin translations. The reference to the man of the Mountain (the dreaming man) is shorter than those of Pipinus and *Novus Orbis* – and than the later Ramusio version) and lacks any reference to the dreaming man. It probably comes from an old Italian version.

The second English translation is contained in the third volume of Samuel Purchas *His Pilgrims* (1625),[8] and it is from Ramusio.[9] Purchas writes that he was induced to prepare his translation after having rejected Hakluyt's version:

> I found this Booke translated by Master Hakluyt out of Latine. But where the blind leade the blind both fall: as here the corrupt Latine could not but yeeld a corruption of truth in English. Ramusio, Secretarie to the Decemviri in Venice, found a better Copie and published the same, whence you have the worke in

manner new: so renewed, that I have found the Proverb true, that it is better to pull downe an hold house and build it anew, then to repaire it; as I also should have done, had I knowne that which in the event I found. The Latine is Latten, compared to Ramusios Gold. And hee which hath the Latine bath but Marco Polos Carkasse, or not so much, but a few bones, yea, sometimes stones rather than bones; thing divers, averse, adverse, perverted in manner, disioynted in manner, beyond beliefe, I have seene some Authors maymed, but never any so mangled and so mingled, so present and so absent, as this vulgar Latine of Marco Polo; not so like himselfe, as the three Polos were at their returne to Venice, where none knew them, as in the Discourse yee shall find. Much are wee beholden to Ramusio, for restoring the Pole and Load-starre of Asia, out of the mirie poole or puddle in which he lay drawned. And, O that it were possible to doe as much for our Countriman Mandevill, who next this (if next) was the greatest Asian Traveller that ever the World had, & having falne amongst theeves, neither Priest, nor Levite can know him, neither have we hope of a Samaritan to releeve him. In this I have indevoured to give (in what I give) the truth, but have abridged some things to prevent prolixitie and tautologie in this so voluminous a Worke, leaving out nothing of substance, but what elsewhere is to be found in this Worke: and seeking rather the sense then a stricter verball following our Authors words and sentence. As for the Chapters I find them diversly by divers expressed, and therefore have followed our owne method.[10]

... In this admirable Voyage of Polo, I confesse, In opem me copia fecit; the Translation which I had of Master Hakluyts from the corrupted Latine, being less then nothing (nimirum damno auctus fui) did me no steed but losse, whiles I would compare it with the Latine, and though to amend it by the Italian; and was forced at last to reiect both Latine and English, and after much vexation to present thee this, as it is, out of Ramusio.[11]

The words used by Purchas about a previous version could lead us to the supposition that an English version had been published in Hakluyt's celebrated Collection, but such a translation did not appear in print either in the editions he published in 1589, 1598, 1599, or in the edition of 1600. The existence of a manuscript version of it by Hakluyt, as William Marsden proposes, is only conjectural, even though possible.[12]

Nevertheless, the 1532 French version of Marco Polo's journeys and the Latin translations of it circulated widely in the Renaissance.[13] This is testified by the existence in England of twelve manuscript versions of it, in Latin, French, and in the Italian vernacular.[14] An Irish translation of the book is contained in the *Book of Lismore*, dated 1460. The book (whose beginning and end are missing) was written about 1460 for Finghin MacCarthy and his wife Catharine Fitzgerald. The text comes from Pipino's Latin version, but it is freely abridged and the reference to the dreaming man is very short.[15]

The popularity of the story is also testified by some analogues of the sixteenth and seventeenth centuries, such as Heuterus in *De rerum Burgundicarum*

(1583),[16] David Chytraeus in *Chronicon Saxoniae* (1593),[17] and Ralph Carr's *The Mahumetan or Turkishe History* (1600),[18] a collection of fragments of Middle East history translated from French and Italian. Similar versions in Latin circulated in the Renaissance and had their common source in a story told by Juan Luis Vives to the Duke Francisco Bejar.[19] The Catalan humanist, in a letter to the Duke, told how of the Duke of Burgundy, walking through the streets at night, met a drunkard. To demonstrate his theory on human vanity, he took him to the court, making him to believe he was a nobleman. After he spent a whole night at court, listening to music and even watching a theatre performance, the drunkard, again asleep, was dressed with his rugged clothes and brought back in the street. The first version of the story in English is told by Richard Barkley in *A Discourse of the Felicitie of Man* (1597),[20] where the Duke of Burgundy becomes the Emperor Charles V and the city of Bruges becomes the city of Gant (pp. 24–36). Later versions can be found in the English translation of Simon Goulart's *Histoires admirables et mémorables* (1606) by Edward Grimstone (1607),[21] and in Robert Burton's *Anatomy of Melancholy* (1621).[22]

Hence the story told in the induction was very popular, and Shakespeare could probably rely on an oral version of it and, according to Thomas Warton, also on a written version contained in a jest book published around 1570. Warton writes that he saw among William Collins's books

> a Collection of short stories in prose printed in the black letter under the year 1570, 'set forth by maister Richard Edwardes' ... Among these tales was that of the Induction of the tinker in Shakespeare's *Taming of the Shrew*; and perhaps Edward's story-book was the immediate source from which Shakespeare, or rather the author of the old *Taming of a Shrew*, drew that diverting apologue.[23]

The story, according to Warton, was the same as told by Heuterus. This suggests how the story not only was a historical-literary anecdote, it was also so popular as to be inserted in a jest book such as that of Edwardes.

Elizabethan drama used a variety of introductory scenes which can be freely defined as inductions, provided that we distinguish their dramatic and theatrical functions. According to Harbage, twenty-one extant plays with inductions were performed or simply entered in the Stationers' Register before 1594. Eight of these plays, such as George Gascoigne's *Jocasta* (1573) and George Peele's *The Batte of Alcazar* (1594), present a dumb-show as introductory scene; another eight plays have what Thelma Greenfield defines as 'occasional inductions', such as that of *The Spanish Tragedy*. Only four plays have the induction as a frame play: *A Shrew*, *The Shrew*, George Peele's *The Old Wives Tale* (1588–94), and Robert Greene's *The Scottish History of James IV* (1590–91). After 1594, the forms of induction registered by Harbage are forty-nine: eight in a dumb-show form (such as John Marston's *Sophonisba or the Wonder of Women*, 1605–6), and only three in the form of frame play: Beaumont's *The Knight of the Burning Pestle* (1607–10), Beaumont and Fletcher and Field's *Four Moral Representations* (1608–13), and Thomas Randolph's *The Muses Looking-Glass* (1630). Seventeen inductions have mainly an introductory function, presenting the play, and sometimes appearing throughout the play; see for instance Thomas Dekker's *If This Be Not a Good Play the Devil Is in It* (1611–12), where the characters in the induction open and close the play. This kind of induction is similar to the frame play, but it lacks the dramatic development of it – see, for instance, the induction to Thomas Middleton's *Michaelmas Term* (1604–06) and that to *Laelia* (1595) an adaptation in Latin of the French translation of *Gl'Ingannati, Les Abusez*, performed at Queens' College, Cambridge, in 1595. The other inductions from 1594 to the Restoration have been classified as 'critical inductions', where 'human spectators appear on stage to watch a play and criticize it. Actors and tiremen rush about it in a last minute *flurry* before the play opens.'[24] Among these inductions, the one written by John Webster for John Marston's *The Malcontent* (1604) is notable, where the 'the persons of the passage' are Dick Burbage, Henry Condell, a theatre patron 'originally played by Will Sly', and Doomsday Jr, 'originally played by John Sinklo'.[25]

Both Shakespeare and the compiler of *A Shrew* did not have many dramatic and theatrical exempla for their frame play. The induction as dramatic and theatrical device was a way to emphasize the gap between stage and audience, between make-believe and actuality, making the audience accept the dramatic illusion. The induction could have been influenced by Italian prologues and epilogues, even though in Italian Renaissance plays they were mainly used to disclose sources and plot, as in the Terencian and Plautine traditions.

It is well known that the wooing subplot and the intrigues in Kate's paternal house have their source in Ariosto's *I Suppositi*, or in George Gascoigne's English version *Supposes* (1566). Ariosto's debt towards Plautus is evident in the *Prologue* to *I Suppositi*, where, in accordance with Terence, the sources are disclosed. Less evident, and still a matter of dispute, is Shakespeare's debt towards Plautus' *Mostellaria*.[26] Shakespeare's use of Latin comedy, and that of Plautus and Terence in particular, is shown by his use of the primary sources in the dramatic construction of the comedies.[27] *Mostellaria*, like most of Plautus' comedies, was not translated in the Elizabethan period, but Latin comedies, as F. S. Boas and G. C. Moore Smith have shown, were performed in the original by University companies at Cambridge and Oxford.[28] According to G. C. Moore Smith, in Cambridge colleges between 1548 and 1583 there were seventeen performances of twelve of Plautus' comedies. Among these there was a performance of *Mostellaria* (Trinity College, 1559–60). Moreover, Plautus' drama, as Baldwin suggests, was part of the Elizabethan school curriculum: 'in Latin, the boys continue to write verses of various types, their poetic models being Horace, Juvenal, Persius, Lucan, Seneca, Martial, and Plautus'.[29] Plautus was studied, according to Hoole, in the final form, where students had to read 'Horace, Iuvenal, Persius, Lucan, Seneca's Tragedies, Martial and Plautus, for afternoon lessons on Mondaies, and Wednesdaies'.[30] That Shakespeare knew *Mostellaria* is evident from the names of Grumio and Tranio in *The Shrew* (but not in *A Shrew*, where their names are Sander and Valeria), servants to Philolaches in Plautus' comedy. Clues to the influence of *Mostellaria* in *A Shrew* are the names of two characters, Simo Senex and, above all, Philematio.[31] In *A Shrew*, the Lord gives his name as Simon ('Simon and it please your honour', A4r, 14), and Christopher Sly decides to call him simply Sim ('Simon, thats as much to say Simion or Simon / Put foorth thy hand and fill the pot. / Giue me thy hand, Sim', A4r, 15–17). In *Mostellaria*, the character of Simo Senex is merely the owner of the house Tranio pretends to have been bought by Philolaches. The coincidence between the two names could be casual, or simply a reminiscence, even though Simo Senex's lines on his wife ('Atque pol nescio ut moribus sient / vostrae: haéc sát scio quam me habet male / peiius posthac foré quam fuit mihi', III, vv. 707–10 – 'I don't know of your wives – are they divers? / I know my case is bad and it's bound to get worse', 1996: 163)[32] resemble very closely lines both about Kate and about Christopher Sly's shrew wife ('*Tapster*. I marry but you had best get you home. / For your wife will course you for dreming here to night', G1v, ll. 1613–14). Sly and Simo Senex, as William E. Harrold writes, have wives who do not allow them 'to take a nap at home' and force them to go out of the house, the former to the tavern, the latter to the Forum.[33] Moreover, in the Italian translation of the *Mostellaria* (*Mustellaria*), made by Geronimo Berardo, published in Venice in 1530, the name of 'Simo Senex' is 'Simon vecchio', and the speech prefix is *Sim*.[34] In the case of Philematio, the influence seems also to be structural. In *A Shrew*, Philema, Alfonso's second daughter – corresponding to Bianca in *The Shrew* – is the object of Aurelius' desire and the cause of the intrigues in Alfonso's house. In *Mostellaria*, Philematio, a courtesan, the object of Aurelius' desire, is freed by him and she is the cause of the dissoluteness and the non-stop carousal at Theopropides' house. Moreover, consider the eavesdropping scene in the first act of *Mostellaria*, where Philolaches overhears Philematio and, having fallen into a rapture over her, reveals his admiration and love:

                      Venu' venusta
haec illa est tempestas mea, mihi quae modestiam omnem
detexit, tectus qua fui, quom mihi Amor et Cupido
in pectus perpluit meum, neque iam umquam optigere possum

                                                                           vv. 162–6

> O queen of Venus!
> Look, there's my storm, the one that unroofed all my reputation.
> I used to have a roof, but Love and Cupid showered on me.
> Love soaked right through my heart, and it's beyond repair.

Philolaches's situation recalls Lucentio's situation in *The Shrew* (1.1), where Lucentio, having seen Bianca for the first time, stands aside overhearing her, telling Tranio of his admiration:[35]

> But in the other's silence do I see
> Maid's mild behaviour and sobriety.
>
> (1.1.70–1)
>
> Hark, Tranio, thou may'st hear Minerva speak.
>
> (84)

The theme of the father who arrives unexpectedly is certainly taken from *I Suppositi*, but there are analogies between Vincentio and Theopropides in *Mostellaria*. For instance, both knock at the door:

> VINCENTIO You shall not choose but drink before you go.
>   I think I shall command your welcome here,
>   And by all likelihood some cheer is toward.   *Knocks.*
> GREMIO They're busy within. You were best knock louder.
> PEDANT What's he that knocks as he would beat down the gate?
> VINCENTIO Is Signor Lucentio within, sir?
>
> (*The Shrew*, 5.1.10–16)
>
> THEOPROPIDES Sed quid hoc? Occlusa ianua est interdius.
>   Pultabo. Heus, ecquís ist? Aperitin fores?
>
> (*Mostellaria*, II, 445)
>
> [I say, what's this? The doors are all locked in day time?
> I'll knock [He knocks] Hello – is someone home? Hey – open up!]

On the contrary, in *I Suppositi* a Ferrarese does it for him, and than Filogono asks him to do it again:

> FERRARESE Ma questa è la casa dove abita Erostrato tuo: io batterò.
> FILOGONO Batti
> FERRARESE Nessuno risponde.
> FILOGONO Batti un'altra volta.
> FERRARESE Credo che costoro dormino.[36]

> FERRARESE Loe you sir here is your sonne *Erostratoes* house, I will knocke.
> PHILOGANO Yea, I pray you knocke.
> FERRARESE They heare not.
> PHILOGANO Knocke againe.
> FERRARESE I thinke they be on slepe.[37]
>
> (Gascoigne's *Supposes*, 3.3)

In *A Shrew*, where the scene of the knocking at Aurelius's door is missing, Jerobel (corresponding to Vincentio), on his arrival in Athens, first meets Ferando and Kate (E4v), then his son, his servant Valeria, the Pedant, Alphonsus and his daughters (Fv–F2r). Finally, both *Mostellaria* and *A Shrew* are set in Athens. If this is logical for *Mostellaria*, whose characters have Greek names, it is not so for *A Shrew*. In *A Shrew*, whose characters have English and Italian names, the setting in Athens maybe is due to imitation.

William E. Harrold lists fifteen dramatic elements in common among *Mostellaria*, *The Shrew*, and *A Shrew*: *Mostellaria* has four similarities with *The Shrew* (the two characters Grumio and Tranio, the servant-beating-servant motif, the knocking at the door by the father, and the banquet); three with *A Shrew* (the setting in Athens, the names of Simo and Philematio); and seven with both *The Shrew* and *A Shrew* (country–town distinctions, music girl, motif of begging pardon from punishment, Tranio or his equivalent as a prompter of vice, drunken man who calls for drink as he falls asleep, man who has a shrew for a wife, young men (wooers) who are friends). Harrold lists eight similarities among *Mostellaria*, *A Shrew*, and *The Shrew*, and five between *Mostellaria* and *The Shrew*, but he is wrong because the 'lover eavesdropping' is present only in *The Shrew*. In *A Shrew* Aurelius expresses his love and admiration to Phylema, not after the eavesdropping, but after having met Alphonsus and his three daughters:

> O might I see the center of my soule
> Whose sacred beautie hath inchanted me,
> More faire than was the Grecian *Helena*
> For whose sweet sake so many princes dide,
> That came with thousand shippes to *Tenedos*
>
> (B2r 5–9)

All these relationships, regarding both plot and dramatic structure, raise the possibility of a double process of revision involving the two *Shrew* plays and a supposed third uncut version. It is possible that most of the similarities between *Mostellaria*, *A Shrew*, and *The Shrew* were all in the uncut version. The Folio version maintains the similarities except those connected with the Athens setting, the Greek names, and the reference to Simo. *A Shrew* does not keep the names of Grumio and Tranio, the servant-beating-servant theme, and the banquet. It seems that, if we accept the revision theory, Shakespeare wrote a version following the folk tradition (the three sisters theme), Plautus, and Ariosto; then, revising the play, he went back to Ariosto, deciding to keep only two sisters as in *I Suppositi*, changing the setting from Athens to Padua, and changing the names of all the characters, except Kate, Grumio, and Tranio. It is impossible to say if he decided to drop Christopher Sly's interludes and the epilogue, or if the dropping was due to new theatrical demands in the 1600s.

Regarding these changes, it seems improbable that both the changes in the setting and names and the adding of one sister are due to the compilers of *A Shrew*.

The intertexts underlying the composition of the two Shrew plays throw light on their relationship. Evidence of possible revision of an uncut version of *The Shrew* might be found in the relationship that both plays entertain with Plautus' *Mostellaria*. Other intertexts underlying the two subplots, *The Journeys of Marco Polo*, George Gascoigne's *Supposes*, and Ariosto's original *I Suppositi* are also significant. From this perspective, the intertexts of *The Shrew/A Shrew* appear to be a sort of palimpsest of quotations, revisions, and translations.

Theatre and drama are necessarily intertextual. The intertext, Roland Barthes has written, is ruled only by its continual and endless quotations. Every encoding clashes with a continual and boundless intertextuality, with its codes of 'already seen'/'already written': 'every text is an intertext; other texts are present in it, at varying levels, under more or less recognisable forms: the text of the previous culture and those of the present culture; the whole text is a new web of reworked quotation'.[38]

Notes

1 I have treated the argument of the textual relationship between the two plays in my article '*A Shrew* and *The Shrew*: Shakespeare, Plautus and the "Bad" Quarto', *Textus*, XI (1998), 235–60. See also Stephen Roy Miller, '*The Taming of a Shrew* and the Theories; or "Though this be badness yet there is method in it"', in Thomas L. Berger and Laurie Maguire, eds, *Textual Formations and Reformations* (Newark, University of Delaware Press, 1999), pp. 251–63; and his edition of *A Shrew, The Taming of a Shrew. The 1594 Quarto* (Cambridge, Cambridge University Press, 1998).

2 For a theoretical and practical approach to Shakespeare's sources see Alessandro Serpieri *et al.*, eds, *Nel laboratorio di Shakespeare: Dalle fonti ai drammi*, 4 vols (Parma, Pratiche Editrice, 1988).

3 Keir Elam, *The Semiotics of Theatre and Drama* (London, Methuen, 1980), p. 93.

4 Michele Marrapodi suggests that Italian prologues could be studied as an intertext for the English induction (see 'Crossdressing, New Comedy, and the Italianate Unity of *The Taming of the Shrew*', *Shakespeare Yearbook*, 10 (1999), 334–41).

5 *In nomine dni nri ihu xpi filij dei viui et veri amen. Incipit [pro]logus i libro dni marci pauli de venecijs de cosuetudinibus et codicionibus orientaliu regionu* (Leeu, Gouda, probably 1484–85).

6 *The most noble and famous travels of Marcus Paulus, one of the nobilitie of the state of Venice, into the East partes of the world, as Armenia, Persia, Arabia, Tartary, with many other kingdoms and provinces* (London, Ralph Newbery, 1579).

7 *El libro del famoso Marco Paulo veneciano delas cosa maravillosa vido en las partes orientales: conviene saber en las indias, Armenia, Arabia, Persia y Tartaria. E del*

poderio del poderío del gran Can y otros reves. Con otro tratado de micer Pogio florentino que trata delas mesmas tierras y islas (Sevilla, 1503).

8 Book One, *Peregrinations and discoveries, in the remotest north and east parts of Asia, celled Tartaria and China*, Chapter III, *The first Booke of Marcus Paulus Venetus, or of Master Marco Polo, A Gentleman of Venice, his Voyages,* §2, p. 72.
9 *Delle navigationi et viaggi*, raccolto da M. Gio. Battista Ramusio, vol. II (Venezia, I Giunti, 1583), pp. 1–60. For the reference to the 'Dreaming man' see pp. 8–9.
10 Samuel Purchas, *Purchas His Pilgrimes* (London, 1625), Book Three, p. 65, folio G3r.
11 Purchas, p. 107, folio K6r.
12 William Marsden, ed., *The Travels of Marco Polo* (London, Longman, 1818), see also pp. xxix–xxx.
13 *La description, géographique des provinces & villes plus fameuses de l'Inde Orientale, meurs, loix, & coustumes des habitans d'icelles, mesmement de ce qui est soubz la domination du grand Cham Empereur des Tartares, par Marc Paule gentilhomme Venetien, Et nouvelment reduict en vulgaire François, Paris, Pour Vincent Sertenas 1556, Avec privilege du Roy.* See chapter XXVIII, 'D'vn grand tyran qui a regné, & des ses adhetens'.
14 Four Latin versions from Pipino and one abridged in Italian at the British Museum Library; one in French at the Bodleian Library, Oxford; one in Latin from Pipino at the Merton College, Oxford; three in Latin from Pipino at Cambridge (University Library, Gonville and Caius College); and two in Latin from Pipino at Glasgow (Hunterian Collection).
15 The whole text with an English translation was edited by Whitley Stoker, 'The Gaelic Abridgment of the Book of Marco Polo', *Zeitschrift für Celtische Philologie*, I (1897), 245–73 and 362–438. The reference to the 'Dreaming man' is on pp. 251–3.
16 Heuterus, *De rerum Burgundicarum*, Antverpiae, 1583, libro VI, p. 150, folio N3.
17 David Chytraeus, *Chronicon Saxoniae & vicinarum aliquot Gentium: ab Anno Christi 1500. Vsque ad M.D.XCIII* (Lipsiae, 1593), folio 110.
18 Ralph Carr, *The Mahumetan or Turkishe history* (London, 1600), pp. 16–17.
19 See Juan Luis Vives (Joannis Ludovici Vivis Valentini), *Opera omnia* (Valencia, 1778), Tomus VII, pp. 144–6.
20 See Richard Barkley's *A Discourse of the Felicitie of Man: or his Summum Bonum* (London, 1598), pp. 24–36.
21 Pages 371–3 (French text) and 587–9 (English translation).
22 Robert Burton's *Anatomy of Melancholy* (London, 1597), part II, Sec. ii, Mem 4.
23 Thomas Warton, *History of English Poetry* (London, 1778), section XXXIV, pp. 292–3. In 1845, H. G. Norton (*Shakespeare Society Papers*, 2 (1845), pp. 292–3) thought to have found a fragment of Edwardes's book. In fact, the fragment, with the title 'The Waking Mans Dreame. The Fifth Event', comes from *Admirable Events*, a collection of stories translated from John Peter Camus by Du Verger in 1639 (see Alfred Edward Thiselton, *The Mystery of The Waking Mans Dreame Revealed* (London, Printed for the Author by Geo. R. Flower, 1913).
24 Thelma N. Greenfield, *The Induction in Elizabethan Drama* (Eugene, University of Oregon Books, 1969), p. 67.

25 See 'Webster's Additions to *QC* of *The Malcontent*', in John Marston, *The Malcontent and Other Plays*, ed. Keith Sturgess (Oxford, Oxford University Press, 1997), p. 343.
26 See Edwin W. Fay, 'Further Notes on the Mostellaria of Plautus', *American Journal of Philology*, XXIV (1903), 245–8, and William E. Harrold, 'Shakespeare's Use of *Mostellaria* in *The Taming of the Shrew*', *Shakespeare Jahrbuch* (West) (1970), 188–94. Robert S. Miola, in *Shakespeare and Classical Comedy* (Oxford, Clarendon Press, 1994), deals with the analogies between Grumio and Tranio in the two comedies (pp. 64–70).
27 On Plautus' influence on Shakespeare and the Elizabethans see Richard Hosley, 'The Formal Influence of Plautus and Terence', in 'Elizabethan Theatre', *Stratford-upon-Avon Studies*, 9 (London, Edward Arnold, 1967), pp. 131–45; Wolfgang Riehle, *Shakespeare, Plautus and the Humanist Tradition* (Cambridge, Cambridge University Press, 1990), Miola, *Shakespeare and Classical Comedy*.
28 F. S. Boas, *University Drama in the Tudor Age* (Oxford, Clarendon Press, 1914); G. C. Moore Smith, *College Plays Performed in the University of Cambridge* (Cambridge, Cambridge University Press, 1923).
29 T. W. Baldwin, *William Shakespeare's Small Latine and Lesse Greeke* (Urbana, Urbana University Press, 1944), vol. I, p. 458.
30 Even though Hoole's book was published in 1660, his system is only a 'clarification of the system in vogue in the latter part of the sixteenth century' (quoted in Baldwin, *William Shakespeare's Small Latine*, vol. I, p. 452), in particular of the 'Eton system'.
31 I do not agree with Rhiele's assumption that Grumio and Tranio come from Shakespeare's reminiscences of grammar school: 'by the time Shakespeare composed *Taming* he had read Plautine and Terentian comedies at school, and he remembered the names Tranio and Grumio from the Plautine *Mostellaria*' (see Riehle, *Shakespeare, Plautus and the Humanist Tradition*, p. 212).
32 All references to the Latin text are taken from Plautus, *Mostellaria*, ed. Edward A. Sonnenschein (Oxford, Clarendon Press, 1907), and, for the English translation, from Plautus' *The Haunted House*, in *Four Comedies*, ed. Erich Segal (Oxford, Oxford University Press, 1996).
33 William E. Harrold, 'Shakespeare's Use of *Mostellaria* in *The Taming of the Shrew*', p. 191.
34 Plautus, *Mustellaria*, translated into Italian by Geronimo Gerardo (Venice, 1530).
35 Quotations from *The Shrew* are taken from the Arden Shakespeare, ed. Brian Morris (London, Methuen, 1981).
36 Ludovico Ariosto, *I Suppositi* (1509), 4.3, in *Tutte le opere di Ludovico Ariosto*, ed. Cesare Segre (Milan, Mondadori, 1964), p. 329.
37 George Gascoigne, *Supposes* (1566), 3.3 in Geoffrey Bullough, *Narrative and Dramatic Sources of Shakespeare* (London, Routledge, 1961), vol. I, p. 139.
38 See Roland Barthes, 'Texte' in *Encyclopædia Universalis*, vol. 15 (Paris, 1973), pp. 1013–17 (p. 1015, my translation).

Part III
Text and ideology

10

'What news on the Rialto': luxury, sodomy, and miscegenation in *The Merchant of Venice*

ANTHONY G. BARTHELEMY

The cumbersome yet extravagant title printed on the first page of the initial printing of Shakespeare's *The Merchant of Venice* may convey to contemporary readers some of the titillation and anticipation felt by sixteenth-century Englishmen as they arrived to see the play at the theatre in the late 1590s or as they handled the quarto printed by Thomas Heyes in 1600.[1] The title promised the purchaser: *The most excellent Historie of the Merchant of Venice. With the extreame crueltie of Shylocke the Iewe towards the sayd Merchant, in cutting a iust pound of his flesh: and the obtayning of Portia by the choyse of three chests. As it hath beene diuers times acted by the Lord Chamberlaine his Seruants. Written by William Shakespeare.* Consistent with the extravagant notions of Venice held by Shakespeare's contemporary, the title of Q1, at least, pledges a play that hints at the wonders of romance, at the same time assuring a stable merchant's world suitable for the mimetic stage of early modern English drama. While the playwright may not have been responsible for selecting the printed title, there is no doubt that he chose Venice as the site of action. And, given the available documentation regarding Venice and the wide public circulation of the 'Myth of Venice', Shakespeare's audience probably entered the playhouse hoping to see some of that city's reputed vices, excesses, and prodigality acted out on the public stage in the play.[2]

Englishmen had been cautioned by many of their compatriots of the dangers that lurked along the Grand Canal. Chief amongst this legion was Roger Ascham, humanist, educator, Greek and Latin tutor to the then Princess Elizabeth, and later Latin Secretary to Edward VI and Queen Elizabeth. According to his own report, the nine days that Ascham spent in Venice exposed him to more vice and sin than he could possibly have encountered in any nine years in London.[3] Ascham, of course, like many other English writers and diarists, seemed to wallow in the pleasures of enumerating the vices that awaited an Englishman who found his way from the sceptred island to the diabolical peninsula. In the opinion of Ascham and others possessed of similar ethnocentric intolerance, the '*Inglesi Italianati*' posed an even greater threat to English morals than the untravelled corrupt because the *Italianati* imported into England those foreign vices that corrupted the mind, body, and soul of true Christians:

> Our Italians [the *Inglesi Italianati*] bring home with them other faults from Italy, though not so great as this of Religion, yet a great deal greater, than many good men can well bear. For commonly they come home, common condemners of marriage and ready persuaders of all others to the same: not because they love virginity, nor yet because they hate pretty young virgins, but, being free in Italy, to go whither so ever lust will carry them, they do not like, that law and honesty should be such a bar to their like liberty at home in England. (Ascham, 235)[4]

To Ascham and others, Venice was literally one hell of a place. One could argue endlessly and fruitlessly about the accuracy of Shakespeare's knowledge of Venice, but the influence of Ascham and the myth of Venice remain undeniable. Shakespeare's acquaintance Thomas Nashe used details from Ascham's work in his 1594 picaresque *The Unfortunate Traveller*. Surely Shakespeare knew the other available sources in English and probably Francesco Guicciardini's 1561 *Storia d'Italia*, first translated into English in 1579.[5] He obviously knew enough Italian popular literature that he was able to borrow stories to turn into plays; the source of *The Merchant of Venice* itself is the fourteenth-century *Il Pecorone* of Ser Giovanni. Popular Italian literature had enough of an impact on contemporary England that Ascham complains about the presence of numerous Italian books recently translated into English. Of course, the Italy of fiction could and did differ radically from sixteenth-century Italy itself. For instance, did the English playwright know of the Venetian government's obsession with rooting out sodomy? Shakespeare probably did not know of Bernardino of Sienna or of the 1420s sermon in which he complained that Italy was the 'mother' of sodomy.[6] However, Shakespeare may well have known of the custom of Venetian prostitutes dressing as men. In other words, many elements of documentable Venetian history could easily inform the play and shed light on the actions and characters. Regardless, Venice's reputation was more complex than Ascham allows. For in addition to being the site of unspeakable carnality, Venice had justly earned the reputation as a centre of wealth, commerce, religious and racial tolerance, and as a place of severe yet impartial justice.[7] Whether Shakespeare knew any, few or all of the specifics, the 'myth of Venice' which finds articulation in so many English plays of the period made the city an appropriate setting for the story of the merchant, his bachelor friend, and the usurer.

Modern readers and scholars, however, should not lose sight of G. K. Hunter's admonition: 'The foreigner could only "mean" something important, and so be effective as a literary figure, when the qualities observed in him were seen to involve a simple and significant relationship to real life at home. Without this relationship, mere observation, however exact, could hardly make an impact on men caught up in their own problems and their own destiny.'[8] Clearly we need be careful not to search out relationships between Italy and England and then abstract them from their relevance to Shakespeare's England. Even though ticket-holders probably hoped to see more of Venice than London, and at play's end they probably thought Venice more spectacular and more boldly wicked than the English capital, *La Serenissma* probably provided a mirror in which the audience could see reflected a little bit of its hometown. After all, Ascham need not have gone all the way to Venice to find the kind of 'liberty' he condemned in Venice. In 1593 Marlowe, a rival playwright whom Shakespeare praises in *As You Like It*, was assassinated and exposed as a blaspheming sodomite. Marlowe's friend Kyd was tortured under the same pretext of being a blasphemer and sodomite. Shakespeare himself was working on his sonnets during the period of composition of *Merchant*; and one of the most overtly homosocial if not homoerotic of the sonnets, number 144 ('Two loves I have of comfort and despair'), appeared in print in 1599. We know that in the 1590s the English were heavily involved in Western trade; that Ralegh had failed at a settlement in Virginia; that Essex, Drake, and Hawkins were plundering Spanish and Portuguese vessels; that Elizabeth I, herself, had invested in the slave trade; and London's trade guilds were investing in argosies of their own. We also know that patriarchy continued to be compromised by the reign of the woman who claimed to have the heart and soul of an 'English Prince'; that Jews and Africans were being expelled from England; that the ambassador from Morocco drew a crowd wherever he went; and that Indians and Africans were on display in public places and in public pageants in the 1590s. Thus even if they desired to, the English could not domesticate all of these phenomena, so a look at Venice might have provided them with ways of mastering their own anxieties about the exotic world that demanded their attention and that seemed to make vulnerable the island nation believed to be a 'fortress built by nature for herself / Against infection and the hand of war' (*Richard II*, 2.1.43–4).[9] Perhaps this fanciful visit to Venice aided Englishmen in imagining a world in which they could continue to be English regardless of the ever changing world around them.

The promised exoticism of the title and setting, however, do not unfold in the play's first moments. Rather than a scene that introduces us to a city of untold splendour and comfort, we find a group of friends anxious about another friend's mental health. The only curiosities arrive in the romantic details of where the merchant's ships might be; he himself, at least according to his friends Salerio and Solanio, has a mind trapped betwixt the fantastic possibilities of the oceans and the sublunary realities of the ledgers. All present seek to comfort Antonio, a man awash in indulgent self-pity. The merchant's friends wonder why he continues to suffer from what they believe to be anxiety but what we latter learn to be melancholy.[10] Antonio's response to the caring inquiry of his friends reveals both the merchant's supposed anxiety and, more importantly, his duplicity:

> In sooth, I know not why I am so sad.
> It wearies me, you say it wearies you;
> But how I caught it, found it, or came by it,
> What stuff 'tis made of, whereof it is born,
> I am to learn;
> And such a want-wit sadness makes of me
> That I have much ado to know myself.
>
> (1.1.1–7)

By emphasizing Antonio's supposed ignorance in the truncated line 5, Shakespeare allows the merchant to pass off his depression as anxiety.[11] But then, with a flare of irony, the playwright's clever use of the reflexive pronoun reveals that Antonio indeed knows himself as well as knows why he will not admit what he knows.[12] In short, Antonio loves Bassanio and awaits his friend to learn of the suit to Portia at Belmont. As soon as Antonio finds himself alone with Bassanio the merchant asks the suitor directly of the 'lady' (1.1.119). Bassanio may be unaware of Antonio's deep feelings, but even if he were, it would be difficult to dismiss Antonio's more then generous and, as we later find out, unhyperbolic offer of 'purse, person and extremest means' (1.1.138). Thus through the conversation of the two friends, we see wedded in that first scene two of the plays most important themes: love and money.

But Bassanio responds to Antonio's extraordinary liberality not with a pledge but with a story of flying shafts, and then the profligate suitor emphasizes the tale's 'innocence' lest Antonio misconstrue 'shaft' as somehow meant to be provocative (1.1.140–53). Once again with emphatic irony, the playwright focuses our attention on Antonio by having him admonish his friend with words that resonate from his earlier melancholy. 'You know me well' (1.1.153), Antonio tells Bassanio, and the audience should recognize that indeed Antonio too knows himself well. However, by Act 2 all doubts of the nature of Antonio's affection seem to be resolved by the merchant's tearful goodbye to Bassanio who leaves Venice for Belmont in pursuit of the lady's hand. From his friend Salerio we hear of how Antonio, with his hand extended behind his back, could not face Bassanio's departure. Perhaps Salerio did not completely comprehend the sentiments of the principal characters of the melancholy scene he witnessed, but he describes it movingly:

> I saw Bassanio and Antonio part.
> Bassanio told him he would make some speed

> Of his return. He answered, 'Do not so.
> Slubber not business for my sake, Bassanio.
> But stay the very riping of the time;
> And for the Jew's bond which he hath of me,
> Let it not enter in your mind of love.
> Be merry, and employ your chiefest thoughts
> To courtship and such fair ostents of love
> As shall conveniently become you there.'
> And even there, his eye being big with tears,
> Turning his face, he put his hand behind him
> And, with affection wondrous sensible
> He wrung Bassanio's hand; and so they parted.
>
> (2.9.36–49)

Indeed Bassanio's return to Belmont may in fact remove him for ever beyond the reach of the man who loves him. Antonio's instructions to Bassanio in line 42 ('Let it not enter in your mind of love') not to let the debt disrupt his courtship of the lady rings of a pathetic plea to remember the love of the creditor to the debtor. This sorrowful farewell made blind by both tears and averted eyes underscores the merchant's refusal to face the truth of his desire, his desperate effort to impress upon his "friend" the depths of this affection, and his unwillingness to admit to himself what he knows of himself.

I have already referred to the myth of Venice and Shakespeare's probable knowledge of at least some documentable facts of Venetian history. However, when we consider the particulars of Antonio's situation, we need look again to both foreign and domestic justifications to explain Antonio's circumspection with regards to expressing the true nature of his affections. Perhaps Shakespeare had heard tales of convicted Venetian sodomites being beheaded and then burned at the stake. Perhaps he knew that Antonio, the older man of the couple, was more likely to have received the more severe punishment for acting on his feelings. But whatever the extent of Shakespeare's knowledge or the reasons for Antonio's reticence, the merchant knows that he has but one love, and that one is of despair (Sonnet 144). Guido Ruggiero and Patricia Labalme document the history of sexual nonconformity in Renaissance Venice and the brutal yet unsuccessful efforts of the government to rid the city of this 'unspeakable' vice. Although prosecutions and persecutions of sodomy did not seem to be as vigorous in England as in sixteenth-century Venice, there were prosecutions and condemnations enough in England to influence Shakespeare's imagination.[13] A direct threat could be found in 1583 in Phillip Stubbes's hysterical condemnation of the theatre. Deploring the homoerotic temptations of playing and the playhouse, Stubbes writes: 'these goodly pageants being done, every mate sorts to his mate, every one brings another homeward and of their way very friendly, and in their secret conclaves (covertly) they play *the Sodomites*, or worse. And these be the fruits of Plays and Interludes for the most part' (pp. 144–5).[14]

Stubbes's overblown reaction to social activity in the playhouse and the social consequences appears to be a *crise de nerfs* or excessive protestation similar to Gertrude's in *Hamlet*. However, research does suggests that there was a germ of truth in Stubbes's protestation. Mary Bly's groundbreaking research reported in her 2000 book *Queer Virgins and Virgin Queans on the Early Modern Stage* documents the homoerotic content found in the repertoire of the Whitefriars Company between 1607 and 1608.[15] Bly asserts that plays performed during that period appealed to cognoscenti who reveled in the sodomitical puns and innuendos of certain plays. Although most of Bly's examples focus on the power of cross-dressed boy actors to reference sodomy, her arguments about a discerning coterie unquestionably extend to other kinds of coded language spoken by other players. The point that Bly so convincingly makes reinforces my argument concerning the cultural climate that surrounded both the Globe and the anxiety of the merchant. A subculture no matter how recognizable but that was required by law to speak its identity and desires in code or risk social disapprobation at best and legal consequences at worst would not only recognize Antonio's disquiet but also sympathize with him. As I have mentioned earlier, accusations of sodomy justified the murder of Marlowe and the torture of Kyd. Thus the theatre proved a locus of sanctuary and a caveat to feeling too comfortable. Mimicking the theatre's ambivalence, Antonio offers and receives comfort and despair from Bassanio.

Antonio's duplicity does not elude the Mistress of Belmont, who quickly discerns it during the trial, and soon she evidences her fear that Bassanio might actually desire playing 'the Sodomite' with Antonio. When her husband's patron implies that the wife of the yet unconsummated marriage is only second in devotion to Bassanio, Portia has to meet the challenge and triumph over the would-be martyr for love in order to save her marriage. In an ostentatiously pathetic manner Antonio commands his lover:

> Give me your hand, Bassanio, fare you well.
> Grieve not that I am fall'n to this for you.
> …
> Commend me to your honourable wife.
> Tell her the process of Antonio's end.
> Say how I loved you, speak me fair in death.
> And when the tale is told, bid her be judge
> Whether Bassanio had not once a love.
>
> (4.1.260–1; 268–72)

Following this little pageant Antonio's challenge to Portia's affectional and spousal supremacy would not end with the merchant's death. In addition to being a martyr, Antonio through his death would precede Portia with the symbolic consummation of his relationship with Bassanio. Not only would the merchant be penetrated to the heart for love, but he would shed first blood to confirm his complete and eternal devotion to Bassanio. The threat of Antonio's shedding of blood, in fact, prevents Portia from shedding her blood first for her husband because Bassanio flees Belmont immediately after the nuptials on a mission of succour to Antonio. It is no wonder then that Portia wants everyone to return to Belmont at trial's end. At least in Belmont she thinks that she will once again be in control and that the threat of Venetian licence and lasciviousness could perhaps be walled out.

The play of the ring reinforces Portia's urgent need to have her husband recommit himself to her. In her disguise as Balthasar, Portia could not persuade Bassanio to surrender the ring even though at that moment both men are indebted to her. But Antonio could. And the tainted wether confirms for Portia that he still holds sway over her husband and her marriage when he intrudes himself into their quarrel. Ironically Bassanio's rejection of Balthasar only confirms for Portia the possibility of homoerotic possibilities between her husband and the merchant. The drollery about adultery and sodomy in Act 5 warns Bassanio that Belmont can become Venice if he does not honour his vows. And the fact that Portia and Nerissa could represent themselves as men escaping the notice and control of their husbands re-emphasizes the dangers of Venetian mores and vices, and that these mores and vices, as Ascham and others warned Englishmen, are not bound by geographic borders.

The drollery of the play's last scene achieves a certain homoerotic intensity, and here again Mary Bly's study proves relevant and instructive: 'The moments in which a boy actor dressed as a young woman jokes about gender attributes which he himself has, within the context of an expression of erotic desire, expand that eroticism from woman to man, to man to man' (Bly, p. 74). Portia goads the audience and prepares it for the gender bending when she promises Nerissa that their husbands shall see them in Venice, but 'they [the husbands] shall think we are accomplished / With that we lack' (3.4.61–2). The later taunting of their husbands about having coupled with Balthasar and his attendant invites the audience into the secret world of the sodomite. Similarly the social disruptions of scenes of a boy cross-dressed as a girl cross-dressed as a boy explodes the mimetic illusion and demands a renegotiation of gender performance and desire.[16] The double encryption of boy as girl as boy ironically makes the secret world of the sodomite suddenly visible and unencrypted. The superimposition of the third layer of enciphering in effect erases the middle term, the variable, the girl. Then the constant, the male, discovers himself to declaim the pleasures of male–male coupling. Moreover, Balthasar (Portia in male drag) reminds us of the covert nature of homoerotic desire and activity and the instability of Bassanio's affections for his wife.

Balthasar's success in having the ring of Bassanio reifies for both Portia and the audience Antonio's sexual desires and their mandatory obfuscation. Thus in yet another ironic twist the proclamation of what can occur on the public stage emphasizes the need to secrete such behaviour in the private sphere.

For Portia the move to Belmont may have occurred too late. Indeed, as Graziano proclaims that he would prefer to skip the explanations in order to consummate his marriage, Portia and her husband retire along with Antonio and everyone else to discuss further the recent incidents in Venice.[17] Portia seems more interested in 'satisfying' the interrogatories of the others rather than 'satisfying' her husband (5.1.295–9). Perhaps she understands or fears that Bassanio has less interest in consummating their marriage than do Graziano and Nerissa.

But the link between Bassanio and Antonio goes beyond the older man's desire for the younger. Indeed, all four of the principal characters as well as Lorenzo and Jessica are linked by a slavish devotion to riches, riches for which Venice was widely reputed. The luxurious improvidence of Bassanio and the prodigal magnanimity of Antonio demonstrate the devotion to luxury that leads both men to the brink of disaster. Bassanio pursues Portia in order to win her riches in marriage, and Antonio finances this adventure. Portia swears faith to her father's will and by proxy to patriarchal prerogative. However, the lyrics of the song performed while Bassanio chooses his casket reveal that Portia will cheat to get Bassanio as her spouse and to keep Belmont and its wealth for herself and her husband.[18] Outright disobedience would have disinherited her, and that is unthinkable. Like Antonio and Bassanio, she chooses to dissemble, a choice that seems to redound to her detriment.

Shylock's famous line 'My daughter! O my ducats' (2.7.15) is frequently used to isolate and opprobriate him. But Shylock's equating of love and money does not differ from Antonio's, Portia's, or Bassanio's behaviour. They are all enamoured of their wealth and use it to accomplish couplings that probably would not have otherwise occurred without the lubricant of lucre. The balance that finally appears in the trial scene of Act 4 has been symbolically present from the start. And the audience should be aware that the scales had already contaminated life at Belmont. Could they not also see that beyond the walls of the theatre ominously lurked the spectre of an enriched England with

> courtesans ... so rich that in a mask, or at the feast of a marriage, or in the shroving time, you shall see them decked with jewels as they were queens. So that it is thought no one city again is able to compare with Venice for the number of gorgeous dames. As for their beauty of face, though they be fair indeed, I will not highly commend them, because there is in manner none, old or young, unpainted.
>
> (Thomas, pp. 82–3)

Frequent visitors to the public theatre already knew the dangers of that venue, and anti-theatrical puritans railed against the lasciviousness they believed resulted from playgoing. The Queen of England had English queans enough amongst her subjects: could the wealth of the new world turn them into sumptuary rivals?

The desire for luxury permeates this play. Lancelot desires to work for Bassanio in part because he gives 'rare new liveries' (2.2.97), and for deserting his former master, the clown will be rewarded with a livery 'More guarded than his fellow' (2.2.140). Luxuriating in his success, the clown see a luscious future in his palm: 'here's a small trifle of wives – alas, fifteen wives is nothing. Eleven widows and nine maids is a simple coming-in for one man, and then to scape drowning thrice, and to be in peril of my life with the edge of a featherbed (2.2.145–8). While we never know if the fifteen wives materialize, Lancelot has at least one mistress whose pregnancy demonstrates the clown's determination to romp in a featherbed and live up to the bawdy pun of his name.

'Four score ducats' spent in a night is Jessica's affront to her father's frugality. And the ring which she trades for a monkey extends the affront by ridiculing her father's sentimental attachment to a symbol of his wife's love. In what may be the most romantic line of the play, the oft-excoriated money-lender laments poignantly: 'I had it [the ring] of Leah when I was a bachelor. I would not have given it for a wilderness of monkeys' (3.2.101–2). Yet his daughter trades it for only one! Jessica's transvestism also contributes to the play's overall concern with luxury. As she elopes loaded down with her father's wealth, Jessica blushes at her transformation and pleads to be 'obscured'. Her soon-to-be husband responds flirtatiously: 'So are you [obscured], sweet, / Even in the lovely garnish of a boy' (2.7.44–5). The disguise, rather than abating the male's desire, stokes it. Even the very word 'garnish' suggests the excess here.[19] And the audience once again finds itself a voyeur in the shrouded world of the ingle and his lover.

Jessica's and Lancelot's couplings also lead us to the important question of miscegenation. Lancelot's smallmindedness with regards to Jessica's marriage and conversion reveals a profound adherence to a kind of racial essentialism that ignores any generosity of spirit; he lacks, in Portia's words, 'an attribute to God himself'. And although he admits that Jessica's conversion will save her from the damnation of being a religious Jew, he refuses to recognize that Jessica is racially other than Jewish. In much the same way, the reader finds unsettling and uncharitable the denouement of the Shylock episode. He is forced to convert to Christianity, but this forced conversion is mean-spirited and intended to punish Shylock and strengthen Christian hegemony. Yet Shylock stands no less an outsider, no less a *racial* other after his baptism than he was before. Shylock's exit conforms to the traditional departure of the *unredeemed* villain and vice characters of earlier English drama. One need think only of Iago's departure or Regan's.[20] The Jew receives no gracious welcome into the confraternity of Christianity, rather his initiation to salvation includes taunts and jeers:

> SHYLOCK I pray you give me leave to go from hence.
>   I am not well. Send the deed after me,
>   And I will sign it.
> DUKE   Get thee gone, but do it.
> GRAZIANO In christ'ning shalt thou have two godfathers.
>   Had I been judge thou shouldst have had ten more,
>   To bring thee to the gallows, not the font.
>
> (4.1.391–6)

While the font is no torture chamber, the intent of baptism is to torture Shylock. And he goes like a man knowing his fate. Shylock's conversion does not transubstantiate him from Jew to gentile. Shylock's otherness is in tack as well as Jessica's. James Shapiro documents historical attitudes towards conversion in *Shakespeare and the Jews*. Notes Shapiro: 'For Shakespeare's contemporaries, Jews were not identified by their religion alone but by national and racial affiliations as well.'[21] Thus even after their conversion, which might entitle them to salvation, Jews still remain a race apart. Like so much else in the play, Jews, even after conversion to Christianity, exist in an uncertain state, hermeneutically, racially, and religiously ungrounded.

While the modern reader may find ambivalence in the conversions of Jessica and Shylock, no such ambiguity exists with the Moors in *The Merchant of Venice*. Lancelot's dalliance with the 'Negro' holds him up for ridicule and possibly even punishment for the breach of fornication laws. Lorenzo's defence of his wife against the clown's insults instruct us in the racial attitudes toward Moors: 'I shall answer that [his interracial marriage to Jessica] better to the commonwealth than you can the getting up of the Negro's belly. The Moor is with child by you, Lancelot' (3.5.31–3). Clearly the miscegenation provokes the taunting, and Lorenzo believes that Lancelot will be scorned by the entire commonwealth for the perceived misalliance. One might be inclined to see this coupling as insignificant, but Portia's earlier dismissal of the Prince of Morocco charges the liaison between the clown and the 'Negro' with greater significance.

Portia's relief at Morocco's departure expresses at least an explicit antipathy towards the man's colour if not an outright racist disapproval. 'A gentle riddance,' she sighs; 'Draw the curtains, go. / Let all of his complexion choose me so' (2.7.78–9). The multiracial society for which Venice was famous may have produced a modicum of tolerance, but not an iota of Christian charity. All the petiteness and mean spiritedness that Shakespeare animates in the play extends to every facet of society and culture of the play's Venice.

I have tried to map English attitudes towards Venice in this famous play. It seems that the ambivalence that is found in English discourse about Italy is also found in the play itself. But I don't think that Shakespeare accepts those ideas uncritically. We see in the characterizations the playwright's discomfort with stereotypes. Yes Shylock whets his knife on his sole – a visual pun on the homonyms – but he offers us the most romantic line of the play. When Shylock pulls out the balance in this context, sentiment and love outweigh all else. He complains about Christian husbands because they seem to be unconcerned about their wives' well-being. Portia will not cheat for Morocco who by analogy holds her to be 'ten times undervalued to tried gold' (2.7.53). Yet she gives all to the bankrupt Bassanio who has exploited his friend's affections so that he (Bassanio) could show 'a more swelling port than [his] faint means would grant continuance' (1.1.124–5). Portia finds eminently more desirable a pretentious white male to a Moroccan prince. The question of miscegenation obscures the real issues of love and marriage: the worth of the beloved, the kind of worth that will never register on scales that weigh material value. And no one in *The Merchant of Venice* seems capable of placing the true value in the balance.

When we look at Shakespeare's work, we discover a playwright who never loses sight of the uncertainties, ambiguities, and imbalances of life. Ever conscious of the constraints on individual liberty, Shakespeare also craves order and stability. So Hermia rebels in *A Midsummer Night's Dream*, but only until she is free to choose her own 'yoke'. Richard II may have been a dishonest king and Bolingbroke a champion of moral rectitude, but the former is the anointed king, the latter a usurper and regicide. So we may ask, what are the moral lessons of *The Merchant of Venice* and how does the play make use of its Italian setting? Perhaps we might turn to William Thomas's 1549 *The History of Italy* for assistance. Thomas offers more admiration for Italy than condemnation:

> my travil at this present hath been to publish unto our own nation in our mother tongue the doings of strangers and specially of the Italian nation, which seemeth to flourish in civility most of all other at this day, methought I could no less do for the encouraging of them that shall take this book in had than partly rehearse what profit they may gather by traveling therein. First, they shall see upon what little beginning many great states have risen, and how they that have had the power to rule, by using their authorities well and prudently, have merited immortal fame of honor and praise and, by suing tyranny and ill governance, have contraiwise borne eternal slander and shame. It encourageth the virtuous men, by examples that they read, to increase in virtue and nobility and showeth the vicious what the fruit of their abuses are and how naughty doings have most commonly naughty ending. (pp. 3–4)

Ascham's moral self-righteousness raises the spectre of moral decline with financial ascendency, but what he condemns already exists in England. Perhaps

Shakespeare hopes that Venice will light the way to and away from the modern world of commerce and cosmopolitanism. English perceptions of Venice, in fact, may have fostered caution, envy, and the desire for emulation. Shakespeare's Venice is a world desired and accessible, a world where hypocrisy corrupts as much as money, and the absence of charity and mercy breeds intolerance. The proper balance eludes everyone in this play: Portia shows no mercy to Shylock; Shylock holds dear the memory of his wife but deliriously longs to plunge the knife in Antonio's chest. And at the end of the play the audience clutches at straws in its desire to find the 'happily-ever-after'. Bassanio's usance of Antonio forces us to re-evaluate the honesty of his friendship for the merchant. Honesty would have saved Antonio, Bassanio, and the rest from the histrionics and near disaster that threatens them all in the courtroom. Bassanio flees to rescue his friend, but his unrepentant prodigality sets everything else in motion. Similarly Portia cannot wall out of Belmont the wickedness of Venice because she embraced it in her own dishonesty. She compromised her fidelity to her father and won for herself a husband who will probably prove to be unworthy of her.

Like Belmont, England must be careful of what it imports from Venice, but unlike Venice it had to learn to control the various forces that were forcing it from a homogeneous culture into a multicultural, wealthy, and cosmopolitan society. A world of honest sodomy stands in stark contrast to the dissembling and dishonest world of Shylock, Bassanio, and Antonio. The same lesson is learned in the sonnets when both lovers seem content to pursue luxury rather than love, and in the end neither finds happiness. In *The Merchant of Venice*, love provides the corrective to luxury, as we see when Graziano seeks to convince Nerissa to wait no longer to consummate their marriage. Graziano proclaims that his sole desire is an honest and chaste wife. Although Stubbes does not, one could learn that lesson from Italy or a play. Perhaps Shakespeare thinks like that early historian of Italy William Thomas: naughty brings forth naughty, and virtue virtue. *The Merchant of Venice* offers the opportunity for both.

Notes

1 The title in the 1623 Folio is simply *The Merchant of Venice*. The play was entered in the Stationers' Register on 22 July 1598 as *The Jew of Venice*. The date of composition is generally agreed to be 1596–97.
2 See Murray J. Levith, *Shakespeare's Italian Settings and Plays* (Basingstoke, Macmillan, 1989), and J. R. Mulryne, 'History and Myth in *The Merchant of Venice*', in Marrapodi *et al.*, ed., *Shakespeare's Italy: Functions of Italian Locations in Renaissance Drama* (Manchester, Manchester University Press, 1993).
3 See *The Scholemaster* in *The English Works of Roger Ascham*, ed. William Wright (Cambridge, Cambridge University Press, 1904), p. 234. It should be noted that Ascham does not initially identify the city as Venice, but later he does.

4 I have modernized the spelling; however, I have allowed Ascham's punctuation to stand unchanged.
5 It should be noted that although *Storia d'Italia* was published posthumously in 1561, twenty-one years after Guicciardini's death. It should be noted that the 1579 translation by Sir Geffray Fenton was not a translation of the original Italian text but a translation of a 1568 French translation of the Italian. Thus the first English version was a translation of a translation.
6 See Michael Rocke, *Forbidden Friendships: Homosexuality and Male Culture in Renaissance Florence* (New York, Oxford University Press, 1996), p. 3.
7 See William Thomas, *The History of Italy*, ed. George B. Parks (Ithaca, Cornell University Press, 1963), pp. 63–84.
8 G. K. Hunter, *Dramatic Identities and Cultural Tradition: Studies in Shakespeare and his Contemporaries* (Liverpool, Liverpool University Press, 1978), p. 13.
9 This and all further citations of Shakespeare's works come from *The Norton Shakespeare*, ed. Stephen Greenblatt (New York, W. W. Norton & Company, 1997).
10 I am using 'anxiety' to mean 'fearful anticipation of impending danger, the source of which is unknown or unrecognized'. By 'melancholia' I mean 'depression or a sense of gloom'.
11 It should be noted that in the Folio edition lines 5 and 6 are joined, thus creating a single fourteen-syllable line. While hexameter lines appear from time to time in all of Shakespeare's plays, there are no fourteen-syllable lines. Even Shakespeare's doggerel written for comic characters is usually iambic pentameter. See George T. Wright, *Shakespeare's Metrical Art* (Berkeley, University of California Press, 1988) for more.
12 We can read 'myself' two ways here. 'Myself' could be used as an emphatic, that is 'Even I, myself, do not know' or as a reflexive pronoun which serves as the object of the verb 'know'.
13 See Guido Ruggiero, *The Boundaries of Eros: Sex Crime and Sexuality in Renaissance Venice* (New York, Oxford University Press, 1985); and Patricia Labalme, 'Sodomy and Venetian Justice in the Renaissance', *The Legal History Review*, 52:3 (1984), 217–54; and Rocke, *Forbidden Friendships*. Also see Alan Bray, *Homosexuality in Renaissance England* (New York, Columbia University Press, 1982).
14 It should be noted that *Anatomy of Abuses* was reissued and enlarged in 1585 and 1595, the year before the generally accepted date of composition for *Merchant*. I have modernized the spelling of the quotation.
15 Mary Bly, *Queer Virgins and Virgin Queans* (New York, Oxford University Press, 2000).
16 See Bly, *Queer Virgins*, pp. 56–7.
17 Act 5 begins with the stage direction 'Enter Lorenzo and Jessica'. Then enter in following order Stefano, Portia, and Nerissa, and finally 'Bassanio, Antonio, Graziano, and their followers'.
18 The rhyming of 'bred', 'head', and the masculine 'nourished' with 'lead' suggest an attempt to lead Bassanio to the right casket (3.2.63–5). The Folio edition of the text does not say who sings the song; the stage directions say only: 'Here Music. A Song

the whilst Bassanio comments on the caskets to himself' (F, p. 174, 106–8). The stage directions offer no speech prefix. It does not seem strange to me that the Mistress of Belmont could be the singer.

19 The word 'garnish' here puts me in mind of the final four lines of Sonnet 20: 'And by addition me of thee defeated, / By adding one thing to my purpose nothing. / But since she pricked thee out for women's pleasure, / Mine be thy love, and thy love's use their treasure.' Sonnet 20, of course, is frequently cited to establish a homoerotic theme in the Sonnets. See Joseph Pequigney, *Such Is My Love: A Study of Shakespeare's Sonnets* (Chicago, University of Chicago Press, 1987). 'Garnish' also foreshadows Portia's use of 'accomplished' in 3.5.62; see p. 000 above.

20 See also Bernard Spivack, *Shakespeare and the Allegory of Evil: The History of a Metaphor in Relation to his Major Villains* (New York, Columbia University Press, 1958).

21 James Shapiro, *Shakespeare and the Jews* (New York, Columbia University Press, 1996), p. 173.

11

Othello italicized: xenophobia and the erosion of tragedy

PAMELA ALLEN BROWN

While Dr Johnson found *Othello* unendurable, Thomas Rymer found it ridiculous. The first attitude wins respect among Shakespeareans, the second mostly scorn. Yet there is something shrewd about Rymer's rude remarks, especially his conclusion that *Othello* contains 'some burlesk, some humor, and ramble of Comicall wit, some shew, and some Mimickry to divert the spectators: but the tragical part is, plainly none other, than a bloody Farce, without salt or savor'.[1] Rymer uses the exasperated rasp of sarcasm, while Johnson deploys the hurt tones of judicious sensibility. Yet both point to the same effect: the work of responding to the play *as tragedy* defeats the critic.

The culprit is generic drift: *Othello* is painfully enigmatic now because it was originally closer to satire than tragedy. Time and critical tradition have effaced the satiric referents, but the mode of irony, mockery, and attack still invades the play. The satiric targets are, I believe, Italy in general, and Venice in particular. *Othello* displays the features of the fabled Republic – from its imperial fleet to its mercenary generals, from its awesome Senators to its potent magnificoes, from its famous actors to its glamorous women – only to tarnish and diminish them. Satire demands a reading that feels for ruptures between statements and meanings, for strange hybrids between texts and intertexts. The satiric irony in *Othello, The Tragedy of the Moor of Venice* is pervasive, shadowing even the title,[2] but its bitter edge is invisible without considering both the anti-foreigner biases of original audiences and the play's debut during an especially fraught moment in English–Venetian relations. In 1604, when *Othello* was first performed, James I re-opened diplomatic relations with Venice, while England pursued a fierce economic rivalry with Venice in two very different arenas: Mediterranean shipping and the professional stage. These rivalries helped spawn deeply antagonistic intertextuality, shaping the play and its reception.

Hatred of foreigners is remarkably productive of intertextuality, if one takes all performances, verbal expressions, and discourses as possible genetic material. The study of Shakespearean intertexts has come to include 'patterns of thought and logic, commonplaces and analogies, habitual figures of speech. … The old notion of particular and distinct sources has given way to new notions of boundless and heterogeneous intertextuality'.[3] Xenophobia relies on an endlessly reinscripted set of stereotypes, parodies, jokes, stories, and insults that have the power to alter and degrade the chastest genre, as graffiti does a tomb. In *Othello*, such adhesive popular narratives may best be understood in relation to audience expectations and beliefs. As Andrew Gurr points out, the 'hermeneutics' of theatre 'depends as much on the audience's state of mind as it does on the author's and players' notions about what, mentally, their audience will be prepared for. That "mindset" is a consequence of the mental furniture the Shakespearean playgoer might have been equipped with,' including his or her education, prejudices, and expectations.[4] For *Othello* critics who address this topic, Iago has long been the key figure. Michael Neill, for example, writes of the process by which Iago 'inseminates' Othello with monstrousness by engaging the audience as collaborators: 'What Iago (along with his collaborators the audience) "discovers" inside Othello is only what he himself has put there, a tautological demonstration of what his audience … have already expected to find.'[5] As I will argue, those expectations, like those that inform many of the play's fictions, are bred out of xenophobic stereotypes and nursed by 'the canker'd muse' of satire.

Hatred of outsiders was deep and abiding in England under Elizabeth and James. New reports of strange cultures over the seas led to 'an excess of distrust' of all foreigners, near or far, because they openly or covertly subverted 'the familiar symbolic universe'.[6] The English were infamous among Europeans for being suspicious, rude, and even violent towards foreigners, an obnoxious trait noted in dispatches from Venetian envoys, in merchants' letters, and in travellers' accounts. Giordano Bruno, who visited England in 1583–85, satirically denounces the brutishness of the English commoners toward Italians. He tells a highly coloured story of being attacked and beaten on the way to Fulke Greville's house, and continues by mocking the boorish manners of his host's hangers-on at dinner.[7] In the last years of the sixteenth century, the backlash against Italy's 'Circean vices' accelerated with the rise of Protestant radicalism. For Italians in London the insults and rebuffs went on and on, prompting John Florio to complain loudly that 'the masses were very discourteous toward strangers'.[8]

The attitude toward Italy expressed in *Othello* does not stem from a simple urge to attack; on the whole, Shakespeare's Italy is altogether less lurid and more tantalizing than it is in Nashe, Webster, or Marston.[9] At the same time that statesmen and travellers were poring over volumes by Lewis Lewkenor and William Thomas and marvelling over the intricacies of Venetian government, playgoers with little hope of meeting a Senator saw *Othello*, which opens the marvellously odd workings of the Most Serene Republic to public view. Interest in Venice would have been running especially high when the play opened at Whitehall in November 1604, just after James had re-established full diplomatic relations with Venice after a gap of forty-four years.[10] The King's top priority was trade relations: Venice had been England's prime rival for supremacy in shipping in the eastern Mediterranean since the founding of the Levant Company in 1581.[11] After decades in which Venice had reigned supreme, England's ships were suddenly penetrating and dominating farflung markets, often through vicious pirate raids on Venetian ships. The Venetians loudly protested against these depradations by English pirates which were so damaging that they contributed to the eventual decline of the Venetian Republic.[12] At this international game, then, the two countries were suspicious rivals, with Venice emerging as the losing player – to the great satisfaction of the English, who by 1604 were 'fast overtaking the Republic as the uncontested masters of Levantine trade'.[13]

On stage, however, Venice could still be painted as a glittering fantasy. The desire was never unmixed: English playgoers tended to view the city with 'an unstable mixture of loathing and attraction', while playwrights created works rife with 'praising contempt' and 'disparaging admiration'.[14] Shakespeare's Venetian plays accommodate both moods: if *The Merchant of Venice* dazzles viewers with the gilded spectacle of Belmont, *Othello* allows them to disparage the proud Venetians at will. Satire is the artful attempt to diminish by ridicule, and *Othello* questions the prime attributes of *La Serenissima* by showing its serenity shattered and its potency challenged from the very start. *Othello*'s unfolding and its protagonist's fall are signs that the state itself is growing unstable. The state's health hinges on hiring foreign-born mercenaries and placing its safety in strange hands – a practice that Machiavelli famously warned his prince against. In the opening act of *Othello* the patriarch is bested by his own daughter, while the heroic bridegroom announces he is 'defunct' on his wedding night ('the young affects / In me defunct' (1.3.265).[15] Satire lurks in the sudden offstage storms that drown the Turks without one Venetian raising a sword. By invoking the Cyprus wars of thirty years past, and inevitably the great Battle of Lepanto, Shakespeare also invites English audiences to recall smugly that the Venetians had since lost control of Cyprus.[16] The English had also 'conquered' the Armada by just such biased weather; yet, in their case, they had managed to hold on to their island entire. Seen in the jaundiced light of Italophobic satire, Brabantio's curt retort to the Duke, who has just advised him to hide his pain, invites the English to sneer at Italianate deception and Venetian political decay: 'So let the Turk of Cyprus us beguile, / We lose it not, so long as we can smile' (1.3.210–11).

Most significant, the play invites English audiences to fault the Venetians for denying justice to one of their own because of their desperate need for a

Moorish general. In England Venice was usually acclaimed for its severe but impartial and incorruptible system of justice. It was not the Venetians' natures but their institutions that were so admired. Lewkenor's 1599 translation of Contarini's *The Commonwealth and Government of Venice* mythologized Venice as 'possess[ing] a set of regulations for decision-making which ensure the complete rationality of every decision and the complete virtue of every decision-maker'.[17] The Venice of *Othello* falls far short of this ideal. The rough music endured by Brabantio in the dead of night is the first sign that the audience is not to pay undue respect to the awesome Signoria. The first punchline in the play comes when an enraged Brabantio tells Iago, 'Thou art a villain!' only to hear: 'You are a Senator!' (1.1.117–18), which ensures a laugh at Brabantio's expense, and cuts at the mighty Senate as well.

Brabantio does not fare much better at the hands of the Duke. Expediency rules the night, and the offended father certainly does not receive the justice he is promised. Brabantio's eventual death must be laid to the Senate's promotion of Othello's desires over his, as much as to his daughter's disobedience. The proof that Venice is dangerously dependent on Othello comes in the Senate's decision to allow Desdemona to go to war with him. The preoccupied Duke waves the matter away with 'Be it as you shall privately determine, / Either for her stay or her going' (1.3.275–6). This abdication is far too casual: the idea of allowing a general's wife to sail with him to a war zone may well have seemed ludicrous to London audiences. Catching out the Venetians in the process of making such an obvious blunder may have tickled spectators not inclined to favour any nation but their own. It is possible that the Venetian ambassadors saw *Othello* at court in 1604, and, if they were present, 'they might have found Shakespeare representation of the Venetian Senator and the myth of Venice strangely ambivalent, particularly in its depiction of the vulnerability underlying the state's apparent strength'.[18] Othello becomes unbalanced and homicidal so quickly precisely because his wife is with him; the Senate has therefore misjudged him as their bulwark. After an enraged Othello strikes his wife in Cyprus, an English audience would not have missed the dig at Senatorial infallibility in Lodovico's plaintive questions: 'Is this the noble Moor whom our full senate / Call all in all sufficient? This the nature / Whom passion could not shake?' (4.1.264–6)

Lodovico's sickened confusion echoes *Othello*'s generic vertigo. On the level of literary genre the play is an elaborate, though far from benign, parody of familiar Italian forms, the *commedia dell'arte* and the tragic *novella*. While scholars have long demonstrated that *Othello* is 'a tragedy built on a comic structure' they have not speculated on the historical motivations or the satiric effects of such a generic crossing; nor have they noted the many parodistic devices in the play.[19] Leon Guilhamet has argued that satire, an inveterate 'borrower of forms', can radically alter the forms it touches; comic diminishment becomes in satire a magnification of evil, for example.[20] Parody is a subspecies of imitation, and can often be benign. When does imitation cross the border into malign parody and satire? I would argue that it happens when texts are combined in such a way that one text renders the other grotesque, producing a deformation appealing to the gaze of a hostile audience.

In the case of *Othello*, which was written during the height of the rage for stage satire, Shakespeare overlays Cinthio's 'Il Moro' with a travesty of *commedia* to produce a deliberately misshapen text.[21] To stage a tragedy Shakespeare chose to deploy stock devices from Italian comedy, ones made familiar by its outstanding professional companies, which were reaching their zenith at just this time. As Louise George Clubb observes, Shakespeare

> begins with comic commonplaces and allows their farthest imaginable psychological weight and consequence to overpower the scenario and subvert all the theatergrams ... The design of the adulterous trickery plot, with jealous cuckold, *malmaritata*, young *innamorato*, and the rest, is transferred to Othello's mind, evoked by Iago.

Maddened by this design, Othello turns an 'obscene farce' to tragedy.[22] Building on Clubb's perception, I would argue that the play transferred the obscene farce to the original audience's minds as well. From the opening action, with Iago and Roderigo flinging rough scurrilities at Brabantio's window, to the overhearing scene of 4.1, in which the horn-mad Othello mistakes what he overhears and falls to spouting frenzied threats, the play shows much indebtedness to *commedia* situations and speeches, from *beffe*, *burle*, and *lazzi* to *contrasti* and *tiratti*. Rymer was more right that he knew when he complained that the Temptation scene of Act 3 resembles nothing so much as Italian farce:

> Whence comes it then, that this is the top scene, the Scene that raises *Othello* above all other Tragedies on our Theatres? It is purely from the Action; from the Mops, and the Mows, the Grimaces, the Grins and Gesticulation. Such scenes as this have made all the world to run after Harlequin and Scaramucchio.[23]

Although they have not been noted as possible intertexts (perhaps, paradoxically, because they are more tragic than comic), *commedia* plays *Flavio's Fortune* and *The Mad Princess* also show strong affinities with *Othello*. In the first a Turkish prince endures shipwrecks and slavery but ends up in Venice, where he converts to Christianity and falls in love with a Venetian *inamorata*; in the second the Prince of Morocco shares a tragic love with a Christian princess and elopes with her by sea; both eventually die, followed by the suicide of the girl's father.[24]

While *contaminatio* and generic hybridizing are prime operations of

Renaissance drama, in *Othello* Italian popular drama and fiction are yoked by violence together. *Commedia*'s cynicism towards women and marriage, and its pervasive cuckoldry humour, turn deadly in Iago's misogynist jesting and plotting. Shakespeare 'ironizes this destructive aspect of *commedia* humor, just as he ironizes the audience's expectations of the "comic" characters' by disposing of those characters with shocking dispatch.[25] The lugubriously conflicting demands of mask-based comedy and tragic fiction produce the spectacle of a Pantalone who dies of grief (Brabantio), a conniving Brighella who is caught and led away to be tortured (Iago), a foolish suitor who is killed in cold blood by his sidekick (Roderigo), a Franceschina whose mischievous prank leads to violent death for herself and her mistress (Emilia), and an *innamorato* whose good looks and charming speeches gain him both dishonour and a maimed leg (Cassio). Othello's character blends aspects of the blustering Capitano at the start,[26] the fearful Pantalone in the middle, and the black-masked Arlecchino at the end, while Desdemona is the *innamorata* who destroys all precedent by falling in love with her middle-aged black husband, rather than her handsome young white admirer, and is herself destroyed. The satire is multiply cannibalistic, wreaking havoc with the masks and roles of the Italian *commedia* players and mutilating the Italian literary forms from which the play is constructed.

The wholesale demotion of tragic *gravitas* is the result. In its original performances, *Othello* may have signalled to spectators that they were free to take 'the tragedy of the Moor' as an opportunity to jeer and mock, producing an experience that would be unbearable to audiences today. As Michael Bristol has argued, a radically mismatched couple, such as an old husband with a young wife, was the traditional target of charivari mockery; and a stage couple perceived as racially mismatched could well have prompted loud scorn, unimpeded by modern pressures of shame and decorum.[27] The play dehumanizes Othello and Desdemona by treating them as grotesque effigies and subjecting them to ritual abuse. By stressing her incoherent artificiality the play exposes Desdemona as a boy actor playing a 'perfect wife' whose transvestite disguise mocks 'her' femininity, while Othello would have be seen as 'a black-faced clown' whose high-flown language produces a lugubrious contrast with his painted exterior.[28] Most English theatregoers who first encountered the noble Moor came to the theatre with deep biases against any dark-skinned foreigners, attitudes they were not ashamed to express in public.[29] Othello's blackness would signal his vulnerability due to his 'weak function' in governing his passions, according to normative contemporary attitudes about skin colour; while a few stage Moors were allowed admirable qualities such as intelligence, virtuousness, and courage, stage representations were overwhelmingly negative, teeming with lust, jealousy, and violence.[30] In *Othello* the negative stereotypes overwhelm the positive ones, operating as intertexts from popular culture in slurs by Iago, Roderigo, Emilia, and others, but also in the form of fixed ideas about skin colour brought to the theatre as part of audiences' 'mental furniture'.[31] Such ideas were highly 'scripted' to begin with, and were not bred out of pure ignorance but out of increasing contact with other peoples. As Kim Hall points out, early modern 'racialism' was provoked by 'England's sense of losing its traditional insularity' by moving from 'geographic isolation into military and mercantile contest with other nations'.[32] Moors and other people of African descent were not unknown in England, but they were hardly made welcome. In 1601 Elizabeth decreed for the second time that 'negars and blackmores' were to be expelled from the country 'where their great number ... are fostered here to the annoyance of her own people'.[33] None the less, in the same period Elizabeth invited a delegation from Barbary to her court, a gesture that grew from her desire to seek a trade agreement rather from any particular feeling of amity. In the reception extended to the sixteen Moorish nobles, the English made it clear they found 'the appearance and conduct of the Moors a spectacle and an outrage'. Courtiers bickered over who was to house them, chroniclers carped about the Moors' bizarre ways of eating and praying, and ship captains refused to give them free passage home.[34] This is an extraordinary case, of course, but, if Moors who were official state visitors endured this treatment, it is unlikely that a Moorish general would meet with a unanimously respectful reception onstage.

It was not only Moors and Africans but Italians who were judged violent owing to the heat of their southern sun, and thus more prone to tyrannical and devilish deeds. Margo Hendricks argues that Italy plays such a key role in English 'racializing discourses', that Venice functions as 'a racial persona' in *Othello*.[35] By placing an outlandish Venetian Moor before his audiences, Shakespeare invites them to read the play in light of their biases about both Venetians and Moors, and to link them in an endless relay of 'othering' centering on the improbable desires of an Italian bride who proudly prefers black to white.

Confronted with this novel idea, the politicians and diplomats who saw *Othello*'s first performance in Whitehall were possibly more polite than were audiences later at the Globe. Our playgoing habits today – sitting silently and anonymously in the dark, and showing respect for the actors – were not those of the early modern theatre, where audiences were used to trading lines with the clowns, hurling catcalls, and hissing, even at a tragedy. Playgoers laughed at endless ethnic jokes about the cheese-loving Welshman, the murderous Italian, and the arrogant Spaniard. As nervous remarks in the Variorum edition show, the ever-present threat of laughter and the grotesque is what makes *Othello* so disturbing for modern audiences. The play is filled with jests, physical humour, and laugh lines, though we have supposedly lost the taste for indulging in cruel laughter at imaginary cuckolds, dark-skinned foreigners, the evils of womankind, or anyone who has fallen to the floor in a fit. For audiences in 1604, however, such moments would have been no threat at all, but an open invitation to mock and laugh.[36]

This laughter was not without a political dimension. When they played the Globe the first Othello, Richard Burbage, and the other actors in the King's Men performed before crowds of apprentices and servants – the same sort of youths who regularly rose up in street riots against foreign workers in London, whom they blamed for shortages and accused of price-fixing.[37] These occurred so often and with such violence that the Italian community repeatedly petitioned the Crown for help. Among their audiences, the players would also find merchants, diplomats, and seamen deeply involved in Mediterranean shipping and trade, and thus with personal stake in England's attempts to wrestle primacy in trade from the mighty Venetians. Some seamen may have been veterans of English attacks on Venetian ships; all would have feared or hated the Barbary pirates who harried Venetians and English alike.

It was not only these men and boys that the actors had to please. They faced a healthy sprinkling of women, well-to-do and humble, married and unmarried. All would have been constantly subjected to surveillance of their sexual conduct by kinfolk, husbands, and neighbours, and many would have been vulnerable to verbal abuse and physical violence by suspicious spouses. These spectators, therefore, could hardly sympathize with any husband who bewhores and then kills his innocent wife on such short notice. When Emilia calls Othello 'the blacker devil' and sneers 'She was too fond of her most filthy bargain' (5.2.131, 157), she may represent this very specific sector of the audience – as racist and Italophobic as the rest, but with different reasons for both empathy and hatred.[38] Of the earliest reactions to the play that have survived, all describe horrified reactions to Desdemona's murder, and two of them mention women's reactions – one weeps, the other cries out as if to stop Othello.[39] Watching Othello's descent into jealous passion, women spectators were far more likely to recall his promise to the Venetian Senate: 'when light-winged toys / Of feathered Cupid seel with wanton dullness / My speculative and officed instrument, / That my disports corrupt and taint my business, / Let housewifes make a skillet of my helm' (1.3.268–72) – in other words, let women mock me as effeminate if I ever let my love for Desdemona cloud my judgement. This self-fulfilling prophecy would alert his very interested jury of women spectators that they are free to 'uncrown' him with mocks and hisses when, inevitably, he loses his self-control.[40]

So far I have looked at *Othello*'s mangled genres and the xenophobic assumptions of audiences as hostile intertexts fuelling its earliest incarnations. But there is still another force behind the play's abundant *ressentiment*, one involving a tiny but crucial special interest group: the professional playing companies. Shakespeare was part of a business that had rapidly established itself, partly through building theatres and charging admission, partly through the creation of companies closely held in shares; but what is little known or studied is how the London professional companies managed to keep the brilliant foreign players from penetrating their lucrative new market. Explaining why the Italian *comici* triumphed in every capital of Europe but rarely crossed the Channel, Kenneth and Laura Richards name 'social, religious and professional impediments, like English anti-Catholic prejudice and hostility to actresses'.[41] Economics as much as national pride mobilized this hostility: 'London was already dominated by highly efficient, organized and competitive native companies resistant to the incursions of foreigners', and it was this resistance that led dramatists to caricature *commedia* as 'vulgar low comedy, while its practitioners were stigmatized as much of the same status as buffoons, mountebanks, and street entertainers'.[42] Some writers called Italians farceurs and clowns; Thomas Heywood went so far as to scorn all continental plays: 'those that frequent are / In Italy & France, even in these dayes, / Compar'd with ours, are rather jigges than Playes'.[43]

In his contemptuous putdown, Heywood undoubtedly refers to bawdy *commedia* farce, like the jig a blend of sung and spoken words, dance, and sexual byplay. This brings us back to Rymer's notorious 'Bloody Farce, without salt or savor'. His catalogue of the salient features of *Othello*, that is, 'burlesk', mimickry, comic wit, and farce, coheres only under the cold glare of satire and irony. If there is some sort of burlesque going on in the play, there must be referents for the burlesque, originals to be mimicked. In my reading the myth of Venetian state perfection is one such referent; the acclaimed mastery of the *commedia* players – another famous Venetian export – is another. It is critically important to sense the hostility in these caricatures, a skewed emphasis that might be called malign 'Italicization'. Envy is desire, if we believe René Girard, but it is envy in league with ignorance and fear that feeds the illogic of xenophobia. The ethnocentrism of the English playgoer, the rising ambition of the English to unseat the Venetians' pre-eminence in trade, and the English players' rivalry with the foreign players, all contributed to the atmosphere in which *Othello* was created and performed. The English may have admired the city that produced these types, and they may have wept for Desdemona, but it is highly unlikely that they could have felt the tense blend of sympathy for Othello and horror at his deeds that later generations have felt so abundantly.

As Bristol has brilliantly argued, this very reaction has been made possible by two centuries of criticism that has laboured to 'beautify' the play, to render it 'cooked' rather than cruel and raw – labour that allows us to enjoy rather than be horrified by our complicity in its violence and racism.[44] The audiences of the first performances would scarcely have felt these pangs. Engineered for a crowd that was consistently and unabashedly hostile to foreigners, *Othello* is a raw play, more raw than anyone has guessed. The critical labour of rendering it a civilized tragedy has caused the satire to vanish like cooking smoke.

Notes

I would like to thank Julie Crawford, Cristine Varholy, Rachel Poulsen, Bianca Calabresi, Nancy Selleck, Melinda Gough, Peter Parolin, Susan O'Malley, and Ian Moulton for their comments on earlier drafts of this chapter.

1 Of Desdemona's murder, Johnson wrote 'I am glad that I have ended my revisal of this dreadful scene. It is not to be endured.' See *Johnson on Shakespeare*, ed. Arthur Sherbo (New Haven, Yale University Press, 1945). Rymer's comments appear in his *A Short View of Tragedy: Its Original, Excellency, and Corruption, With Some Reflections on Shakespeare* (London, 1693), p. 146. Rymer's judgements about *Othello* are sharply satiric and often Italophobic, though he does not recognize the possibility that Shakespeare has similar ends in view.

2 Thomas Goffe's *The Couragious Turk, or Amvrath the First* (c. 1613–18) also culminates in the horrifying onstage murder of an innocent Christian woman in her bed by a dark-skinned foreigner who claims to be courageous. As a title, *Othello, The Tragedy of the Moor of Venice* is not as obviously ironic, but the hero's actions do undercut of the heroic expectations raised by its title. For an intriguing appraisal of Goffe's play in relation to *Othello* see Daniel J. Vitkus, 'Turning Turk in *Othello*: The Conversion and Damnation of the Moor', *Shakespeare Quarterly*, 48 (1997), 171–4.

3 Stephen J. Lynch, *Shakespearean Intertextuality: Studies in Selected Sources and Plays*, Contributions in Drama and Theatre Studies 86 (Westport, Conn., Greenwood, 1998), p. 1.

4 Andrew Gurr, *Playgoing in Shakespeare's London* (Cambridge, Cambridge University Press, 1987), p. 6.

5 Michael Neill, 'Unproper Beds: Race, Adultery, and the Hideous in *Othello*', *Shakespeare Quarterly*, 40 (1989), 383–412.

6 Richard Marienstras, 'The Near and the Far: The Calvin Affair and the Status of Foreigners under James I', in *New Perspectives on the Shakespearean World*, tr. Janet Lloyd (Cambridge, Cambridge University Press, 1985), pp. 126–7.

7 Giordano Bruno, *La Cena de le Ceneri: The Ash Wednesday Supper*, ed. and tr. Edward A. Gosselin and Lawrence S. Lerner (Toronto, University of Toronto Press, 1995), pp. 120–6. See also Lewis Einstein, *The Italian Renaissance in England* (New York, Columbia University Press, 1907), pp. 156, 174; and G. K. Hunter, 'Elizabethans and Foreigners', *Shakespeare Survey*, 17 (1964), 37–52 (esp. 43, 45).

8 Quoted in Einstein, *Italian Renaissance in England*, p. 174.

9 Angela Locatelli, 'The Fictional World of *Romeo and Juliet*', in Michele Marrapodi et al., eds, *Shakespeare's Italy: Functions of Italian Locations in Renaissance Drama* (Manchester, Manchester University Press, 1997), pp. 69–87.

10 Jonathan Goldberg, *James I and the Politics of Literature* (Stanford, Stanford University Press, 1989), p. 75.

11 Talk of the Levant Company would be in the air at this time because from 1600 to

1605 its members wrangled with Elizabeth and then James over renewing its charter. See Alfred C. Wood, *A History of the Levant Company* (New York, Barnes & Noble, 1935), pp. 38–9.
12 Fernand Braudel, *The Mediterranean and the Mediterranean World in the Age of Philip II*, vol. I (New York, Harper & Row, 1966), p. 629.
13 Gigliola Pagano De Divitiis, *English Merchants in Seventeenth-Century Italy* (Cambridge, Cambridge University Press, 1990), pp. 29–30.
14 Ann Rosalind Jones, 'Italians and Others', in David Scott Kastan and Peter Stallybrass, eds, *Staging the Renaissance: Reinterpretations of Elizabethan and Jacobean Drama* (New York, Routledge, 1991), p. 251; Locatelli, 'Fictional World', p. 74.
15 William Shakespeare, *Othello*, *The Riverside Shakespeare*, ed. G. Blakemore Evans *et al.* (Boston, Houghton Mifflin, 1974). All quotations from the play are taken from this edition.
16 Emrys Jones, '"Othello," "Lepanto," and the Cyprus Wars', *Shakespeare Survey*, 21 (1968), 47–52 (p. 50).
17 J. G. A. Pocock quoted in Goldberg, *James I*, p. 76.
18 Virginia Mason Vaughan, *Othello: A Contextual History* (Cambridge, Cambridge University Press, 1994), p. 21.
19 Barbara Heliodora C. de Mendonça, 'Othello: A Tragedy Built on a Comic Structure', *Shakespeare Survey*, 21 (1968), 31–8; Susan Snyder, *The Comic Matrix of Shakespeare's Tragedies* (Princeton, Princeton University Press, 1979).
20 Leon Guilhamet, *Satire and the Transformation of Genre* (Philadelphia. University of Pennsylvania Press, 1987), pp. 14–15.
21 The Bishops' Ban on, and the public burning of, verse satires in 1599 drove satire on to the stages, where it flourished for more than a decade, taking the form of 'comical satires' or 'tragical satires'. See Lynda E. Boose, 'The Bishops' Ban, Elizabethan Pornography, and the Sexualization of the Jacobean Stage', in Richard Burt and John Archer, ed., *Enclosure Acts in Early Modern England* (Ithaca, Cornell University Press, 1994), pp. 185–200. Othello's date of first performance was a watershed year for the form: 1604 also saw Jonson's *Every Man Out* and Marston's *Malcontent*. Edward Pechter usefully reads Iago as a kind of Malcontent in *Othello and Interpretive Traditions* (Iowa City, University of Iowa Press, 1999), p. 33; Alvin Kernan, *The Cankered Muse: Satire of the English Renaissance* (New Haven, Yale University Press, 1959), calls Iago a 'satirist-intriguer'. Kernan does not mention *Othello* in his discussion of Shakespeare's 'tragical satires' (*Timon of Athens* and *Troilus and Cressida*) but *Othello* has all the identifying marks of the mode: an exotic locale, often Italianate; fools who are conned by a villain; a sinister satirist who can be 'the flatterer, the Machiavel, the parasite, the traitor' and who combines 'an absolute pride in self and absolute loathing of all other creatures' with a 'compulsive hatred, mixed with an unhealthy fascination' for the body and sexuality; and who seems driven by 'some dark complex of pride, fear and loathing' (pp. 194–7). In this type of drama, the satirist's role is 'twisted and contradictory' (p. 207). This fits Othello and Iago down to the ground, of course, though scholars have tended to see Iago more as English Vice or Devil than Italianate satirist-intriguer.

22 Louise George Clubb, *Italian Drama in Shakespeare's Time* (New Haven, Yale University Press, 1989), p. 25.
23 Rymer, *A Short View of Tragedy*, p. 119.
24 Flaminio Scala, *Scenarios of the Commedia dell'arte: Flaminio's Scala's Il Teatro Delle Favole Rappresentative*, trans. Henry F. Salerno, 3rd edn (New York, Limelight, 1996), pp. 11–21 and 313–20.
25 Theresa J. Faherty, 'Othello dell'Arte: The Presence of *Commedia* in Shakespeare's Tragedy', *Theatre Journal*, 43 (1991), 192.
26 Faherty, 'Othello', p. 192. Faherty's major thesis is that Othello resembles the Capitano in general and Francesco Andreini in particular.
27 Michael Bristol, 'Charivari and the Comedy of Abjection in *Othello*', *Renaissance Drama*, 21 (1990), 4, 10.
28 Bristol, 'Charivari', p. 9.
29 Vaughan, *Othello: A Contextual History*, p. 63.
30 Anthony Gerard Barthelemy, *Black Face Maligned Race: The Representations of Blacks in English Drama from Shakespeare to Southerne* (Baton Rouge, Louisiana State University Press, 1987), pp. 72–146; Hunter, *Elizabethans and Foreigners*, p. 45; Hunter, 'Othello and Colour Prejudice', in *Dramatic Identities and Cultural Tradition: Studies in Shakespeare and His Contemporaries* (Liverpool, Liverpool University Press, 1978), pp. 32–40.
31 Gurr, *Playgoing*, p. 6.
32 Kim F. Hall, *Things of Darkness: Economies of Race and Gender in Early Modern England* (Ithaca, Cornell University Press, 1995), p. 4. Also see Vaughan, *Othello: A Contextual History*, p.58.
33 Quoted in *Othello*, ed. E. A. J. Honigmann, The Arden Shakespeare, third series (Walton-on-Thames, Thomas Nelson, 1997), p. 29. Also see Hall, *Things of Darkness*, pp. 11–14.
34 Bernard Harris, 'A Portrait of a Moor', *Shakespeare Survey*, 11 (1958), 89–97.
35 Margo Hendricks, '"The Moor of Venice," or the Italian on the Renaissance English Stage', in Shirley Nelson Garner and Madelon Sprengnether, eds, *Shakespearean Tragedy and Gender* (Bloomington, Indiana University Press, 1996), pp. 193–209.
36 Nicholas Brooke, *Horrid Laughter in Jacobean Tragedy* (London, Harper & Row, 1979), pp. 3, 8.
37 Einstein, *Italian Renaissance in England*, p. 249; Marienstras, 'The Near and the Far', p. 102.
38 Emilia also says she will cry 'as liberal as the North', possibly a reference to the greater liberties proverbially enjoyed by Englishwomen. A similar comparison occurs in Dekker and Webster's *Westward Ho!*, in which the Italian merchant tells a London city wife 'how happy be our Englishwomen that are not *troubled* with Italian husbands; why your Italians in general are so Sun-burnt with these Dog-daies, that your great Lady there thinkes her husband loves her not if hee bee not jealous: what confirms the liberty of our women more in *England*, then the Italian Proverbe, which saies if there were a bridge over the narrow Seas, all the women in Italy would shew their husbands a Million of light paire of heeles, and flie over into *England*' (3.3.81–8).

39 *Othello*, ed. Honigmann, p. 101. No theatregoer on record mentions the sufferings of 'the griev'd Moor', the compliment given to Burbage by his male colleagues, which has been used to argue for audience empathy for the character from the earliest performances.
40 Note that Othello's promise is constructed precisely like that of another imaginary cuckold, Master Ford of *Merry Wives*, who says 'If I suspect without cause, why then make sport at me. Then let me be your jest; I deserve it' (3.3.137–9). Both become the butts of laughter, just as they promise.
41 Kenneth Richards and Laura Richards, *The Commedia dell'arte: A Documentary History* (Oxford, Blackwell, 1990), p. 194.
42 Kenneth Richards, 'Inigo Jones and the *Commedia dell'arte*', in Christopher Cairns, ed., *The Commedia dell'arte from the Renaissance to Dario Fo* (Lewiston, Edwin Mellen Press, 1989), pp. 220–1.
43 K. M. Lea, *Italian Popular Comedy: A Study in the Commedia dell'arte, 1560–1620, with Special Reference to the English Stage*, 2 vols (Oxford, Clarendon Press, 1934), vol. II, p. 380.
44 Bristol, 'Charivari', p. 16.

12

The politics of plot: *Measure for Measure* and the Italianate disguised duke play

MICHAEL J. REDMOND

In considering the intertexts of *Measure for Measure*, the radical expansion of the role of the Duke is the most striking innovation that Shakespeare makes in his appropriation of the traditional monstrous ransom story.[1] Previous versions of the tale represent the Duke, or monarch, as an *a posteriori* judge, punishing the corrupt official after the fact for his lewd treatment of the condemned criminal's wife. What Shakespeare does instead, by placing his Duke in the disguise of a friar, is give the head of state an active role in the outcome of the action. Rather than responding to events, the Duke of Vienna covertly manipulates them, becoming the most prominent character in terms of the number of lines allocated to him by the dramatist. The surveillance of the Duke, staging the standard happy ending of New Comedy, ensures that the moral integrity of his government and the physical integrity of Claudio and Isabella are never really at stake, in contrast to the betrayed promises, executed husbands, and violated wives of the sources. The play becomes about the tension between the public performances of the ruler, observed by 'millions of false eyes', and the maintenance of power by covert direction, exposing the corruption of Angelo and the treasonous slanders of Lucio.[2] The Duke continually defines his public role in theatrical terms:

> I love the people
> But do not like to stage me to their eyes.
> Though it do well, I do not relish well
> Their loud applause.
>
> (1.1.68–71)

Yet, although he resists casting himself as an actor, he does relish a behind the scenes role in determining the outcome of the action, gleefully recounting how his 'craft against vice' will force an unwitting Angelo to 'perform an old contracting' via the bed-trick (3.1.531, 536). The use of a disguised duke, reflecting dramatic strategies current amongst Shakespeare's contemporaries, changes the focus of the established ransom story from Isabella's moral crisis to the voyeurism of the ruler. After the Duke's proposal of marriage at the end of the play, a significant departure from the traditional resolution of the erstwhile victim's plight, the conspicuous silence of Isabella embodies the inherent generic tensions between the concern with power in the disguised duke plot, the challenge to oppressive authority in the ransom story, and the celebration of individual choice in standard New Comedy.

Critics of *Measure for Measure* have felt obliged to acknowledge the manner in which Shakespeare's revision of the Duke's role places the play within a so-called 'theatrical vogue' that emerged in the first 'five or six years' following the accession of James I to the English throne.[3] Historical evidence and claims in the frontispieces of published editions make it clear that, prior to the staging of *Measure for Measure* before James on Boxing Day, 1604, there had already been court performances of Thomas Middleton's *The Phoenix* and John Marston's *The Malcontent*. Each of these works treats disguise as an opportunity for political reform, where the ruler must abandon the flattery and isolation of the court to discover abuses in secret. While *Measure for Measure* went unpublished until 1623, Marston's tale of Genovese court intrigue was one of the most influential and popular works of the time, a success on the public and private stages and available in three published quartos in 1604 alone.[4] The persistence of the disguised duke plot in subsequent years, becoming the object of self-conscious parody in comedies such as Edward Sharpham's *The Fleire* (1606) and John Day's *Humour Out of Breath* (1608), underlines its utility in dealing with issues of corruption and royal authority. None the less, in stating that 'the disguised ruler was fashionable in the theatre', traditional studies have not gone on to consider how Shakespeare's version of an established narrative structure with such explicit political concerns fits within the dynamic appropriation, citation, and revision of the structure in the plays of his contemporaries.[5] What is at stake in such an approach is the extent of audience recognition of generic intertextuality, involving specific dramatic conventions and ideological issues. For although regular theatregoers may not have recognized the relationship of the ransom story to individual sources, such as a novella in Cinthio's *Hecatommithi*, the disguised duke plot of *Measure for Measure* draws on the immediate context of the evolving Jacobean theatre repertory.

By the time that Beaumont wrote *The Woman Hater*, usually dated 1607, the Italianate disguised duke play had become a cliché. Indeed, his prologue openly concedes a lack of originality: 'a Duke there is, and the Scene lyes in Italy, as those thinges lightly we never miss'.[6] The startling effect of the opening scene, where the Duke of Milan asks some courtiers to discern his latest covert endeavour, is contingent upon entrenched audience expectations. The courtiers, obviously frequent theatregoers, immediately assume that their ruler must be preparing 'to cure / Some strange corruptions in the commonwealth' (1.1.11–12). The speculation onstage about a 'waightie court plot', adding to the impression given by the prologue, encourages a complacent acceptance of the work's generic affiliation (1.1.9). The Duke, however, abruptly dismisses any political motives: 'You are my friends, and you shall have the cause; / I breake my sleeps thus soone to see a wench' (1.1.28–9). The parodic implications of the ruler's anticlimactic denial of political reform are telling when placed alongside the self-justifications of Shakespeare's Duke, who denies 'that the dribbling dart of love / Can pierce a complete bosom' (1.3.2–3). For the ruler of Vienna, disguise is a pretext for reconstructing order in an upside-down society where

> liberty plucks justice by the nose,
> The baby beats the nurse, and quite athwart
> Goes all decorum.
>
> (1.3.29–31)

Yet, despite the extent of his declared ambitions, Shakespeare's Duke ends up seeking a woman as well.

Apart from its critical insight, underlining the tension between politics and romantic comedy, Beaumont's parody presupposes an audience capable of appreciating the misleading allusions to a typical disguised duke plot. What stands out in the theatre's treatment of political disguise, as the opening of *The Woman Hater* suggests, is the focus upon reform and surveillance within the context of a specific Italian city state. In *The Phoenix*, for example, the future ruler of Ferrara qualifies himself for power through his effort 'to look into the heart and bowels of [the] dukedom, and, in disguise, mark all abuses ready for reformation and punishment'.[7] The portrayal of a vigorous young prince eager to stem the corruption permitted by his predecessor would have appealed to the hopes of domestic reformers in the immediate aftermath of the accession of James VI of Scotland to the English throne.[8] Yet placing the action in Ferrara, a state which lost its independence in 1598 after the failure of the ruling Este family to produce a suitable heir, adds particular resonance to Middleton's handling of the potential dangers of royal succession.[9] For although Marston took care to deny the relevance of location in his prologue to *The Malcontent*, disclaiming any topical references even to distant Genoa, the Italian settings of such plays exploited the historical and cultural associations that individual states had already acquired in England.[10] It is significant that *The Fawn* (1604), Marston's second use of a disguise plot, features another Duke of Ferrara's surreptitious observation of the court of Urbino. The decline of the two states, as Thomas Gainsford noted in *The Glory of England*, provided a cautionary vision of failed leadership and the loss of sovereignty: 'you see, how pitifully *Ferrara* and *Urbine* have lost their reputation of courtshippe, and offered their coronets on the altar of Clergie man's usurpation'.[11] Marston's contemptuous depiction of Urbino, the state that Baldassare Castiglione presented as a model for courtly conduct and judicious government in *Il Libro del Cortegiano*, forms an integral part of his satiric strategy. The disguised ruler's study of Castiglione's court, consistent with the frequent mockery of the precepts of 'the absolute Castilio' in other plays and satires by Marston, exposes the 'A, B, C, of courtship' as mere sycophancy.[12] The argument of the play becomes how the Duke of Ferrara learns good government from the errors he finds in Urbino: 'Another's court shall show me where and how / Vice may be cured' (2.1.565–6).

Marston's approach to the standard disguised duke plot, siting the surreptitious investigation of the ruler in a different state, dramatizes the process of cultural comparison implicit in the English fascination with the Italian political scene. The fragmentation of the Italian nation into 'royall That and Duchie This', as William Warner put it in *Albion's England*, gave domestic political theorists a laboratory of failed statecraft.[13] In spite of all the preoccupation in the culture at large about Sir Politic Would-bes eager to emulate the *sprezzatura* of Castiglione and the subtle schemes of Machiavelli, early modern English political writing deals with Italian practices as cautionary models of how not to govern a state. An understanding of what had gone wrong in Italy, as the title of an abridged 1591 translation of Guicciardini promised, was '*verie necessarie for Parliament, councell, treatises, and negotiations*'.[14] Through the study of the 'mutation, disorder, and utter ruine' of individual Italian states, Thomas Bedingfield notes in dedicating his 1595 translation of Machiavelli's *Florentine History* to the Lord Chancellor of England, those 'becalled to the consultation of publike affaires and government' could better avoid the causes of 'domesticall discords'.[15]

Enterprising courtiers made careers by displaying their knowledge of Italian political failures. On the heels of self-appointed Tudor experts on Italian government such as William Thomas and Charles Merbury, there was a proliferation of translations and studies of Italy by those eager for preferment under the Stuarts. The case of Sir Robert Dallington, who was one of the few courtiers to serve in the households of both Prince Henry and Prince Charles, marks the tangible benefits of being an expert on Italian politics in Jacobean England.[16] Dallington wrote two texts on judicious government, each of which used Italian precedents as examples of how not to rule. At the opening of his *Aphorismes Civill and Militarie*, he cites Francesco Guicciardini's history of Florence as a warning for his royal readers:

> About the year 1490, Italy the most glorious and goodliest countrie of Europe, stood in fairer termes of happiness and prosperitie, then ever it had done since the first declination of the Romane Empire: she was not subject to any command, but of naturall Italians ... All of which faire flowers of peace were soddainly

blasted: most of the governments changed: the people wasted: the wealth exhausted: the cities demolished: Arts and Armes decayed: and all by the heart burning and jealousie of her own Princes, which set that noble countrie in combustion; and being once on fire, ministred so much fuell of herselfe, as in fortie years space it could not be quenched.[17]

Here, with its contempt for the factionalism and blind self-interest of the rulers, Dallington's citation draws on the nostalgia for the past and the disgust for the shame of Italy that characterizes the works of Guicciardini, Machiavelli, and even Castiglione. In his *Survey of the Great Dukes State of Tuscany*, Dallington casts the state's loss of its tributary cities and, finally, its very independence as an instructive lesson in political incompetence:

I could not finde where that great wit of theirs lay, whatsoever either by Macciavel his report in his historie, or in his person may to the contrary be alleadged … I dare say that if Macciavel were again living, and should see them, that were wont to rule a state, now not [fit] to bring a few Lettice from their Villa … he would unsay that which hee had formerly said, and sweare that they had no witte.[18]

As he disclaims that he acquired any useful 'matter of pollicy, or history or Art' during his time in Florence, Dallington refuses to derive any positive knowledge from Italian culture.[19]

The morbid curiosity with which such early modern English treatises of government survey the disorder of Italian states comes to the fore in the disguised duke plays of Marston, Middleton, and Sharpham, where concealed observers learn how to renew their hold on power by studying the errors of other leaders. Disguise becomes a process of political education, demonstrating how to overcome instability. Even as these plays register discontent with corruption on a wider level, reflecting domestic unease about the court, they are rooted in conventional representations of precarious Italian states. Despite the attention paid to individual abuses, the motives for concealment have little to do with mere voyeurism or capriciousness. The disguised dukes, faced with internal treason and the territorial ambitions of neighbouring states, have no choice but to abandon their public roles. The protagonist of *The Malcontent*, a deposed Duke of Genoa, 'lie[s] in ambush for conveniency', spying on conspiracies in the usurper's court as a means of regaining his title (3.3.22). The erstwhile ruler bitterly laments being compelled to take on the guise of Malevole: 'O God, how loathsome this toying is to me!' (5.3.41). In *The Phoenix*, the inability of the ageing Duke to see beyond the flattery of the court obliges his son to act in secret against treasonous conspirators. The cynical ex-Duke of Florence in Sharpham's *The Fleire* profits from the sexual abuses permitted by the weak government of his new abode. For although Ivo Kamps has argued that the disguised monarch figure is 'a wishful image of the Christian God', unaffected by temporal events, the rulers in these plays are subject to political tumults beyond their control.[20] It is telling that the unseen Duke of Florence, deposing and reinstating rulers of Genoa at will, is the most powerful leader in *The Malcontent*. The historical context of Italian crisis, where the status of the ruler and the state are always under threat, demands a new understanding of the realities of power.

The lack of an Italian setting in *Measure for Measure* marks a departure from the handling of disguised duke plots by period dramatists. What stands out immediately in Shakespeare's approach is the security of the ruler's own position. It is significant that, although the Duke's public absence creates the potential for state violence and sexual exploitation, the consequences of misrule threaten only the subjects of Vienna. For although the Italianate plays deal with the fragility of political power, the fate of the Duke of Vienna is never at stake. Confident in his ability to return, Shakespeare's Duke chooses of his own accord to avoid the popular view for a brief period. In spite of Angelo's eagerness to abuse his temporary position, once given 'Mortality and mercy in Vienna', he does not show any ambition to seize permanent authority (1.1.44). The combination of a disguised duke plot with the traditional ransom story has much to do with the limited focus on the correction of a subordinate's abuses. As Vincentio adopts the costume of a friar, allowing him to spy unobserved, he admits a desire to test his followers: 'Hence shall we see / If power change purpose, what our seemers be' (1.3.53–4). The ruler's curosity reflects what Foucault has called the changing economy of power with the decline of absolutism, moving from the production of royal spectacle to an invisible strategy of surveillance that 'imposes on those whom it subjects a compulsory visibility'.[21] For all its reputation as a problem play, as Franco Moretti has argued, *Measure for Measure* might be better seen as the '"de-problematizing" play par excellence … a comedy written by the Duke'.[22] Denied any private space, the populace of Vienna becomes the spectacle.[23] Isabella's principled rejection of Angelo, 'Dressed in a little brief authority', does not offer a precedent for resistance to legitimate power (2.2.120). Apart from Barnadine's refusal to die, an exception that proves the rule, Vincentio disposes of the bodies of his subjects as he sees fit.

While *Measure for Measure* draws on the portrayal of surveillance in early Jacobean political drama, it leaves the ruler's place at the head of the established social hierarchy in Vienna unquestioned. The intertextual density of Shakespeare's plot construction, merging sources from diverse ideological positions and circumstances, complicates the transmission of individual genres. The more than legitimate paranoia of Italian dukes on the Jacobean stage, constantly menaced by treason, has little to do with Vincentio's blithe manipulation of his subjects. When Shakespeare came to depict the trials of an usurped duke in *The Tempest*, a later work with remarkable similarities to disguised ruler narratives, he was careful to site the action amidst a context of

Italian state intrigue. For although Gary Taylor has recently contended that *Measure for Measure*'s references to Vienna are the product of posthumous adaptation, envisioning a more typical Italianate version based in Ferrara, the anomalous setting highlights the distance separating the providential vision of the ransom story from the staging of crisis in other political disguise plays.[24] The active surveillance of officials is a logical expansion of the Duke's role in the ransom plot as the ultimate guarantor of justice, permitting the prevention of abuses before they occur.[25] At the end of the play, a chastened Angelo makes manifest the outcome's association with theories of the ruler as a proxy for God:

> O my dread lord,
> I should be guiltier than my guiltiness
> To think I can be undiscernable,
> When I perceive your grace, like power divine,
> Hath looked upon my passes.
>
> (5.1.367–71)

Given the importance of the ransom plot, the textual history of the location has potential ramifications for our understanding of the play's assimilation of material from outside the disguised duke tradition. The most immediate English source for the sexual blackmail story, George Whetstone's *Promos and Cassandra* (1578), takes place '*In the Cyttie of* Julio *(sometimes under the dominion of* Corvinus *Kinge of* Hungarie, *and* Boemia*)*'.[26] It is noticeable that Lucio's gossip at the beginning of the play, in a passage whose provenience Taylor has disputed, emphasizes the central European setting: 'If the Duke with the other dukes come not to composition with the King of Hungary, why then all the dukes fall upon the king' (1.2.1–3).[27]

With the recognition in the Jacobean theatre community of the disguised duke play as a distinct genre, the continuities and discontinuities of Shakespeare's approach emerge from within the context of a wider repertory. Though critics often tend to idealize the ability of Shakespeare to interrogate existing forms, rather than merely reproducing them, generic parody became part of the satiric strategies of many playwrights. The ideological implications of rewriting disguise plots come to the fore in Edward Sharpham's *The Fleire*, where the great innovation is to bring a super-sophisticated deposed Duke of Florence to a clearly defined Jacobean London. Composed after the works of Marston, Middleton, and Shakespeare, as underlined by the wealth of allusions to entrenched conventions and plot structures, the satire exploits audience recognition of the disguised ruler figure. In Sharpham's version, performed in 1606 by the Children of the Queen's Revels, Duke Antifront explicitly observes the court of James himself, rather than a distant Italian state or a city in central Europe. The novelty of a domestic setting emphasizes the rhetorical function of location in previous plays. When asked why he came 'out of *Italy* into

England, the Florentine provides a self-reflexive gloss on the early modern drama's treatment of political issues within an Italian context: 'Because *England* would not come into *Italy* to me.'[28] The emphasis on Italy underlines how anomalous the Viennese setting of *Measure for Measure* really is, falling outside conventional strategies of political commentary.

In so far as *The Fleire* is a product of a series of citations and revisions of other dramatists, the pleasure of the audience, especially for the cognoscenti, must have come from the possibility it offers for intertextual interpretation.[29] By repatriating the Italian stereotypes of political error, forcing the Jacobean audience to watch a Florentine mock the domestic scene, Sharpham challenges the manner in which previous plays rehearse English anxieties within a foreign setting. Explicit allusions to the genre, as in *The Woman Hater*, underline its association with political transition under James I. The play devotes much of the second act to the Florentine's response, as an expert on statecraft, to the Jacobean court:

> I saw a Farmers Son sit newly made a courtier, that sat in the presence at cardes, as if the chaire of state had bin made of a peece of his fathers Barne-doore:
> O tis a shame:
> I would have state be state in earnest and in game.
>
> (2.1.223–8)

Here, as in *The Fawn*, a foreign expert contemptuously reviews the practices of a fellow ruler. The reference to 'the presence', denoting that the events described took place before the English monarch, ensures that the disguised duke's criticisms of the court appear to be directed at King James himself. The association of 'the chaire of state' with a country squire's 'Barne-doore' targets his failure to maintain appropriate standards of royal decorum.[30] The specific criticism of the behaviour of a 'newly made' courtier picks up, of course, on the widespread unease about James's prodigality with honours.[31]

While *Measure for Measure* does not hazard such obvious topical allusions to the English scene, Sharpham's demystification of the genre shows that disguised duke plots had already acquired specific political connotations. Given the potential associations with the domestic monarch, Shakespeare's depiction of the Duke of Vienna deserves particular attention. Without the threat of Italian crisis, the absence of any sense of personal danger discourages Vincentio from undergoing the same process of education as the rulers in contemporary plays. Despite regular denials of any yearning for the approval of his subjects, where he notes that 'the man of safe discretion' will not affect it, the Duke's actions are continually motivated by the fear of libel (1.1.72). Even before Angelo demonstrates his lack of integrity, as part of the ransom plot, the Duke has already cast him as the front man for his new campaign against vice: 'Sith 'twas my fault to give the people scope, / 'Twould be my tyranny to strike and gall them' (1.3.35–6). In explaining his decision to adopt the disguise of a friar, as Vincentio seeks to persuade a doubting Friar Thomas, he points to the advantages of disassociating himself from the implementation of unpopular measures:

> I have on Angelo imposed the office,
> Who may in the ambush of my name strike home,
> And yet my nature never in the fight
> To do in slander.
>
> (1.3.40–3)

The importance that libel acquires for the ruler is such that the enforced marriages imposed by Vincentio at the end of the play equate the conduct of Lucio, guilty of trading in malicious gossip, with the human cost of the moral abuses of Angelo. In staging the normalizing happy ending, the Duke pointedly excludes Lucio from the general amnesty: 'And yet here's one in place I cannot pardon' (5.1.502). He makes it clear that the courtier's unpardonable offence consists in the description of him as 'a fool, a coward, / One all of luxury, an ass, a madman' (5.1.502–3).

The anxiety about slander in *Measure for Measure*, where the ruler seeks public acquiescence, has nothing to do with the didactic concerns of Marston and Middleton. As a professional satirist, incurring official wrath under both Elizabeth and James, it was unlikely that Marston would encourage fears about libel. Indeed, as Brian Gibbons has noted, the disguised duke of *The Malcontent* 'is a dramatic metaphor for the imaginative art of the satiric poet, encouraging vice and folly in order to exhibit their true nature and contrive their exposure and correction'.[32] Marston depicts surveillance in terms of education, where the study of error brings the ruler to correct his own weaknesses. In *The Fawn*, after participating in the sycophancy at the court in Urbino, the disguised Duke of Ferrara emphasizes that the experience has forced him to confront his own susceptibility to flattery:

> By Him by Whom we are, I think a prince
> Whose tender suffrance never felt a gust
> Of bolder breathings, but still liv'd gently fanned
> With the soft gales of his own flatterers' lips,
> Shall never know his own complexion ...
> Mortal till now, I scarce had known myself.
>
> (1.2.306–14)

Instead of legitimating authority, these plays argue, public shows of deference beguile the ruler. Middleton represents the Duke of Ferrara's political weakness in *The Phoenix* as a failure to interpret the body politic. After seeing the political education disguise has offered his son, the aged ruler acknowledges the epistemic value of surveillance:

> To thee let reverence all her powers engage,
> That art in youth a miracle to age!
> State is but blindness; thou hast piercing art:
> We saw only the knee, but thou the heart.
>
> (5.1.176–80)

Here, with the physical opposition of the knee and the heart, the abdicating Duke employs synecdoche to privilege the covert vision of the prince, able to determine the disposition of the individual subject. The political illegibility of the 'knee', representing an obligatory performance of reverence, demands that the ruler discount the external gestures of his subjects.

The importance of corporeal synecdoche in plays like *Measure for Measure*, as Elizabeth Hanson has noted, is that it 'seems to promise access to unseen essences – things whose nature is to elude mediation'.[33] The surveillance of Middleton's Phoenix, rhetorically depicted as seeing the heart, overcomes the divide between the public and private spaces of the subject. Yet, when disguise permits Shakespeare's Duke to hear himself ridiculed by Lucio, he resists the unmediated version of his reputation:

> No might nor greatness in mortality
> Can censure scape; back-wounding calumny
> The whitest virtue strikes. What king so strong
> Can tie up the gall in the slanderous tongue?
>
> (3.1.442–5)

The corporeal synecdoche used by Vincentio, asserting that the tongue of the subject menaces the ducal back, point to the desire of the ruler to protect himself by silencing the opinion of the individual subject.

For although the Duke of Vienna uses surveillance to consolidate his hold on power, exploiting the information he acquires, he resists placing himself in discussion. Indeed, contrary to the disguised ruler plays of Marston and Middleton, what *Measure for Measure* makes clear is the extent to which the Duke demands outward praise and deference. Unsettled by Lucio's disrespect, Vincentio actually laments the absence of 'dearer love' (3.1.411). The fake friar's defensive portrayal of the Duke as an archetypal Renaissance man has the air of self-flattery about it:

> Either this is envy in you, folly, or mistaking. The very stream of his life, and the business he hath helmed, must upon a warranted need give him a better proclamation. Let him be but testimonied in his bringings- forth, and he shall appear to the envious a scholar, a statesman, and a soldier. (3.1.401–7)

Here, Vincentio's complaint recalls the narcissism of Gonzago, the Duke of Urbino in *The Fawn* who continually trumpets his own sagacity and learning. In searching for topical allusions in Marston's play, critics have argued that Gonzago's appetite for flattery forms part of a satirical depiction of King

James.[34] The emphasis that the ruler of Urbino places upon his qualifications as 'a philosopher' and a prince 'of discerning wit' certainly corresponds with period accounts of the Stuart king's proud evaluation of his voluminous writing and scholarship (1.2.171, 147). The appeal by Shakespeare's Duke to the value of his public statements, with the reference to 'his bringings-forth', may also allude to the royal authorship of works such as *The True Law of Free Monarchies* and *Basilikon Doron*. The English publication of *Basilikon Doron* in 1603, permitting James's new subjects to anticipate his agenda, reflected the same cultural interest in the issue of royal authority that fostered the popularity of disguised duke plots.[35] However, as the similarity to the inept ruler in *The Fawn* suggests, the ideological posturing of Shakespeare's Duke does not go unchallenged.

In his clueless way, incurring the wrath of the disguised ruler with his playful malice, Lucio crushes the Duke's delusions of popular consent.[36] It is significant that there is no equivalent figure to Lucio in the other relevant plays, except perhaps for Malevole. What condemns the gallant is his failure to offer a consistent performance of loyalty, anticipating the possibility that he might be watched. In looking at the 'culture of suspicion' implicit in early modern Italian theories of courtiership, Harry Berger Jr has persuasively outlined the importance that 'self-surveillance' has in Castiglione's and Della Casa's precepts for social advancement.[37] The Duke's final punishment of the character, forcing him to marry the 'punk' who bore his child, does not come from the desire for moral reform. Rather, he intones that 'Slandering a Prince deserves it' (5.1.527). After all his efforts for the good of Vienna, at least as he sees it, Shakespeare's Duke is unable to accept the lack of public affection for him:

> O place and greatness, millions of false eyes
> Are stuck upon thee; volumes of report
> Run with their false and most contrarious quests
> Upon thy doings; thousand escapes of wit
> Make thee the father of their idle dream,
> And rack thee in their fancies.
>
> (4.1.58–63)

Here, as N. W. Bawcutt notes in his edition of the play, the repetition of 'false' does not refer to the artifice of the flatterer, but to the treachery of unlove.[38] Confronted with the epistemic distance between private contempt and public deference, the heart and the knee that the aged ruler in *The Phoenix* identifies, Vincentio's response is to compel displays of affection. The early modern idea of power, as Stephen Greenblatt has argued, is about more than social position and wealth: '[its] quintessential sign is the ability to impose one's fictions upon the world'.[39] Yet what makes the encounters with Lucio so traumatic for the Duke is that he had not fully recognized that the apparent love of his subjects was only an act. In returning to his outward role, after his disguise is removed, Vienna's ruler regains the authority to suppress dissent and exact affection. The marriage he demands for himself at the end, set alongside the enforced unions, comes as his ultimate revendication of authentic love.

The vanity of the Duke of Vienna lies behind another significant departure from the conventions established in the Italianate plays: the choice of disguise. While other disguised rulers depart from their usual position of respect, casting themselves as disreputable figures on the fringes of the court engaged in flattery or conspiracy, Vincentio maintains his dignity 'Like a true friar', claiming the honour due to a religious elder (1.3.48). The irony about the choice of a disguise granting moral authority is that Shakespeare's Duke requires his subjects to engage in disquieting physical actions such as the bed-trick, a sexual bait and switch involving a would-be religious novice, and the desperate attempt to find a 'convenient' corpse to substitute for Claudio (4.3.100). In accepting to perform in the Duke's deception of Angelo, hazarding their bodies and personal reputations in the scheme, both Isabella and Mariana make it clear that they are relying upon the assurances of the supposed friar that ''tis no sin' (4.2.71). What is at stake in such covert manoeuvring is that enforcing the rule of an absolute monarch can be a messy business even in the best of disguised duke plays.

When we look beyond Shakespeare things get even messier. One of the most striking aspects of the later parodies of the genre, alongside the topical satire, is the squalid means by which power is obtained and preserved. Instead of merely observing folly and vice, the deposed Duke of Florence in *The Fleire* exploits the activity of his two daughters as prostitutes, installing himself unbeknownst to them as their enterprising pimp. Aware that the son of the usurping ruler of Florence is one of their most enthusiastic clients, Antifront uses the sexual labour of his daughters to gain access to the Jacobean court and search for the information he needs to regain his dukedom. Needless to say, many critics have found that the play lacks 'serious moral pressure'.[40] In noting that the entrance of the daughters into the stews, 'varied by attempts to poison some of their clientele, proves no impediment to a concluding journey to the altar', Alfred Harbage has declared that it would be difficult 'to imagine Shakespeare dealing in such ware'.[41] However, as Mary Bly's recent study of the repertory of the Whitefriars theatre has argued, the popularity of plays with bawdy language and situations proves that sexual material did have a commercial appeal in the London theatre marketplace.[42] Critical approaches based on subjective values such as morality and dramatic quality distract from the manner in which Sharpham's bawdy satire, designed to satisfy the particular tastes of his fellow students at the Inns of Court, offers an insightful reading of the political strategies of the disguised duke plays written by his predecessors. At the very least, *The Fleire* is important because it documents what one of Shakespeare's contemporaries thought were the weak points in the theatre's treatment of disguise and sovereignty. The blatant moral lapses of Antifront's cynical will to power suggest that, for Sharpham, control over the body politic was not divorced from the fate of individual bodies.

Given the interest in recent studies of *Measure for Measure* in what Stephen Cohen has described as 'the ideological schizophrenia of the play's conclusion', where romantic comedy seems to clash with the disguised duke plot, Sharpham's self-reflexive handling of comic closure in *The Fleire* offers a valuable Jacobean critical precedent.[43] In the twelve lines of rhyming couplets which conclude the play, by this time a sign of parody, Duke Antifront quickly marries his unwilling daughters to their most pathetic clients, loudly claiming that the marriages fulfil all the requirements of New Comedy: 'And now since everie thing so well doth sort, / Let all be pleas'd in this our comic sport' (5.5.112–13). The only confirmation that there is a happy ending comes from the Duke, since his chatter about genre drowns out any potential opposition from the couples. For all his blustering at the end, however, Antifront makes no effort throughout the course of the action to hide the fact that the need to 'regaine our right in *Florence*' outweighs anything else (2.1.430). Sharpham treats the Duke's efforts to match his daughter Florida with Piso, the son of the dead usurper of power in Florence, as part of a perverse inversion of a standard romantic comedy plot, where the heavy father succeeds in imposing his wishes in spite of the resistance of his daughters and the disgust of the grooms. As in *Measure for Measure*, the transition from the very real threat of execution to a series of enforced marriages serves a clear political function. Brought to desperation by his condemnation to death, after a trial engineered by Antifront, a distraught Piso unwittingly renounces his new title:

> Let them call back the banisht Signior *Antifront,* whome they and we, and al have wrong'd: O could I live but to enquire him out, in satisfaction of his wronges, ide marry his eldest Daughter and whilst a liv'd a should be restored to his estate, but O hee's – (5.5.100–4)

The spontaneous disavowal of a dukedom, overheard by the disguised ruler, closely follows a similar scene in *The Malcontent*.[44] At this point, taking up the offer, Antifront reveals his true identity and marries Piso to his daughter, a prostitute who has already shown her contempt for him. For both Antifront and Piso, the marriage with Florida is a function of political expediency. While Piso has limited information about the identity of the actual bride, his long-term intention is to ensure his legitimate succession to power in Florence after Antifront. The conclusion's reminder of the role of dynastic marriages in consolidating the fortunes of a royal house would not have scandalized the Jacobean audience, since English political life for the final half of the sixteenth century was conditioned by the interminable discussion of Elizabeth's wedding prospects.[45] The absurdity arises from the ruler's unconvincing effort to represent a sleazy political alliance as romantic comedy, a genre promoting ideals of love and personal autonomy.

Such generic tension is at the heart of what modern audiences and critics have come to see as the disturbing outcome of the final scene in *Measure for Measure*, where Shakespeare seeks to resolve the three different plotlines he derived from his array of sources. The uncomfortable silence of Isabella at the conclusion, after receiving the abrupt proposal of marriage from the Duke of Vienna, feels like 'a rent in the play's coherence, a site of unspeakable confusion in its discourse'.[46] It is important to note that the silence of a female character, eliding the absence of a coherent dramatic motivation, is not unique in Shakespearean comedy. At the end of *Twelfth Night*, as Alan Sinfield has cogently noted, Shakespeare distracts from the inadequacies of his plot by leaving Olivia 'improbably silent at just the moment when anything she might possibly say would disrupt the normalizing patriarchal closure'.[47] The lack of any response by Isabella, as with Olivia, naturalizes her impromptu betrothal to an unexpected suitor. The difference between the silences of the two women, however, comes from the generic context in which they are set. While Olivia's seeming acceptance of marriage to the male twin of the disguised woman that she had been courting serves to complete the reassuring final tableau of happy couples, leaving only the comic victim Malvolio excluded, the power relations involved in the Duke of Vienna's desire evoke the broader pattern of enforced marriages at the conclusion of *Measure for Measure*. After continuing to renounce Mariana when she appears before him, Angelo himself offers no response when ordered to 'marry her instantly' (5.1.378). While Mariana and Isabella come to plead for the remission of his execution, his only further comment is that he 'crave[s] death more willingly than mercy' (5.1.479). Angelo's own silence about his new wife smooths over the fact that, to paraphrase Mariana, the Duke is mocking her with a husband. Among the none too happy couples in this tableau of unconvincing reconciliation, only Lucio enunciates his disgust at the Duke's match making: 'Marrying a punk, my lord, is pressing to death, whipping, and hanging' (5.1.524–5). Placed at the climax of this sequence of unwanted unions, as Lucio is forcibly taken away to wed in prison, the proposition to Isabella threatens to betray the ideological antagonisms dividing the romantic ideal of personal choice, the ruler's incarnation of state power, and his role in the sexual blackmail plot as the defender of female chastity. It is telling that, despite Vincentio's frequent denials of sexual motives, Friar Thomas suspected right from the beginning that the ruler was led by the 'ends / Of burning youth' (1.3.5–6). Isabella remains voiceless because she is the bond holding together Shakespeare's unstable amalgam of the traditional ransom story, the disguised duke plot, and romantic comedy. Anything she says could upstage the ostensible closure, exposing the conflicts of interest

172   Text and ideology

between the different roles that Vincentio is attempting to perform simultaneously. The intertextual background of *Measure for Measure*, mediating sources with diverse ideological visions of the individual subject, precludes a harmonious comic resolution to the political discourses it attempts to manage.

Notes

1 For accounts of the intertextual background of the ransom story and its use by Shakespeare see Mary Lascelles, *Shakespeare's* Measure for Measure (London, Athlone Press, 1953), Geoffrey Bullough, *Narrative and Dramatic Sources of Shakespeare*, vol. 2: *The Comedies, 1597–1603* (London: Routledge and Kegan Paul, 1958), pp. 399 ff., and Kenneth Muir, *The Sources of Shakespeare's Plays* (London, Methuen, 1977), p. 174.
2 William Shakespeare, *Measure for Measure*, The Oxford Shakespeare, ed. N. W. Bawcutt (Oxford, Oxford University Press, 1991), 4.1.58. All further references are placed within the text.
3 Thomas A. Pendleton, 'Shakespeare's Disguised Duke Play: Middleton, Marston, and the Sources of *Measure for Measure*', in John W. Mahon and Thomas A. Pendleton, eds, *'Fanned and Winnowed Opinions': Shakespearean Essays Presented to Harold Jenkins* (London, Methuen, 1987), p. 82. Recent accounts of the role of the disguised duke (or disguised ruler) plot structure in Shakespeare's play include Stephen Cohen, 'From Mistress to Master: Political Transition and Formal Conflict in *Measure for Measure*', *Criticism*, 41 (1999), 431–64; Ivo Kamps, 'Ruling Fantasies and the Fantasies of Rule: *The Phoenix* and *Measure for Measure*', *Studies in Philology*, 92 (1995), 248–73; Leonard Tennenhouse, 'Representing Power: *Measure for Measure* in its Time', in Stephen Greenblatt, ed., *The Power of Forms in the English Renaissance* (Norman, Pilgrim, 1982), pp. 143–56; and Rosalind Miles, *The Problem of* Measure for Measure (New York, Barnes and Noble, 1976), pp. 134–60.
4 The popularity of *The Malcontent* in 1604, following upon its revival by the King's Men, does not preclude an earlier composition date. While James's accession raised hopes for reform, as shown by the emergence of similar plays, satire of the court had already become prominent in the waning years of Elizabeth's reign.
5 Geoffrey Bullough, *Narrative and Dramatic Sources*, vol. 2, p. 411.
6 Francis Beaumont, *The Woman Hater*, in *The Dramatic Works in the Beaumont and Fletcher Canon*, ed. Fredson Bowers (Cambridge, Cambridge University Press, 1966–89), Prologue, ll. 17–9. Although he does not consider the play in detail, Albert Tricomi has cited the line as proof that 'Francis Beaumont clearly perceived something of the pattern' established in previous disguise plays. See Tricomi, *Anticourt Drama in England, 1603–1642* (Charlottesville, University Press of Virginia, 1989), p. 13.
7 *The Works of Thomas Middleton*, ed. A. H. Bullen (rpt New York, AMS Press, 1964), 1.1.100–2.
8 There has been extensive critical discussion of the relationship between Middleton's play and the new monarch: significant accounts include Tricomi, *Anticourt Drama*, pp. 15–16; N. W. Bawcutt, 'Middleton's *The Phoenix* as a Royal

Play', *Notes and Queries*, 201 (1956), 287–8; and D. B. Dodson, 'King James and *The Phoenix* – Again', *Notes and Queries*, 203 (1958), 434–7.

9 After the death of Alfonso II in 1597, the Este were left without a legitimate heir and the Papacy took direct control of Ferrara. See Luciano Chiappini, *Gli Estensi: Mille anni di storia* (Ferrara, Corbo, 2001), and Bonner Mitchell, *1598: A Year of Pageantry in Late Renaissance Ferrara* (Binghamton, Medieval and Renaissance Texts and Studies, 1990).

10 See John Marston, *The Malcontent*, ed. M. L. Wine (Lincoln: University of Nebraska Press, 1964), Prologue, ll. 4–12.

11 Gainsford, *The Glory of England* (London: 1618), p. 227.

12 John Marston, *Certaine Satyres* in *The Poems of John Marston*, ed. Arnold Davenport (Liverpool, Liverpool University Press, 1961), l. 27 (see also, for example, the comments in *The Malcontent* (1.4.87) and the sycophantic character named 'Castilio Balthazar' in *Antonio and Mellida*), and *The Fawn*, ed. Gerald A. Smith (Lincoln, University of Nebraska Press, 1964), 4.1.167.

13 William Warner, *Albion's England*, 3rd edn (London, 1597), p. 307.

14 See *A briefe collection or epitomie of all the notable and material things contained in the hystorie of Gucciardine being verie necessarie for Parliament, councell, treatises, and negotiations* (London, T. Purfoote, 1591).

15 N. Machiavelli, *The Florentine History*, trans. T[homas] B[edingfield] (London, 1595), sig. A2r.

16 See Karl Josef Holtgen, 'Sir Robert Dallington (1561–1637): Author, Traveler, and Pioneer of Taste', *Huntington Library Quarterly*, 47 (1984), 167ff.

17 Sir Robert Dallington, *Aphorismes Civill and Militarie: Amplified with authorities, and exemplified with historie out of the first quatrne of Fr. Guicciardine* (London, 1613), sigs B1r–v.

18 Sir R. Dallington, *A Survey of the Great Dukes State of Tuscany* (London, 1605), pp. 61–2.

19 The vehemence of Dallington's attack was such that the Duke of Florence protested to the English authorities. See Anna Maria Crinò, *Fatti e figure del seicento anglo-toscano* (Florence, Leo S. Olschki, 1957), pp. 41–8.

20 See Ivo Kamps, 'Ruling Fantasies', pp. 250–60. Leonard Tennenhouse also sees the disguised ruler plays as staging the ideology of absolutism. See 'Representing Power', pp. 143–6.

21 Michel Foucault, *Discipline and Punish: The Birth of the Prison*, trans. Alan Sheridan (New York, Vintage, 1979), p. 187.

22 Franco Moretti, *Signs taken for Wonders: Essays in the Sociology of Literary Forms* (London, Verso, 1983), pp. 57–8.

23 Jonathan Goldberg notes the Duke's violation of religious privacy when he acts as a confessor to Mariana. See *James I and the Politics of Literature: Jonson, Shakespeare, Donne, and Their Contemporaries* (Baltimore, Johns Hopkins University Press, 1983), p. 233 note. See also Jonathan Dollimore, 'Transgression and Surveillance in *Measure for Measure*', in Jonathan Dollimore and Alan Sinfield, eds, *Political Shakespeare* (Manchester, Manchester University Press, 1985), pp. 72–87.

24 Taylor argues that the location must have been changed by Thomas Middleton, as

a response to English hostility in 1620 towards Ferdinand II's persecution of Protestants on the continent. See Gary Taylor, 'Shakespeare's Mediterranean *Measure for Measure*', in Tom Clayton and Susan Brock, eds, *Shakespeare and the Mediterranean* (Newark, University of Delaware Press, 2004). (I thank Professor Taylor for sending me a copy of his paper before publication.)

25 See Richard Proudfoot, '"It is an accident that heaven provides": Shakespeare's Providence in *Measure for Measure*', in Sergio Rossi and Dianella Savoia, eds, *Italy and the English Renaissance* (Milan, Unicopli, 1989), pp. 155–66.

26 George Whetstone, *Promos and Cassandra* in Bullough, *Narrative and Dramatic Sources*, vol. 2, p. 444.

27 See John Jowett and Gary Taylor, 'With New Additions: Theatrical Interpolation in *Measure for Measure*', in Taylor and Jowett, *Shakespeare Reshaped 1606–1623* (Oxford, Clarendon Press, 1993), pp. 151–5.

28 Edward Sharpham, *A Critical Old Spelling Edition of the Works of Edward Sharpham*, ed. Christopher Gordon Petter (New York, Garland, 1986), 1.3.258, 259. All further citations will be placed within the text. Albert Tricomi has noted the relation of this passage to the disguised duke tradition. See *Anticourt Drama*, p. 23.

29 See Michael J. Redmond, '"Tis common knowledge": Italian Stereotypes and Audience Response in *Much Ado About Nothing* and *The Novella*', *Shakespeare Yearbook*, 13 (2002), 419–41.

30 Tricomi, *Anticourt Drama*, p. 23.

31 In just the first year of his reign, James tripled the number of knights. See Linda Levy Peck, *Court Patronage and Corruption in Early Stuart England* (Boston, Unwin Hyman, 1990), p. 32.

32 Brian Gibbons, *Jacobean City Comedy*, 2nd edn (London, Methuen, 1980), p. 69.

33 Elizabeth Hanson, *Discovering the Subject in Renaissance England* (Cambridge, Cambridge University Press, 1998), pp. 80–1.

34 See Albert W. Upton, 'Allusions to James I and his Court in Marston's *The Fawn* and Beaumont's *The Woman Hater*', *PMLA*, 44 (1929), 1048–65, and Tricomi, *Anticourt Drama*, p. 22.

35 See Ivo Kamps, 'Ruling Fantasies', pp. 248ff.

36 Dollimore notes that 'perhaps the most subversive thing in the play is the most casual, namely Lucio's slurring of the Duke's reputation'. See 'Transgression and Surveillance', p. 83.

37 See Harry Berger, Jr, *The Absence of Grace: Sprezzatura and Suspicion in Two Renaissance Courtesy Books* (Stanford, Stanford University Press, 2000), pp. 12–13.

38 See *Measure for Measure*, note 58, p. 180.

39 Stephen Greenblatt, *Renaissance Self-Fashioning: From More to Shakespeare* (Chicago, University of Chicago Press, 1980), p. 13.

40 Alexander Leggatt, *Citizen Comedy in the Age of Shakespeare* (Toronto, University of Toronto Press, 1973), p. 120. See also G. K. Hunter, 'English Folly and Italian Vice: The Moral Landscape of John Marston', in *Dramatic Identities and Cultural Traditions* (Liverpool, Liverpool University Press, 1978), pp. 103–32.

41 Alfred Harbage, *Shakespeare and the Rival Traditions* (New York, Macmillan, 1952), pp. 196, 208.

42 See Mary Bly, *Queer Virgins and Virgin Queans on the Early Modern Stage* (Oxford, Oxford University Press, 2000).
43 See Cohen, 'From Mistress to Master', pp. 452ff, and Tennenhouse, 'Representing Power', p. 147.
44 The spontaneous renunciation, overheard by the disguised ruler, echoes that of Pietro in *The Malcontent* 4.4.119–30. For the possible dramatic and personal relations between the two authors, contemporaries at the Middle Temple, see Christopher Gordon Petter's prefatory material to his edition of Sharpham, pp. 33, 185–8, and 201–3.
45 See Susan Doran, *Monarchy and Matrimony: The Courtships of Elizabeth I* (London, Routledge, 1996).
46 Elizabeth Hanson, *Discovering the Subject*, p. 74.
47 Alan Sinfield, *Cultural Politics–Queer Reading* (London, Routledge, 1994), pp. 37–8. I thank Professor Sinfield for suggesting this reference.

13

'The three-fold world divided': *Julius Caesar* in the light of *Theologia Platonica*

CLAUDIA CORTI

As the most influential exponent of the Renaissance Neoplatonic philosophy of man, Marsilio Ficino belongs both to the history of the diverse fortunes of what has been called Ancient Wisdom, or Perennial Philosophy, and to the evolution of those ideas and attitudes which we term modern.[1] Under the patronage of the Medici family in Florence, he devoted himself to the task of reviving Platonism not only as a distinct philosophical doctrine but also as an intellectual movement with the same vitality and community of interests which characterized the 'prisca philosophia'. In the Platonic Academy in the villa at Careggi, Ficino had an opportunity to promote the study of Platonism among a congenial group of thinkers, artists, and literary men. Through his teaching and through his writings, particularly the *Theologia Platonica*, he was able to inspire a new attitude towards the Platonic material as a comprehensive framework within which the dominant ideas of Renaissance humanism might be expressed and its dominant problems resolved.

According to Ficino's own statements, the choice of Platonism as both source and structure for a philosophic system was determined by the harmony he believed existed between it and Christianity. What he wanted to demonstrate is that the ultimate end of all human desire and activity can only be 'boundless truth and goodness', that is, God. Hence, the central role played in Ficino's system by the soul: because it is the soul that must be able to reach this end. The assertion that the soul must be directed towards some end peculiar to it, and be able to attain that end, depends upon the theory of natural movement, or natural desire, i.e. *appetitus naturalis*; while the idea that this end of the soul can be attained only in the afterlife depends upon the unique nature of the soul, its universality and dual inclination.

The attainment of the appropriate end is guaranteed by the relationship between the creator, God, and the created being, either Man in his singularity or the World in its multiplicity. Just as the order and good of all human creatures is ultimately dependent on their creator, so the order of the physical universe is a necessary consequence of the highest 'Order' of divinity. No created thing could exist without contributing to the general order and good of the whole, and any natural desire unaccompanied by the strength to reach one's proper end would be worthless in this respect, and contrary to any naturalistic order.

The soul, being par excellence the human, unperfect thing that longs for a direction towards an end in which it can be perfected, must likewise possess an energy, a natural desire for an end identified with its good. And since this desire is platonically grounded in the nature of the desiring thing, the specification of the ultimate end and good of the soul becomes based upon the unique metaphysical position of the soul. In Ficino's hierarchy of Being, the soul is 'the third or middle essence' and 'the fountain of motion' as well. With its central position, the soul has an affinity with all things above and all things below it; because of its self-motion, the soul is able to move in either direction. Therefore, through the intellect the soul strives to *know* all things, while through the will, it strives to *enjoy* all things.

Like all other created things, the soul must be able to attain its own desired end; but, unlike all other creatures, the attainment of this end is not predetermined by its *natural* impulse. Indeed, the human soul is made up of a dual nature: with lower forms of nature, it shares the powers of generation, nutrition, and sensation, and these comprise the lower, or irrational soul. The higher soul includes both the power of intellectual contemplation – which Man shares with God *in primis* and with Angels *in secundis* – and the discursive, logocentric power of reason which is peculiar to Man alone. Accordingly, the soul itself has two tendencies: one associated with body and sense, and the other with mind and abstract speculation. Because human reason is free, it can either oppose the senses or be misled by them, but in either case can it attain its own end. Thanks to its rational soul, the essence of Man is more perfect than that of all other creatures, which are determined by motion and possess some desires, but, in being below God and the angels, it cannot achieve the final perfection corresponding to happiness. This paradox can be resolved either in the afterlife, when the soul satisfies one of its inclinations, that towards God, or in this life, with the satisfaction of its second inclination through the possession of its own body 'made everlasting'.

These, then, are, in brief, the distinguishing characteristics of Ficino's philosophy of Man that spread among European thinkers and literary men, and that one can find in an aesthetic form in many English writers of the Renaissance, with Shakespeare in the lead: not only did Shakespeare, like Spenser and Marlowe, for example, express his personal knowledge about Man in the terms of Ficino's philosophy, but he was actually influenced by Ficino's works, creating poetry and dramas which, no matter how secular they seem, nevertheless embody and communicate a very particular 'mythical' dimension, as well as a 'divine' or 'daemonic' one.

As is widely known, one of Ficino's correspondents in England had been John Colet. It was he who helped to promote Ficinio's teaching in England and it was not long before his books were to be found in all the country's greatest libraries. By the time Shakespeare was growing up, Ficino's philosophy was well known in academic and artistic circles, and had begun to inspire the poets and artists of the English Renaissance. The prestigious work of John Erskine Hankins, *Backgrounds of Shakespeare's Thought*,[2] has exhaustively demonstrated the presence of Ficino's works in Shakespeare's poetic and dramatic production, particularly in relation to the *Commentarium in Convivium*, the *Compendium in Timaeum*, and the *Theologia Platonica* (or *De immortalitate animorum*). Some years ago, I analysed the relevance of the theory of *spiritus phantasticus*, as transmitted by the *Theologia Platonica*, to the text of *Macbeth*.[3]

Ficino brought together the many threads of Ancient Wisdom or Perennial Philosophy; among them the Platonic teachings from the Greek and Roman worlds, the Egyptian writings of Hermes Trismegistus, and Christianity from the Middle East. At the heart of this tradition is the concept of the *unity*, the Platonic *One*, whom Ficino refers to as God.

Unity, or the Platonic One

All Ficino's thought oscillates between two poles: God and the Soul. Both the world at large and human existence in particular can make sense because the human soul is united with divinity, and because the link between God and Soul is given by Love, the supreme quality shared by Heaven and Earth. Unity is, then, the fundamental rule that governs any sort of relationship between the upper and the lower world, because the latter tends to overcome its own fragmentary disposition, searching to re-establish – on Platonic terms – a lost compactness with the primeval integrity previously guaranteed by its divine origin.

Thus, unity is the stable reference of all human existence, and it is unity that implies, in a special, unique way – being a heavenly category – both truth and goodness: 'Unitas, veritas, bonitas, idem sunt, et super ea nihil est' (2.1.73).[4] Nothing can be above unity, because the elementary, substantial (and lexematic as well) series One-True-Good is the qualification of God Himself: 'Unus ergo est Deus, et simplex, nempe una summa unitas, una summa veritas atque bonitas, Deus unus' (2.2.77). But although unity is the unique prerogative of divinity, none the less it is by it that earthly fragmentation is derived. God could not lose its own primary integrity in creating the material world, and so the created universe had to reveal its secondary, derived origin, in manifesting itself as *divided*. The whole universe appears in a graduation into five degrees: from the lowest to the utmost, Body, Quality, Soul, Angel, God: 'Proinde cum huc ascenderimus, hos quinque rerum omnium gradus, corporis videlicet molem, qualitatem, animam, angelum, Deum' (1.1.39). Of these five degrees of existence, only quality and soul concern Man. However, they concern mankind in its rational dimension only, separated as it is from the corporeal or vegetative one which is restricted to the body.

However, on the operative level (Ficino was, humanistically, very pragmatic and he could not envisage too complex a system), the theoretical, abstract five-part articulation of his *Sein* universe, is limited to the threefold structure that concerns the *Dasein* of his humanly oriented and resolved world of creation. So, he posits the hypostasis of a human universe divided up into three fields, respectively governed by Mind, Soul, and Body; in other words, by Reason, Perception, and Passion. The 'Angelic World of the Mind', as Ficino calls it, is the finest, and most abstract form of existence, while the most dense and physical is of course the corporeal Body of the World. Between them lies the Soul, where heaven/mind and earth/body come together in harmony. Soul is not – by definition – either body, or divisible like bodies – 'Anima non est corpus aut forma divisa in corpore' (6.3.238). In not being like the body, but surely in not being like the mind, the soul has a double nature, animate-inanimate: 'Neque corpus animatum est anima neque inanimatum' (6.5. 240); or, in pure Platonic terms, thick-thin: 'Neque crassum corpus est, neque subtile' (6.6.242).

Transferred to a pure existential level, the threefold nature of the human universe becomes active on – again – a triple stucture. Indeed, Ficino envisages a triple differentiation of the Soul into: 'anima sphaerarum' (related to the intellect); 'anima mundi' (related to emotions and passions); 'anima animalium' (related to physical drives and natural causes): 'Tres sunt animarum rationalium gradus. In primo est anima mundi, in secundo animae sphaerarum, in tertio animae animalium quae in sphaeris singulis continentur' (4.1.144).

In this conceptual scheme, the major role is played by the central section – *anima mundi* – because it concerns that typical human prerogative which is emotional and passional life, able to connect the high, 'pure' life of the angelic mind to the low, 'base' life of the bodily functions. Ficino does not disregard any section of this threefold structure; but he foregrounds the relevance of passions or human existence. Human nature is fundamentally composed – once more – of three elements, which are reason, localized in the brain, anger, localized in the heart, and desire, localized in the liver: 'Vitam agunt homines per rationem cerebro assignatam, per iram cordi, per concupiscentiam iecori attributam' (4.1.153). All these three elements are indispensable to the growth of the soul. None can be avoided, or rejected, because – as Ficino clearly explains – if a person would like to eliminate, or even more simply not to use, one of his rational/passionate functions, he would have to renounce his very human nature, as though expecting to live without breathing: 'Si quis nulla harum virium uti dicatur, ne spirabit quidem; si quis ratione sola, non amplius erit homo' (4.1.153). It is impossible to limit one's functions to the sole intellectual area, because no man has a mind separated from his body: 'Immo impossibile est animam corpori coniunctam sola incedere ratione' (4.1.153). At the same time, it is impossible to respond uniquely to passional drives because anger is always stimulated either by a rational justification or by an uncontrollable impulse of desire. Desire itself is on its own part oriented either by a 'depraved' reason, or by a choleric drive: 'Sola quoque irascendi vi uti nequit, quia haec semper vel rationi servit, vel cupiditati. Sola etiam cupiditate non potest, haec enim roboratur semper vel a ratione depravata, vel ab iracundia' (4.1.153).

So human nature too requires a subsidiary integrity, no less fundamental than the unity assigned to God. The human soul continuously searches for a primary connection between the angelic prerogatives of the mind and the physical assumptions of the body, ever trying to elevate itself towards the being's superior powers, and simultaneously projecting itself downward to its inferior qualities: 'Anima est medius rerum gradus atque omnes gradus tam superiores quam inferiores connectit in unum, dum ipsa et ad superos ascendit et descendit ad inferos' (3.2.137).

Ficino names this particular tendency of the soul to observe synchronically up and down, and to move upward and downward at its will, *essentia tertia*, that is intermediary essence, because 'it is both intermediary and the third one everywhere': 'ad omnia media est et undique tertia' (3.2.137). Its being 'the third one everywhere' – meaning the soul's capacity of going up and down the degrees of human nature – depends on its natural, original, essential mobility. The soul's mobility is what permits any sort of relation between the superior mind and the inferior body, determining a series of partial, momentary fusions which, taken all together, make up what Ficino calls, in a wonderful, both emotionally and sexually charged metaphor, 'copula mundi', the union of the three worlds:

> Illinc cum superioribus, hinc cum inferioribus [anima] convenit. Si cum utrisque convenit, appetit utraque. Quapropter naturali quodam instinctu ascendit ad supera, descendit ad infera. Et dum descendit, inferiora non deserit. Et dum descendit, sublimia non relinquit. Nam si alterutrum deserat, ad extremum alternum declinabit; neque vera erit ulterius mundi copula. (3.2.138)

Stabilty versus Mobility

The first and foremost differentation between divinity and humanity resides precisely in the opposition between stability, firmness, constancy – on the part of God, or even partially of the Angels – and mobility, change, fluctuancy, on the part of human nature and its most prominent feature, the soul. If God is static and unitary in his perfection, being the unmovable One, and if Angels, although not one, but a multitude, are none the less characterized by a substantial immobility (due to their proximity to God), the Soul – the human soul – is made up of a 'mobile multiplicity', because men and women are many, and each soul is, through its original constitution, attracted to movement: 'Super angelum est Deus, quoniam anima est mobilis multitudo, angelus multitudo immobilis, deus immobilis unitas' (1.6.67).

Just because the human soul stays in between, with respect to the high, stable mind, and low, movable body, it partakes of a double, ambiguous nature, both movable and unmovable, static and dynamic as well. Ontologically static, being determined by God, it is at the same time dynamic on both a practical and theoretical human level, its constitutive dimension being at the same time operative and conceptual: 'Anima rationalis per substantiam immobilis est; per operationem est mobilis; per virtutem est partim immobilis, partim mobilis' (1.4.56).

This is due to the three components of the human quality, that is substance (or ontologically determined status), power (or the complex of the soul's potentialities), and action (that is, its pragmatic/performative actualization): 'Tria in qualitate sunt: essentia, virtus et actio' (1.4.56). What gives an operative turn to the implicit dynamic potentiality of the soul, is motion: 'Haec omnia versantur in motu' (1.4.56). Proceeding further into *Theologia Platonica*, one can discover that natural, human mobility is also reversedly invested of the function of permitting vital movement to the heavenly universe, otherwise devoid of any substantial energetic impulse, and thus – one might construe – doomed to self-centred and narcissistic consumption: 'Quid tandem est istud per se mobile quod proxime caelum volvit? Nihil est aliud praeter animam. Haec enim est quae et per seipsam est mobilis, et talis motionis vestigium praestat corporibus' (4.1.158).

Ficino seems to be enthusiasic about the free, natural, undetermined, and intrinsically vitalistic attitude of the soul towards its own essentially dynamic being; as a matter of fact, he takes this as the exterior sign of an authentic and very exuberant inner life: 'Nonne motus, ut ita loquar, spontaneus, ubicumque est, vitae interioris est signum?' (4.1.159).

This dynamic quality of the soul, firstly due to its passionate component, also becomes operative in public, social and political affairs, because the *res publica* is a composite but harmonious organization of single elements which must search for unity and cohesion: 'Omne opus quod constat ex pluribus tunc est perfectissimum, quando ita ex suis membris conglutinatur, ut unum fiat undique, sibi constet et consonet, neque facile dissipetur' (3.2.138).

Such harmonious consonance of the state comes from the members' conviction that 'the parts should serve the whole, not the whole the parts'; it is not by chance that one of the principal signs of the soul's immortality, the special 'tertium signum', is the practice of government, or 'gubernationis industria' (13.3.223).

The neoplatonic structure of *Julius Caesar*

The political overtones of Ficino's epistemological commitment offer us an elementary access to Shakespeare's *Julius Caesar*, a drama where politics and philosophy are intertwined, as far as a typically Renaissance conception of humanity is at stake. Shakespeare's interest in humanity, the microcosm or 'little world' – as defined by Lear (*King Lear*, 3.1.10) – is always paralleled by an interest in the macrocosm or 'great world' – as defined by Portia (*The Merchant of Venice*, 1.2.2) – of which humanity, according to the Platonists, is the undiscussed model. The idea of such a resemblance or 'cosmic sympathy' seems to be ubiquitous in Shakespeare's plays, and contributes to their 'larger than life portrayals'.[5] The physical world seems to echo disasters in the world of humanity: this is a most evident theme in *Julius Caesar*, where, after Caesar's murder, 'men, wives, and children stare, cry out and run, / As it were doomsday' (3.1.96–7).[6] Doomsday, or the world's destruction, is seen by Ficino – particularly in the *Commentarium in Convivium* – as the return of ancient chaos, from which the universe was enhanced by the unique strength of Love; Love is the creative force whose impulse brings order and harmony out of the confusion of chaos. But Love is dual: if moderate, from it come temperance, tranquillity, and fertility; if immoderate, their opposites. The superabundance of love, in personal, political, and universal senses, which one can find in *Julius Caesar* offers a second elementary access to a reading of the play according to neoplatonic principles. Love is obsessively mentioned in this play, all characters speak about love: not only Antony, who is Love itself (as we shall see), but Brutus too, and Portia, and even the unloving Cassius; not to mention such an incidental character as the anonymous poet who briefly appears in Act 4.

The interconnection between politics and the Renaissance philosophy of man, no less active in Shakespeare than in Ficino, finds a symbolic manifestation in a phrase pronounced by Antony in 4.1.14, which acquires a paradigmatic relevance. The 'threefold world divided' mentioned by the character indicates, although in a political context (the division of the Roman empire in three parts, following the division of political leadership among the triumvirs), the intrusion of an exquisite humanistic philosophical concept, concerning the triple nature of humanity, and the triple configuration of the physical world as well, according to Ficino's tripartite structure of the created universe.

Finally, it is difficult to read *Julius Caesar* without noticing the clamorous occurrence of terms linked to the paradigm of motion-change, in opposition to the paradigm of stability-constancy and its related terms, suggesting the author's knowledge of one of Ficino's central conceptual implements. The absolute redundancy of the mobility/stability theme calls attention to a specific philosophical and epistemological ground: the one divulged by the humanistic conception of the mobile Soul.

We have sufficient elements to attempt an analysis of this Shakespearean text keeping an attentive eye on the *Theologia Platonica*.

The threefold world of *Julius Caesar*

Let us begin with a most elementary scheme, provided by the principal characters of the play, which can be devided into three classes, reminiscent of Ficino's triple division of human nature: mind–soul–body. In Shakespeare's application of the Ficinean outline, it is easy to evince that Caesar, the sun-god leader and would-be king, should stand for the mind, theoretically the stable God-angelic mind, but in being a human tripartite being he represents the human soul, although in its highest degree, that of *anima sphaerarum*. The *anima mundi*, the human soul depending on the mobility of ideas and the fluctuation of sensations and emotions, is embodied by the most problematic and contorted characters, namely – although in different ways – Brutus and Cassius. Antony, in his passionate psychological constitution, can be easily construed as the representative of *anima animalium*, the section of the soul chiefly affected by the impulses of physiological and biological life. At the same time Antony, whom the text often refers to as the only one who can love, is also the Neoplatonic and Ficinean *amor* as *primum mobile*, the agency of mobility between lover and beloved. Such is the inner philosophical content of Antony's passionate rhetoric, performed (no less for the audience than for the Roman populace) upon the corpse of Caesar, the privileged object of his love. As Ficino thought, when one loves, one's own soul leaves the body and transmigrates on to the body of the beloved. When the beloved is dead, when the body is no more to be loved, the soul of the lover is also dead, with nowhere to live.

A very peculiar comment can be made about Portia, who seems to partake of all three levels of the rational soul. Constant in her love to Brutus, she can be compared to an *anima sphaerarum*. Lively in her emotions, and sympathetic to her husband's feelings, always dynamic in her responses to situations, never passive or static, she is undoubtedly a model of the genuinely mobile *anima mundi*. Full of passions, up to the point of giving herself a physical wound as a narcissistic sacrifice, she represents the *anima animalium* at its human best.

The quality of the soul: reason versus passions

An analogous tripartite Ficinean scheme can be applied to the play's principal characters, as far as the Platonic opposition between reason and passions is concerned. We have already read Ficino's passage where a further threefold variant of Man's constitution is stated, and indicated as the inner division of Man's functions among reason (the function of the intellect), anger (the function of the heart), and desire (the function of the liver) (4.1.153). This combination of intellectual and passionate activity is what primarily distinguishes Man from God, and this combination is such that no living creature can give up one of its three components, without running the risk of altering or upsetting his human nature as a harmonious whole. A harmonious cohabitation of reason and the two fundamental passions makes Man *neuter*, that is well-balanced. But, when one of the three elements overruns another, we find peculiarities of behaviour, singular discrepancies and contradictions (the Platonic *discrasia*), and Man becomes a type, identified with a humour.

In *Julius Caesar*, it goes without saying that Brutus claims to represent reason; not only is he a philosopher, and more specifically a Stoic, more attracted by speculative thought than by action. The most intense scenes of the play dominated by his figure (before and after the conspiracy, before and after the murder, before and after the civil war) always show him lost after his own trains of thinking. These are the 'perturbations' and 'deviations' of the mind that, according to Ficino, affect reason in its relation to the will. Ficino is very clear about this: the most common conflict within the soul is that between reason and affections for control of the will. The will, itself an instrument of the pure and active power of the mind, finds itself compelled to use the emotions of the heart as a physical instrument. Thus, understanding and will are distinct 'offices' of the soul:

> Since Cassius first did whet me against Caesar,
> I have not slept.
> Between the acting of a dreadful thing
> And the first motion, all interim is
> Like a phantasma, or a hideous dream:
> The genius and the mortal instruments
> Are then in council; and the state of man,
> Like to a little kingdom, suffers then
> The nature of insurrection.
>
> (2.2.61–9)

'Acting' – to act – is used here in the sense of 'to enact', or 'to decide for action', meaning a decision, of course made by the will. The 'first motion' begins the actual execution of that decision, while the 'Genius' is the Platonic 'guardian spirit' which accompanies Man through his life and counsels him by means of his own intellect. The 'moral instruments' seem to be all the powers of the soul, except the intellect, or *sphaerarium anima*, and therefore they include the will, the affections, and all the internal senses, beyond judgement on one side, and the animal spirits on the other. It is significant that other possible physical 'instruments' are not included in the 'council' that represents the workings of Brutus' mind. It is significant, because the organs of the body and the external senses seem to be the 'instruments' of a lower order only.

It is also interesting to note the parallel between the human mind and a commonwealth or state, which one can detect in Brutus' comparison of himself to a 'little kingdom' threatened with insurrection, to which the 'council' of his internal senses is seeking a solution. Here we can find further proof of the interrelations between humanistic philosophy and Renaissance political doctrine, so active in this philosophical/political play.

But one could object that Brutus the thinker, the speculative mind and the moral spirit of this play, 'noble Brutus', as he is usually denominated, often proposes a melancholic strain of his psychological outlook, as Cassius first and Portia soon after acutely perceive. Says Cassius: 'You bear too stubborn and too strange a hand / Over your friends that loves you' (1.2.34–5). Portia notes: 'No, my Brutus; / You have some sick offence within your mind' (2.1.267–8). Brutus himself recognizes this: 'Vexed I am / Of late with passions of some difference, / Conceptions only proper to myself, / Which give some soil, perhaps, to my behaviours' (1.2.38–41). The link between passions and conceptions helps to understand the character, in whom predominant reason has slight leanings towards melancholy by force of outward occurrences (here, the conspiracy against Julius Caesar). This becomes easily explicable in the light of Ficino's system; having himself a melancholic temperament, he restated and developed the pseudo-Aristotelian doctrine that links the productive work of intellectuals and thinkers with melancholy and with the planet Saturn.[7] By turning away from external perceptions, and by an interior ascent towards pure contemplation, in the solitary meanders of the mind, the rational soul can arrive at a deep knowledge of the intelligible word and also at a firm ethical attitude which is the secure foundation of all opinions and actions (as Brutus' are).

The second principal human function, according to Ficino, is anger, or choler, located in the heart. In *Julius Caesar*, the angry or choleric temperament par excellence is of course Cassius: lean, greedy, swift, bold, wrathful, agile, as Timothy Bright – whose authoritative *Treatise of Melancholy* (1586) presents some of the explanations given by Ficino – would have classified him. The theme of Cassius' choler occupies a whole section of Brutus' indictment of him during the war, in the camp near Sardis: 'Must I give way and room to your rash choler?' (4.3.39); 'Go show your slaves how choleric you are' (4.3.43). Then he is accused by his relative and political partner as well of being under a 'testy humour' (4.3.6), and of having an 'ill-temper'd blood' (4.3.114). In Bright's reflexed and refined rearrangement of Ficino's theory, Cassius' temperament would be more precisely identified as the choleric-melancholic man, in whom the yellow bile of choler is mixed with the black bile of melancholy. Although he is described as 'choleric', he commits suicide because of an error in judgement caused by melancholy; his imagination causes him to think that the horsemen surrounding Titinius are the enemy, and in that mistaken belief he dies. As the messenger says, 'Mistrust of good success hath done this deed. / O hateful error, *melancholy*'s child, / Why dost thou show to the apt thoughts of men / The things that are not?' (5.3.66–9). It is exactly such a choleric-melancholic mixture of Cassius' disposition that so frightens Caesar: Cassius 'has a lean and hungry look', 'he is a great observer', 'he loves no plays', 'he hears no music', and, moreover, 'Seldom he smiles, and smiles in such a sort / As if he mock'd himself, and scorn'd his spirit / That could be mov'd to smile at any thing' (1.2.191–204). Cassius' leanness and greediness are characteristics of the angry man, while his deep thought, wakefulness, and extensive reading are characteristics of the melancholic man.

In Ficino's psychological system, the supreme function of the soul is love, physiologically determined by the chemical operations of the liver; and the individuals dominated by love are called 'sanguine'; Timothy Bright describes them as merry, sympathetic, talkative. In the Ficinean scheme of *Julius Caesar*, love is undoubtedly represented by Antony. Even the acid, choleric Cassius must admit that Antony bears to Caesar an 'ingrafted love' (2.1.184). The whole action of Act 3, turning around Caesar's corpse, is overflooded by the theme of love, unarrestingly enunciated by Antony, a theme that finds both a lexematic and semantic climax in his funeral oration. One can say that, in neoplatonic terms, Antony not only represents love but *is* Love itself. Indeed, he possesses all the characteristics of the sanguine man: cheerfulness and empathy with people, in being a 'gamesome' (1.2.27), one 'given to sports, to wildness, and much company' (2.1.188–9), a theatregoer (1.2.201), and one 'that revels long a-nights' (1.2.116). As far as his talkative and communicative capacities are concerned, they are ostensibly signified by the outstanding rhetoric of the funeral oration. Moreover love, in Ficino's terms, is synonymous with desire, or *concupiscentia*, and it is evident that Antony's way of loving owes much to passion and amatory disposition, as Brutus – rather scornfully – hints to Cassius, contrasting Antony's nature to his own: 'I am not gamesome: I do lack some part / Of that quick spirit that is in Antony' (1.2.27–8). It is worth noting that the lexeme '*quick* spirit' denounces the character's association with the paradigm of mobility, notoriously the quality of man in its *anima mundi* constituent.

Exactly according to mobility or changeableness, as opposed to stability or constancy, it becomes possible to pursue a further line of composition in *Julius Caesar* that can relate the play to an overall Ficinean structure.

Firmness versus change/motion

'I am constant as the northern star', says Caesar of himself (3.1.60). Not only he, as the actual political leader and the virtual moral guide of the community, but also the other characters who feel devoted to a 'higher' world insist that they are stable and motionless, just like Ficinean *animae sphaerarum*. Constancy, firmness, unchangeabilty, is perceived by all as the typical Roman virtue, which has rendered the Romans 'noble'; in such a guise 'noble Brutus' invites the conspirators to behave, 'with untir'd spirits and formal constancy' (2.1.227). Brutus himself is deeply convinced of the firmness of his disposition (1.2.164–5), but the most convinced of all is Caesar. When requested by Cimber to recall his banished brother home, Caesar answers his courteous adulations with a rigid denial of any possibility of being influenced, or *moved*: 'Be not fond, / To think that Caesar bears such rebel blood / That will be thaw'd from the true quality / With that which melteth foods' (3.1.39–42). And when Cimber's prayer is supported by Cassius, Caesar, the would-be monarch, the one assigned by Fate to the Angelic-Divine World, replies devoting a whole, intense speech to constancy; where I am graphically going to emphasize the clamorous co-occurrence of terms related to the paradigmatic opposition *stability/mobility*:

> I could be well *mov'd*, if I were as you;
> If I could pray *to move*, prayers would *move* me;
> But I am *constant* as the northern star,
> Of whose *true-fixed and resting quality*
> There is no fellow in the firmament.
> The skies are painted with unnumber'd sparks,
> They are all fire, and every one doth shine;
> But there's but one in all *doth hold his place*.
> So in the world: 'tis furnish'd well with men,
> And men are flesh and blood, and apprehensive;
> Yet in the number *I do know but one*
> *That unassaible holds on his rank,*
> *Unshak'd of motion*; and that I am he,
> Let me little show it, even in this,
> That I was *constant* Cimber should be banish'd,
> And *constant* do remain to keep him so.
>
> (3.1.58–73)

By the end of this inflamed speech, Caesar is certain not only of having placed himself in the Angelic World but also of establishing his own divinity, and, as the leader of Rome, his position as God's representative on earth. But, as we shall see, this is not the truth.

The truly constant character in this play is of course Portia. She is upset by her noble, reasonable husband's strange behaviour:

> Y'have ungently, Brutus,
> Stole from my bed; and yesterday at supper
> You suddenly arose, and walk'd about,
> Musing, and sighing, with your arms across;
> And when I ask'd you what the matter was,
> You star'd upon me with ungentle looks.

> I urg'd you farther; then you scratch'd your head,
> And too impatiently stamp'd with your foot;
> Yet I insisted, yet you answer'd not,
> But with an angry wafture of your hand
> Gave sign for me to leave you.
>
> (2.1.237–47)

Brutus' reduction from well-balanced to choleric-melancholic man cannot be understood by his wife, who knows nothing about the workings of his mind upon the conspiracy into which he is reluctant to be drawn. But having a strong, stable nature, not only is she Brutus' wife, but Cato's daughter too, Portia decides to regain her husband's confidence by physically exhibiting a firm, solid, impregnable – and therefore reliable – temperament. So, she proudly wounds herself by her own hand:

> I have made strong proof of my *constancy*,
> Giving myself a voluntary wound
> Here, in the thigh: can I bear that with patience,
> And not my husband's secrets?
>
> (2.1.299–302)

The same constancy that urges her to remain true to her husband conditions her actions towards the conspirators; sending young Lucius as a messanger to the Capitol, she appeals to the firmness of her own character not to betray her fear of failure: 'O *constancy*, be strong upon my side; / Set a huge mountain 'tween my heart and tongue!' (2.4.6–7).

Portia's voluntary wound is a precognition of her suicide, referred to Brutus during the civil war, and transmitted by him to Cassius:

> Impatient of my absence,
> And grief that young Octavius with Mark Antony
> Have made themselves so strong; for with her death
> That tidings came. With this she fell distract,
> And, her attendants absent, swallow'd fire.
>
> (4.3.151–5)

Portia's suicide is of great philosophical and epistemological relevance. On the one hand, it confirms the belonging of her soul to that *anima sphaerarun* which is so clearly indicated by her very constancy: because the rational soul longs to be reunited to its divine origin, which – Ficino says – can be completely attained only in the afterlife, when the soul itself loses the physical burden of its bodily linkages. On the other hand, her suicide, preceding that of her husband, alludes to one of Ficino's beliefs, chiefly expressed in the *Commentarium in Convivium*, but everywhere implied in the *Theologia Platonica*: in mutual love there is a double death and a double revivification within each other. As the soul of a lover is a mirror in which shines the image of the beloved, the lover's soul must desert its hearthly domicile to cross over into the body of the beloved. This seems to happen in the double, interrelated, and cross-referenced suicides of Portia and Brutus.

We have previously recalled how Brutus believes in his unmovable intellectual and psychological disposition. He disdainfully rejects being solicited either by his relative Cassius or by any of the conspirators (1.2.164–5), because, no less than Caesar, he too is 'noble', and therefore uninfluenceable and unchangeable. None the less Cassius – who knows very well the profundities of his friend's soul – thinks otherwise, convinced as he is that even Brutus can be brought to change and motion; musing within himself, as the typical choleric-melancholic man does, he states just that:

> Well, Brutus, thou art noble; yet I see
> Thy honourable mettle may be wrought
> From that it is disposed: therefore 'tis meet
> That noble minds keep ever with their likes;
> For who so firm that cannot be seduc'd?
>
> (1.2.305–9)

After all, mobility and changeability are – following the Platonists – inherent in human nature as well as in the material world. It is not surprising, then, that Man, no less than the physical universe, is subject to unpredictable variation: ' Are you not mov'd' – Casca asks the philosopher Cicero – 'when all the earth / Shakes like a thing unfirm?' (1.3.3–4). Leaving aside the mind, which aspires by its own constitution to the stableness guaranteed by its original angelic dimension, the human soul, both rational and corporeal, can live and explicate its own potentialities only if given the opportunities of moving, that is climbing or descending up and down its ontological configuration. Thus, all human creatures depend on movement; and movement, in a political as well as philosophical text such as *Julius Caesar* aspires to be, cannot but affect – both symbolically and pragmatically – all the agonists. It seems that everybody is subject to changeability. The senators may change their mind and withdraw the crown they now are likely to offer Caesar, as Decius warns Caesar himself to induce him to go to the Capitol (where the conspirators are waiting to kill him, 2.2.93–6). Also the conspirators, although their spirits are linked by a common aim, give proof of fickleness in deciding whether to co-opt Cicero or not in the conspiracy, and whether to kill Antony or not (2.1.141–91). In a very short time, successively influenced one by another, they continuosly change their opinions in a real vortex of contrasting judgements. Cassius oscillates in his faith in Epicureanism (5.1.77–9), and he is overtly accused by Brutus of inconsistency in his conduct of the war (4.2.6–9). Brutus himself, as we have already noticed, although he believes in his own firmness, becomes an easy prey to Cassius' seductive rhetoric. Later, during the civil war (Act 4), he has frequent moments of irresolution and at the end of the play finds himself compelled to admit that he has become less sure about the legitimacy of Caesar's murder (4.2.8–9).

In Caesar's case, although he continuously endeavours to establish the statutory firmness that everyone is likely to expect from God's representative on earth – on the grounds both of Neoplatonism and of Tudor political doctrine – Caesar himself is all but mentally and psychologically stable. We soon learn – instructed by the very attentive Cassius – that he has recently changed his mind about the reliability and practical incisiveness of premonitions and dreams: 'he is superstitious grown of late, / Quite from the main opinion he had once / Of fantasies, of dreams, and ceremonies', 2.1.195–7). Brutus can be easily induced by the performance of a sycophant to change his attitudes to people (2.1.207–8) and that is why Cassius is so confident in being able to adjust Caesar's nature to his own expectations: 'Let me work, / For I can give his humours the true bent' (2.1.209–10). Later on, Caesar's mental and psychological pliability is dramatically shown to the audience when he cannot make up his mind whether to go to the Capitol (where the Senate is waiting to give him the imperial crown) or stay indoors, following Calphurnia's admonitory vision of her husband's assassination. In this particular case (2.2.55–107), his Ficinean 'fluctuation of the mind' develops such a restless series of self-contradictions – 'I will not come' versus 'I will go' – that, were it not oriented to his own death, it would reach an almost comic anticlimax.

If it is true that all mutability derives from the passionate nature of *anima mundi*, as Cassius believes, 'all things change from their ordinance', he observes in 1.3.66, following almost verbatim the *Theologia Platonica* 4.1.153, one may easily expect that changeable and movable should be the pathemic character by excellence of this play, namely Antony, who is – as we have seen – the embodiment of Love itself. It appears as if exactly the excited vulnerability due to his hot-tempered psyche is what makes Brutus so perplexed about him, both before and after Caesar's death. We remember how Brutus disdains Antony's 'quick spirit' at the very beginning of the play (1.2.28): that quickness, which is primarily perceived by Brutus as a frivolous disposition, is also, on philosophic grounds, the typical essence of the human temperament in which love-desire wins over the other two contrasting powers of reason and anger, as Ficino clearly explains. Of the six possibilities in which the soul expresses its inner tendency to motion, Antony seems to represent the sixth and last, the one that owes much to desire, very little to anger, and little to reason: 'multum libidine, ira parum, paulum ratione' (4.1.154). After Caesar's assassination, Brutus is bewildered by Antony's vacillating intelligence of the regicide's purpose: 'But what compact mean you to have with us? / Will you be prick'd in number of our friends, / Or shall we on, and not depend on you?' (3.1.215–17). Brutus' nervousness may be easily understood, given Antony's straight acknowledgement of his own irresoluteness and emotional vulnerability: 'Therefore I took your hands, but was indeed / *Sway'd from the point* by looking down on Caesar' (3.1.218–19). While Antony is naturally subject to change of affections and consequently to conversion of ideas, he is all but reluctant to believe that he can, in his own turn, influence or alter others' psychological and intellectual positions. That is why Antony is so confident in his own power to move and direct his fellow Lepidus' behaviour in the management of the civil war, as he confidently announces to the third triumvir, Octavianus: 'It is a creature that I teach to fight, / To wind, to stop, to run directly on, / His *corporal motion govern'd by my spirit*' (4.1.31–3).

However, the most movable or changeable agent of all in this play is, from beginning to end, the Roman mob. When the play opens, Caesar has the support of the body of Rome, i.e. the working people; they wish to 'make holiday to see / Caesar, and to rejoice in his triumph' (1.1.30–1) over the sons of Pompey. But the body – Ficino warns us – is the most loosely moved of all the three worlds and the tribunes have little trouble in deflecting their celebrations and sending them back to work: 'See where their basest mettle be not mov'd', says tribune Flavius to his partner Marullus (1.1.61). Cassius' objection to allowing Antony's funeral oration on the corpse of Caesar is founded upon his fear that the agile ('quick' again) rhetorical dynamics of Caesar's pupil could influence the movable populace: 'Know you how much the people may be mov'd / By that which he will utter?' (3.1.234–5). Brutus feels that he must appease 'the multitude, besides themselves with fear' (3.1.180); Antony himself is well aware of the active, operative potentialities of his ceremonial talk about Caesar's generosity to the people, upon the people's psychological configuration, 'how I had mov'd them' (3.3.273); while the entire, long dramatic section made up of scenes 2 and 3 in Act 3 (during which Brutus first and Antony later offer to the people/audience their respective, opposite interpretations of Caesar's murder) is a perceptible demonstration of the mob's fickleness both on an emotional and on an intellectual level. As everyone knows, Shakespeare's mob responds emotionally – and pragmatically as well – to the succeding solicitations of the two orators: from 'Caesar has had great wrongs', enhanced by Brutus' oration, to the general revenge/mutiny cry urged by Antony's. The fluctuating passions of the multitude are carefully portrayed: the plebeians are swayed back and forth, finally reaching fever pitch and destroying without regard to guilt or innocence.

The dark side of the moon

The soul of Brutus speaks to him through his conscience, telling him that, for love of Caesar, he should not be his assassin. While Antony acts from love, the prime mover of the universe that should not be sacrificed at any cost, Brutus acts for the sole good of the state. Instead of remaining constant to his love towards his virtual father (*Et tu, Brute?*), he has been persuaded by the reasonable arguments of Cassius. This means that instead of following his own noble and stable mind, he has become susceptible to the movable world of nature, as Cassius is well aware. Shakespeare stresses the mutual love between Brutus and Cassius. In many respects, their friendship unites them – Platonically speaking – as One Being, with Cassius reflecting what the Platonists would have called the 'dark side' of Brutus' nature – and, by extension, the dark side of the Universe:

> Therefore, good Brutus, be prepar'd to hear;
> And since you know you cannot see yourself
> So well as by reflection, I, your glass,
> Will modestly discover to yourself
> That of yourself which you yet know not of.
>
> (1.2.65–9)

This darkness is Chaos, the unformed matter from which the whole threefold world arises, and is often described by the Platonists as 'the dark side of the moon'. In allowing himself to be moved into joining the conspiracy to murder Caesar, the nature of Brutus' soul falls into this primeval darkness, and the logocentric harmony of his *anima sphaerarum* disrupts into ontological disorder: almost before he has made up his mind to become the leader of the conspiracy, God, or the powers of Nature, display their anger in a series of unnatural events in the physical world. Casca arrives breathlessly to report of fire tempests, earthquakes, and strange happenings beyond the rule of nature: men with burning hands, lions strolling in the Capitol, men on fire walking up and down the streets of Rome (1.3.15–32). In neoplatonic terms, the physical world is a reflection of the Heavenly or Angelic World, and the lower, materialistic world should reflect the harmony of the ideal, higher one. Therefore, any agitation in this most movable, corporeal world, which includes the nature of Man and his emotions, needs to be tempered or reordered by the power of love, in accordance with divine or celestial disposal. This maturation may require some sort of cosmic upheaval. In political terms, before harmony can be restored in the state of Rome after Caesar's murder, the strife of war can be necessary so that the balance of nature may be rectified. Such a process begins with Antony's funeral oration, during which he enlists the powers of love to incite the mob into action against the conspirators, who, in turn, take up arms in civil war.

The rest of the play is not so much the revenge of Caesarism as the playing of the forces of nature to restore harmony on earth, or, more simply, to recover order in Rome. What really matters, in Ficinean terms is that the metaphysical heaven may once again be in concord with the physical world. The final symbolic act that brings this about is Brutus' death by his own hand. His entry into the Platonic 'dark side of the moon' – of his inner nature – is brief, and his quarrel with Cassius over the taking of bribes in 4.3 signifies his return to constitutional nobility. However, his part in the Renaissance of Rome requires the final sacrifice. Before there can be rebirth, there has to be death.

Brutus and his mirror image Cassius, respectively the light and dark sides of the moon (or of human nature), die of their own volition, not long after they hear of the voluntary death of Portia, the only firm, immovable person in the play and their truly constant soul.

Notes

1 The most exhaustive studies of Ficino's philosophy, and of its European influence, are notoriously those by Paul Oscar Kristeller, especially: *The Philosophy of Marsilio Ficino*, trans. Virginia Conant (New York, P. Smith, 1943); *Studies in Renaissance Thought and Letters* (Rome, Edizioni di Storia e Letteratura, 1956); *Renaissance Thought* (New York, Harper and Row, 1961), and *Renaissance Thought II* (New York, Harper and Row, 1965); *Renaissance Thought and Its Sources*, ed. M. Mooney (New York, Columbia University Press, 1979); *Renaissance Concepts of Man and Other Essays* (New York, Harper and Row, 1972). For the conceptualization of 'Perennial Philosophy' the classic study is Frances Amalia Yates, *Giordano Bruno and the Hermetic Tradition* (London, Routledge, 1964). Other relevant studies are: N. A. Robb, *Neoplatonism of the Italian Renaissance* (London, Octagon Books, 1935), R. Klibansky, E. Panofsky and F. Saxl, *Saturn and Melancholy* (London and New York, Basic Books, 1964), Robert Klein, *La Forme et l'intelligible* (Paris, Gallimard, 1970).
2 John Erskine Hankins, *Backgrounds of Shakespeare's Thought* (Hamden, Conn., Archon Books, 1978).
3 See Claudia Corti, *'Macbeth': la parola e l'immagine* (Pisa, ETS, 1983); see also Claudia Corti, ed., *Silenos: Erasmus in Elizabethan England* (Pisa, ETS, 1998).
4 All quotations are from *Théologie platonicienne de l'immortalité des âmes*, Texte critique établi et traduit par Raymond Marcel (Paris, Le Belles Lettres, 1964), 3 vols. The first number refers to the book, the second to the chapter, while the third number indicates the page in the three-volume edition.
5 See John Erskine Hankins, *Shakespeare's Derived Imagery* (New York, Octagon Books, 1967), p. 33.
6 Quotations are from the Arden Shakespeare edition, ed. T. S. Dorsch (London, Methuen, 1964).
7 The classic study for these themes is Klibanski, Panofsky and Saxl, *Saturn and Melancholy*.

Part IV

Stage and spectacle

14

Cleopatra's barge and Antony's body: Italian sources and English theatre

J. R. MULRYNE

In one of the most famous speeches in Shakespeare, Enobarbus describes Cleopatra's barge:

> ENOBARBUS I will tell you.
>   The barge she sat in, like a burnished throne
>   Burned on the water; the poop was beaten gold;
>   Purple the sails, and so perfumed that
>   The winds were love-sick with them; the oars were silver,
>   Which to the tune of flutes kept stroke, and made
>   The water which they beat to follow faster,
>   As amorous of their strokes. For her own person,
>   It beggared all descriptions: she did lie
>   In her pavilion, cloth-of-gold, of tissue,
>   O'erpicturing that Venus where we see
>   The fancy outwork nature. On each side her
>   Stood pretty dimpled boys, like smiling cupids,
>   With divers-coloured fans, whose wind did seem
>   To glow the delicate cheeks which they did cool,
>   And what they undid did.
> AGRIPPA   O, rare for Antony!
>
> (2.2.200–15)[1]

By looking at this passage, along with a few other moments in *Antony and Cleopatra*, this chapter considers a juncture in the broad transition of cultures with which this collection of essays is concerned. I shall necessarily describe a large arc, from the ancient Greek writer and thinker Plutarch, who became an honorary Roman by virtue of history and choice (and is thus implicated in the transition of cultures between Italy and England), through Florentine marriage-entertainments of the late 1580s, on to that vector of Italian culture in England, Inigo Jones. This exploration will come to rest in a brief discussion of the characteristic theatrical art of Shakespeare himself. One could begin with the improbability, to a modern eye and ear, of the comparison of barge to throne: 'The barge she sat in, like a burnished throne'. 'Barge' is the word Thomas North, Shakespeare's source, uses in his 1579 translation of a French version of Plutarch's *Life of Marcus Antonius*. In adopting the word, Shakespeare follows North in a detail of expressions, as he so frequently does. Modern commentators find the word awkward. That excellent scholar and critic David Bevington offers in his New Cambridge edition (1990) the view that 'The barge burning on the water is reminiscent ... of a representation of the battle of Actium in Edward Fairfax's translation of Tasso's *Jerusalem Delivered* under the English title *Godfrey of Bulloigne* (1600)'. He quotes Peter Dronke[2] for what he calls the 'intriguing parallel passage' in a late-twelfth-century epic of Troy by Joseph of Exeter, a passage that refers to Tyrian purple, a golden poop and rival winds swelling the sails. But Bevington and Dronke, and many other critics and commentators, may be looking in the wrong direction, with their attention directed towards books, or on occasion towards easel painting, rather than towards the performance world of Shakespeare's contemporaries. Bevington goes on to notice, it is true, that 'Barges in Shakespeare's day were often used for cerimonial official visits rather than for towing merchandise'. But even here, one might think, he does not quite identify the context which gives meaning to Enobarbus' lines. Shakespeare's audience, and their European contemporaries, had in their mind's eye not just official visits but those lavish occasions of pageantry with which the whole of Europe celebrated festivals events. The occasions for these events might be of several kinds: dynastic marriages or the birth of royal heirs, the entry of dukes and princes into capital cities, royal christenings or funerals. When such events took to the water, as they often did, the semi-technical word for the floating scenic element in which grandees played mythological persons was 'barge' (Italian *barca*). Cleopatra's barge on the Cydnus, one might propose, is a visual reminiscence of such pageants, on the Thames or the Arno or the other rivers of Europe, on those occasions when aristocracy sought to dazzle elite and popular audiences by taking on the appearance of gods.

Bevington edges close to identifying the appropriate visual reference for the barge when he includes in a footnote, illustrates, and fleetingly mentions in his Introduction, the so-called 'progress entertainment' which took place in the presence of Queen Elizabeth at Elvetham in Hampshire in September, 1591. This was the occasion when the Queen, visiting the Earl of Hertford, observed with her entourage and local bystanders a highly ambitious water-pageant presented for her entertainment on a crescent-shaped artificial lake. The Queen, sitting under an elaborate canopy of green satin, watched and responded while Nereus, five Tritons, and assorted sea creatures approached and addressed her. A pinnace carrying three Virgins, a Nymph of the Sea, and various musical attendants accompanied Nereus and the others, and was followed by two further boats and an assortment of Sea-gods, wading breast-high in the water. Much else took place at other points in the lake.[3] The 'iconography of royal pageants' as Bevington calls the symbolism of such occasions, provides an appropriate matrix for commentary on Cleopatra's barge. In order to widen the discussion, it could be suggested that Elvetham represents a facet of the transition of cultures from Italy to England. Interpretation of Enobarbus' speech is most fruitfully undertaken in a European, not only an English, context. Florence and the Arno offer just as apt cultural references as Elvetham and its lake.[4]

In considering the visual allusions to the Italian water-pageants and the cultural referents, it is obvious at first reading that the accent is on ostentation. The poop, that is to say the ship's stern (or a deck above the stern), 'was beaten gold', an arrangement highly impractical but undoubtedly eye-catching. Both the poop and the prow of the pageant-boat at Elvetham were manned, with an allegorical person in each, the prow being occupied by Neaera and the poop by an unidentifiable male. In this arrangement, the significant feature is the prow, where Neaera is about to present Elizabeth, according to the accompanying text, with a 'sea-jewell' or 'fanne'. The peculiar profile of the typical Italian pageant-ship or *barca* of the period, by contrast (and of its land-based parallel), is all poop and no prow. In the leading ship of the *Argonautica*, staged on the river Arno in November 1608, for example, a huge statue of Pallas Athena, goddess of war, presides on the poop deck above the seated Jason (played by Prince Cosimo in full armour). In another, Vulcan presides, in another Cupid, in another Scylla, and so on, all positioned on the poop. One engraving, for a ship which in the event was not realized, shows Maria Magdalena, Archduchess of Austria, seated on the poop under a canopied baldachino, with the symbols of rule of the Habsburgs and of Florence displayed around her.[5]

In Shakespeare's play, Enobarbus does not specify that Cleopatra's 'pavilion', like Maria Magdalena's baldachino, occupied the poop deck, even if he mentions these as the two prominent features of the 'barge'. But perhaps Shakespeare saw in his mind's eye just such a poop-dominated vessel as the pageanteers of Florence and elsewhere favoured. In any case, he saw a sumptuous spectacle, of the kind associated with the grander festivals of the Italian renaissance and baroque. The sails of Cleopatra's barge were purple, the blood-red of Elizabethan usage, signifying royalty, rather than the more acidulous colour of modern use. The oars were silver, another spectacular if highly impractical piece of technology, if the vessel were used for anything other than display. And so it goes on, sumptuous, dazzling and wholly without utility. Such a description may conjure up for the modern reader the Venetian *bucentoro*, the state barge from which the doge confirmed each Ascension Day the wedding of his city with the sea. The association is not wholly inappropriate.

Amidst all this splendour, Cleopatra lies nestled in her pavilion, an erotic focus for the extravagant display. A 'pavilion' seems an unusual term for a feature of the barge, taking its origin, as it does, from the ornate tents of medieval warfare. For pageantry it is entirely fitting, like the pavilions that covered Queen Elizabeth during her excursions on the Thames, or were held over her head by courtiers during processions on land – or like the *baldachino* under which Maria Magdalena sat. Plutarch in his *Life of Antony*, from which both North's translation and Shakespeare's play ultimately derive, uses for Cleopatra's covering the fairly commonplace Greek word *skias*, meaning anything that offers shade, a canopy. North, and with him Shakespeare, uses the more technical pageantry term 'pavilion'. Nor is it an ordinary pavilion, but one of exactly specified luxury: cloth of gold, of tissue. Plutarch wrote *chrusopastoi*, sprinkled with gold, or shot with gold. North and Shakespeare intensify Plutarch's vision by evoking the Elizabethan textile trade in its most luxurious form. 'Cloth of gold' is silk interwoven with gold threads; 'tissue' means that the threads are twisted, rather than plain, 'being thus of doubly rich texture'.[6] If one sees in one's inner eye the costume and stage designs of Buontalenti or Carracci for the Florentine *intermedi*, or those of Inigo Jones for the Jacobean masque, the mental picture conjured up is not far out of the way. Of course, this Venus of the river eroticizes everything around her, from lovesick winds to amorous water. Her attendant 'pretty dimpled boys, like smiling Cupids' are on the one hand physically attractive children, and on the other naked Cupids, thus exemplifying the borderline status of the performers of Renaissance pageantry, on the cusp between mythology and real persons. Bevington offers us as possible analogy for this Cleopatra-Venus 'a famous picture by Apelles, "Venus Anadyomene", or Venus Rising from the Sea', a subject, as he notes, painted in the Renaissance by Botticelli. Renaissance fascination with mythologizing is the right context, but we do not need to go to easel painting in search of an appropriate analogy. The figures in Shakespeare's lines are figures from a pageant or a masque, or from a waterborne procession, with the lesser deities disposed around the recumbent figure of the goddess to express her seductive power.

I have referred once or twice to the 'onelie begetter' of the Enobarbus passage, the ancient historian, or historian-biographer, Plutarch. It is worth spending a few moments reflecting on the transition of cultures from Plutarch's Roman Empire to the England of Shakespeare and Sir Thomas North, Plutarch's Elizabethan translator, before returning to comment again on Enobarbus. Plutarch's artistry, it is evident, deeply impressed Shakespeare. Indeed, as T. J. B. Spencer puts it, 'The reading of North was rather a serious thing for a busy man of the theatre, probably his most serious experience of the bookish kind.'[7] The acknowledgement of influence is right, yet the terms could be misleading. Shakespeare's debt to Plutarch is not only 'of the bookish kind', but a tribute to the vividly theatrical qualities of the ancient author's rendering of history.

Even in the merely descriptive mode of the barge passage, Shakespeare's indebtedness to Plutarch, and his divergence from him, are evident. Plutarch's mind was Greek, not Roman.[8] He explicitly disapproved of what he considered Roman lack of taste. Though he served the Roman state, he exhorted his readers to shun Roman politics and serve instead their native cities, within the far-flung Roman Empire. Perhaps the most congenial post he occupied was priest of the Delphic Oracle, an office that stemmed from and led to an immense knowledge of Delphic antiquities. What all this means, to offer an indefensible generalization, is that Plutarch's depiction of Cleopatra's barge displays Greek pleasure in sensory experience and extravagant display, in contrast to Rome's fastidious unease. This rift in sensibility is an issue central to the Cleopatra/Antony story, and one with which Shakespeare had to engage. Plutarch may have been drawn to Cleopatra because, like him, she was a Greek, in her case from Macedonia. His treatment of Antony may have been softened by the historic Antony's philhellenism. These tastes and prejudices result in a biography of the two main characters fed more by sympathy than recrimination, especially in the case of Cleopatra, whose treatment in Plutarch's sources had been uniformly hostile. In the passage we are focusing here, Plutarch delights in the scene's vivid colouring, allowing himself a degree of elaboration characteristic of no Roman writer, with the possible exception of Ovid. It is easiest to see this in the latter half of the passage, following on from the Shakespearean lines already quoted. The Plutarchan passage runs as follows:

> Her ladies and gentlewomen also, the fairest of them, were apparelled and at tired like the nymphs Nereides (which are the mermaids of the waters) and like the Graces, some steering the helm, others tending the tackle and ropes of the barge, out of the which there came a wonderful passing sweet savour of perfumes, that perfumed the wharf's side, pestered with innumerable multitudes of people. Some of them followed the barge all alongst the river's side; others also ran out of the city to see her coming in; so that in the end there ran such multitudes of people one after another to see her that Antonius was left post-alone in the market-place in his imperial seat to give audience. And there went a rumour in the people's mouths that the goddess Venus was come to play with the god Bacchus, for the general good of all Asia. (*Shakespeare's Plutarch*, p. 201)

The parallel Shakespearean passage runs like this:

> Her gentlewomen, like the Nereides,
> So many mermaids, tended her i'th'eyes,
> And made their bends adornings. At the helm
> A seeming mermaid steers. The silken tackle
> Swell with the touches of those flower-soft hands,
> That rarely frame the office. From the barge

> A strange invisible perfume hits the sense
> Of the adjacent wharfs. The city cast
> Her people out upon her; and Antony,
> Enthroned i'th'market-place, did sit alone,
> Whistling to th'air, which, but for vacancy,
> Had gone to gaze on Cleopatra, too,
> And made a gap in nature.
>
> (2.2.216–28)

There is close indebtedness here, but the divergences are, for present purposes, more telling. Plutarch brings his passage to a close with a reference to the mystery religions, with Antony and Cleopatra in the form of Greek and Roman gods (Plutarch says Aphrodite and Dionysus, North translates Venus and Bacchus) standing in as agents of cultural transformation on a grand scale ('for the general good of all Asia' – Plutarch's phrase is even barer: *ep' agathoi tes Asias*). Shakespeare dispenses with such superstition, substituting what reads like a thorem from an early scientific text ('but for vacancy ... made a gap in nature'). Moreover, a cultural *translatio studii* takes place in the imagining of the event. Where Plutarch maintains his characteristic stance of documentary observer, Shakespeare elaborates the observations into Mannerist art. Plutarch serves, that is, as the inspiration for a distinctively Renaissance style. In Shakespeare's account, *all* the gentlewomen, not just the fairest of them, are assimilated to the condition of Nereides, becoming, we are told, 'so many mermaids'. Mermaids serve as iconography for an ambiguous land-and-water existence that signified in Renaissance performances (in Florence, Paris, or London) a mysterious spiritual knowledge. In this amplification, one could say mistranslation, of Plutarch, Shakespeare was anticipated by North. Plutarch refers to the Nereides, not to mermaids. The Nereides were in Roman mythology human in form, rather than, like mermaids, half human, half fish. In this fashion, North and Shakespeare substitute for Plutarch's Greek sensibility the visual and symbolic vocabulary of the late Renaissance, using an idiom perfectly familiar to makers of pageants and writers of masques.

The transforming tendency evident in the treatment of the Nereides is more widely distributed. In Shakespeare account, a strange animation seizes on the ship-borne tableau, with the mermaids' gestures of subservience ('bends') becoming a form of clothing for their mistress ('adornings'). The reciprocal, indeed inseparable, energy that flows between physical posture, costume, and iconographic significance exactly evokes the practices and the ideals of baroque performance art. A line or so later, the ship's rigging, transformed from the rough textures of rope to the luxury of silk, responds to the caresses of delicate hands, as though sensate ('Swell with the touches of those flower-soft hands'). Perhaps it is a step too far to discern in this animated tableau the impress of that eroticized delight in luxury which Lisa Jardine identifies as a distinguishing mark of Renaissance art.[9] Even if this is to generalize too boldly, the characteristic notes are present, and the transformation is vividly evident from Plutarch's observant if elaborated idiom to the etherealizing wish-fulfilment of the baroque. We cannot be far wrong if we find analogies in Shakespeare, if not in North, with the notoriously expensive, richly ornamented spectacles of the European courts, delighting as they do in every aspect of ostentation, luxury, and erotic suggestion. The animated ensemble of Cleopatra's barge is directly reminiscent of baroque self-aggrandizement as it is figured, for example, in the *tableaux vivants* of Florentine entertainments of the 1580s.

It may be appropriate to draw attention to one of those Florentine occasions, on or by the Arno, which may serve as Italian analogue for Shakespeare's treatment of Cleopatra on the Cydnus. Medici Florence was much given to festivals, especially festivals in celebration of dynastic marriage. The most splendid of these was the festival marking the 1589 marriage of Ferdinand de' Medici and Christina of Lorraine. The marriage was important for political reasons. By choosing a bride from France, Ferdinand was marking a decisive shift in Medici policy towards Spain, still a great European power, but now on the defensive (especially in view of the humiliation of the Armada at the hands of the English in the previous year). But there were other objectives in view beyond Euro-politics in mounting the magnificent wedding entertainments. In the words of James M. Saslow, whose book represents a landmark in festival studies, Ferdinand used 'elaborate public and courtly spectacles ... as a way to sacralise the monarchy and the persons of the ruling family by surrounding them with an aura of mystery and pomp'.[10] This was a practice by no means confined to Florence. Rather, as Roy Strong and others have shown, it was Europe-wide, from Hungary and Poland–Lithuania in the east to Spain, France, Germany, the Netherlands, Britain, and the Scandinavian countries in the west. In the absence of efficient forces of law and order, kingly and ducal authority in the late sixteenth century was largely a matter of *performance*, a focus in the equations of politics which both invited, and exercised pressure on, the stage performance of history. In the case of Florence, there lurked always in the background the unnerving presence of the most notorious Florentine of the century, practitioner and critic at once. As Saslow remarks, 'Since Machiavelli, Italian political theorists had held that the prince's essential art is "looking the part" – that is, playing the public role of statecraft with conviction and splendour' (p. 15). Ferdinand de' Medici, in staging the 1589 festival, was doing just that. Remarkably, for a few days, and longer in the memory, Florence became a stage, with Ferdinand through the artistic achievements of his creative team achieving what Saslow calls 'the theatricalization of the whole spatial environment' of the city (p. 15): the streets, the palaces, the churches, the river Arno.

Two elements of the festival seem especially germane in providing a cultural matrix in which to read aspects of *Antony and Cleopatra*. The lesser, for reasons which will become clear, is the *naumachia*, a mock sea-battle between Christians and Turks staged (with difficulty) in the courtyard of the Palazzo Pitti. One or two details from Saslow's accounts vividly evoke the occasion:

> The court was covered with a single huge awning in red cloth, suspended on ropes held with pulleys ... The whole arena was illuminated by hundreds of lamps and torches, both freestanding and fixed to the walls. Technologically, the most complex task was hydraulic: flooding the court while holding the water back from the seating under the arcade. The 'ocean' was pumped in via the grotto piping, and two river gods were modeled in clay ... with working spouts ... Barricades were erected within each of the 18 ground-floor arches, topped by balustrades ... built of a double wall of used planks ... filled with fuller's earth, an absorbent powder. (p. 96)

Cavillino, one of the chroniclers of the event, describes the noise, smoke, and commotion of the battle itself. Saslow comments:

> Fireworks and artillery bombardments resulted in much splashing about of wounded or panicked fighters in what must have been a very crowded courtyard; the defenders realistically cried out in Turkish, no doubt familiar to sailors. As always in this conventionalized combat, the Christian assailants were victorious, storming the citadel and raising their ensign. (p. 168)

It is not difficult to imagine the chaos. It is clear from Orazio Scarabelli's etching that everything must have been pretty much of a shambles, as with a real naval battle, at Actium (the naval battle in *Antony and Cleopatra*), for example, or at the defeat of the Armada. In any case, the Florentine mock battle, like the real battles, stands aesthetically at a great distance from the serene showmanship of other elements of the Florentine celebrations – or of Cleopatra in her barge. No doubt the aim of the event's organizers was ceremonial order, or a sub-variety of it, confirming in pageantry the superiority of Christian to Turk and honouring the commitments of politics and belief of the house of Medici. The reality must have been very different. The discrepancy between art and actuality represents an aesthetic concern of *Antony and Cleopatra*.

The more obvious parallel to the imaginative world of Cleopatra's barge comes in the form of the *intermedi* performed for the Florentine wedding celebrations at the Uffizi Theatre during the intervals of Girolamo Bargagli's play *La pellegrina*. *Intermedi* originated from the brief musical tableaux offered in the intervals of prose comedies, but by the date of the Uffizi performance they had begun to take over as the major attractions of these events. Six were performed, each displaying notable musical and performance skills. For the appearance of the shows, in the briefest form, we might turn to Intermedio 5, *Arion and the Dolphin*:

Rocky cliffs frame an undulating sea over which dolphins pull a shell that bears Amphitrite, queen of the ocean, accompanied by tritons and nereids; they pronounce a marital blessing and predict for the royal pair 'such a brilliant progeny that it will adorn the earth from pole to pole.' The sea creatures vanish as a giant galley approaches, bearing several dozen sailors and the poet-singer Arion, whose legendary musical prowess had been invoked earlier by the Pierides. The ship, bobbing realistically, turns and strikes its sails in reverence to the grand duke. Arion, who has been threatened with death by the sailors, covetous of his treasure, sings a farewell lament, then escapes their drawn knives by jumping overboard. The crew, presuming him drowned, merrily divide up the spoils, but Arion, saved by a dolphin who admires his song, is borne safely to shore. (pp. 32–3)[11]

It is not necessary to point out the parallels with Cleopatra's barge. Amphitrite's shell and her entourage of tritons and nereids recall Cleopatra, her barge and her attendants. If Amphitrite, in contrast to the serene Cleopatra, seems distinctly insecure in the pen-and-brown-ink sketch after Buontalenti, that may be interpreted as no more than a warning against going to sea in a shell. There is no Arion in *Antony and Cleopatra*, but Arion's power of taming the sea is recollected in the peculiar enchanted and erotic harmony of sea and oars in Shakespeare: 'the oars were silver, / Which to the tune of flutes kept stroke, and made / The water which they beat to follow faster, / As amorous of their strokes' (2.2.204–7). The complete series of *intermedi*, in fact, anticipate and elaborate Shakespeare in celebrating music's power, from *musica mundana*, the 'music of the spheres' to *musica humana*, music's effect on humans and gods.

When we turn to costumes, we find in the Florentine entertainments illustrative parallels for the luxury that attaches to Shakespeare's Cleopatra. Drawings and written records attest the elaboration and costliness of the fabrics (at least those of the outer garments) and the expensive fantasy of the tailoring. The ethereal effects aimed at are explained by Saslow: 'skirts and bodices were covered in materials – silk, satin, taffeta, and *ermisino* (sarsanet, a light silk) – that were thinner and more fragile than street wear'. He goes on: 'The single largest acquisition was some 1,200 *braccia* of *velo di Bologna*, a Bolognese import used for the thin, gauzy veils of various colors that hang from the headdresses of most female characters.' These veils made possible some delightful theatrical effects because they 'would ripple elegantly when the loose hands of the veils were held in the hands of dancing or gesturing characters'. Referring to the floor-length veils of the hamadryads in Intermedio 1, the chronicler Sebastiano Rossi says that they 'swelling [*gonfiando*] with each puff of breeze, made that noble and rich costume more magnificently embellished' (p. 61). The reminiscence (for us) of the swelling silken tackle of Cleopatra's barge is mere chance, but the aesthetic preferences which the *intermedi* and Enobarbus express dovetail perfectly. Shakespeare's winds, love-sick with the barge's purple sails, gesture towards that same wished-for harmony between an eroticized heaven and earth as the writers and composers of the *intermedi* envisaged. A further intriguing parallel arises when Harmony in the *intermedi* addresses the married couple, Ferdinand and Christine, as 'the new Minerva and mighty Hercules', thus envisaging a marriage of female wisdom and male heroic action. We shall return to the association of deities with the play's protagonists. Cleopatra and Antony are in no sense married, and Antony, instead of sitting in the barge by his bride, or at the least receiving her on land, was (in North's vivid phrase) 'left post-alone in the market-place' (*Shakespeare's Plutarch*, p. 201). Perhaps the alert observer of Shakespeare's play would perceive in Antony's solitariness the ironic inversion of a standard wedding trope. In any case he (or she) would recognize the festival idiom which (at this point) the play shares with the *intermedi*.

The leading vector for the introduction of Florentine culture, or at any rate festival culture, into England in Shakespeare's day was the architect and stage designer Inigo Jones. A remark by James Saslow may help to trace the political path that led from the Arno to the Thames. 'It was during Ferdinando's [Ferdinand de Medici's] reign that the theory of divine right entered Florentine discourse. Its objective was to create legitimacy by assimilating the ruler to a sacred realm of meaning and fixed authority outside space and time' (p. 34). As is well known, the virtuoso of absolutist thought among English political figures was James VI and I, at whose court, and the courts of his wife Anne and son Henry, Inigo Jones served. It will seem scarcely surprising, then, that the art of James's court, especially its masques, offers marked similarities to the *intermedi* of Ferdinand's court in Florence. The good political relations between Ferdinand and England (Ferdinand died in 1609, two or three years after the composition of *Antony and Cleopatra*), and the marked influence Florence exercised on English art and manners in the early seventeenth century, especially at the court of Henry, Prince of Wales, will have promoted the parallel development of masque and *intermedi* culture in Florence and London.[12]

However that may be, it requires no deep scholarship to perceive the creative influence Florentine court theatre exercised on the work of Inigo Jones. John Peacock has traced every thread of the connection in his splendid and learned book, *The Stage Designs of Inigo Jones: The European Context*.[13] It is true, as Peacock points out, that Jones was most decisively influenced by Florence during the 1630s, more than twenty years after the first performance of *Antony and Cleopatra*, especially by the work of Berbardo Buontalenti, who, in Peacock's words, 'had made the Medici court theatre the wonder of Europe' (p. 188), and even more by his successor Giulio Parigi. Yet the broad influence of Florentine stage and costume design is evident, to take a pertinent example, in the costume for the Naiad, a close relative of the Nereid (my Latin dictionary calls one a water nymph and the other a sea nymph), which Jones drew for *Tethys' Festival* in 1610. The drawings derives from an engraving of Temperance prepared by Marcantonio, after Raphael. As Peacock notes, 'Jones has thinned and elongated Raphael's sturdy, sculptural figure, transposing her into a mannerist key' (p. 125). We have met just such etherealizing tendencies in the 1589 *intermedi*. Jones is an eclectic artist, drawing on a variety of traditions for his costume and scenic designs, but it would not be out of order to say that his main sources are Italian, if not purely Florentine. The similarities between Buontalenti's work and Jones's may be seen by comparing Buontalenti's Siren of the Eighth Sphere with Jones's Naiad. In any case, the major point must be that Shakespeare's mannerist portrait of Cleopatra (in her barge that is) belongs recognizably to the same pictorial tradition as the masque figures drawn and designed by Jones.

This claim needs a little more substance through reference to one or other of the Jones-designed masques of the time of *Antony and Cleopatra*. The *Annals of English Drama* dates the play 1606–8. Bevington thinks 'the likeliest date for *Antony and Cleopatra* is some time in 1606, probably late in the year' (p. 2). It was a busy period for Jones and the court masque, following *The Masque of Blackness* of January 1605, which gained Queen Anne notoriety and some disapproval (she appeared made up as a blackamoor). A year later the great spectacular masque of *Hymenaei* was performed, in which Ben Jonson laid out the classical precedents for contemporary wedding lore. The fact that the masque embarrassingly honoured, with Jonson's learning, and with Inigo Jones's brilliant designs, an aristocratic marriage that turned out to be anything but ideal, is no more than a reminder of the fragile relationship between vision and actuality that can be read as one of the subtexts of Shakespeare's play. In 1608 came *The Masque of Beauty* (10 January), a successor for *Blackness*, and *The Masque at Lord Haddington's Marriage* (9 February), followed in 1609 by *The Masque of Queens* (2 February). This was the heyday of brilliant and expensive masque performance, enjoying the backing of Queen Anne and the young Prince Henry. Any of these shows (or other masques of the time) would serve to make the points we want, but it is perhaps worth referring to *The Masque of Beauty*, as a lesser-known piece close in date to the first performance of Shakespeare's play. The Venetian Ambassador, Zorzi Giustiniani, wrote home telling us almost all we need to know:

> I must just touch on the splendour of the spectacle, which was worthy of her Majesty's greatness. The apparatus and the cunning of the stage machinery was a miracle, the abundance and beauty of the lights immense, the music and the dance most sumptuous. But what beggared all else and possibly exceeded the public expectation was the wealth of pearls and jewels that adorned the Queen and her ladies, so abundant and splendid that in everyone's opinion no other court could have displayed such pomp and riches. So well composed and ordered was it all that it is evident the mind of her Majesty, the authoress of the whole, is

gifted no less highly than her person. She reaped universal applause, and the King constantly showed his approval. At the close of the ceremony he said to me that he intended this function to consecrate the birth of the Great Hall [i.e. the new Banquetting House in Whitehall] which his predecessors had left him built merely in wood, but which he had converted into stone.[14]

It is handsome praise, coming, if not from a Florentine, then from a Venetian, one who must have known the splendour of civic processions and spectacles in his own city, and in all probability those of Florence too.

The most remarkable sentence in the despatch is the one attributing the invention of the whole spectacle to the Queen. Jonson's authorship and Jones's designs go for nothing, not to mention the professionals who composed the music and choreographed the dances. Surely a sophisticated court-commentator such as Giustiniani must have known the real facts? Yet so intimately were these spectacles identified with the life of the court that it must have seemed appropriate, or at least not inappropriate, to credit them in their entirety to the royal person who commissioned them and supported them financially (Giustiniani says elsewhere that the masque was at the Queen's own charges).[15] The Queen's masques were occasions of self-display, like Cleopatra's pageant-barge. She initiated them and she appeared in them.

Stephen Orgel has written that 'Masques were essential to the life of the Renaissance court; their allegories gave a higher meaning to the realities of politics and power, their idealized fictions created heroic roles for the leaders of society'.[16] In the present masque, the Queen and her ladies (almost all of them Catholics, as the French diplomat La Boderie interestingly notes) appeared on an island 'floting on a calme water',[17] with the sixteen ladies personating various aspects of Beauty, each of them seated on 'a seate of state, call'd the throne of beautie' (p. 186). Each lady was splendidly dressed, in a fashion reminiscent of the Florentine figures we have already noted. The steps of the throne were 'couered with a multitude of Cupids (chosen out of the best, and most ingenuous youth of the Kingdome, noble, and others) that were the *Torch-bearers*; and all armed, with *Bowes, Quiuers, Wings*, and other *Ensignes of loue*' (p. 188). These are not the 'pretty dimpled boys, like smiling Cupids' who fanned Cleopatra's cheeks and made them glow, but they belong to the same Renaissance mode of fanciful classicism. Jonson, and Jones with him, together with other masque writers and designers, were responsible for a specific transition of cultures between Italy and England, in this masque and elsewhere. Shakespeare cannot have been unaware of what they were doing, given that he was a member of the acting company (the King's Men) who took the speaking roles in these very performances. His Cleopatra, or rather her barge-pageant, transfers to the public stage the aesthetic values and preferences of the masque culture of his time.

In a stimulating article, Harold Fisch wrote: 'Shakespeare is dealing *directly* in this play with a pair of characters who lay claim to mythological status and who at every turn adopt the posture of figures in a fertility ritual'.[18] 'The first such myth pattern', he continues, 'is that concerned with the names of Mars and Venus. From the first scene the personalities of Antony and Cleopatra are mythologically inflated and presented in terms of the conjunction of the god of war and the goddess of love' (p. 59). Fisch points to the explicit reference to Venus in the barge passage: 'O'erpicturing that Venus where we see / The fancy outwork nature'. He could have added, in line with the case we have just been developing, that Shakespeare's terms fit, with cunning precision, the aesthetic assumptions of the court masque, where Queen Anne (to take her as example) seeks for herself and her ladies of the court a power to 'o'erpicture' Beauty, and in performance to lead fancy to outwork Nature.

Fisch goes on to propose an even grander matrix for understanding the Antony and Cleopatra fable. The two protagonists, he says, 'merge into another mythological grouping of much greater significance for Shakespeare's purpose, namely the Isis-Osiris-Set triangle with Cleopatra functioning as Isis, goddess of nature and fertility, and Antony as Osiris, the dying sun-god who is resurrected in eternity' (p. 61). Fisch thinks that Shakespeare may have drawn on Plutarch's *Of Isis and Osiris*, which had been translated into English by Philemon Holland in 1603. He mentions the further possibility that Shakespeare picked up this Egyptian mythology from Spenser's *The Faerie Queene*, and is particularly tempted to argue for Apuleius' *The Golden Ass* as a source (translated into English by Adlington, with four editions published by the end of the sixteenth century). Hewever these speculations may be, Fisch points to the specific mention of Isis in Act 3, scene 6, where Cleopatra is once more play-acting, as she is in the barge: 'She / In th'habiliments of the goddess Isis / That day appeared' (16–18). As for Antony, Fisch thinks his association with Osiris is endorsed by his metaphoric connection with the sun. Cleopatra cries out 'O sun / Burn the great sphere thou mov'st in (4.15.10–11); she re-creates him in memory in similar terms: 'His face was as the heavens, and therein stuck / A sun and moon which kept their course and lighted / The little O, the earth' (5.2.78–80).

Where one begins to question this mythological reading of the play is the point at which Fisch reaches a judgement such as this: 'Antony's ritual death has all the slow elaborate ceremonial we would expect' (p. 61). Notoriously, Antony's death is a messy, ill-executed affair, of which he himself is bitterly ashamed. Cleopatra, says Fisch, following a similar line, 'joins in mythic union the principle of love and death: she represents the *Liebestod*, the downward drag of nature into unconsciousness and death' (p. 62). Mythology entirely takes over the critic's mind as he reads the play's closure: 'Shakespeare has somehow penetrated into this region of ancient belief; creating for us in the last act of the play a dramatic realisation of the active attainment of immortality' (p. 63). This judgement is expanded a little later on: 'Shakespeare presents in the fifth act a ritual of apotheosis in which Antony and Cleopatra in the most ceremonial fashion put off mortality and announce their union as god and goddess eternally united in the field of peace' (p. 63). We are bound to ask whether Shakespeare's dramatic tactics quite so simply endorse a reading that seems willing, as Fisch appears to do, to accept in full the aesthetics of the masque.

It would be inaccurate to portray Fisch's article as so simplistically univocal as I have made it seem. He analyses, for example, the Clown episode of Act 5, finding that its opening words 'parody the Egyptian myth of immortality in the fields of peace … which forms the very essence of the Isis-Osiris legend' (p. 64). He notes that the episode 'brings a Biblical realism vigorously to bear on the dream-world of Paganism' and concludes that 'a cold, sharp, but morally bracing wind of realism blows through this dialogue' (p. 64). He writes earlier that 'Shakespeare … presents the whole apotheosis of Antony and Cleopatra within a framework of irony' (p. 63), and shows how a preoccupation with history, largely associated with Rome, qualifies the inclination towards mythology which he finds otherwise so pervasive. Fisch is surely right to enter these qualifications. What is puzzling is that a mind so attuned, as it seems intermittently to be, to the paradoxes of the play's language, should express itself so uncritically as to describe the fifth act as a 'ritual of apotheosis', or to talk of Antony and Cleopatra putting off mortality 'in the most ceremonial fashion'. Anyone with a feel for theatre will notice how insistently Shakespeare has crafted the dramatic structures of the final act as a series of interrupted and episodic moments, how he has repeatedly varied the focus of the audience's attention, how he has called on his actors to alter pace, emphasis, and emotional stance, and how he has perplexed our settled estimates of Cleopatra, Caesar and others by giving these characters unexpected twists of attitude and intent (Cleopatra's petty concern with money, for example, as she behaves like a tax-dodger unsuccessfully calling on an accountant to verify a fraudulent tax declaration). The episodes of Proculeius, Dolabella, and Seleucus, as well as much else, make it impossible to adopt towards the play's action the simple attitude characteristic of, say, the audience at a pageant or masque, consorting with the performers in an uninterrupted act of homage. The article throws into relief Shakespeare's indebtedness to Plutarch as an aspect of that transition of cultures where retention of the earlier culture serves as implicit critique of contemporary modes.

Act 4, scene 15 of *Antony and Cleopatra* is the nightmare episode for any director of the play. The raising of Antony's body to Cleopatra's monument poses such awkward questions of staging that most directors shirk the practicalities involved. To raise a full-grown man, sufficiently imposing physically to play Antony, but with his dying body now no more than a slack weight, to the elevated position where Cleopatra and her maids await him, implies strenuous effort and untidy performance. On the Elizabethan stage, as on any stage that mimics it, the effect must have been one of clumsy awkwardness. The best guess of those who reconstructed Shakespeare's Globe in Southwark is that the upper stage rose about nine feet above the stage floor.[19] To work an actor through that elevation and over the rail that fronted the upper stage could only be done with the greatest difficulty, and with maximum emphasis on the sheer factuality of stage performance. No other Elizabethan dramatist asked his company of players to attempt such a feat, and nowhere else in his work does Shakespeare replicate it. With the shortage of rehearsal opportunity for an Elizabethan company (of which an experienced dramatist such as Shakespeare in 1606 will have been acutely aware), the inclusion of such an episode can only be the result of deliberate calculation and deliberate courting of hazard. Shakespeare prepares for it very consciously. The stage direction near the conclusion of the previous scene specifies 'Enter four or five of the Guard of Antony', who subsequently, bear the dying body off stage and re-enter with it at the foot of the monument. Cleopatra, Charmian, and Iras are reinforced 'aloft' in the monument by 'Maids' (presumably boy actors) who are unmentioned elsewhere in the play. Between both parties, the feat of raising Antony is undertaken, though evidently with difficulty and at some length, for the text refers to 'weight' and 'heaviness', and twice (lines 14 and 30–2) Cleopatra begs the assistance of the others in accomplishing the task. Shakespeare clearly envisaged a stressful piece of performance.

Plutarch's account of the event makes vivid in words what Shakespeare has realized in action. North's translation must have considerably influenced his conception of the staging:

> When he [Antony] heard that she was alive, he very earnestly prayed his men to carry his body thither; and so he was carried in his men's arms into the entry of the monument. Nothwithstanding, Cleopatra would not open the gates, but came to the high windows, and cast out certain chains and ropes, in the which Antonius was trussed; and Cleopatra her own self, with two women only which she had suffered to come with her into these monuments, triced Antonius up.
>
> They that were present to behold it said they never saw so pitiful a sight. For they plucked up poor Antonius, all bloody as he was and drawing on with pangs of death, who holding up his hands to Cleopatra raised up himself as well as he could. It was a hard thing for these women to do, to lift him up. But Cleopatra stooping down with her head, putting to all her strength to her uttermost power, did lift him up with much ado and never let go her hold, with the help of the women beneath that bade her be of good courage, and were as sorry to see her labour so, as she herself.[20]

It is noticeable that Shakespeare departs from the detail of this only where the practicalities of theatre demand, for example in specifying more than two women to assist Cleopatra, or where these practicalities allow the author to remain silent (in not mentioning the 'certain chains and ropes' or the blood-covered body and supplicating hands, matters that stage action would take care of). Plutarch emphasizes strenuous effort as much as Shakespeare. The episode is, to put the matter in a convenient way, *theatre*, not pageant or masque. Another dramatist might have avoided the sheer staging difficulties. Shakespeare embraces them. Because he wishes to acknowledge in his theatre-writing the actualities which masque and pageant avoid. It is a commitment which is carried forward into the play's conclusion, and which casts its influence retrospectively into our reading of everything that is implied by Cleopatra's barge.

If the barge is affiliated to the Renaissance tradition of baroque spectacle, with its roots in Italian and earlier pageantry, the monument scene finds its source in the English vernacular theatre of mystery play and morality. That vernacular theatre attends to factuality as it realizes, for a popular audience, a metaphysical understanding of human destiny – as Bill Bryden's production of the Tony Harrison *Mysteries* at London's Royal National Theatre so eloquently showed.[21] Shakespeare theatre inherits, that is to say, competing traditions, one of them the Renaissance admiration for a theatre of ritual, the other the theatre of emphatic physical presence. *The Tempest* may be read as Shakespeare's culminating reflection on the conflicting tendencies of the two traditions.

Act 5 of *Antony and Cleopatra* reminds us more than once of the tensions within the theatre of spectacle. The Roman triumph to which Caesar would subject Cleopatra is envisaged from the victim's viewpoint, rather than the conqueror's. Caesar's anticipated triumph is not presented as the glorification of Caesar, except where the glory arises from the humiliation of Cleopatra:

>   Shall they hoist me up
> And show me to the shouting varletry
> Of censuring Rome?
>
> (5.2.54–6)

> Now, Iras, what think'st thou?
> Thou an Egyptian puppet shall be shown
> In Rome as well as I. Mechanic slaves
> With greasy aprons, rules and hammers shall
> Uplift us to the view ...
>   Saucy lictors
> Will catch at us like strumpets, and scald rhymers
> Ballad us out o' tune ...
>
> (5.2.206–15)

The festivals of Renaissance Florence or London trace their origins to the triumphs of ancient Rome, but for Shakespeare's play, or at least this facet of it, triumph implies not idealization but degradation. The public spectacle of Cleopatra's imagining, as she nears her death, with its full complement of mechanic slaves and saucy lictors, may serve as ironic commentary on the self-presented and self-isolating spectacle of the barge.

Cleopatra, however, remains dedicated to the cause of self-display. The strategies she adopts for her death scene are those of royal funeral. She will present herself, or so she desires, like the effigies of kings and emperors, dressed in royal robes for her people's admiration. Funeral festivals of the Renaissance took great care to dress the body of the deceased, and to robe his or her effigy, in the royal garments worn in life. The effigy that was carried in the funeral procession of Queen Elizabeth was dressed in either her Coronation or Parliamentary robes, and wore the imperial crown and carried the orb and sceptre.[22] In a similar spirit, Cleopatra attempts to pre-arrange her own lying in state:

> Give me my robe. Put on my crown. I have
> Immortal longings in me.
>
> (5.2.279–80)

She attempts, that is to say, in a kind of physical ellipsis, to overstep the facts of mortality. This bargaining with death conjures up in her mind her previous occasion of self-ritualization:

> Show me, my women, like a queen. Go fetch
> My best attires. I am again for Cydnus
> To meet Mark Antony.
>
> (5.2.226–8)

But the physical world takes its revenge by implicit commentary. Cleopatra's carefully composed lying-in-state is disrupted by events and by gravity:

> CHARMIAN Your crown's awry;
>   I'll mend it, and then play.
>
> (5.2.317-18)

Caesar's Guard come 'rustling' (i.e. clattering) in. He himself enters with forensic enquiries like a Roman Sherlock Holmes. The play ends with his generous tribute to 'a pair so famous', but the juxtaposition of ritual dressing-up and the stark facts of death remain in our minds as the double impression of the play's conclusion.

This chapter has attempted to show some of the sources of influence which imaginatively configure Shakespeare's play. It is the case that lack of scholarly interest in the theatre of ritual and pageant, so marked a feature of Renaissance political and cultural life, has led us to read the concerns of *Antony and Cleopatra* less than fully. A more thorough study of the matter would require us to situate the play within a culture where the theatre of the city and the court, and in particular, in England, the masque and civic pageant, with their European affiliation, drew performance resources and public attention almost equally with mainstream theatre. Shakespeare, though he must have performed in masques (his company certainly did), and though he incorporated them in his plays, did not commit his career to the masque in the manner of Ben Jonson. Yet the culture to which he responded so comprehensively did so commit itself, not only among the elite at court but in the city too. The Italian component, and especially the Florentine component, in this culture, as suggested above, was pervasive. Shakespeare's *Antony and Cleopatra* allows us a sensitive glimpse of that transition of cultures between Italy and England which so marked the imaginative life of the Elizabethan and Jacobean period.

Notes

1. *Antony and Cleopatra*, ed. John Wilders, The Arden Shakespeare, Third series (London, Routledge, 1995).
2. *Notes and Queries*, 225, n.s. 27 (1980), 172–4.
3. See Jean Wilson, *Entertainments for Elizabeth I* (Woodbridge, D. S. Brewer, 1980), pp. 96–118, and Edmund A. Bowles, *Musical Ensembles in Festival Books, 1500-1800* (Ann Arbor, UMI Research Press, 1989), pp. 123–8.
4. The most famous of all Elizabethan progress entertainments, that given for the Queen at the Earl of Liecester's castle at Kenilworth in 1575, also has a watery element, involving the Lady of the Lake, but no barge or 'pinnace'.
5. See Arthur R. Blumenthal, *Theater Art of the Medici* (Hanover, N.H. and London, University Press of New England, 1980), pp. 30–86.
6. Linthicum, quoted in *Antony and Cleopatra*, ed. David Bevington (Cambridge, Cambridge University Press, 1990), 2.2.209 n.
7. T. J. B. Spencer, *Shakespeare's Plutarch* (Harmondsworth, Penguin, 1964), p. 14.
8. For an excellent account of Plutarch and his career and values see C. B. R. Pelling, *Plutarch: Life of Antony* (Cambridge, Cambridge University Press, 1988), pp. 1–18.
9. Lisa Jardine, *Wordly Goods: A New History of the Renaissance* (London, Macmillan, 1996).
10. James M. Saslow, *The Medici Wedding of 1589: Florentine Festival as 'Theatrum Mundi'* (New Haven and London, Yale University Press, 1996), p. 14.
11. A representation of the performance, using modern television techniques, was broadcast for Thames Television on Channel 4 in 1992, under the direction of Andrew Parrott and Hugh Keyte. The music was recorded and made available under the title *Una stravaganza dei Medici*.
12. See Roy Strong, *Henry Prince of Wales: England's Lost Renaissance* (London, Thames and Hudson, 1986), *passim*.
13. Cambridge, Cambridge University Press, 1995.
14. *Calendar of State Papers, Venetian*, XI (1607–10), p. 86, quoted in C. H. Herford and Percy and Evelyn Simpson, eds, *The Collected Works of Ben Jonson* (Oxford, 1925–52), vol. X, p. 457.

15 Herford and Simpson, *Ben Jonson*, vol. X, p. 455.
16 John Harris, Stephen Orgel and Roy Strong, *The King's Arcadia: Inigo Jones and the Stuart Court* (London, Arts Council of Great Britain, 1973), p. 35.
17 Herford and Simpson, *Ben Jonson*, vol. VII, p. 186.
18 Harold Fisch, '*Antony and Cleopatra*: The Limits of Mythology', *Shakespeare Survey*, 23 (1970), 59–67.
19 See Ronnie Mulryne and Margaret Shewring, eds, *Shakespeare's Globe Rebuilt* (Cambridge, Cambridge University Press, 1997), especially the discussions by Jon Greenfield and John Ronayne.
20 Judith Mossman, ed., *Plutarch: The Lives of the Noble Grecians and Romans*, trans. Thomas North (Ware, Wordsworth, 1998), p. 748.
21 See Jason Barnes, 'The Mysteries: Staging and Scenography at the Cottesloe and Elsewhere', in Ronnie Mulryne and Margaret Shewring, *The Cottesloe at the National: Infinite Riches in a Little Room* (Stratford-upon-Avon, 1999), pp. 72–80.
22 For an excellent discussion of the rituals of royal funerals see Jennifer Woodward, *The Theatre of Death* (Woodbridge, Boydell, 1997). For a description of the rituals used at Elizabeth's funeral see especially chapter 5, pp. 87–117.

15

Intertextuality and the chess motif: Shakespeare, Middleton, Greenaway

JEFFREY A. NETTO

In reading *The Tempest*, it is important to look at that all too brief and seemingly incidental moment in Act 5 of the play, the moment when 'Prospero discovers Ferdinand and Miranda playing at chess' (5.1.171–5).[1] This tiny, inset scene effectively condenses the self-reflexive functions of the play at large while simultaneously marking the locus of the play's intertextual relation to a certain discursive pattern that is similarly elaborated in other works and in other media – namely, in the chess motif informing various works of Renaissance portraiture, Thomas Middleton's *A Game at Chess*, and Peter Greenaway's *Prospero's Books*.

Before analysing the moves and variations of this intertextual game, it is worthwhile to consider the dramatic context of the chess scene in Shakespeare's play. The scene occurs just after the wedding plans for Ferdinand and Miranda are put on hold so that Prospero can direct the play's darker plots of political intrigue to their final conclusion. At this point Prospero intervenes, warning Ferdinand not to break Miranda's 'virgin knot' until he has arranged things so that 'all sanctimonious ceremonies … with full and holy rite be ministered' (4.1.15–17). In the meantime, he cautions Ferdinand:

> Look thou be true; do not give dalliance
> Too much the rein. The strongest oaths are straw
> To th' fire i' th' blood. Be more abstentious,
> Or else good night your vow!
>
> (4.1.51–4)

While this is undoubtedly sound advice, it nevertheless begs an important question: exactly how much 'rein' is 'too much' where dalliance is concerned? Outright fornication is obviously ruled out, but Prospero's warning suggests that there are other variations of recreational intercourse available to curb an appetite for dalliance. As it turns out, there are two such variations offered on the island – theatre and chess – and they are both quickly brought into play.

Accordingly, in the space of this romantic interruption Prospero magically conjures forth a cast of spirits who promptly stage a marriage masque for the amusement and edification of the chaste pair. Here theatre intervenes, and the dallying lovers are rendered safely passive in so far as they are cast by Prospero's spectacle into the role of spellbound audience. Thus, theatre is explicitly offered as a safely sublimated form of sensual dalliance.

Immediately following the masque, the lovers then settle down to a quiet game of chess. The transition from theatre to chess is all but seamless as the intervening action of the conjured players *walking the boards* easily gives way to the interposition of moving pieces at play on the chessboard. The game, like the preceding masque, here assumes the status of a familiar Shakespearean *mise en abyme*, a scene of playing within the play akin to the players' scenes in *Hamlet* and *A Midsummer Night's Dream*. In such scenes, theatre self-reflexively stages itself and thereby proposes a paradigmatic alignment between the playing *of* the drama and the playing *within* it. And by virtue of this kind of interpolated mirror-imaging of the play at large by a single reflexive element within it, various subtleties that are all too easily overlooked in the overall production might suddenly find clearer expression when reflected *en abyme*. Here, for example, one notes that those subtler feints and evasions attendant upon the couple's love-play are more clearly framed when played out in sublimated form above the board, as it were, in their dalliance over a game of chess.

Furthermore, on a broader narrative level, this reflexive scene also reflects the more serious political counterplay between Prosper and Antonio (as well as that between Alonso and Sebastian). And in this light, Miranda's playful remark 'Sweet lord, you play me false' (5.1.172) darkly resonates with the more serious schemes of foul play that are elsewhere afoot upon the island. But it is finally at a deeper, specifically semiotic level of the play that the reflexivity of the chess motif is ultimately played out. At this level, the chess game hearkens back to Prospero's 'We are such stuff as dreams are made on' soliloquy, which pointedly offers a meta-poetic commentary – apropos the conjured masque – on the transcendental function of aesthetic signs with regard to the verbal and gestural medium of theatre.

> These our actors,
> (As I foretold you) were all spirits, and
> Are melted into air, into thin air,
> And like the baseless fabric of this vision,
> The Cloud-capp'd tow'rs, the gorgeous palaces,
> The solemn temples, the great globe itself,
> Yea, all which it inherit, shall dissolve,
> And like this insubstantial pageant faded
> Leave not a rack behind. We are such stuff
> As dreams are made on.
>
> (4.1.147–56)

Here, Prospero gives voice to a certain, well established conception of the aesthetic sign, a conception according to which all artistic signification is predicated upon the exhaustion of the signifier's materiality (the sign's sensuous aspect – of which not a rack is left behind), as it accedes to the immaterial realm of signified meaning (which is to say, the intelligible or spiritual aspect of the sign – the conjured dreams of which Prospero speaks).

This conception of the aesthetic sign's transcendence over its material basis is a familiar theme for those Renaissance portraits that likewise deploy the chess motif. Such paintings iconographically present the scene of chess – the materiality of the game (that is, the board, pieces, furniture, etc.) – as the occasion for an intellectual transcendence of the physical domain of things and a movement towards the realm of pure, unencumbered ideas. Focusing for a moment on a first group of well-known paintings by Karel van Mander (c. 1603), Ludovico Carracci (c. 1590), and Paris Bordone (c. 1550–55), one readily notes that in the paintings by van Mander and Carracci the players are preoccupied by the game to the point where they seem to transcend the rendered scene.[2] They seem to be transported elsewhere, to be abstracted from the physical setting of the game as it appears on the canvas. The paintings thereby gesture towards, without quite explicitly rendering, the purely mental landscape on which these players contend.

Van Mander's painting, ostensibly a portrait of Ben Jonson and William Shakespeare,[3] explicitly equates chess-playing with literary aesthetics by allegorically depicting the well-known professional rivalry between these figures in terms of a battle of wits played out upon the miniature stage formed by their chessboard. Here the transcendental iconography of the chess motif readily lends itself to such an allegorical representation of mental abstraction at the moment of aesthetic creation. And even if we grant that the portrait of the two dramatists is perhaps not genuine (i.e., taken from life), the sceptical move to discredit the positive identification of the painting's material referents (seated somewhere behind the canvas) only retraces the allegorical thrust of the composition and the transcendental thematics conventionally signalled by the chess motif.[4]

Carracci's portrait similarly demonstrates the thematics of ideational transcendence signalled by the chess motif. In stark contrast with the small dog who seems to stare directly at the painting's viewer and thereby establishes a kind of connection between the rendered setting of the painting and the site of its current viewing (i.e., the gallery and its gazing visitors), the two chess players are completely oblivious to their surroundings, both within and beyond the painting's frame. They are instead absorbed in a state of deepest contemplation – reflecting the kind of aesthetic contemplation explicitly courted by the overall painting (*qua* work of art in the Kantian sense). Here Carracci's painting and the chess motif that informs it thus intertextually anticipate

Kant's third critique, wherein he elaborates his conception of the transcendental function of art. The rendered players, like the viewers of a work who judge it to be beautiful, are absorbed in a contemplation of pure form – above and apart from any particular contents that may appear on the surface of either the canvas or the playing surface. Rather, the mind of both viewer and player transcends all such phenomenal features of things as they appear in the real world in order to achieve a *disinterested* state of abstract appreciation in which both perceiving subject and perceived object are momentarily abstracted from the material world of sensible phenomena.[5]

In the painting by Bordone, by contrast, the players seem all too aware of their immediate setting. However, Bordone's portrait illustrates the same transcendental thematic associated with the chess motif in van Mander and Carracci, albeit in a more roundabout and backhanded manner. Bordone's players stare fixedly and impatiently at the painter/viewer, whose distracting presence has evidently drawn these men back out of the abstract play of ideas somewhere above and beyond the board. In regarding this painting, the viewer is decidedly not invited to identify his or her own aesthetic abstraction with the players' momentarily interrupted absorption in the game. Rather our very presence, coldly acknowledged by the players' irritated stare, seems to freeze the mental and physical activity of the game into a tableau of disdainful impatience for our actual departure. Here, the transcendental thematic associated with the chess motif is all the more pronounced, rather than checked, by the momentary suspension of play as we contemplate the players who, in their turn, pause to contemplate us before resuming their inward focus upon the game.

The scene of chess in Shakespeare's play is a kind of citation of this iconographic convention which articulates the distinction of the aesthetic sign into its sensible and intelligible aspects. The scene thus marks a peculiar point of *ekphrastic intertextuality* – the textual recital of a figurative scheme that is initially elaborated elsewhere in the plastic arts. In so far as Shakespeare's scene draws upon the iconographic conventions of the chess motif in Renaissance portraiture, it invokes a system of intertextual relays between the medium of painting and that of theatre. Thus, by way of this system of intertextual relays, Shakespeare's inset scene of pieces and players is able to draw upon the iconographic conventions of Renaissance portraiture, while at the same time painting, as we saw in the case of Bordone, is able to stage a dramatic encounter between the intellectual abstraction (of the players) and real world interruptions (by us). This intertextual citation and cross-fertilization accordingly infuses each medium with new, hybrid forms of signification – making it henceforth possible for us to speak of *dramatic painting* and *iconographic theatre.*

However, any consideration of the intertextual relays between *The Tempest* and the iconography of the chess motif in Renaissance portraiture must also take into account the equally prominent counter-thematic of foregrounded material sensuousness that several paintings also invoke by way of the chess motif. This counter-thematic effectively deconstructs the particular conception of the aesthetic sign that the iconography of chess conventionally invokes. Instead of postulating the absorption of the material signifier into the signified meaning of the aesthetic sign, this counter-thematic treatment of the chess motif focuses on the insistence of the sensuous, material aspect of the sign – that tactile aspect of the game that can legibly foreground itself, even and especially in those moments when, by convention, the materiality of the image's rendering is supposedly absorbed or eclipsed by the imposition of meaning. In the tradition of the chess motif in Renaissance portraiture, this insistence of a sensuous materiality in excess of the transcendental vocation of the sign is frequently rendered in the erotically charged portraits of chess-playing women or lovers who are by no means fully absorbed by the pure abstractions of the game. The conventional iconography of chess notwithstanding, these portraits underscore the more immediate, sensuous characteristics of the game's players and setting.

Focusing now on a second group of paintings by Sofonisba Anguissola (c. 1555) and by Girolamo da Cremona (c. 1475–80), one might note that in Anguissola's portrait of her sisters at the chessboard, there is a marked emphasis upon the physical rather than intellectual aspects of the rendered scene.[6] The three sisters appear to glow with vitality and emotion: Lucia, on the left, is flushed with victory; Europa, in the centre, is smiling with delight over the game; and Minerva, at the right, is raising her hand in resignation as she stares bewilderedly at her smirking opponent. Even the sensuous materiality of the board and pieces is here accentuated by the tantalizing daintiness with which they are caressed by these nubile players. Also worth noting here is the degree to which the reflexive character of the chess motif is literally foregrounded by the placement of the artist's signature – located on the facing edge of the chessboard. The peculiar placement of this signature paradigmatically equates the board's framed rectangular surface with that of the overall painting, and the effect of this equation is that the co-ordinated composition of the game itself becomes infused with some of the players' vitality as it is depicted in the composition of the overall work.

The other painting in this group similarly accentuates the sensuous vitality of the players, heightening it by incorporating a more explicit sense of eroticism, a sense that is then metonymically transferred on to the game. Here, the conventions of transcendental iconography in the chess motif are effectively overwritten by palpable signs of erotic love-play on the plane of everyday material existence. In the portrait by Girolamo da Cremona, the newly married couple seated at the chessboard gently caress one another as they play. But chess is not here simply an intellectual counterpoint to the rendered materiality and physicality sumptuously detailed in the scene. Rather, chess here serves as the very occasion for that rendering. What the painting accordingly suggests is that certain formal conventions which typically underwrite such intellectually rarified activities as aesthetic engagement and games of chess are similarly mobilized to provide social and domestic coherence to the more down-to-earth experience of marriage. Here the transcendental abstraction of chess sets the stage where physical and material aspects of the game might be brought into play, rather than vice versa.

In the chess motif in Renaissance portraiture, we are thus routinely confronted with the residual insistence of the material signifier, a vicious mole in the nature of signs that similarly runs rampant throughout the text of *The Tempest*. For this play (like all of Shakespeare's plays) likewise foregrounds the materiality of its medium – the tactile texture of its text – by way of an elaborate play upon and across its own signifying surface of words. From the constant verbal jesting of Trinculo, to the punning reparetee between Antonio and Sebastian, to Ferdinand's anagrammatic play upon his lover's name ('Admired Miranda!'), and on to Prospero's punning references to the theatrical context of the play's performance in his epilogue, *The Tempest* persistently rages against the simple subsumption of signifier to signified. And accordingly, wherever the signifier's accession to the transcendental sphere of signified meaning stalls, there the sensuous, material aspect of the medium holds court.

One of the more pronounced instances of the signifier's insistent materialization in the play occurs, appropriately enough, in the scene of Ferdinand and Miranda playing at chess. There, the transcendental iconography of the chess motif notwithstanding, the scene of their chess-playing is overcoded with the more down-to-earth games of sexual and international politics that each must learn to play. This signifying convergence of games and contexts – chess, marriage, and politics – is rendered through Shakespeare's own game of words:

> *Here Prospero discovers Ferdinand and Miranda playing at chess.*
> MIRANDA Sweet lord, you play me false.
> FERDINAND No, my dearest love,
>   I would not for all the world.
> MIRANDA Yes, for a score of kingdoms you should wrangle
>   And I would call it fair play.
>
> (5.1.171–5)

Here, with a stroke of punning triple-entendre, Shakespeare overloads the conventional significations of false and fair play in chess by activating the erotic and political senses of these terms, all within a single exchange. Miranda's assertion that Ferdinand's cheating ('wrangling') will henceforth be accepted as 'fair play' by her when a kingdom (or, hyperbolically, a score of kingdoms) is at stake is punningly suggestive of her willingness to acquiesce to any political wrangling Ferdinand may have occasion to commit in managing their joint estates. And at the same time, this assertion also hints at her probable acquiescence to any extra-marital wrangling, in the form of sexual dalliance, that her future husband may desire. This three-pronged fork in the passage towards a single, straightforward meaning renders the precise signified intention of the exchange ambiguous and thereby subverts the transcendental sign-function of the lover's exchange. In other words, the ambiguity renders their discourse over the game 'playful' and situates the locus of this playing squarely upon the punning excesses of the signifiers they exchange over the board. Thus, the direct accession to a determinate signified meaning of this game momentarily stalls, and accordingly it is the signifier, that is, the linguistic material that renders this scene, which comes to assume an air of heightened, if uncertain, significance. Here the apparent fair play of straightforward communication confesses to a nefarious complicity in an act of semiotic foul play – if not the murder, then at least the dismemberment of signs under the weight of an excess of the material signifier at the point of its expected exhaustion. It is this excess of the signifier that provides a surface upon which the foul play of aberrant senses is inevitably traced within the sign in the wake of straightforward signification.

The strictest attention to such semiotic dismemberment is a large part of the intertextual inheritance that Shakespeare bequeathed to Thomas Middleton, who similarly explored the deconstruction of signs in a scene of fair and false play over a chessboard. In *A Game at Chess*, Middleton accordingly elaborates and expands upon the self-reflexive characteristic of the chess motif that Shakespeare had earlier invoked in *The Tempest*. But instead of rendering this self-reflexive element *en abyme*, as Shakespeare had done in confining the chess scene to an inset tableau, Middleton stretches the edges of the chessboard to the point where the game played out upon it now encompasses the entire action of the play. Thus, Middleton intertextually invokes the conventional world-as-stage conceit most famously given voice in Shakespeare's *As You Like It*.[7] Aside from the obvious pun on the Globe Theatre (where both *The Tempest* and *A Game at Chess* were originally staged), this conceit posits an allegorical relationship between the formal conventions of Renaissance stagecraft and the social and political conventions according to which the ideological script of everyday life is played out.

In this light, readers cannot fail to recognize that several of Middleton's chess-pieces characters are drawn from the actual persons who played key roles in what came to be called 'the Spanish marriage plot'. The allegorical rendering of the Spanish marriage plot in the second half of *A Game at Chess* focuses for the most part on the political manoeuvrings of the White Knight and the Black Knight as each tries to checkmate his opponent. Here White designates Protestant England under the rule of James I, and Black represents Catholic Spain under Philip IV. The strategy of the Black Knight (representing the Conde de Gondomar, the Spanish ambassador to England) consists in luring the White Knight (Prince Charles) to join ranks with the Black House. This allegorically corresponds to the actually proposed match between Charles and the Infanta of Spain, who would agree to marry the English prince only on the condition that he first convert to her religion and thereby subject the English throne to Papal influence. The White Knight's strategy consists in luring the Black Knight into betraying the hypocritical tactics by way of which he pursues his own strategy. It is here, in the juxtaposition of these two figures and their respective modes of foul and fair play, that Middleton's own play effectively engages with the transcendental and materialist thematics pertaining to the chess motif.

In casting the game between Charles and Gondomar in terms of a contest between White and Black Knights, Middleton immediately draws upon the obvious iconographic clichés conditioned by countless intertexts: White stands for virtue – a transcendental value – while Black designates the corruption of this value and the pursuit of more immediate, earthly material. Against the White Knight's sense of virtue and fair play, the Black Knight cites as his motto, '*Qui cauté, caste*,' which is to say, 'Whoever acts prudently, acts virtuously' (2.1.171n.). Virtue is thus debased in the Black House to the point where it answers only to prudence (i.e., the practical and efficient execution of earthly designs). The Black Knight then shows himself ready to practise what he preaches, describing himself as a polymorphous being capable of altering his outward, material shape to suit the momentary exigencies of his immediate plots: 'I will change / To any shape to please you, and my aim / Has always been to win our love in all this game' (5.5.42–4). So committed to the outcome of this game is the Black Knight that, with an intertextual nod to Shakespeare's *Tempest*, he claims that in the foulness of his schemes he feels 'no tempest, not a leaf-wind stirring / To shake a fault; [his] conscience is becalmed rather' (4.2.38–9). This is in obvious contrast to Shakespeare's Antonio and Sebastian who *do* feel the tempestuous stirrings of conscience by the end of *The Tempest*.[8]

In the White Knight's eventual triumph over the Black Knight, it would appear that the transcendental value of virtue unequivocally triumphs over the material ambitions allegorically embodied by members of the Black House. However, upon closer analysis the outcome of this match is not quite so clear-cut. The trouble with such a straightforward reading of the allegory's ending arises as soon as one recognizes the evident traces of Black's foul play in the tactical manoeuvres of the White Knight. In his final, winning combination, the White Knight and his companion, the White Duke (Buckingham), confess to a variety of vices, all of which mark these figures of fair play and transcendental virtue with the taint of those material obsessions proper to the Black House. And even if we allow that the White Knight and Duke are only pretending to indulge in these vices in order to discover and expose them in the Black House, the last and apparently darkest of them – a penchant for dissembling – is stamped all the more legibly upon the whiteness of these characters. That is, in executing his final gambit by placing himself and his Duke *en prise*, the White Knight adopts that very tactic of shape-shifting dissemblance that most clearly characterizes Black's policy of foul play. In other words, the White Knight here underscores the ambiguities traced into himself, *qua* material signifier of virtue, by effectively drawing upon the theatrical display of his outward, material shape rather than his putative transcendental significance in order to achieve his victory. To triumph over the Black Knight, it would thus appear that the White Knight has to meet him on his own terms and beat him at his own foul game – a game played out in the playfulness of the corrupted material signifier once it has loosened itself from its transcendental ties to a signified concept of value.

By way of resuming and bringing up to date our analysis of the chess motif informing *The Tempest*, it is useful to consider Peter Greenaway's 1991 film adaptation of the play. The title of Greenaway's film, *Prospero's Books*, clearly announces the filmmaker's critical agenda as a self-reflexive exercise in intertextual analysis. And, in the film's foregrounded focus upon the cultural intertexts informing Shakespeare's play, it indeed manages to live up to its title. As the film unfolds, Shakespeare's play is divided into discrete episodes, each prefaced by an explicit citation of a particular text from Prospero's library. Prefacing the scene in which Prospero unveils Ferdinand and Miranda playing chess, Greenaway presents us with a telling reference to *A Book of Games*. The significance of this referenced title and the scene it prefaces is readily apparent once we give the title a playful twist of a chiastic about-face. Read backwards (and with an intertextual nod to the film's earlier citation of *A Book of Mirrors*), *A Book of Games* now references that overarching *game of books* that Greenaway has set out to play. Thus, at this peculiar moment of chess-inspired self-reflection, Greenaway seems to take his cue from Prospero, deciding at this point that it is high time to give the game away. Here, then, the unveiling of the chess motif signals the confrontation of transcendental and materialist thematics pertaining the aesthetic signifiers of the cinema. This, indeed, is what Greenaway has consistently trained his camera on throughout the film.

The chess scene in Greenaway's film follows Shakespeare's text in presenting the lovers at the conclusion of their game as Prospero reveals them in order to announce their betrothal. As the lovers stand, the camera moves in to frame a close-up of their clasped hands. A drawing of a chessboard is then superimposed over the shot of their clasped hands, its rectangular field almost totally filling the screen's frame, leaving only a slight marginal border in which we can still see the edges of the shot of Ferdinand and Miranda. The pieces upon the drawing of the board are animated, and they move smoothly about by themselves, playing out an endgame combination even after Ferdinand and

Miranda have broken off their game. At the conclusion of this game without players, the drawing of a pair of hands, clasped in cordial acknowledgement of the game's resolution, materializes on the board, and the superimposed chess set then dissolves to reveal the clasped hands of Ferdinand and Miranda as they confront their proud fathers.

By way of this elaborate display of artifice and cinematic technique, Greenaway effectively drafts the transcendental and materialist thematics of the chess motif into the service of a critique of the film medium and its own peculiar aesthetic signifiers. Here we are reminded that the magic of cinema, at its basis, lies in the trick of transcending the stasis of its photographic material in order to render the illusion of movement. In superimposing an animated drawing over the cinematic image, Greenaway literally marks and thus lays bare the film's celluloid substance, the stuff of the signifier on which rests the signified construct of cinema's 'motion pictures'.

But there is one more move in Greenaway's self-reflexive analytic of the transcendental and materialist elements of his signifying medium. For while the plastic substance of the filmic frame is markedly showcased by the accentuated materiality of the drawn board and pieces, the progress of the self-played game seems to be driven by an intentional design that transcends the materiality of the graphically rendered scene. However, a closer scrutiny of the endgame combination played out on the superimposed chessboard reveals the material source of this design. The combination is itself an intertext, taken from the recorded annals of so-called 'chess literature'. It is the conclusion of a game well known to chess enthusiasts the world over and heralded with the title 'The Game of the Century' in the wake of its debut when Bobby Fischer (then thirteen years old) defeated chess's grandmaster Donald Byrne at the 1956 Rosenwald Tournament. What this surprising intertext accordingly reveals is that the apparent transcendence of the aesthetic signifier's materiality by the enigmatic designs of unseen players is actually the occasion of that materiality's intertextual displacement. Here the material basis of the game is not so much transcended by an occult intentional design as it is transposed into the site of another material inscription – in other words, the insistence of the signifier shunted out of one book and into another. Thus, what *Prospero's Books* ultimately illustrates for us is the degree to which the material signifier (rather than simply the senses of the signified) can pass through those intertextual circuits which deepen and defer signification.

The point in all this is not simply that there are allusions to painting, contemporary politics, and chess in Shakespeare, Middleton, and Greenaway. Rather, the chess-inspired scenes in their works effectively elaborate a system of intertextual citation – a kind of textual communication by way of which Shakespeare's romance, Middleton's allegory, and Greenaway's film participate in the play of reiterations, of cultural rehearsals and revisions, that is always at work behind every act of aesthetic signification. Here the alternating lines of chess-inspired reflections on the transcendental and sensuous nature of aesthetic media are made possible to the extent that these lines are both played out on a chequerboard of intertexts, that board on which the meaning of painted, enacted, and projected scenes is configured only amidst the clutter of material excesses which inevitably gesture towards variations of sense beyond any canonical imposition of intentional meaning.

Notes

1 *The Tempest*, in *The Riverside Shakespeare*, ed. G. Blakemore Evans (Boston, Houghton, 1974). Line references are taken from this edition.
2 Karen Van Mander, *Ben Jonson and William Shakespeare Playing at Chess*, 1603, private collection of Frank de Heyman, New York; Ludovico Carracci, *The Chess Players*, 1590. Picture Library Preussischer Kulturbesitz, Berlin; Paris Bordone, *The Chess Players*, 1550–5. Picture Library Preussischer Kulturbesitz, Berlin.
3 For an account of the efforts of art historians to validate or discredit the authenticity of van Mander's portrait see Bryan Loughrey and Neil Taylor's 'Jonson and Shakespeare at Chess?' *Shakespeare Quarterly*, 34:4 (1983), 440–7.
4 That is, in discrediting the idea that Shakespeare and Jonson themselves were actually present for van Mander's painting, sceptical art historians tend to cast interest away from the actual scene of the game and its players, focusing instead on the painting's signified meaning as it is allegorically (rather than referentially) given to us. The precise physical rendering of the players is thus downplayed and critical emphasis is given to the abstract idea of their rivalling aesthetic principles.
5 Immanuel Kant, *Critique of Judgement*, trans. J. H. Bernard (New York, Hafner, 1951), pp. 37–45.
6 Sofonisba Anguissola, *The Chess Game*, 1555, Norodwe Museum, Posnan; Girolamo da Cremona, *The Game of Chess*, 1475–80, Metropolitan Museum of Art, New York.
7 Echoing the famous 'All the world's a stage, / And all the men and women merely players' monologue from *As You Like It*, Middleton's White Queen's Pawn remarks that 'The world's a stage on which all parts are played' (*A Game at Chess*, ed. T. H. Howard-Hill, Manchester, Manchester University Press, 1993, 5.2.19). For a discussion of the extensive intertextual history of the world-as-stage conceit see Swapan Chakravorty, *Society and Politics in the Plays of Thomas Middleton* (Oxford, Clarendon Press, 1996), pp. 166–92.
8 Earlier in *A Game at Chess*, the Black Knight gives a similar intertextual nod to *The Tempest*, noting that the agents of his plots are so committed to their tasks that 'The loudest tempest that authority rouses / Will hardly shake 'em off' (3.1.95–6).

16

'Rare Italian master(s)': Roman art in *Romeo and Juliet, Antony and Cleopatra,* and *The Winter's Tale*

FRANÇOIS LAROQUE

Above and beyond his Roman plays, where Rome is the centre of the Roman world in its cultural and political sense, and refers to classical antiquity rather than to contemporary Italy, Shakespeare used a number of specific Roman allusions for a variety of effects and purposes.

The needs of dramatic construction as well as a desire to introduce possible parallels between the ancient and the modern worlds are among these effects and purposes; aesthetic allusions to contemporary styles and manners, if not always to specific painters, may also be significant. Finally, and this is certainly the most tricky or uneasy side of the topic – this may be part of a system of cryptic references to Roman Catholicism, to its cult of saints and images as well as to its style of prayer and religious ritual. I would like to examine these various hypotheses in three plays where Italy, or Sicily (even if it was supposed to be part of Greece in the classical age), is woven into the text or part of its background, namely *Romeo and Juliet, Antony and Cleopatra,* and *The Winter's Tale,* in order to emphasize Shakespeare's rich inter- and intra-textual combinations, allusions, or collages. These rely on a complex interweaving of myth, of toponyms, and of patronyms that have always sounded intriguing to editors and critics.

Name games in *Romeo and Juliet*

Shakespeare's first love tragedy, it is to be remarked, begins and ends with the name 'Romeo' where the concluding couplet echoes the title of *Romeo and Juliet*:

> For never was a story of more woe
> Than this of Juliet and her Romeo.
>
> (5.3.308–9)[1]

So, *Romeo and Juliet* as a title leads to 'Juliet and her Romeo', an ending which repeats the title in an inverted way, as in a perfect chiasmus. This may be considered as a stylistic or rhetorical mirroring of the 'star-crossed lovers' pattern, which governs the play as a whole. It is mostly a means of calling attention to the name Romeo, which contains and foregrounds 'Rome'.

What is intriguing is the fact that the play takes place in Verona and only in part in Mantua, where the banished pilgrim or 'roamer' (the meaning of the name) never even thinks of making it to Rome, were it only to fly away from the plague. But the Elizabethan spectator may have kept in mind the fact that Rome was the seat of Shakespeare's first tragedy, *Titus Andronicus*, where the name of the empress of the Goths, Queen T*amo*ra, contains the anagrammatic, reversible names of 'Amor' and 'Roma'. Although her love affair with the Moor Aaron is developed in one of the subplots in this Senecan tragedy of horror and revenge, the second aspect is not given pride of place. As to the rape and mutilation of Lavinia, it is taken up again in *The Rape of Lucrece*, also situated in ancient Rome.

Joseph A. Porter examines the significance of the name Romeo in his book on Mercutio when he argues that 'Virgil's Mercury … is amplified by the "Rome" in Romeo, and fainter Trojan–Roman overtones … in the names Paris and Juliet.'[2] In *Romeo and Juliet*, Shakespeare initially quibbles on the lovers' names (Juliet as July, Jule and 'jewel', Romeo as 'roamer' and 'pilgrim') just as Petrarch, in his *Canzoniere*, plays on the various meanings contained in the name Laura, which he successively parses as 'laurel', 'l'aura', 'l'oro', etc. Love and religion are also put in parallel. As in the companion piece to *Romeo and Juliet*, *A Midsummer Night's Dream*, where Helena is said 'to dote in idolatry', Juliet says that Romeo's 'gracious self' is 'the god of [her] idolatry' (2.1.156–7).

As to Romeo, he describes the fair Rosaline in terms of pagan and mythological imagery:

> She'll not be hit
> With Cupid's arrow, she hath Dian's wit,
> And, in strong proof of chastity well armed,
> From love's weak childish bow she lives unharmed.
> She will not stay the siege of loving terms,
> Nor bide th'encounter of assailing eyes,
> Nor ope her lap to saint-seducing gold.
>
> (1.1.205–11)

This description of Rosaline as Diana protected by the proof of her chastity and as some anti-Danaë who will not be seduced by the power or even by a shower of gold as in Ovid (a myth often represented in the Renaissance by painters such as Titian) assimilates her to one of those 'deities' or 'court nymphs' who were then part of what André Chastel has called the 'eroticism of cold beauty': 'Le cycle de Diane s'accomplit dans cette célébration grandiose de la féminité voluptueuse et méprisante, parfaite et inaccessible.'[3] Benvolio would like to tempt Romeo away from this local Diana, who also seems quite inaccessible and certainly remains invisible all along the play, and thus he urges him to

> Compare her face with some that I shall show,
> And I will make thee think thy swan a crow.
>
> (1.2.88–9)

To which Romeo retorts:

> When the devout religion of mine eye
> Maintains such falsehood, then turn tears to fires,
> And these who, often drowned, could never die,
> Transparent heretics, be burnt for liars.
>
> (1.2.90–3)

Romeo swears that he is ready to be burnt at the stake, to die for love and his faith, rather than prove a heretic. But Benvolio was right. As soon as he sees Juliet, Romeo singles her out as a 'snowy dove trooping with crows' (1.5.47). And when he actually meets her, the pair share a love sonnet where he becomes a pilgrim coming to touch the holy shrine of her saint-like body.

In these images, Juliet metaphorically appears as the statue of some virgin saint which he has come to adore, so that Marian or Roman idolatry is here being transposed to the field of profane love and dramatic lyric.

In an earlier sonnet, Lady Capulet had used a conceit to praise the beauty of Paris and encourage her daughter to love him, by comparing the young man to a book in need of a cover:

> This precious book of love, this unbound lover,
> To beautify him only lacks a cover.
> The fish lives in the sea, and 'tis much pride
> For fair without the fair within to hide.
> That book in many's eyes doth share the glory
> That in gold clasps locks in the golden story.
>
> (1.3.87–92)

The words 'gold' and 'golden' here ironically hark back at the image of the 'saint-seducing gold' that could not persuade the chaste and serious Rosaline. But the phrase 'the golden story' probably also evokes the famous book of saints and martyrs of the Church, namely *The Golden Legend* by James de Voragine, bishop of Genoa, one of the first books printed by Caxton. At the same time, the image looks ahead to the golden statues of the two lovers that will be raised by the parents after their 'untimely death':

> MONTAGUE For I will raise her statue in pure gold,
>   That whiles Verona by that name is known,
>   There shall no figure at such rate be set
>   As that of true and faithful Juliet.

> CAPULET As rich shall Romeo's by his lady's lie,
>   Poor sacrifices of our enmity.
>
> (5.3.298–303)

In other words, the double death of the title parts is assimilated to a form of martyrdom, to the choice of paying the heavy price of their young lives for their faith and love. Romeo and Juliet become the 'saints' of the medieval and early modern cult of love and passion.

Reading the clouds: *Antony and Cleopatra*

Antony and Cleopatra is another, later companion piece to *Romeo and Juliet*, giving a picture of mature, adult passion also based on social transgression. Here the 'Roman' element seems quite remote from the world of love, especially when embodied by young Octavius Caesar who is an ambitious general and a cold-headed calculator. The expression 'Roman thought', used by Cleopatra to describe the sudden change in Antony at the news that he must return to Rome after the death of his wife Fulvia, suggests severity and strict discipline.[4] Octavia's portrait by the Messenger in Act 3 gives a good illustration of what is meant by this in terms of beauty and aesthetics:

> Her motion and her station are as one.
> She shows a body rather than a life,
> A statue than a breather.
>
> (3.3.19–21)[5]

As we shall see later, this satirical vignette is both an antithesis and an anticipation of Hermione's 'breathing', living statue. But in these lines from *Antony and Cleopatra* Octavia stands poles apart from Cleopatra herself who, according to Enobarbus, 'did make defect perfection,/ And, breathless, pour breath forth' (2.2.241–2). In the imbricated as well as antithetical pictures, which are painted of Rome and Alexandria, Rome clearly corresponds to the outer frame while Egypt represents the painting proper. This dramatic distancing consists here in pushing back the main action into a perspective frame as in the use, at the beginning of the play, of two choric figures like those of Philo and Demetrius, who comment on the current 'dotage' of the general. Antony's addiction to a 'gypsy's lust' is mocked as the general and the gypsy enter followed by a train of eunuchs fanning Cleopatra. This is a dramatic counterpart of the gestures of the *Sprecher* figure in Mannerist painting.[6] The sonnet prologues in *Romeo and Juliet* and the indirect or deflected information provided in the second scene of Act 5 in *The Winter's Tale*, where the highly emotional scene of *anagnorisis* is described in the course of a long conversation between three anonymous 'Gentlemen', are equivalents of and variations on this same technique of alienation.

Another characteristic mode, which uses allusion while avoiding depiction as such, is found in Enobarbus' famous narrative of Cleopatra's arrival on her barge on the river Cydnus in 2.2. The whole passage depends upon an aesthetics of absence or emptiness, since Cleopatra herself is described only indirectly through her entourage and exotic apparatus.[7] When it comes to describing 'her own person', Enobarbus resorts to an intriguing association of tropes that combines ellipsis and hyperbole, since her appearance is said to 'beggar all description':

> she did lie
> In her pavilion, cloth-of-gold of tissue,
> O'erpicturing that Venus where we see
> The fancy outwork nature.
>
> (2.2.208–11)[8]

By using the deictic pronoun 'that', Shakespeare titillates his audience by seeming to allude to a supposedly well-known Venus whose real identity remains in fact totally vague. Such tantalizing allusions in matters of art are evocative of the Mannerist technique known as *non finito*. In this particular perspective, the painted or carved body remains hazy or in the making in order to create a sense of transience and relativity. Beauty lies in the eye of the beholder. This very same feeling is emphasized in 4.14, when Mark Antony faces his own sunset and reads the signs in the clouds:

> Sometime we see a cloud that's dragonish,
> A vapour sometime like a bear or lion,
> A towered citadel, a pendent rock,
> A forked mountain, or blue promontory
> With trees upon't that nod unto the world
> And mock our eyes with air. Thou hast seen these signs?
> They are black vesper's pageants.
>
> (4.14.2–8)

These figures in the clouds, already mentioned as a game in *Hamlet*, depend on the belief that there is a *disegno* in nature, an idea exploited by Mantegna (1431–1506) in two well-known pieces, *The Martyrdom of St Sebastian*, which is hanging in the Kunsthistorisches Museum in Vienna, and *Minerva Expelling the Vices* in the Louvre. A similar technique is also used in the tree trunks suggesting human shapes in Piero di Cosimo's paintings.[9] The theory behind all this is Leonardo's *Treatise on Painting*, where the author requires the artist to pay attention to the

> power of confused shapes, such as clouds or muddy water ... You should look at walls stained with damp, or stones or uneven colour. If you have to invent backgrounds, you will be able to see in these mountains, ruins, rocks, plains, hills and valleys ... and then battles and figures in violent action, expressions of faces,

and an infinity of things you will be able to reduce to their complete and proper forms. The same thing happens as in the sound of bells, in whose stroke you may hear every word you can imagine.[10]

Michelangelo's unfinished statues which were used to adorn the walls of the artificial grotto of Buontalenti in Florence, or Piero Mati's human shapes in the same place, represent an interesting endeavour to apply those principles which were aiming at blending or reconciling the two contrary poles of art and nature. In the grotto, the human figure emerges from the wall in a confusion of motifs of petrified chalk, thus giving the impression that they are indeed images made by chance, miraculously resulting from the creative moulds of *natura naturans*. It is as if they came straight out of the womb of Mother Nature.[11]

If we now go back to Antony's cloud images, it is interesting to establish a possible link between the passage and Mantegna's St Sebastian, especially with the mention of the horse at the end:

> That which is now a horse, even with a thought
> The rack dislimns and makes it indistinct
> As water is in water.
>
> (4.14.9–11)

Indeed, Antony's mention of a horse and a rack introduces a possible pun on the word rack as a torture instrument, so that the verb 'dislimns' can also be heard as '*dislimbs*' in the sense of 'dismembers'. So, the quibble introduces an effect of duplication or equivocation, which superimposes images of physical torture over the illusions of the masque. The word 'rack' was indeed the technical term used to designate the cloud machine of the Stuart masque, so that this is probably to be connected with Jonson's *Masque of Blackness* performed on Twelfth Night 1605, a piece which offers intriguing parallels with Shakespeare's tragedy.[12] Mantegna's St Sebastian shows in the foreground the saint's body pierced with arrows while the background clouds on the left-hand side, above, reveal the image of a horse, or rather of a man riding a white horse, so that the painting does look like a visual illustration of Antony's lines. Did Shakespeare know of this painting for which he gave a verbal, if not a verbatim translation? This is just another wild hypothesis for which there is of course no answer, but the parallel is rather striking.[13] For Darriulat, Mantegna's horse in the clouds is ultimately to be read as an allegory of painting while, for Yves Peyré, 'Antony's meditation on the dissolution of matter … is appropriate in a tragedy in which two civilizations, Rome and Alexandria, clash, with one of them doomed to disappear'.[14] The ruins, the torment of Sebastian, and the horse are then to be read as a kind of 'writing on the wall', or apocalyptic message, foreshadowing the end of Ptolemaic Egypt and the rise of the Roman Empire.

But the image of the horse rider may also be interpreted as part of the play's internal symbolism. Indeed, when Cleopatra is alone, she imagines Antony on his horse:

> Stands he, or sits he?
> Or does he walk? Or is he on his horse?
> O happy horse, to bear the weight of Antony!
> Do bravely, horse, for wot'st thou when thou mov'st?
> The demi-Atlas of this earth, the arm
> And burgonet of men!
>
> (1.5.20–5)

The horse image may be a reminder of Cleopatra's dream or erotic fantasy, a sort of fuzzy signature in the fleeting vapours of the setting sun. This may be reminiscent of the then current theory of the 'maternal print' (in the writings of the Aristotelian philosopher Pomponazzi as well as in Ambroise Paré) which established a link between a pregnant woman's 'longings' and the imagination of the artist who had both the power, as it were, to shape their fantasy on the flesh of the child or on their canvas or marble block. The word 'horse' may also be a double-entendre suggesting 'whores', a usual Elizabethan pun of which Frankie Rubinstein gives many examples in *A Dictionary of Shakespeare's Sexual Puns*.[15] As such it looks ahead to Cleopatra's refusal to see 'Some squeaking Cleopatra boy my greatness / I'th' posture of a whore' (5.2.219–20). The word 'horse' also anticipates her heroic or maniloquent dream of Antony as 'emperor' of the world when Cleopatra says to Dolabella that Antony's 'legs bestrid the ocean' (5.2.81), thus turning him into a cosmic rider. As in Leonardo's fine image of the 'sound of bells, in whose stroke you may hear every word you can imagine', Shakespeare's imagery and diction combine visual with acoustic anamorphosis. Like Antony, who, according to Cleopatra, is 'painted one way like a Gorgon, / The other way's a Mars' (2.5.118–19), Shakespearean language moves in a double direction, one way towards the grotesque and the obscene, the other way towards a form of transcendence or sublimity. This is congruent with the succession of masque and antimasque forms and themes evolved by Ben Jonson in the preface to *The Masque of Queens*, performed at court in 1609. But the technique had already been used by Shakespeare in *A Midsummer Night's Dream*.[16] So the two love tragedies of *Romeo and Juliet* and *Antony and Cleopatra* share these alternating modes and moods as well as these silent references to the visual arts where specific authors are never mentioned except in a roundabout way in the tentative traces or signatures that may be retrieved or deciphered in a few select textual images. But when we leave the world of the 'Romans' for that of the 'romances', things seem to work the other way round.

'Her natural posture'

A play like *The Winter's Tale* is indeed known for its wild charades or odd singularities, like the 'sea-coast of Bohemia', the stage direction 'Exit Antigonus pursued by a bear', as well as for its riddling allusion to the 'statue … newly performed by that rare Italian master, Julio Romano' (5.2.94–6).[17] Leonard Barkan and Stephen Orgel explain that the mistake may be due to Giulio's epitaph quoted by Vasari: 'Jupiter saw sculpted and painted bodies breathe and the houses of mortals made equal to those in heaven through the skill of Giulio Romano'.[18] For Orgel, 'the problem as far as Shakespeare is concerned is solved. Giulio was known in the Renaissance as a sculptor'.[19] Leo Salingar is more cautious. For him, it is quite possible that Shakespeare

> made his choice of a 'rare Italian master' because of his reputation for *trompe l'œil* effects; in any case, his genuine but generic sounding name, Julius the Roman, contributes to that sleight-of-hand of flickering ambiguity between actuality and impossibility characteristic of his romance where Sicilians have been wrecked on the sea-coast of Bohemia and the Delphic oracle has been consulted about a Russian princess.[20]

This may well be so. But I think that Shakespeare's strategy of vagueness and evasion has now changed. By naming the supposed author of the wonderful piece, he wants to call attention to the signifier 'Giulio Romano' as such.

The little we know, through Vasari, of the life of Giulio Romano (1499–1546) is that he was the disciple of Raphael who became a master of Italian Mannerism. He left Rome for Mantua in 1524 in order to work for the Duke of Gonzaga. This is the city where he built the famous Palazzo del Tè, which he then decorated with mythological frescoes representing the 'Battle of the Giants'. Some critics suggest that the Mantuan exile was due not, like Romeo's, to manslaughter in a duel but to the scandal caused by the publication, this very same year, of his erotic drawings for Aretino's sixteen *Sonetti lussuriosi*. These infamous pornographic pieces were widely known in the Renaissance and referred to as Romano's *posizioni*.[21] The book was censored on publication and the original prints were destroyed. But a number of copies were made by a certain Waldeck and were then widely circulated.[22]

Now, when in the final scene Paulina draws the curtain and reveals the statue, Leontes' first words are the exclamation 'Her natural posture' (5.3.23). The word 'posture', reminiscent of Cleopatra's 'i'th'posture of a whore', is almost certainly a hint at Romano's well-known erotica. Of course, this comes as a bit of a shock in the almost sacred atmosphere of the family reunion and quasi-miraculous motion of the stonework. But this shocking association also corresponds to the Mannerist style, which was born in a period of crisis and to a taste for what Frederick Hartt has called a 'special emphasis on abnormal and spectacular attitudes, on acute physical strain, and on frustration' which he regards as significant for the psychology of early Mannerism.[23] So, once Leontes' double entendre is perceived, it may be thought of as iconoclastic and even blasphemous in the miraculous, moving moment of Hermione's reapparition from the dead as it were. In fact, it adds a comic touch to a highly solemn moment, very much in the style of tragicomedy, just like Paulina's attempt to rein in Perdita's enthusiasm by referring to the fresh coat of paint on the statue:

> O, patience!
> The statue is but newly fixed, the colour's
> Not dry.
>
> (46–8)

Interestingly, the situation sounds like an inversion of Romeo's misprision when he sees 'dead' Juliet in the Capulets' monument:

> O my love, my wife,
> Death, that hath sucked the honey of thy breath,
> Hath had no power yet upon thy beauty.
> Thou art not conquered; beauty's ensign yet
> Is crimson in thy lips and in thy cheeks,
> And death's pale flag is not advanced there.
>
> (5.3.92–7)

The 'dead' body, which he describes here, shows no sign of death because it is still alive, a conclusion which he somehow comes to at a subconscious level, as the imagery ironically reveals, without clearly realizing it in his brain. Indeed, Shakespeare introduces a dissociation between what Romeo says and feels on the one hand, and what he thinks and 'knows' on the other, just as he reinforces the gap between the audience's awareness and the character's passionate blindness. The same holds true of Leontes' comparison between the statue and 'her' daughter where 'stone' and 'spirits' are interchanged:

> O royal piece!
> There's magic in thy majesty, which has
> My evils conjur'd to remembrance, and
> From thy admiring daughter took the spirits,
> Standing like stone with thee.
>
> (5.3.38–42)

For the King of Sicilia, this is the sign of artistic perfection since the illusion of life itself has been created: 'The fixure of her eye has motion in't, / As we are mock'd with art' (67–8).

This may be read as the Sicilian answer to Perdita's desire for an art that is nature itself contrary to the 'pied gillyflowers' in her exchange with Polixenes in the course of the sheep-shearing feast in Bohemia. This fusion of nature and art is achieved also in the last act of *The Winter's Tale* in the criss-crossing of geographic and cultural signs: the pastoral is staged in Bohemia and the picture gallery (which may hint at Rudolph II's famous *Wunderkammer* in Prague) is set in Sicilia. And, in Mantua, the 'famous sculptor' Giulio Romano stands in between as it were.

So, from Romeo to Romano, the whole process of Roman allusion and diffuse presence of Italian art has come full circle and has been completely reversed. Instead of 'a statue in pure gold', to commemorate the tragedy of the 'star-crossed lovers', Hermione's living statue offers a metaphor of the wonders of dramatic illusion in keeping with the ekphrastic powers of the Jacobean masque.

'What's in a name', Juliet asked in order to exorcize the dire fate of the family feud in Verona. In *The Winter's Tale*, the question of the name becomes very meaningful since the Third Gentleman's allusion to Giulio Romano serves to moralize and modernize the Ovidian myth of Pygmalion. This combines topical reference (the scandal of Romano's *posizioni*) with an emphasis on the female rather than on the male as the Pygmalion myth is now emblematized on stage as '*Hermione*'s statue'. Giulio Romano is thus another case of 'Ovid moralisé' where the pagan fable is translated into a Christian and, possibly, into a Roman Catholic allegory. Art becomes a means to 'awake [our] faith', a device which anticipates Roman baroque and Counter-Reformation churches, fountains, or statues, which, like the flamboyant *mise-en-scène* of St Theresa's ecstasy in the Cornaro chapel in Santa Maria della Vittoria in Rome, are meant to prompt in the spectator a blending of mystic élan and erotic frisson.

In *Antony and Cleopatra*, the end transcends the sharp successive polarities opposing Rome and Egypt in order to achieve something like an alchemical fusion of contraries. Mark Antony dies after reading the signs in the clouds of his own sunset, an experience in fragmentation and dissolution ('Here I am Antony, / Yet cannot hold this visible shape' (4.14.13–14). Contrary to this form of almost feminine *jouissance*, where Eros and Thanatos meet, Cleopatra decides to die 'after the high Roman fashion' (4.15.91) and she becomes 'marble constant' with 'nothing / Of woman in [her]' (5.2.237–8). So it is paradoxically through Cleopatra that Roman art is rehabilitated in the end as a symbol of stoic or heroic death. This combines the pagan with the Christian ideals and reconciles Plutarch's *Lives* with *The Golden Legend* in what looks like an eclectic but truly humanist stance. In other words, Roman art in Shakespeare, whether it is exiled in Mantua or in Alexandria, remains a model and a source of inspiration. Most of all it is an overarching means to unify a number of fragmentary, odd references or correspondences scattered in plays written over a period of some sixteen years, from 1595 to 1611. It is intriguing that 'the wide gap of time' between the Sicilian events, the Bohemian interlude, and the young lovers' return to the court of Leontes, where Hermione's statue is unveiled, roughly corresponds to the interval between the writing of *Romeo and Juliet* and *The Winter's Tale*. It is tempting to conclude on the suggestion that in Giulio Romano's stone statue the name of the Roman artist may after all work as the quibbling counterpart of the gold statue of Romeo and Juliet. Rome, Romeo, Romano are of one place as well as of everywhere: 'Infinite riches in a little room' but also 'Rome indeed and room enough'.[24]

Notes

1 *Romeo and Juliet*, ed. Brian Gibbons (London, Methuen, 1980)
2 Joseph A. Porter, *Shakespeare's Mercutio* (Chapel Hill and London, University of Carolina Press, 1988), pp. 102–3.
3 André Chastel, *Mythe et crise de la Renaissance* (Geneva, Skira, 1968–69, repr. 1989), p. 341: 'The Diana cycle is completed in the grand celebration of a voluptuous, distant femininity, which is both perfect and inaccessible.'
4 See G. K. Hunter, 'A Roman Thought: Renaissance Attitudes to History Exemplified in Shakespeare and Jonson', in Brian S. Lee, ed., *An English Miscellany: Presented to W. S. Mackie* (Cape Town, London, New York, Oxford University Press, 1977), p. 94: 'When Cleopatra uses the phrase "a Roman thought" she means one that is "soldierly, severe, self-controlled, disciplined"'.
5 *Antony and Cleopatra*, ed. John Wilders, The Arden Shakespeare (London, Routledge, 1995).
6 See Michael Neill, introduction to *Anthony and Cleopatra*, The World's Classics (Oxford, Oxford University Press, 1994), p. 89.
7 In this connection, see my '*Antoine et Cléopâtre* ou l'esthétique du vide', *Etudes Anglaises*, 4 (octobre–décembre 2000), 400–12.
8 In a note to his edition of the play (Cambridge, Cambridge University Press, 1990), David Bevington writes: 'Surpassing the picture or statue of Venus. Whether Shakespeare had a particular work in mind is unknown. Pliny's *Natural History* ... mentions a famous picture by Apelles, "Venus Anadyomene" or Venus Rising from the Sea – a subject also painted by Botticelli' (pp. 124–5).
9 See H. W. Janson, 'The Image Made by Chance', in *Sixteen Studies* (New York, 1972), pp. 53–69.
10 Quoted by Ernst Gombrich, *Art and Illusion: A Study in the Psychology of Pictorial Representation* (London, Phaidon, 1960), pp. 154–61.
11 On this see Philippe Morel, *Les grottes maniéristes en Italie au XVIe siècle* (Paris, Macula, 1998), pp. 48–64.
12 See Philippa Berry, '"The crown o'th'earth doth melt": The Alchemy of States in *Antony and Cleopatra*', in Pierre Iselin, ed., *William Shakespeare: 'Antony and Cleopatra'* (Paris, Didier Erudition, 2000), pp. 50–1.
13 See Jacques Darriulat, *Sébastien le Renaissant* (Paris, Lagune, 1998), pp. 115–30; Yves Peyré, '"Travels in the clouds": Metamorphosis, Doubt, and Reason in the Renaissance', in Jean-Marie Maguin and Michèle Willems, eds, *French Essays on Shakespeare and His Contemporaries* (London, Cranbury, NJ and Mississauga,

Ontario, Associated University Presses, 1995), pp. 11–15.
14 Peyré, 'Travels in the clouds', p. 15.
15 *A Dictionary of Shakespeare's Sexual Puns and their Significance* (London, Macmillan, 1984).
16 See my 'Masque et antimasque dans *A Midsummer Night's Dream*', in Pierre Iselin and Jean-Pierre Moreau, eds, *Le songe d'une nuit d'été et La Duchesse de Malfi* (Limoges, Trames, 1989), pp. 113–41.
17 *The Winter's Tale*, ed. J. H. P. Pafford (London, Methuen, 1963).
18 Leonard Barkan, 'Living Sculptures: Ovid, Michelangelo and *The Winter's Tale*', *ELH*, 48 (1981), 639–67; Stephen Orgel, ed., *The Winter's Tale*, World's Classics (Oxford, Oxford University Press, 1996), pp. 221–2 (footnote).
19 'Introduction', p. 57.
20 'Shakespeare and the Italian Concept of Art', in his *Dramatic Form in Shakespeare and the Jacobeans* (Cambridge, Cambridge University Press, 1986), p. 15.
21 See David O. Frantz, *Festum Voluptatis: A Study of Renaissance Erotica* (Columbus, Ohio, Ohio University Press, 1989), p. 2.
22 See Frantz, *Festum Voluptatis*, figures 1 and 2, after p. 139.
23 Frederick Hartt, *Giulio Romano* (New Haven, Yale University Press, 1958), 2 vols, I, p. 282. Paul Barolsky, *Infinite Jest: Wit and Humor in Italian Renaissance Art* (Columbia, University of Missouri Press, 1978), sees *Posizioni* as sexual comedy.
24 Christopher Marlowe, *The Jew of Malta* (1.1.37) and Shakespeare, *Julius Caesar* (1.2.156).

17

Shakespeare in the *bottega*: art works, apocrypha, and the stage

GIORGIO MELCHIORI

> A hand, or eye
> By *Hilliard* drawne, is worth an history,
> By a worse painter made;
>
> John Donne, *The Storme*, 3–5

A history can be told by different means. Painting is a visual representation of it, but a stage play combines the visual and the verbal elements in the telling. What matters is the hand or the touch of the artist who undertakes the narration. Can we really distinguish Shakespeare's hand from that of lesser artists who presented such a wealth of stage plays in the Elizabethan and Jacobean ages?

The problem of attribution has engaged both literary and art historians for centuries; in fact art scholars were the first in the field, since establishing whether a painting or a sculpture came from the hand of a famous artist or not made for a substantial difference in assessing the work's commercial or market value. Art merchants entrusted experts with the task of vouching for the authenticity of a work to a prospective buyer. The experts in turn devised most sophisticated methods of determining the age of the canvas or stone, the characteristic touch of different artists, their use of colour, of brush-work, their techniques in carving or modelling and so on. But long before modern technology put new scientific instruments such as X-rays or computerized tests of the materials at the disposal of the experts, a very simple notion was present in their minds: that of the 'school' or *bottega*.

This notion was suggested by a consideration of the social status of the artist from the early Renaissance onward: he was a skilled craftsman working for a patron – the merchant, the Church, the nobleman's palace. He did not work in splendid isolation in a private studio: he had a workshop (his *bottega*), and one or more helpers – generally apprentices to his trade. It is common knowledge that Giotto as a boy was apprenticed to Cimabue; and when in turn, having become a recognized master in the trade, he was commissioned to decorate the Scrovegni Chapel in Padua, it would be foolish to think that Giotto worked at that impressive cycle of frescos single-handed – while there is no question that the general design, layout and execution of each single picture is due to him, art historians have detected in several of them the brush strokes of *aiuti*. This practice, already common in the fourteenth century, was the norm throughout the early and high Renaissance, the most splendid age of European art.

Now, if we turn to consider the status of the English playwright in that extraordinary period of the history of the theatre which was the Elizabethan age, we find that it did not differ in any marked measure from that of his contemporaries, the continental visual artists. The theatre 'poet' was an expert craftsman who provided scripts for a sponsor: not of course the merchant or the Church, but the theatre manager and the playhouse audiences (significantly, theatre companies in turn sought the patronage of the nobility). Like their status, the working methods of the English playwright and the continental artist were parallel. Let us put it in this way: a skilled dramatist (the 'master') would devise the plot and write out a script, but in giving it its final form he had a number of *aiuti*, younger playwrights (they could be called 'apprentices') and especially his fellow actors. In the most precious document of the theatrical practices in the Elizabethan age, Philip Henslowe's *Diary*, until as late as 1598 no payment for a play 'book' is made to a single author, but always to several who contributed to its writing; and it records even later payments for 'additions' to existing plays written by other authors. As in the art market, so in the publishing trade of the early seventeenth century, when an author – artist or playwright – had reached an outstanding reputation, unscrupulous, or at times even *bona-fide* traders attributed to him works in which he had had no hand, or perhaps, as Thomas Heywood said of his own production, only a little finger. In the art field these are normally called 'fakes', in that of the Elizabethan theatre and especially of Shakespeare, 'apocrypha'.

When nearly a century ago C. F. Tucker Brooke published an impressive volume under the title *The Shakespeare Apocrypha*[1] he listed no fewer than forty-two plays which had been at different times attributed to Shakespeare but did not figure in the first Folio of 1623, claimed by Heminge and Condell to contain all the Comedies, Histories, and Tragedies that he had written 'cur'd, and perfect in their limbes … as he conceiued the[m]'.[2] Brooke felt the need to justify the absence from his 'catalogue' of one Folio play, *Titus Andronicus*, that many at the time considered spurious, and of *Pericles*, not included in the Folio: '*Pericles* and *Titus Andronicus* are designedly omitted because they have established their position in practice, if not in universal opinion, among the genuine works.' The absence from the list of *Edmund Ironside* merely indicates that by 1908 nobody had as yet suggested the name of Shakespeare as its author.

Out of these forty-two plays Tucker Brooke granted to only thirteen the claim to be considered 'doubtful plays' of Shakespeare and published them together with *Sir Thomas More*. It should be noted that among them there is *The Two*

Noble Kinsmen, a play that is now regularly included in all editions of the complete plays of Shakespeare as a collaboration with John Fletcher. Brooke issued a warning: 'The exact likelihood of Shakespeare's connexion with any member of this various group must be determined by careful individual examination. On the whole, it may be said, the reader will be impressed more with the unlikeness of the doubtful to the authentic plays than with their likeness.'

On the strength of the scanty evidence available to him, Brooke's diffidence, rather than caution, was more than justified. Now, I have been involved in providing critical editions of two of the plays that figure in Brooke's volume: *The Reign of Edward the Third* and *The Book of Sir Thomas More*. This entailed a close study of the theatrical practices in the Elizabethan age and more specifically in the 1590s.

Before attempting to relate the conclusions I reached about the nature of these plays, I wish to refer to a recent case in the parallel field of Renaissance art studies that served to confirm the opinion I had matured in respect of the Elizabethan plays I edited. The case is that of a statue of *Cristo Redentore* (figure 17.1 below) which, after having been for more than three centuries on the main altar was confined some thirty years ago to the sacristy of the Church of San Vincenzo Martire in the countryside near Bassano Romano, a church built in the seventeenth century by the nobleman Vincenzo Giustiniani. It had been taken for granted that a minor artist (supposedly Ippolito Buzio, 1562–1634) had sculpted it in the early years of the seventeenth century as a copy with variants of the well-known *Cristo Risorto* by Michelangelo in the church of Santa Maria sopra Minerva, Rome (figure 17.2 below). Being considered a mere late copy of the work of a master, the Bassano Christ had escaped the notice of scholars and was never publicized, until very recently art historian Silvia Danesi Squarzina, after years of research in the archives of the Giustiniani family (with the help of her pupil Irene Baldriga who searched the correspondence of the Buonarroti descendants), was able to reconstruct beyond any reasonable doubt the true history of the origin of the statue.[3]

The Roman patrician Metello Vari had commissioned the statue of *Cristo Risorto* on 14 June 1514 from Michelangelo for the church of Santa Maria sopra Minerva. As usual, Michelangelo started to work on the marble block from the base, and had more than roughed-out the feet, the legs, the torso and the left hand of the statue (as Donne recognized, the treatment of a hand is the hallmark of the artist), when he detected a serious flaw in the top part of the block (figure 17.3 below). Michelangelo left the work unfinished, and the next year went to Florence; there he got a new block of marble and worked on the statue in 1519–20, so that in 1521 his assistant Pietro Urbano carried it to Rome and, after Urbano had given it some rather poor finishing touches, the *Cristo Risorto* was placed, with the help of Federico Frizzi, in the Minerva church. The unfinished statue, instead, was donated in January 1522 to Metello Vari, who housed it in the courtyard of his house in Rome, near the Minerva church, and another nobleman, Ulisse Aldrovandi, recorded seeing it there in 1549–50. About a century later this sculpture became available for purchase, and the Giustiniani – a family of art collectors – bought the unfinished block and placed it at first in their Roman palace and set some able artist or artisan in their service to complete it, in spite of the flaw in the marble, which is still clearly visible. In 1644, respecting the will of the late Marquis Vincenzo Giustiniani, his heirs took it to Bassano Romano to place it in the San Vincenzo church. I will discuss this sculpture in more detail later in the chapter.

If this were not a sculpture but a play it would certainly qualify to be included among the Michelangelo Apocrypha. What I want to point out is the analogy in the process of production of figurative and dramatic works in the late Renaissance. The main difference is in the fact that while in the case of the sculpture Michelangelo was the originator, the 'plotter' of a work completed by other hands, in the two plays I edited young William Shakespeare was merely one of the *aiuti* called upon to complete a work plotted by others.

I had the privilege of being entrusted, together with Vittorio Gabrieli, with an edition of *The Book of Sir Thomas More*.[4] It was not included in any of the current series devoted to Shakespeare's dramatic works, but it appeared among the Revels Plays, a series that, in the words of its founder, Clifford Leech, aimed 'to apply to Shakespeare's predecessors, contemporaries and successors the methods that are now used in Shakespeare editing'. The play of *Sir Thomas More* had already appeared in some editions of the complete works of Shakespeare such as those edited by C. J. Sisson (1953), where it figured as an appendix edited by Harold Jenkins, and the Nonesuch Press edited by Herbert Farjeon (1953), while the Tudor Shakespeare (ed. Peter Alexander, 1951), The London Shakespeare (ed. John Munro, 1958), the Riverside Shakespeare (ed. G. Blakemore Evans, 1974) and the Oxford Shakespeare (ed. Stanley Wells and Gary Taylor, 1986), included only those scenes of the play which were thought to be Shakespeare's. It is today generally acknowledged that at least part of one scene of the play is Shakespeare's – three pages which are the only surviving evidence of Shakespeare's handwriting.[5]

We thought that presenting the Shakespearean scene(s) of the play out of their natural context, i.e. the whole dramatic structure into which he had fitted them, was seriously misleading. The only justification for such a procedure was the state in which the manuscript had reached us, that had induced previous scholars to consider it rather as an extremely interesting theatrical document than as a fully elaborated and complete performable playtext. With the single exception of Harold Jenkins's modern-spelling edition, *The Booke of Sir Thomas Moore* had been reproduced diplomatically, conveying the impression of a fragmentary and unfinished text – an impression emphasized in the otherwise admirable edition of 1911 by W. W. Greg for the Malone Society where the additions in different hands were printed as appendices to an original in the hand of Anthony Munday which presented most conspicuous gaps, evidencing the fact that some parts of the original version of the play were irretrievably lost. Obviously Greg's edition with Harold Jenkins's later corrections of some misreadings of the manuscript (further misreadings of the same nature were privately pointed out to us by Peter Blayney) was our starting point; but we confronted our task with a precise aim: to ascertain the stageworthiness of the text once all the substitute passages, cancellations, and corrections in the manuscript were put in their proper places, disregarding at first the different hands contributing them and the question of authorship. A play after all is a vehicle for acting and what matters is its effectiveness in performance. In other words we considered *Sir Thomas More* as any other script intended for the stage in the form it had reached after the intervention of several highly skilled professionals intent on providing serious entertainment for an appreciative audience.

I hope that in our edition we produced enough evidence for the origin and the stages of composition of the play, undertaken by Anthony Munday possibly in collaboration with Henry Chettle and young Thomas Dekker. Munday furnished a fair copy for submission to a company of actors who required a number of changes and improvements to render the script more stageworthy and to avoid trouble with censorship. It was at this point that Thomas Heywood added a new part for a clown, absent in the original, Chettle rewrote parts of some scenes, and Shakespeare was asked to rewrite completely the scene representing a popular rebellion. A bookkeeper was entrusted with the task of inserting the new contributions into the script and providing suitable directions; but even after the replacement of a number of scenes, amounting to a re-structuration especially of the central part of the play, it was felt that further linking passages were needed to render the stage action more fluid. The job was undertaken by Dekker, Heywood, and a third writer whose identity cannot be established with any certainty because his contribution was transcribed in the bookkeeper's hand – several scholars suspect him to be Shakespeare himself. The result was a well constructed play running smoothly and dramatically effective – so effective in fact that the Master of the Revels thought it politically dangerous, and that is presumably why it never reached the stage.

The experience with editing *Sir Thomas More* was an object lesson when I came to edit my second 'apocryphal' play: *King Edward III*.[6] From the *More* manuscript I had learned a lot on how collaboration worked in the plays for the public theatre: in the first place, such plays in the 1590s might have been planned by a single mind but were the result of the contributions of several writers, in the same way as now a number of scriptwriters collaborate on a film or television script. The disadvantage in this case was that I had at my disposal only printed copies so that I missed the guidance of the different hands that appeared in the manuscript of *More*. I had learned as well the impossibility of discriminating and identifying the different contributors because the final result was a coherent actable text. The only clues were provided by some irregularities in the print such as confusions in stage divisions and speech prefixes as well as the frequency of obvious printer's misreadings of the manuscript copies in some specific sections of the playtext. What stood out was that the scenes in which scholars had suggested the presence of Shakespeare's hand (Act 1 scene 2 and the whole of Act 2) appeared only loosely linked with the rest of the play, and that most of the printer's misreadings of the original manuscript were concentrated in them, as if the printer had been confronted in such pages with a different hand from that which had written the rest of *Edward III* – and some of these misreadings were due to the peculiar spellings of words that had their counterpart in the three Shakespearean manuscript pages of *Sir Thomas More*. This suggests that they were printed from manuscript pages in Shakespeare's hand; they amount in other words to what Greg called 'additions'. As in the case of *Sir Thomas More*, also in that of *Edward III* William Shakespeare, a young actor whom his fellows had begun to appreciate for his skill at playwriting, had been asked to contribute a scene or a sequence of scenes to replace a part of the play that for some reason was considered unsuitable or dramatically ineffectual. This does not rule out the possibility that he might at the same time have been one in what a reviewer has called the 'syndicate' responsible for the original writing of the play. Is this reason enough to promote *Edward III* from apocryphal to canonical status? And does it – this promotion, I mean – really matter?

As in the case of a work by Michelangelo or Giotto, what matters, beyond all question of the attribution to individual authors, collaborators or *aiuti*, is that a fresco or a statue should strike us as an integrated whole, and that a play should be dramatically effective. I feel that, like the Scrovegni chapel or the Giustiniani Christ, both *Sir Thomas More* and *Edward III* fulfil this requirement.

An excursus on hands

I have been concerned in the previous pages with the analogy between theatrical practice in the Elizabethan age and the working conditions of visual artists in the Italian Renaissance. How do these similarities reflect on the critical and philological approaches to the same fields of study? This brief excursus is meant to illustrate and document precisely this point.

The textual scholar and the art critic must in the first place collect any scrap of evidence offered by the works they examine, taking into account two elements: the general conditions, historical, social, professional, under which the works were originally produced on the one hand, and on the other the physical conditions of the works themselves, i.e. the state in which a manuscript or a printed book or a piece of sculpture or a painting is found at present. This is largely detective work and it must be stated from the outset that the conclu-

Shakespeare in the bottega

17.1 *Cristo Redentore*, in the Church of San Vincenzo Martire at Bassano Romano, Viterbo. First version of the marble statue of Christ in the Minerva church (figure 17.2), left unfinished by Michelangelo Buonarroti in 1514–16 and completed by other hands in the seventeenth century, with the further addition of a metal loincloth which has now been removed. Height 201 cm. without the cross.

17.2 *Cristo Risorto*, by Michelangelo Buonarroti in the Church of Santa Maria sopra Minerva, Rome. Marble sculpture, 1618–21. Height c. 205 cm.

sions reached cannot be considered absolute truths: the quality of the single work examined is the only warrant for undertaking the enquiry into its origin and nature. The main question is that of authorship, which is particularly relevant in cases like those I have been dealing with, that is to say works resulting from some form of collaboration, which is exactly the case of most works produced in the two areas under consideration.

Let me look at the evidence for considering the Bassano statue (figure 17.1) not just as a late copy with variants, but as an earlier version of the *Cristo Risorto* by Michelangelo in Santa Maria sopra Minerva (figure 17. 2).

The search into the documents connected with the art collections of the Giustiniani brought to light an inventory of their works of art compiled in 1638, containing a description of precisely the Bassano statue.[7] The next step in assessing the early history of the Bassano statue was the already mentioned discovery, through a number of other documents, that Michelangelo had not completed the first version of his Christ for the Minerva church because of a serious flaw – a dark vein – in the marble block he was working on, and, about a century later, the unfinished statue became available for sale. The fact that just such a black vein in the marble is clearly visible on the face of the Bassano statue (figure 17.3) strongly suggests that the Giustiniani Christ was not simply what, in the language of show business, would be called a 'remake' – a new and possibly improved production or copy of a successful previous work – but rather an attempt by other hands to present as complete the early version of a work left unfinished by the original author.

In the parallel field of dramatic art it is possible to find similar cases, though the most common practice is that of the remake, of which Shakespeare was a past-master.[8] Apart from *The Book of Sir Thomas More* and *Edward III*, I had the good fortune in my experience as an editor to come across another play that underwent a process of completion and re-elaboration of exactly the same nature as that to which the unfinished Michelangelo statue in Bassano was subjected. *The Insatiate Countess* is not one of the Shakespeare apocrypha but a play that another major Elizabethan dramatist, John Marston, had undertaken in the early Jacobean age. Marston had plotted the play and sketched out the first act when in 1608 he renounced the theatrical profession. A patient search based on merely circumstantial evidence suggested that a young actor, William Barkstead, together with a hanger-on of the theatrical profession, Lewis Machin, endeavoured to complete the play, of which Marston had only roughed out the first scenes (like Michelangelo, he had started from the 'base'), in order to have it presented on the stage by a company of boy actors. An unscrupulous publisher managed to assemble a wretched text of the performed play, and in 1613 handed it over to the printers in such a chaotic state that it took a long time to make sense out of it.[9] *The Insatiate Countess* is an apocryphal work by Marston in the same way that the Giustiniani Christ is an apocryphal version of Michelangelo's statue in the Minerva church.

We are back to the problem of editing apocryphal works whether in the dramatic or in the field of visual arts. The basic criterion is the identification of the author's hand. In a manuscript what is meant by 'hand' is the characteristic handwriting peculiar to each writer. In *The Book of Sir Thomas More* we can see clearly how also the three pages which are recognized to be in Shakespeare's

248 *Stage and spectacle*

17.3 Detail of the *Cristo Redentore* (figure 17.1), showing a black vein in the marble on the face of the statue.

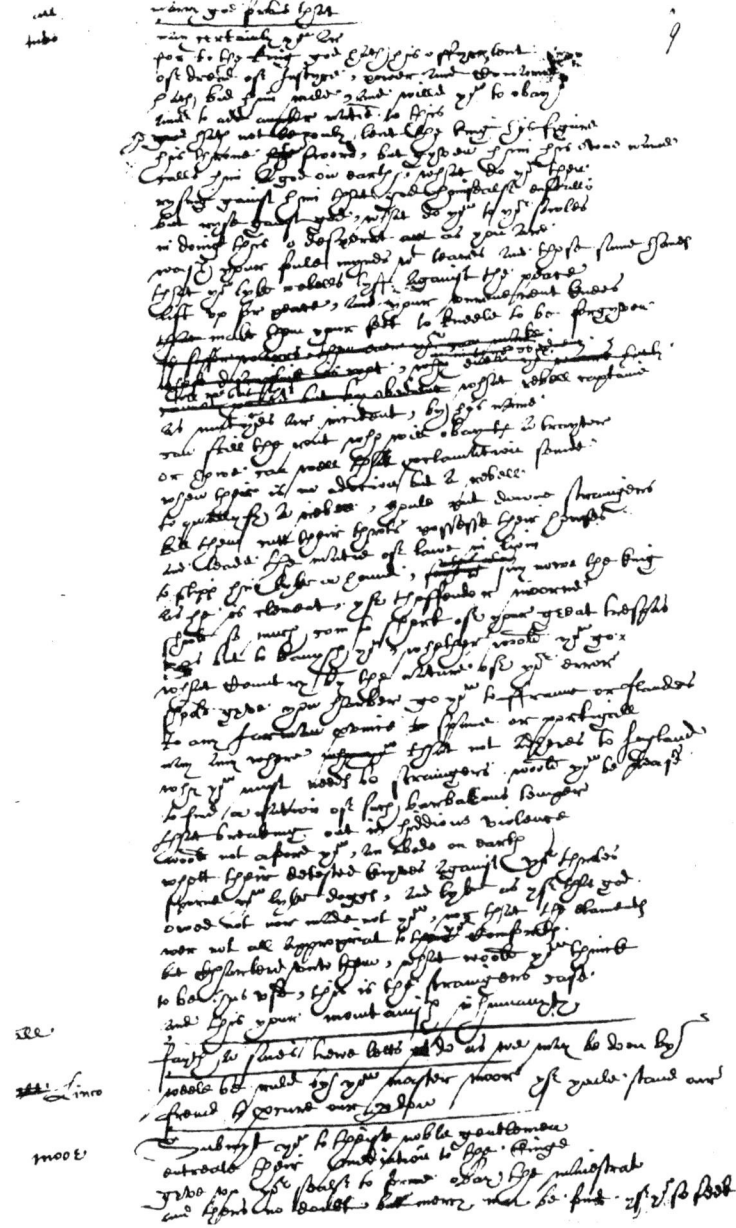

17.4 The third of the three pages known as Addition in Hand D (probably Shakespeare's) in the manuscript *Booke of Sir Thomas Moore*, Harl. MS 7368 in the British Library, fol. 9r. This page corresponds to 2.3.104–59 in the Gabrieli/Melchiori edition. Most of the intrusions of Hand C (presumably the bookkeeper's) in the passage misinterpret the intentions and meanings of the original writer in Hand D.

250 *Stage and spectacle*

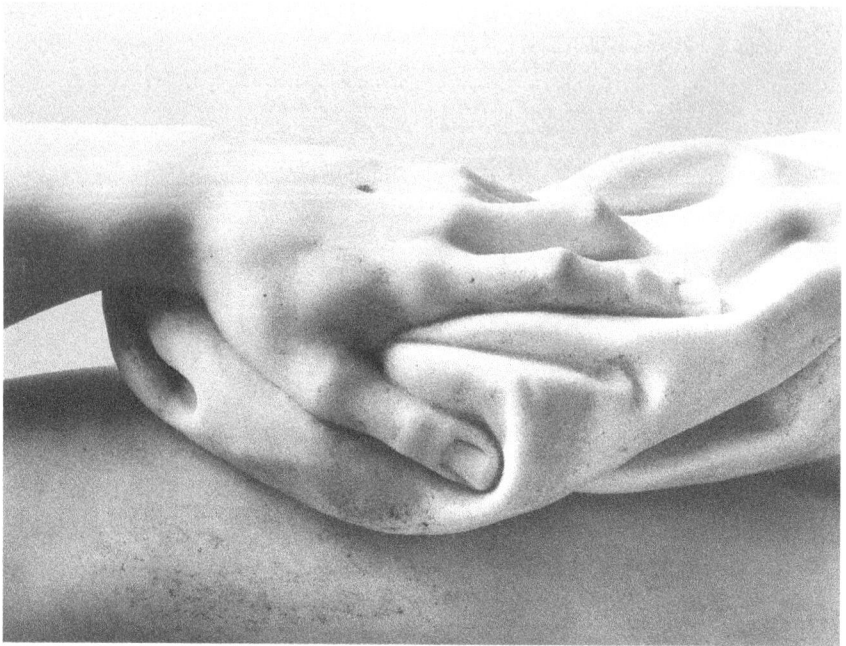

17.5 Detail of the left hand of the *Cristo Redentore*.

17.6 A hand drawing a hand, attributed to Michelangelo Buonarroti. Drawing in pen and sepia ink on paper, 18 by 28.6 cm. Paris, Musée du Louvre, inv. 717, n.63522.

hand have been interfered with by other hands (figure 17.4).[10] Evidence of the presence of different handwriting can be detected also in printed texts. The fact that, in *Edward III*, by far the greatest part of that printer's howlers are concentrated in the pages containing the so-called 'Countess scenes' attributed to Shakespeare strongly suggests that in that section of the play the printer was confronted with copy in an unfamiliar hand, markedly different from that in which the rest of the play was written.[11]

But by 'hand' is meant not only the graphic habits but also the characteristic spellings of an author as well as his peculiar use of words and constructs which can be taken as his stylistic hallmarks. This is what allows us to establish without manuscript evidence the extent of Shakespeare's contribution to *Edward III* or Marston's to *The Insatiate Countess*.[12] In the same way in the case of a drawing or a sculpture the treatment of hands is a way to identify the artist.

The Giustiniani Christ is the best instance of this. A particularly fine detail of the standing figure is the left hand that holds a folded loincloth against the left side of the body (figure 17.5) – a feature that disappeared from the Minerva version, where the left arm is folded across the chest to hold the cross.[13] The hand and the general posture of the figure in the Bassano church are very similar to that of a youthful work by Michelangelo, the *Bacco* in the Bargello in Florence. But the clinching argument for the attribution of the initial work on the Giustiniani Christ to Michelangelo is a sepia drawing, now in the Louvre, of a hand exactly in the same posture (figure 17.6). The peculiarity of this drawing is that it shows the hand in the act of being drawn by a much smaller hand. Professor Danesi observes that there is the same proportion between the larger and the smaller hand in the drawing as that between the size of an average human figure and that of the Christ statue, which is definitely larger.

Granting the collaborative nature of most art works in the Renaissance and dramatic works in the Elizabethan age, the study of hands is crucial in settling basic questions of authorship.

Notes

1 C. F. Tucker Brooke, ed., *The Shakespeare Apocrypha, Being a Collection of Fourteen Plays which Have Been Ascribed to Shakespeare* (Oxford, Clarendon Press, [1908] 1967). Quotations from p. xi.
2 *To the great Variety of Readers*. 1623 Folio, sig. A3.
3 I am greatly indebted to Professor Silvia Danesi Squarzina for calling my attention to the Giustiniani Christ, discussing with me and placing at my disposal a full documentation of her remarkable findings. See her contributions to *The Burlington Magazine*, CXL (1998), 'The Collections of Cardinal Benedetto Giustiniani, Part II', p. 113, and CXLII (2000), 'The Bassano "Christ The Redeemer" in the Giustiniani Collections', pp. 746–51; the second is accompanied in the same issue of the *Burlington Magazine*, pp. 740–5, by the article by Irene Baldriga 'The First Version

of Michelangelo's Christ for S. Maria Sopra Minerva'. In Italian see in *Ars*, 4, 12 (December 2000), the richly illustrated articles by S. Danesi Squarzina, 'Un Cristo in piedi nudo' (pp. 114–22), and by I. Baldriga, 'Michelangelo ritrovato: la prima versione del Cristo di Santa Maria sopra Minerva' (pp. 124–30).

4 *Sir Thomas More: A Play by Anthony Munday and Others, Revised by Henry Chettle, Thomas Dekker, Thomas Heywood and William Shakespeare*, edited by Vittorio Gabrieli and Giorgio Melchiori. The Revels Plays (Manchester, Manchester University Press, 1990).

5 In her recent *Ungentle Shakespeare: Scenes from His Life* (London, Arden Shakespeare, 2001), based on unquestionable documentary evidence, Katherine Duncan-Jones refuses to take into consideration the addition in Hand D to *Sir Thomas More*, arguing that 'half a dozen late signatures do not seem to me to provide an adequate sample on which to base an identification of Shakespeare's secretary hand' (p. xii). Obviously in these matters 'ocular proof' at second hand may well be deceptive, as Othello learnt at his own expense.

6 William Shakespeare, *King Edward III*, ed. Giorgio Melchiori. The New Cambridge Shakespeare (Cambridge, Cambridge University Press, 1998).

7 See the already mentioned *Burlington Magazine* article by S. Danesi Squarzina, 'The Collections of Cardinal Benedetto Giustiniani, Part II'. The inventory of the works then in the Giustiniani palace in Rome lists a '*Christo in piedi nudo con panno traverso di metallo moderno che abbraccia con la dritta un tronco di Croce con corda e spongia e tre pezzi di croce in terra alto palmi 9*'. The 'modern' addition of a metal loincloth (*panno traverso di metallo moderno*) has now been removed; the height of the statue is 201 cm, corresponding exactly to the 9 *palmi* indicated in the inventory. A further treatment of the statue and its history is in the Catalogue of the exhibition held in Rome, January to February 2002, *Caravaggio e i Giustiniani*, ed. S. Danesi Squarzina (Milano, Electa, 2002), pp. 246–51.

8 See G. Melchiori, 'The Corridors of History: Shakespeare the Re-maker', *Proceedings of the British Academy*, 72 (1986), 67–85.

9 John Marston and others, *The Insatiate Countess*, ed. Giorgio Melchiori, The Revels Plays (Manchester, Manchester University Press, 1984).

10 See on this point G. Melchiori, 'Hand D in *Sir Thomas More*: An Essay in Misinterpretation', *Shakespeare Survey*, 38 (1985), 101–14.

11 The best example is at 2.2.154–5, where the allusion to the story of Hero and Leander, 'But I will through a Hellespont of blood / To arrive at Sestos where my Hero lies', is misread by the printer of the 1596 Quarto (sig. D4v) as 'But I will *throng a hellie spout* of bloud / To arriue at Cestus where my Hero lyes'.

12 The evidence (obviously merely circumstantial) for identifying Shakespeare's hand in the so-called 'Countess scenes' of *Edward III* is set out in the section 'Textual analysis' of my edition of the play, pp. 171–7. For *The Insatiate Countess* see the section on 'Authorship' in the Introduction to my edition of it, pp. 9–16.

13 Probably in the years between the first (1514–16) and the second version (1518–21) of the *Cristo Risorto* Michelangelo developed the principle that Giovanni Paolo Lomazzo relates in his *Trattato della pittura* [1598]: according to Michelangelo, the artist 'should always make a figure Pyramidall, Serpentlike, and multiplied by one two and three' (quoted from the English translation by Haydocke of Lomazzo's *Trattato* in William Hogarth, *The Analysis of Beauty* (London, 1753), pp. v–vi).

18

Afterword:
Italy as intertext

KEIR ELAM

'Intertextuality' has proved to be an extraordinarily fortunate and fertile critical concept since its original formulation by Julia Kristeva (inspired by Bakhtin) in the 1960s. Unlike much structuralist and post-structuralist terminology, it has been accepted unreservedly into the mainstream of literary critical discourse and beyond. This favourable reception has probably to do in part with the strategic openness of Kristeva's original definition, which embraces potentially all modes of textual production and exchange: 'the text is ... a productivity, and this means: first, that its relationship to the language in which it is situated is redistributive (destructive-constructive) ... and second, that it is a permutation of texts, an intertextuality: in the space of a given text, several utterances, taken from other texts, intersect and *neutralize* one another'.[1] The success of the concept is doubtless due also to the fact that ours is an exquisitely intertextual era, since all postmodern culture is unmistakably the expression of relations between cultural texts in the broadest sense. As a result, nearly all criticism today has a degree of textual and intertextual awareness – i.e. the recognition that all literary and dramatic discourse is culturally mediated – that was certainly not present fifty or even twenty years ago.

Apart from postmodernism itself, the most fruitful area of intertextual enquiry has been without doubt the Renaissance, above all Renaissance drama. It might be said that this in itself is not entirely a recent phenomenon, if one extends the field of investigation into relations between texts to include 'source study' of the kind that has been a mainspring of Shakespeare criticism since the nineteenth century. In practice, however, it is precisely the Kristevan or Bakhtinian conception of intertextuality as a dissemination or permutation of texts that has led to the crisis of the traditional quest for single sources. In terms of Robert Miola's 'seven types of intertextuality' in this volume, there has been a shift, as it were, towards the bottom half of Miola's list. In other words, where intertextual studies (although they were not called that at the time) once occupied almost exclusively the top half of his typology, especially the 'book on the shelf' category – regarding quotations, translations, and especially one-to-one relationships with privileged sources – these 'philological' priorities, founded on the criterion of the verifiability of textual debts, have been altogether overturned in the last two decades or so.

Miola mentions the impact of contemporary critical theory – and in particular cultural materialism and new historicism – on intertextual enquiry. A crucial factor in this respect has been the opening up of the very notion of textuality, above all under the influence of Foucault, whereby the 'text' becomes in a general sense the entire formation or conformation of Renaissance culture, transforming every mode of cultural production into a textual event. Foucault's epistemological and semiological model – most explicitly in *The Order of Things* – is that of the *liber naturae*, the great book of nature in which all natural and cultural phenomena are potentially readable to the trained eye: 'There are no resemblances without signatures ... This is why the face of the world is covered with blazons, with characters, with ciphers and obscure words – with "hieroglyphics" ... And the space inhabited by immediate resemblances becomes like a vast open book; it bristles with strange figures that intertwine and in some places repeat themselves.'[2] The interpretation of the world thus becomes a matter of close reading, a search for textual resemblances: 'The sixteenth century', affirms Foucault, 'superimposed hermeneutics and semiology in the form of similitude.'[3]

This totalizing conception of textuality, which has been taken up by new historicists and to a certain extent by cultural materialists, makes every microhistorical document, event, or object fair critical game, in the sense that textual relations are no longer monogamous (Shakespeare and Ovid, Shakespeare and Holinshed, and so on) but can happily and 'promiscuously' comprehend any kind of cultural contamination, direct or indirect. This has been very clear in recent developments in Shakespearean criticism, where the tendency, or, as it were, the 'Greenblattian' gesture of forming rapports between remote aspects of a given historical moment, has been for example to take a document which is geographically or culturally as far removed as possible from Shakespeare's actual dramatic practice, and then to work out (at times, perhaps, to force) relationships between the two.

The idea of culture as an endless productivity of textual exchange, without predefined boundaries, has proved highly attractive to critics of early modern drama, no longer restrained or restricted by the scholarly necessity of demonstrating likely influences. Some of the more beneficial results of this emancipation of the intertext are visible in this volume, while the more questionable effects – the arbitrary juxtaposition of texts or events linked at most (and not always) by their contemporaneity – are happily absent.

Only two of the papers collected here belong – at least apparently – to

Miola's first, 'book on the desk', category, i.e. that of close philological study of a text in relation to a privileged source: namely, Jason Lawrence's discussion of *Othello* and Cinthio and Alessandro Serpieri's examination of *Julius Caesar* with reference to Plutarch. In practice both contributions, however, go well beyond a static, one-to-one approach to literary influence. Lawrence sets up a quadrangular model of textual mediation: his concern is not simply with Shakespeare's Cinthio but rather with Ariosto adopted by Shakespeare as a means of reading Cinthio via Greene. This four-way network of exchange underlines dramatically the complexities of influence in the Renaissance. Alessandro Serpieri, instead, suggests criteria for examining the relationship between text and source as a dynamic process of transformation and transcodification, allowing us to observe, as it were, the playwright at work in making his strategic dramaturgical and discursive choices.

Perhaps the most fertile notion linking many of the papers gathered here is that of Renaissance Italy *tout court* as a great cultural intertext for Shakespeare and his contemporaries. What is at stake here is the fact that not only Italy represented a treasure trove of literary and dramatic sources (thus becoming itself a sort of meta- or mega-source), but that it was perceived as a sort of generative machine producing powerful models – cultural models, political models, ideological models, iconographic models, behavioural models and so on – which could be freely taken up and transformed by the early modern English.

The most literal sense in which Italy itself was assumed by Shakespeare as intertext can be seen in two chapters dedicated to the epistemological and theological poetics of place, with particular reference to Rome. Claudia Corti, in suggesting certain metaphysical affinities between *Julius Caesar* and Florentine neoplatonism, takes Shakespeare's Rome as an allegorical counterpart to Platonic man, composed of different constituent worlds; François Laroque, instead, reads references to Rome in various plays as part of a system of cryptic allusions to Roman Catholicism, via the mediation, among other cultural influences, of Italian Mannerist painting.

The other main intertextual space in the volume is Venice. Anthony Barthelemy's paper on forms of Venetian vice, for example, sets out from the idea of Italy itself as a paradigm for certain modes of what he terms 'unspeakable carnality', that is then transmitted through a long series of texts. What is of interest to Barthelemy is not so much Shakespeare's use of specific textual material but his adoption and adaptation of Italian cultural archetypes or stereotypes. An analogous concern with Venetian ideological models emerges in Pamela Allen Brown's paper on the generative force of xenophobia, which traces the ways in which Venice as cultural space gave rise to a chain of interconnected texts, both written and oral (including the *vox populi*, the archetypes and even the prejudices of Elizabethan society) which then constitute for Shakespeare a kind of discursive net into which he can weave his own dramaturgy. As in several other contributions, the emphasis here is on Italy as a primarily negative ideological model, in regard to which Shakespeare positioned his plays in a revisionist or reactive relationship. 'The pleasant garden of great Italy', *The Taming of the Shrew*, becomes an unpleasant garden of vices, a sort of Boschian inferno, with which Shakespeare's texts entertain at best a problematic rapport.

Other contributors, in addressing the question of the intertextuality of political practice, posit Italy as the chief venue not only of political theory but of actual (often highly questionable) modes of government, so much so that all plays dealing with political subjects sooner or later have to come to terms, directly or otherwise, with the great Italian models of political theory and practice. This is particularly evident in Michael J. Redmond's and Michele Marrapodi's chapters on *Measure for Measure*, a play which addresses both the political and the moral tensions inherent in the relationship between governor and governed.

If Italy as body politic proves to be eminently quotable, so too is the Italian body proper. My own contribution regards the 'textuality' of the Italian bodily behaviour, which came to constitute a prestigious cultural model that the English strove with difficulty to adopt and adapt. The particular corporeal practice that I examine – the exquisitely Italianate art of fencing – represents a point of encounter between Anglo-Italian texts proper (Saviolo, Silver), an imported ideological habitus (the discourse of the courtier or gentleman), and a specific stage skill, whereby the performance itself necessarily 'cites' its Italian influences.

A further aspect of the perception of Italy as prime intertext is its role in the creation and dissemination of semantic paradigms that are widely imported and re-elaborated within early modern English culture. The study of such thematic 'imports' implies, among other things, a revisiting and revalorizing of E. R. Curtius's celebrated – but in recent years somewhat neglected – notion of the *topos*,[4] subsequently varied in Louise George Clubb's highly productive notion of the 'theatregram', according to which semantic *topoi* of Italian derivation become codified and crystallized in the form of specific dramatic situations and specific modes of stage business within early modern drama.[5]

Various chapters address Shakespeare's reworking of Italian literary, iconographic, or discursive *topoi*. Mario Domenichelli's discussion of *la bella morte*, for example, charts the European and English fortune of an important commonplace of Renaissance chivalric romance and epic that finds late expression, but also unsparing deconstruction, in Shakespeare's *Troilus and Cressida*, revisited here in the light of its striking parallelisms with Aretino's disenchanted mock-epic *L'Orlandino*. Michele Marrapodi finds antecedents to the ransom plot of *Measure for Measure* – with its accompanying 'lewd magistrate' theatregram – in Cinthio and, more surprisingly, in Luther in the wider context of post-Reformation debate, while the same plot in the same play is examined by Michael Redmond with regard to its 'unstable' marriage with the disguised duke subgenre and the conventions of New Comedy.

In the field of iconographic *topoi*, Jeffrey Netto's linking of the inset chess scene in *The Tempest* to a series of Renaissance pictorial representations of the same theme allows Shakespeare's romance to take part in what Netto terms a 'play of reiterations'. J. R. Mulryne's chapter on the classical archetypes transmitted to English drama through Italian scenography takes us from the *intermedi* of the 1589 Medici wedding in Florence to Shakespeare's *Antony and Cleopatra*, via Inigo Jones. It might be noted that Mulryne's identification of possible iconographic intertexts rests on the opposite procedure from Alessandro Serpieri's dramaturgic approach: here it is the play's discursive divergences from Plutarch that become significant clues to other possible antecedents. Still within the field of iconography, and still with reference to collective participation, Giorgio Melchiori, affirming what he terms 'the collaborative nature of most art works in the Renaissance', proposes an affinity between Shakespeare's participation in plays by several hands (*The Book of Sir Thomas More*, *King Edward III*) and the Italian artistic *bottega*. Here intertextuality translates into a form of polyphonic intratextuality: a dialogue of authorial voices, or a meeting of artistic as well as calligraphic hands, within a 'single' text.

A further form of horizontal engagement with shared models is the adoption and rethinking of 'Italian' literary or dramatic genres, a mode of inter- or trans-textuality that has to do not so much with specific debts as with the rules and conventions governing textual production. Again, Italy was acknowledged as the primary fount of all the main modern literary and dramatic genres – from the sonnet to the modern epic poem to neoclassical tragedy and comedy to pastoral tragicomedy, etc. – which were often notoriously reformulated on their arrival from the continent: see in this regard Pamela Brown's questioning of the genre label applicable to *Othello* (tragedy/satire), against the background of Italian and English Renaissance cultural *auctoritates*, as well as Mario Domenichelli's comments on 'Shakespeare's generically indefinable' *Troilus and Cressida*. A dialogical or dialectical approach to relations between genres is adopted by Charlotte Pressler, who sees the *novella* as a narrative go-between mediating two strictly dramatic corpuses, the Italian and the English, as in the case of *Twelfth Night*, whose most direct source is not *Gl'Ingannati* but Riche's version of Bandello's prose narrative derived from the Sienese comedy. It is the narrative representation of the conventions of erudite comedy that makes them accessible to English audiences, thereby making possible – almost paradoxically – their re-dramatization.

One of the principal reasons for the emphasis in this volume on non-canonical forms of intertextuality is the sheer difficulty, in the early modern period, of distinguishing between sources proper and analogues, parallelisms, or other textualized material belonging to the cultural matrix in the form of the great Renaissance mingle-mangle of shared plots, thematic commonplaces or archetypes. In Mulryne's chapter, for example – as Mulryne himself observes – the issue is not really whether Shakespeare in *Antony and Cleopatra* was directly 'borrowing' iconographical and scenographical precedents, but that these had in any case become cultural givens that the dramatist was able to draw on; and, as Fernando Cioni demonstrates with regard to Shakespeare's *Shrew* and its analogues, it is often arduous to chart in this period the actual temporal or genealogical relationship between, as it were, precedence and subsequence. As a result, much of the discussion in this book is in effect dedicated to what Cesare Segre has called interdiscursivity, i.e. the exchange of modes, fragments, topics, or genres of discourse, beyond the bounds of immediate derivation or citation.

Another factor in the opening up of textual boundaries is the manner in which the theatre multiplies in exponential fashion the whole question of inter-artistic dialogue, due to the potentially innumerable modes of textuality on which it can feed. As Cioni, Laroque, and Mulryne, among others, suggest the drama is an exquisitely transversal form that enables the playwright to employ a polyphony of simultaneous discourses: to dramatize a narrative source, allude to iconographic tradition, draw on discursive commonplaces, resort to performative conventions from, say, the *comedia dell'arte*, etc. There is in theory no limit to the number of artistic or cultural modes that the theatre can at the same time both use and mention – to adopt a distinction from the philosophy of language – a fact that makes life for students of Renaissance drama eventful but also somewhat complicated.

Such expressive riches were more often than not exploited in the borrowed (or used, or mentioned) name of Italy, adopted as a supremely enabling or liberating symbolic space that authorized dramatists and others to create whatever textual or intertextual domains they pleased.

Notes

1 Julia Kristeva, *Desire in Language: A Semiotic Approach to Literature and Art* (Oxford, Basil Blackwell, 1984), p. 36.
2 M. Foucault, *The Order of Things: An Archeology of the Human Sciences* (New York, Pantheon Books, 1970), pp. 26–7.
3 Foucault, *The Order of Things*, p. 29.
4 E. R. Curtius, *European Literature and Later Middle Ages*, tr. Willard R. Trask (New York, Harper & Row, 1963).
5 Louise George Clubb, *Italian Drama in Shakespeare's Time* (New Haven, Yale University Press, 1989).

Select bibliography of recent publications

Allen, G. *Intertextuality*, London, Routledge, 2000.
Andrews, R. *Scripts and Scenarios: The Performance of Comedy in Renaissance Italy*, Cambridge, Cambridge University Press, 1993.
Angenot, M. 'Intertextualité, interdiscursivité, discours social', *Texte* 2 (1983).
Ascoli, A. R. and V. Kahn (eds), *Machiavelli and the Discourse of Literature*, Ithaca, N.Y., Cornell University Press, 1993.
Barasch, F. K. 'Shakespeare and the Italians', in W. R. Elton and John M. Mucciolo (eds), *The Shakespearean International Yearbook*, Aldershot, Ashgate, 1999.
Bárberi Squarotti, G. *Machiavelli o la scelta della letteratura*, Roma, Bulzoni, 1987.
Barthes, R. *Empire of Signs*, tr. Richard Howard, London, Cape, 1982.
Bate, J. 'Ovid and the Mature Tragedies', *Shakespeare Survey*, 41 (1989).
Bate, J. 'Ovid and the Sonnets; or, Did Shakespeare Feel the Anxiety of Influence?', *Shakespeare Survey*, 42 (1990).
Bate, J. *Shakespeare and Ovid*, Oxford, Clarendon Press, 1993.
Bate, J. 'The Elizabethans in Italy', in Jean Pierre Maquerlot and Michèle Willems (eds), *Travel and Drama in Shakespeare's Time*, Cambridge, Cambridge University Press, 1996.
Beecher, D. and M. Ciavolella (eds), *Comparative Critical Approaches to Renaissance Comedy*, Ottawa, Dovehouse Edition, 1986.
Berger, H. Jr. *The Absence of Grace: Sprezzatura and Suspicion in Two Renaissance Courtesy Books*, Stanford, Stanford University Press, 2000.
Bloom, H. *Agon, Towards a Theory of Revisionism*, Oxford and New York, Oxford University Press, 1982.
Braden, G. *Renaissance Tragedy and the Senecan Tradition: Anger's Privilege*, New Haven, Yale University Press, 1985.
Branca, V. and C. Ossola (eds), *Cultura e società nel Rinascimento tra Riforme e Manierismi*, Florence, Olschki, 1984.
Brand, P. 'Disguise, Deception and Concealment of Identity in Ariosto's Theatre', in Eileen A. Millar (ed.), *Renaissance and Other Studies: Essays Presented to Peter M. Brown*, Glasgow, University of Glasgow, 1988.
Braunmuller A. R. and J. C. Bulman (eds), *Comedy from Shakespeare to Sheridan:*

Change and Continuity in the English and European Dramatic Tradition. Essays in Honor of Eugene M. Waith, Newark, University of Delaware Press, 1986.

Briggs, J. *This Stage-Play World: English Literature and Its Background 1580–1625*, Oxford, Oxford University Press, 1983.

Brockbank, P. *Urban Mysteries of the Renaissance: Shakespeare and Carpaccio*, Occasional Paper 4, Hertford, International Shakespeare Association, 1989.

Broich, U. and M. Pfister (eds), *Intertextualität Formen: Funktionem, anglistische Fallstudien*, Tübingen, M. Niemeyer, 1985.

Bryson, N., 'Intertextuality and Visual Poetics', *Style*, 22:2 (1988).

Burke, P. *The Fortunes of the Courtier: The European Reception of Castiglione's Cortegiano*, Cambridge, Polity Press, 1995.

Burrow, C. *Epic Romance: Homer to Milton*, Oxford, Clarendon Press, 1993.

Butler, L. E. 'The Structural Uses of Incest in English Renaissance Drama', *Renaissance Drama*, n.s. XV (1984).

Carron, J.-C. 'Imitation and Intertextuality in the Renaissance', *New Literary History*, 19 (1988), 565–79.

Castagno, P. C. *The Early Commedia dell'arte (1550–1621): The Mannerist Context*, New York, Peter Lang, 1994.

Clayton, J. and E. Rothstein (eds), *Influence and Intertextuality in Literary History*, Madison, University of Wisconsin Press, 1991.

Clubb, L. G. *Italian Drama in Shakespeare's Time*, New Haven, Yale University Press, 1989.

Clubb, L. G. and R. Black, *Romance and Aretine Humanism in Sienese Comedy*, Florence, La Nuova Italia, 1993.

Clubb, L. G. 'Italian Stories on the Stage', in Alexander Leggatt (ed.), *The Cambridge Companion to Shakespearian Comedy*, Cambridge, Cambridge University Press, 2002.

Cole, H. C. *The 'All's Well' Story from Boccaccio to Shakespeare*, Urbana, University of Illinois Press, 1981.

Cope, J. I. *Dramaturgy of the Daemonic: Studies in Antigeneric Theater from Ruzante to Grimaldi*. Baltimore, Johns Hopkins University Press, 1984.

Corti, C. (ed.), *Silenos: Erasmus in Elizabethan England*, Pisa, ETS, 1998.

Cox, V. *The Renaissance Dialogue: Literary Dialogue in its Social and Political Context*, Cambridge, Cambridge University Press, 1992.

Cruciani, F. and D. Seragnoli (eds), *Il teatro italiano nel Rinascimento*, Bologna, Il Mulino, 1987.

Culler, J. *The Pursuit of Signs: Semiotics, Literature, Deconstruction*, London, Routledge and Kegan Paul, 1981.

Curtius, E. R. *European Literature and Later Middle Ages*, tr. Willard R. Trask, New York, Harper & Row, 1963.

Dembowski, P. 'Intertextualité et critique des textes', *Littérature*, 41 (1981).

Dashwood, J. R. and J. E. Everson (eds), *Writers and Performers in Italian Drama from the Time of Dante to Pirandello*, New York, Edwin Mellen Press, 1991.

Davico Bonino, G. *La commedia italiana del cinquecento e altre note su letteratura e teatro*, Turin, Tirrenia Stampatori, 1989.

David, J. G. (ed.), *Studies in the Commedia dell'Arte*, Cardiff, University of Wales Press, 1993.
Davidson, C. et al. (eds), *Drama in the Renaissance: Comparative and Critical Essays*, New York, AMS Press, 1984.
Desens, M. C. *The Bed-Trick in English Renaissance Drama: Explorations in Gender, Sexuality, and Power*, Newark, University of Delaware Press, 1994.
Elam, K. 'The Fertile Eunuch: *Twelfth Night*, Early Modern Intercourse, and the Fruits of Castration', *Shakespeare Quarterly*, 47:1 (spring 1996).
Elam, K. and F. Cioni (eds), *Una civile conversazione: Lo scambio letterario e culturale anglo-italiano nel Rinascimento / A Civil Conversation: Anglo-Italian Literary and Cultural Exchange in the Renaissance*, Bologna, Clueb, 2003.
Elton, W. R. and W. B. Long (eds), *Shakespeare and Dramatic Tradition: Essays in Honor of S. F. Johnson*, Newark, University of Delaware Press, 1989.
Evans, J. X. 'Erasmian Folly and Shakespeare's *King Lear*: A Study in Humanist Intertextuality', *Moreana*, 27:103 (1990).
Faas, E. *Tragedy and After: Euripides, Shakespeare, Goethe*, Kingston and Montreal, McGill-Queen's University Press, 1984.
Falletti, C. 'Il comico non integrato e la frantumazione degli statuti', in Fabrizio Cruciani and Daniele Seragnoli (eds), *Il teatro italiano nel Rinascimento*, Bologna, Il Mulino, 1987.
Fatherty, T. J. '*Othello dell'Arte:* The Presence of *Commedia* in Shakespeare's Tragedy', *Theatre Journal*, 43 (1991).
Ferroni, G. *Il testo e la scena: saggi sul teatro del Cinquecento*, Rome, Bulzoni, 1980.
Fitzpatrick, T. 'Commedia dell'arte and Performance: The Scenarios of Flaminio Scala', *Renaissance Drama Newsletter*, Supplement 5, University of Warwick, 1985.
Foucault, M. *The Order of Things: An Archeology of the Human Sciences*, New York, Pantheon Books, 1970.
Fowler, A. *Kinds of Literature: An Introduction to the Theory of Genres and Modes*, Cambridge, Mass., Harvard University Press, 1982.
Fox, A., *The English Renaissance: Identity and Representation in Elizabethan England*, Oxford, Blackwell, 1997.
Frantz, D. O. *Festum Voluptatis: A Study of Renaissance Erotica*, Columbus, Ohio State University Press, 1989.
Freedman, B. 'Frame-up: Feminism, Psychonalysis, Theatre', *Theatre Journal*, 40:3 (1988).
Frow, J. 'Intertextuality and Ontology', in Michael Worton and Judith Still (eds), *Intertextuality: Theories and Practices*, Manchester, Manchester University Press, 1990.
Gatti, H. *The Renaissance Drama of Knowledge: Giordano Bruno in England*, London and New York, Routledge, 1989.
Gatti, H. 'Giordano Bruno and the Stuart Court Masques', *Renaissance Quarterly*, 48 (winter, 1995).
Gaudet, P. '"A little night music": Intertextuality and Status in the Nocturnal Exchange of Jessica and Lorenzo', *Essays in Theatre/Etudes théâtrales*, 13 (1994–95).
Genette, G. *Palimpsestes: La littérature au second degré*, Paris, Seuil, 1982.

Genette, G. 'Transtextualités', *Magazine Littéraire*, 192 (1983).
Genette, G. 'Structure and Functions of the Title in Literature', *Critical Inquiry*, 14 (1988) 692–720.
George, D. J. and C. J. Gossip (eds), *Studies in the Commedia dell'Arte*, Cardiff, University of Wales Press, 1993
Gillies, J. *Shakespeare and the Geography of Difference*, Cambridge, Cambridge University Press, 1994.
Goodman, A. and A. Mackay. *The Impact of Humanism on Western Europe*, London and New York, Longman 1990.
Goyet, F. '*Imitatio* ou intertextualité? (Riffaterre Revisited)', *Poétique*, 18:71 (1987).
Grafton, A. *Forgers and Critics: Creativity and Duplicity in Western Scholarship*, Princeton, Princeton University Press, 1990.
Grafton, A. and L. Jardine (eds), *From Humanism to the Humanities: Education and the Liberal Arts in Fifteenth- and Sixteenth-Century Europe*, London, Duckworth, 1986.
Grassi, E. *Renaissance Humanism: Studies in Philosophy and Poetics*, Binghamton, N.Y., Medieval and Renaissance Texts and Studies, 1988.
Greenblatt, S. *Renaissance Self-Fashioning: From More to Shakespeare*, Chicago, University of Chicago Press, 1980.
Greenblatt, S. (ed.), *The Power of Forms in the English Renaissance*, Norman, Okla., 1982.
Greenblatt, S. *Shakespearean Negotiations: The Circulation of Social Energy in Renaissance England*, Oxford, Clarendon Press, 1988.
Greenblatt, S. *Learning to Curse: Essays in Early Modern Culture*, London, Routledge, 1992.
Greene, T. M. *The Light in Troy: Imitation and Discovery in Renaissance Poetry*, New Haven, Yale University Pres, 1982.
Greenwood, J., *Shifting Perspectives and the Stylish Style: Mannerism in Shakespeare and His Contemporaries*, Toronto, University of Toronto Press, 1988.
Grendler, P. F. *Culture and Censorship in Late Renaissance Italy and France*, London, Variorum Reprints, 1981.
Grendler, P. F. *Books and Schools in the Italian Renaissance*, Alderrshot, Variorum, 1995.
Grewar, A. 'The Clowing Zanies: Shakespeare and the Actors of the *Commedia dell'Arte*', *Shakespeare in Southern Africa: Journal of the Shakespeare Society of Southern Africa*, 3 (1989).
Grewar, A. 'Shakespeare and the Actors of the *Commedia dell'Arte*', in D. J. George and C. J. Gossip (eds), *Studies in the Commedia delll'Arte*, Cardiff, University of Wales Press, 1993.
Guidotti, A. *Il modello e la trasgressione: Commedie del primo '500*, Rome, Bulzoni, 1983.
Gurr, A. 'Intertextuality at Windsor', *Shakespeare Quarterly*, 38 (1987).
Haber, J. *Pastoral and the Poetics of Self-Contradiction*, Cambridge, Cambridge University Press, 1994.
Hainsworth, P. et. al. (eds), *The Languages of Literature in Renaissance Italy*, Oxford, Clarendon Press, 1988.
Hanning, R. W. and D. Rostand (eds), *Castiglione: The Ideal and the Real in Renaissance Culture*, New Haven, Yale University Press, 1983.

Harty, E. R. 'Text, Context, Intertext', *Journal of Literary Studies*, 1:2 (1985).
Harvey, E. D. and K. Maus Eisaman. *Soliciting Interpretation*, Chicago, University of Chicago Press, 1990.
Hebel, U. J. *Intertextuality, Allusion, and Quotation: An International Bibliography of Critical Studies*, Westport, Conn., Greenwood Press, 1989.
Heck, T. F. *Commedia dell'Arte: A Guide to the Primary and Secondary Literature*, New York, Garland, 1988.
Henke, R. '*The Winter's Tale* and Guarinian Dramaturgy', *Comparative Drama*, 27 (1993).
Henke, R. *Pastoral Transformations: Italian Tragicomedy and Shakespeare's Late Plays*, Newark, University of Delaware Press, 1997.
Henke, R. *Performance and Literature in the Commedia dell'Arte*, Cambridge, Cambridge University Press, 2002.
Hendricks, M. '"The Moor of Venice", or the Italian on the Renaissance English Stage', in S. N. Garner and M. Sprengnether (eds), *Shakespearean Tragedy and Gender*, Bloomington, Indiana University Press, 1996.
Hilman, R. *Intertextuality and Romance in Renaissance Drama: The Staging of Nostalgia*, Basingstoke, Macmillan, 1992.
Holland, M. 'De l'intertextualité: Métacritique', *Texte*, 2 (1983), 177–92.
Holland, P. 'Theseus' Shadows in *A Midsummer Night's Dream*', *Shakespeare Survey*, 47 (1994).
Holquist, M. *Dialogism: Bakhtin and His World*, London, Routledge, 1990.
Hutcheon, L. 'Literary Borrowing and Stealing: Plagiarism, Sources, Influences, and Intertexts', *English Studies in Canada*, 12 (1986).
Jones, A. R. 'Italians and Others: Venice and the Irish in *Coryat's Crudities* and *The White Devil*', *Renaissance Drama*, 18 (1987).
Jones, A. R. 'Italians and Others', in D. S. Kastan and P. Strallybrass (eds), *Staging the Renaissance: Reinterpretations of Elizabethan and Jacobean Drama*, New York, Routledge, 1991.
Jones-Davies, M. T. 'Paroles intertextuelles: Lecture intertextuelle de Parolles', in '*All's Well That Ends Well*': *Nouvelles perspectives critiques*, Montpellier, Publications de l'Université Paul Valéry, 1985.
Kahn, V. *Machiavellian Rhetoric: From the Counter-Reformation to Milton*, Princeton, Princeton University Press, 1994.
Karrer, W. 'Titles and Mottoes as Intertextual Devices', in H. F. Plett (ed.), *Intertextuality*, Berlin and New York, De Gruyter, 1991.
Kastan, D. S. '"The Duke of Milan / And his Brave son": Old Histories and New in *The Tempest*', in *Shakespeare After Theory*, New York, Routledge, 1999.
Kennedy, G. 'Ancient Antecedents of Modern Literary Theory', *American Journal of Philology*, CX:3 (1989).
Kibédi, V. A. 'Pour une histoire intertextuelle de la littérature', *Degrés*, 12:40 (1984).
Kirkpatrick, R. *English and Italian Literature from Dante to Shakespeare: A Study of Source, Analogue and Divergence*, London, Longman, 1995.
Kristeva, J. *Desire in Language: A Semiotic Approach to Literature and Art*, Oxford, Basil Blackwell, 1984.

Kristeva, J. 'Word, Dialogue, and Novel', trans. as *Desire in Language* in Toril Moi (ed.), *The Kristeva Reader*, Oxford, Blackwell, 1986.
Langher, U. 'The Renaissance Novella as Justice', *Renaissance Quarterly*, LII (summer, 1999).
Larivaille, P. *Pietro Aretino fra Rinascimento e Manierismo*, Rome, Bulzoni, 1980.
Lawrence, J. '"The whole complexion of *Arcadia* chang'd": Samuel Daniel and Italian Lyrical Drama', *Medieval and Renaissance Drama in England* (1999).
Leitch, V. B. 'Versions of Textuality and Intertextuality: Contemporary Theories of Literature and Tradition', in V. B. Leitch (ed.), *Deconstructive Criticism: An Advanced Introduction*, New York, Columbia University Press, 1983.
Lepage, R. 'A Study in Dramatic Transposition and Invention: Della Porta's *La Sorella*, Rotrou's *La Soeur*, and Middleton's *No Wit, No Help Like a Woman's*', *Comparative Literature Studies*, 24 (1987).
Levith, M. J. *Shakespeare's Italian Settings and Plays*, Basingstoke, Macmillan, 1989.
Lewalski, B. K. (ed.), *Renaissance Genres: Essays on Theory, History, and Interpretation*, Harvard English Studies, no. 14, Cambridge, Mass., Harvard University Press, 1986.
Lombardo, A. (ed.), *Shakespeare a Verona e nel Veneto*, Verona, Grafiche Fiorini, 1987.
Lynch, S. J. *Shakespearean Intertextuality: Studies in Selected Sources and Plays*, Westport, Conn., Greenwood, 1998.
McMullan, G. and J. Hope (eds), *The Politics of Tragicomedy: Shakespeare and After*, London, Routledge, 1992.
McPherson, D. C. *Shakespeare, Jonson and the Myth of Venice*, Newark, University of Delaware Press, 1990.
Margolin, J.-C. and M.-M. Martinet (eds), *L'Europe de la renaissance, cultures et civilisations: Melanges offertes à Marie-Thérèse Jones-Davies*, Paris, Jean Touzot, 1988.
Marrapodi, M. *La Sicilia nella drammaturgia giacomiana e carolina*, Rome, Herder, 1989.
Marrapodi, M. (ed.), *Il mondo italiano del teatro inglese del Rinascimento: Relazioni culturali e intertestualità*, Palermo, Flaccovio Editore, 1995.
Marrapodi, M. (ed.), *The Italian World of English Renaissance Drama: Cultural Exchange and Intertextuality*, Newark, University of Delaware Press, 1998
Marrapodi, M. 'Shakespeare and Italy: Past and Present', in H. Klein and M. Marrapodi (eds), *Shakespeare Yearbook*, X (1999).
Marrapodi, M. (ed.), *Shakespeare and Intertextuality: The Transition of Cultures Between Italy and England in the Early Modern Period*, Rome, Bulzoni, 2000.
Marrapodi, M. (ed.), *Intertestualità shakespeariane: Il Cinquecento italiano e il Rinascimento inglese*, Roma, Bulzoni, 2003.
Marrapodi, M., T. Hoenselaars, M. Cappuzzo and L. Falzon Santucci (eds), *Shakespeare's Italy: Functions of Italian Locations in Renaissance Drama*, rev. pbk edition, Manchester, Manchester University Press, 1993.
Martin, C. 'Retrieving Jonson's Petrarch', *Shakespeare Quarterly*, 45 (1994).
Martinez, R. L. 'The Pharmacy of Machiavelli: Roman Lucretia in *Mandragola*', *Renaissance Drama*, n.s. XIV (1983).
Mattioli. E. 'Intertestualità e traduzione', *Testo a fronte*, 5 (1991).
Melchiori, G. '"In fair Verona", *Commedia erudita* into Romantic Comedy', in M. Marrapodi *et al.* (eds), *Shakespeare's Italy: Functions of Italian Locations in Renaissance Drama*, rev. pbk. edition, Manchester, Manchester University Press, 1993.

Melchiori, G. 'Falstaff's Ancestry: From Verona to Windsor', in *Shakespeare's Garter Plays: Edward III* to *Merry Wives of Windsor*, Newark, University of Delaware Press, 1994.
Mellamphy, N. 'Pantaloons and Zanies: Shakespeare's "Apprenticeship" to Italian Professional Comedy Troupes', in M. Charney (ed.), *Shakespearean Comedy*, New York, New York Literary Forum, 1980.
Miller, O. 'Intertextual Identity', in M. J. Valdés and O. Miller (eds), *Identity of the Literary Text*, Toronto, University of Toronto Press, 1985.
Miola, R. S. *Shakespeare and Classical Tragedy: The Influence of Seneca*, Oxford, Clarendon Press, 1992.
Miola, R. S. *Shakespeare and Classical Comedy: The Influence of Plautus and Terence*, Oxford, Clarendon Press, 1994.
Miola, R. S. *Shakespeare's Reading*, Oxford, Oxford University Press, 2000.
Molinari, C. *La commedia dell'arte*, Milan, Mondadori, 1985.
Moretti, W. 'La novella di Epitia e *Measure for Measure*', in M. Tempera (ed.), *Measure for Measure: Dal testo alla scena*, Bologna, Clueb, 1992.
Morgan, T. E. 'Is There an Intertext in this Text? Literary and Interdisciplinary Approaches to Intertextuality', *American Journal of Semiotics*, 3 (1985).
Moyer, A. E. *Musica Scentia: Musical Scholarship in the Italian Renaissance*, Ithaca, N.Y, Cornell Unversity Press, 1992.
Mulryne, J. R. and M. Shewring (eds), *War, Literature and the Arts in Sixteenth-Century Europe*, Basingstoke, Macmillan, 1989.
Mulryne, J. R. and M. Shewring (eds), *Theatre of the English and Italian Renaissance*, Basingstoke, Macmillan, 1991.
Net, M. 'Towards a Pragmatics of Poetic Intertextuality', *Cahiers de Linguistique Théorique & Appliquée*, 20 (1983).
Neuhaus, H. J. 'Shakespeare Hypertext', *Deutsche Shakespeare-Gesellschaft West* (1990).
Osborne, L. 'Dramatic Play in *Much Ado About Nothing*: Wedding the Italian *Novella* and English Comedy', *Philological Quarterly*, 69 (1990).
Patterson, A. M. *Censorship and Interpretation, the Conditions of Writing and Reading in Early Modern England*, Madison, University of Wisconsin Press, 1984.
Pellegrini, G. *Dal Manierismo al barocco: studi sul teatro inglese del XVII secolo*. Florence, Olschki, 1985.
Pfister, M. 'Comic Subversion, a Bakhtinian View of the Comic in Shakespeare', *Deutsche Shakespeare-Gesellschaft West* (1987).
Pieri, M. *La scena boschereccia nel rinascimento italiano*, Padua, Liviana Editrice, 1983.
Pietropaolo, D. (ed.), *The Science of Buffoonery: Theory and History of the Commedia dell'Arte*, Ottawa, Dovehouse Editons, 1989.
Pigman III, G. W. 'Versions of Imitation in the Renaissance', *Renaissance Quarterly*, XXXIII (1980).
Pinciss, G. M. *Literary Creations: Conventional Characters in the Drama of Shakespeare and His Contemporaries*, Wolfeboro, N.H., Boydell & Brewer, 1988.
Pitkin, H. F. *Fortune is a Woman: Gender and Politics in the Thought of Niccolò Machiavelli*. Berkeley, University of Calfornia Press, 1984.
Plett, H. F. (ed.), *Intertextuality*, Berlin, De Gruyter, 1991.

Prescott, A. L. 'Intertextual Topology: English Writers and Pantagruel's Hell', *English Literary Renaissance*, 23 (1993).
Pucci, P. 'Decostruzione e intertestualità', *Nuova Corrente*, 93–4 (1984).
Pugliatti, P. 'Intertextuality, Interdiscursivity, Dialogism', in T. Pugliatti, G. Barbera, and C. Zappia (eds), *Studi in onore di Alessandro Marabottini*, Rome, De Luca, 1997.
Quint, D. *Epic and Empire: Politics and Generic Form from Virgil to Milton*, Princeton, Princeton University Press, 1993.
Redmond, M. J. '"I have read them all": Jonson's *Volpone* and the Discourse of the Italianate Englishman', in M. Marrapodi (ed.), *The Italian World of English Renaissance Drama: Cultural Exchange and Intertextuality*, Newark, University of Delaware Press, 1998.
Redmond, M. J. '"My Lord, I fear, has forgot Britain": Rome, Italy and the (Re)Construction of British National Identity', *Shakespeare Yearbook*, X (1999).
Redmond, M. J. '"'Tis common knowledge": Italian Stereotypes and Audience Response in *Much Ado About Nothing* and *The Novella*', *Shakespeare Yearbook*, 13 (2002).
Rhu, L. 'Agons of Interpretation, Ariostan Source and Elizabethan Meaning in Spenser, Harington, and Shakespeare', *Renaissance Drama*, n.s. XXIV (1993).
Richards, K. 'The *Commedia dell'Arte* and the Caroline Stage', in S. Rossi and D. Savoia (eds), *Italy and the English Renaissance*, Milan, Edizioni Unicopli, 1989.
Richards, K. and L. Richards. *The Commedia dell'Arte: A Documentary History*, Oxford, Blackwell, 1990.
Richmond, H. M. 'Shaping a Dream', *Shakespeare Studies*, XVIII (1985).
Riehle, W. *Shakespeare, Plautus and the Humanist Tradition*, Cambridge, D. S. Brewer, 1990.
Riffaterre, M. 'Intertextual Representation: On Mimesis as Interpretive Discourse', *Critical Inquiry*, 11 (1984).
Riffaterre, M. 'The Intertextual Unconscious', *Critical Inquiry*, 13 (1986).
Rocke, M. *Forbidden Friendships: Homosexuality and Male Culture in Renaissance Florence*, New York, Oxford University Press, 1996.
Rossi, S. and D. Savoia (eds), *Italy and the English Renaissance*, Milan, Edizioni Unicopli, 1989.
Rothstein, E. *Influence and Intertextuality in Literary History*, Madison, Wisconsin University Press, 1991.
Rougé. B. 'Ironie et répétition dans deux scènes de Shakespeare: Crise du *degree* ou tournant du *mischief*?', *Poétique*, 87 (1991).
Rudd, N. *The Classical Tradition in Operation*, Toronto, University of Toronto Press, 1994.
Ruggiero, G. *The Boundaries of Eros: Sex, Crime and Sexuality in Renaissance Venice*, New York, Oxford University Press, 1985.
Ruprecht, H.-G. 'Intertextualité', *Texte*, 2 (1983).
Ryan E. N. 'Robortello and Maggi on Aristotle's Theory of Catharsis', *Rinascimento*, XXII (1982).
Salingar, L. 'Postscript: Elizabethan Dramatists and Italy', in J. R. Mulryne and M. Shewring (eds), *Theatre of the English and Italian Renaissance*, London, Macmillan, 1991.

Schnierer, P. P. *Rekonventionalisierung im englischen Drama 1980–1990*, Tübingen, Niemeyer, 1994.
Schoeck, R. J. *Intertextuality and Renaissance Texts*, Bamberg, H. Kaiser, 1984.
Scott, M. 'Machiavelli and the Machiavel', *Renaissance Drama*, n.s. XV (1984).
Scragg, L. *Shakespeare's 'Mouldy Tales': Recurrent Plot Motifs in Shakespearean Drama*, London, Longman, 1992.
Segre, C. *Teatro e romanzo: Due tipi di comunicazione letteraria*, Turin, Einaudi, 1984.
Seragnoli, D. *Il teatro a Siena nel cinquecento*, Rome, Bulzoni, 1980.
Serpieri, A. 'Reading the Signs: Towards a Semiotics of Shakespearean Drama', tr. Keir Elam, in J. Drakakis (ed.), *Alternative Shakespeares*, London, Methuen, 1985.
Serpieri, A. *Retorica e immaginario*, Parma, Pratiche, 1986.
Serpieri, A. *et al. Nel laboratorio di Shakespeare: Dalle fonti ai drammi*, 4 vols, Parma, Pratiche Editrice, 1988.
Shaheen, N. 'Shakespeare's Knowledge of Italian', *Shakespeare Survey*, 47 (1994).
Smarr, J. L. *Italian Renaissance Tales*, Rochester, Mich., Solaris Press, 1983.
Smith, A. J. *The Metaphysics of Love: Studies in Renaissance Love Poetry from Dante to Milton*, Cambridge, Cambridge University Press, 1988.
Smith, R. 'Admirable Musicians: Women's Songs in *Othello* and *The Maid's Tragedy*', *Comparative Drama*, 28 (fall, 1994).
Sorelius, G. *Shakespeare's Early Comedies: Myth, Metamorphosis, Mannerism*, Studia Anglistica Upsliensia 83. Uppsala, Uppsala University, 1993.
Sorelius G. and M. Srigley (eds), *Cultural Exchange between European Nations during the Renaissance*, Uppsala, Uppsala University, 1994.
Sorella, A. *Magia, lingua e commedia nel Machiavelli*, Florence, Olschki, 1990.
Steele, E. *Shakespeare and the Italian Professionals*, Taipei, Bookman, 1993.
Still, J. and M. Worton. 'Introduction', in J. Still and M. Worton (eds), *Intertextuality: Theories and Practices*, Manchester, Manchester Unversity Press, 1990.
Tarantino, E. *Le metamorfosi dell'amore: Lyly, Greene, Shakespeare e le origini della commedia romantica*, Rome, Bulzoni, 1995.
Tessari, R. *Commedia dell'Arte: La maschera e l'ombra*. Milan, Mursia, 1981.
Tonelli, F. 'Machiavelli's *Mandragola* and the Signs of Power', in J. Redmond (ed.), *Drama, Sex and Politics*, Cambridge, Cambridge University Press, 1985.
Turner, J. G. *Sexuality and Gender in Early Modern Europe: Institutions, Texts, Images*, Cambridge, Cambridge University Press, 1993.
Vickers, B. *Appropriating Shakespeare*, New Haven, Yale University Press, 1993.
Vultur, S. 'A propos des configurations intertextuelles', *Cahiers Roumains d'Etudes Littéraires*, 11:4 (1984).
Vultur, S. 'La place de l'intertextualité dans les théories de la réception du texte littéraire', *Cahiers Roumains d'Etudes Littéraires*, 13:3 (1986).
Weiner, A. D. 'Sidney/Spenser/Shakespeare: Influence/Intertextuality/Intention', in J. Clayton and E. Rothstein (eds), *Influence and Intertextuality in Literary History*, Madison, University of Wisconsin Press, 1991.
Whigham, F. *Ambition and Privilege: The Social Tropes of Elizabethan Courtesy Theory*, Berkeley, University of Calfornia Press, 1984.
Worton, M. 'Intertextuality: To Inter Textuality or to Resurrect It?', in D. Kelley and I.

Llasera (eds), *Cross-References: Modern French Theory and the Practice of Criticism*, Leeds, Society for French Studies, 1986.

Yates, F. A. 'Intertextualität', in *Textsoziologie: Eine kritische Einführung*, Stuttgart, J. B. Metzler, 1980.

Zepp, E. H. ,The Criticism of Julia Kristeva: A New Mode of Critical Thought', *Romanic Review*, 73 (1982).

Zumthor, P. 'L'intertexte performanciel', *Texte*, 2 (1983).

Index

Accademia Senese degli Intronati, 116
    Gl'Ingannati, 5, 107, 108, 109, 111, 114, 116, 122, 257
Adams, H. H., 88
Adlington, 209
Albrecht, Louis, 104
Aldrovandi, Ulisse, 242
Alexander, Peter, 242
Alighieri, Dante, 22, 24
    Divina Commedia, 24
Allen Brown, Pamela, 6, 145, 255, 257
Allen, Graham, 10
Anagnorisis, 230
Anamorphosis, 8
Anguissola, Sofonisba, 220, 226
Anima animalium, 183
Anima mundi, 183, 186, 190
Anima shaerarum, 183, 184, 186, 188, 192
Apelles, 200
Apius and Virginia, 75, 88
Appian, 51
Apuleius, 209
    Golden Ass, 209
Arabian Nights, 118
Archer, John, 155
Aretino, Pietro, 60, 65, 66, 69, 234, 256
    L'Astolfeide, 65, 67, 70
    L'Orlandino, 65, 66, 70, 256
    Lettere, 69
    Ragionamenti d'Amore, 66
    Ragionamenti delle Corti, 66
    Sonetti lussuriosi, 234
Arion and the Dolphin, 204
Ariosto, Lodovico, 1, 2, 5, 9, 21, 61, 67, 94, 95, 96, 99, 100, 101, 118, 122, 125, 126, 255
    Cassaria, 1

    Lena, 1
    Orlando Furioso, 5, 94, 95, 96, 97, 99, 100-2, 104
    Suppositi, 1, 9, 118, 122, 124, 125, 126
Aristotle, 1, 112, 113
    Rhetoric, 112
Ascham, Roger, 6, 131, 132, 133, 142, 143
    Scholemaster, 132, 142
Asor Rosa, Alberto, 88

Badaloni, Nicola, 88
Bakhtin, Mikhail, 2, 10
Baldriga, Irene, 241, 252
Baldwin, T. W., 122
Baldwin, William, 18
    Treatise of Moral Philosophy, 18
Ball, Robert H.,103, 104
Bande Nere, Giovanni, 60
Bandello, Matteo, 92, 93, 94, 95, 110, 111, 114, 117
Novelle, 110, 111, 117
Barbera, G., 9
Bargagli, Girolamo, 204
    Pellegrina, 204
Barilli, Renato, 88
Barkan, Leonard, 234, 238
Barkley, Richard, 121, 127
    Discourse of the Felicitie of Man, 121, 127
Barkstead, William, 247
Barnes, Jason, 215
Barolsky, Paul, 238
Barthelemy, Anthony, 6, 131, 156, 255
Barthes, Roland, 10, 13, 126
Bate, Jonathan, 25
Bawcutt, N. W., 87, 168, 172
Bayard, 60

Beaumont, Francis, 122, 159, 160, 172
  Knight of the Burning Pestle, 122
  Woman Hater, 159, 160, 165, 172
Bedingfield, Thomas, 161, 173
  Florentine History, 161, 173
Beecher, Donald, 106, 117
Belleforest, 92, 93
Bennington, Geoffrey, 112, 113, 117
Berger, Harry Jr., 168, 174
Berger, Thomas L., 126
Bernard, J. H., 226
Bernini, Anna, 57
Berry, Philippa, 237
Bevington, David, 24, 69, 70, 109, 116, 198, 200, 207, 214, 237
Bibbiena, 21
Blakemore Evans, G., 155, 226, 242
Blayney, Peter, 243
Blount, Edward, 32
Blumenthal, Arthur R., 214
Bly, Mary, 136, 137, 143, 169, 175
Boas, F. S., 122
Boccaccio, Giovanni, 2, 4, 62, 63, 64, 74, 75, 82, 87, 94, 104
  Decameron, 74, 82, 87, 88, 94
  Filostrato, 62, 63
Boitani, Piero, 69
Bolkonsky, Andréy, 60
Bonaparte, Napoleon, 60
Bondini, Francesco, 111
  Lezioni sopra il Comporre delle Novelle, 111
Book of Lismore, 120
Book of Sir Thomas More, 240, 241, 242, 243, 244, 247, 249, 257
Boorde, Andrew, 27, 34
  Fyrst Boke of the Introduction of Knowledge, 43
Boose, Lynda E., 155
Bordone, Paris, 218, 219, 226
Borsellino, Nino, 74, 87
Botticelli, 200
Boughner, Daniel C., 25
Bourdieu, Pierre, 26, 31, 32, 43, 44
Bowers, Fredson, 172
Bowles, Edmund A., 214
Braden, Gordon, 25
Bramble, Bartholomew, 33
Braudel, Fernand, 155
Bray, Alan, 143
Bright, Timothy, 185, 186
  Treatise of Melancholy, 185

Bristol, Michael, 150, 153, 156, 157
Brock, Susan, 174
Brognoligo, Gioachino, 9, 88, 117
Brooke, C. F. Tucker, 240, 241, 251
Brooke, Nicholas, 20, 25, 156
Brown, John Russell, 43, 88
Bruno, Giordano, 146, 154
  Cena de le Ceneri, 154
Bryden, Bill, 212
Budd, Frederick E., 103
Bullen, A. H., 172
Bullough, Geoffrey, 74, 87, 92, 103, 104, 116, 172, 174
Bunny, Edmund, 15
Buontalenti, B., 200, 206, 207
Burbage, Richard, 36, 122, 152, 157
Burrow, Colin, 105
Burt, Richard, 155
Burton, Robert, 121, 127
  Anatomy of Melancholy, 121, 127
Buzio, Ippolito, 241
Byrne, Donald, 225

Cairncross, Andrei S., 95, 104
Cairns, Christopher, 157
Calabresi, Bianca, 154
Caldwell, Mark, 69
Callaghan, Dympna, 106
Calvin, Thomas, 16
Camus, John Peter, 127
Caretti, Lanfranco, 104, 105, 106
Carr, Ralph, 121, 127
  Mahumetan or Turkish History, 121
Carracci, Ludovico, 200, 218, 219, 226
Castelvetro, Jacopo, 65
Castelvetro, Lodovico, 1
Castiglione, Baldassare, 161, 162, 168
  Libro del Cortegiano, 161
Cavillino, 204
Caxton, William, 62, 63, 70, 229
  Recueyll, 70
Celli, Aldo, 57
Cenni, Serena, 57
Chakravorty, Swapan, 226
Chapman, George, 16, 17, 18, 19, 62
  Bussy D'Ambois, 18
  Euthymiae Raptus, 16
  Iliad, 16
Chappuys, 94
Charney, Maurice, 25
Chastel, André, 237
Chaucer, Jeffrey, 62, 63, 64, 66

Troilus and Creseyde, 62, 66, 70
Chettle, Henry, 243
Chiappini, Luciano, 173
Chytraeus, David, 120, 127
  Chronicon Saxoniae, 120, 127
Cibber, 16
Cicero, 113
Cimabue, 239
Cioni, Fernando, 5, 118, 258
Clayton, Tom, 174
Clubb, Louise George, 9, 10, 21, 25, 76, 77, 88, 107, 116, 149, 156, 256, 258
Cohen, Stephen, 170, 172, 175
Cohen, Walter, 116
Colet, John, 7, 178
Colie, Rosalie, 112, 117
Collins, William, 121
Commedia dell'arte, 6, 148, 149, 150, 153, 258
Commedia erudita, 5, 77, 107, 110, 116
Commedia grave, 77, 80
Commedia nova, 2
Complicatio, 2
Conant, Virginia, 193
Condell, 240
Condell, Henry, 122
Consoli, Joseph P., 117
Contaminatio, 1, 2, 27, 77, 149
Contarini, 148
  Commonweath and Government of Venice, 148
Corneille, 59
Corti, Claudia, 7, 57, 176, 193, 255
Craik, T. W., 44, 103
Crane, Mary Thomas, 117
Crawford, Julie, 154
Crinò, Anna Maria, 173
Curtius, E. Robert, 69, 256, 258

Daalder, Joost, 25
D'Alembert, 59, 68
Dallington, Robert, 161, 162, 173
  Aphorismes Civill and Militarie, 161, 162, 173
  Survey of the Great Dukes State of Tuscany, 162, 173
D'Amico, Jack, 108, 116
Danesi Squarzina, Silvia, 241, 251
Daniel, P. A., 105
Daniell, David, 58
D'Argental, 59
Darriulat, Jacques, 232, 237

Davenport, Arnold, 173
Day, John, 159
  Humour Out of Breath, 159
De Caritat, J. A. Nicolas, 68
De la Harpe, 68
De' Medici, Ferdinand, 203, 206
De' Medici, Giovanni, 60, 69
De Mendonça, Barbara H., 155
Dekker, Thomas, 122, 156, 243
  If This Be Not a Good Play the Devil Is in It, 122
  Westward Ho!, 156
Della Casa, Giovanni, 168
Delle Colonne, Guido, 62, 63, 70
  Historia destructionis Troiae, 62, 63, 70
Derrida, 13
Desens, Marliss C., 89
Devereux, Robert, 32
Di Girolamo, Costanzo, 10
Dodson, D. B., 173
Dolce stil novo, 23
Dollimore, Jonathan, 173, 174
Domenichelli, Mario, 4, 59, 256, 257
Donne, John, 239, 241
  Storme, 239
Doran, Madeleine, 104
Doran, Susan, 175
Dorsch, T. S., 193
Drake, Francis, 133
Dronke, Peter, 198
Dryden, John, 16, 69
  Troilus and Cressida, 69
Duncan Jones, Katherine, 90, 252

Edmund Ironside, 240
Einstein, Lewis, 154, 156
Eisaman Maus, Katharine, 116
Ekphrastic intertextuality, 8, 219
Elam, Keir, 2, 3, 9, 26, 57, 58, 116, 118, 126, 253
Eldridge, Elaine, 69
Elizabeth I, 6, 23, 28, 133, 146, 151, 155, 166, 170, 172, 198
Elton, W. R., 88
Emerson, Caryl, 10
Emulatio, 1
Erasmus, 18, 24
  Adagia, 18
Essex, Earl of, 133
Exemplum (*exempla*), 111, 112, 113, 114

Faherty, Theresa J., 156

Fairfax, Edward, 61, 69, 198
  Jerusalem Delivered, 61, 198
Farjeon, Herbert, 242
Farley-Hills, David, 106
Farmer, Richard, 91, 103
Fenton, Geffraie, 117
  Certain Tragical Discourses, 117
Ferdinand II, 174
Ficino, Marsilio, 7, 176, 177, 178, 179, 180, 182, 183, 184, 188, 193
  Commentarium in Convivium, 178, 182, 188
  Compendium in Timaeum, 178
  Theologia Platonica, 176, 178, 181, 183, 188, 190
Field, John, 122
Fiorentino, Giovanni, 75, 132
  Pecorone, 75, 132
Fisch, Harold, 209, 210, 215
Fischer, Bobby, 225
Fiston, William, 62
Flavio's Fortunes, 149
Fletcher, John, 122, 241
  Two Noble Kinsmen, 241
Florio, John, 36, 44, 91, 103
  First Frutes, 91
  Second Frutes, 91
Foucault, Michel, 68, 163, 173, 254, 258
Fowler, Bridget, 43, 44
Frampton, John, 119
Frantz, David O., 238
Freud, Sigmund, 21
Frizzi, Federico, 241
Frye, Roland M., 89

Gabrieli, Vittorio, 242, 249, 252
Gainsford, James, 160, 173
  Glory of England, 160, 173
Garner, Shirley Nelson, 156
Garrick, David, 16
Gascoigne, Gorge, 118, 121, 122, 126
  Jocasta, 121
  Supposes, 118, 122, 124, 126
Gibbons, Brian, 166, 174, 237
Gilbert, Allan H., 117
Giotto, 239, 244
Giraldi Cinthio, G. B., 1, 2, 4, 5, 9, 73, 74, 79, 80, 81, 82, 84, 85, 86, 87, 88, 91, 92, 93, 95, 97, 100, 101, 110, 112, 113, 117, 159, 255
  Dialoghi della Vita Civile, 80
  Discorso Intorno al Comporre delle Commedie e delle Tragedie, 1, 9, 80
  Discorso intorno al Comporre dei Romanzi, 113, 117
  Epitia, 73, 74, 81, 82, 92, 93, 103
  Hecatommithi, 73, 79, 80, 82-4, 88, 92, 94, 96, 104, 110, 159
  Orbecche, 80, 88
  Tragedie, 92
Girard, René, 153
Girolamo (da Cremona), 220, 226
Giustiniani, Vincenzo, 241, 242
Giustiniani, Zorzi, 207, 208
Goffe, Thomas, 154
Goldberg, Jonathan, 154
Goldberg, Jonathan, 173
Gombrich, Ernst, 237
Gosselin, Edward A., 154
Gough, Melinda, 154
Goulart, Simon, 121
  Histoires admirables et mémorables, 121
Grafton, Antony, 24, 25
Gratian, 24
  Decretum, 24
Greenaway, 8, 216, 224, 225
  Prospero's Books, 216, 224, 225
Greenblatt, Stephen, 2, 10, 68, 116, 143, 168, 172, 174
Greene, Robert, 5, 62, 70, 96, 97, 98, 99, 100, 105, 106, 121, 255
  Arrenopia, 97
  Euphues, His Censure to Philautus, 62
  Historie of Orlando Furioso, 96, 97, 98, 105
  Historie of Iames the Fourth, 96, 97, 121
  Pandosto, 96
Greene, Thomas M., 16
Greene, Thomas M., 24
Greenfield, Thelma, 121, 127
Greg, W. W., 105, 242, 244
Greville, Fulke, 60, 146
Griffin, N. E., 70
Grimstone, Edward, 121
Grynaeus, Simone, 119
  Novus Orbis, 119
Guarini, Giambattista, 1, 9, 80, 88
  Compendio della Poesia Tragicomica, 1, 9, 80, 81
  Pastor Fido, 22, 81, 88
Guerrieri Crocetti, C., 9
Guicciardini, Francesco, 7, 132, 143, 161, 162
  Storia d'Italia, 132, 143

Guilhamet, Leon, 148, 155
Guizot, F., 69
Gurr, Andrew, 44, 146, 154, 156

Hakluyt, 119, 120
Hall, Kim F., 151, 156
Hankins, John E., 178, 193
Hanson, Elizabeth, 167, 174, 175
Happé, Peter, 88
Harbage, Alfred, 169, 174
Harington, 94, 95
Harker, Richard, 43
Harris, Bernard, 156
Harris, John, 215
Harrison, Tony, 212
Harrison, William, 26, 27, 28, 29, 30, 31, 32, 33, 34, 43, 44
    Description of England, 26, 27, 28
Hartt, Frederick, 234, 238
Harvey, Gabriel, 19
Hawkins, 133
Haydocke, 252
Heminge, 240
Hendricks, Margo, 151, 156
Henke, Robert, 9, 108, 116
Henley, W. E., 87
Henslowe, Philip, 240
    Diary, 240
Herbert, George, 24
Herford, C. H., 214, 215
Herford, James, 70
Herrick, Marvin T., 88
Heuterus, 120, 121, 127
    De rerum Burgundicarum, 120, 127
Heyes, Thomas, 131
Heywood, Thomas, 76, 153, 240, 243
    Rape of Lucrece, 76
Hoepfl, Harro, 87
Hogarth, William, 252
Holinshed, 26
Holland, Peter, 25
Holland, Philemon, 76, 209
Holquist, Michael, 10
Holtgen, Karl Joseph, 173
Homer, 16, 17, 19, 62
    Iliad, 4, 59, 62, 65
Homily against Excess of Apparel, 28, 29
Honigmann, E. A. J., 104, 105, 106, 156, 157
Hooker, Richard, 23
    Laws of Ecclesiastical Polity, 23
Horace, 123
Horne, P. R., 103

Howard, Jean E., 116
Howard-Hill, T. H., 24, 226
Hunter, G. K., 132, 143, 154, 156, 174, 237
Hunter, R. G., 89
Huttich, Giovanni, 119

Imitatio, 1, 19
Innocenti, Loretta, 57
Intermedi, 204, 205, 206, 207, 257
Inventio, 39
Iselin, Pierre, 238

Jackson, James L., 44
Jaggard, William, 24
James I, 23, 102, 146, 147, 155, 159, 165, 166, 168, 172, 174, 206, 222
    Basilikon Doron, 168
    Lepanto, 102
    True Law of Free Monarchies, 168
Janson, H. W., 237
Jardine, Lisa, 214
Jenkins, Harold, 44, 242, 243
Johnson, Samuel, 19, 145, 154
Jones, Ann Rosalind, 155
Jones, Emrys, 14, 24, 102, 106, 155
Jones, Inigo, 197, 200, 206, 208, 257
    Hymenaei, 207
    Masque of Beauty, 207
    Masque of Blackness, 207
    Tethy's Festival, 207
Jonson, Ben, 15, 19, 36, 44, 155, 207, 208, 214, 218, 232, 233
    Every Man in His Humour, 15, 36
    Every Man Out is Humour, 155
    Hymenaei, 207
    Masque at Lord Haddington's Marriage, 207
    Masque of Beauty, 207
    Masque of Blackness, 207, 232
    Masque of Queens, 19, 207, 233
Jowet, John, 174
Juvenal, 123

Kamps, Ivo, 162, 172, 173, 174
Kant, Immanuel, 219, 226
Kernan, Alvin, 155
Keyte, Hugh, 214
Kirkpatrick, Robin, 90, 110, 117
Klein, Robert, 193
Klibansky, R., 193
Knolles, Richard, 102
    Generall Historie of the Turkes, 102

Kristeller, Paul Oscar, 193
Kristeva, Julia, 10, 13, 253, 258
Kurosawa, Akira, 16
Kyd, Thomas, 20, 133, 136
  Spanish Tragedy, 3, 18, 121

Labalme, Patricia, 135, 143
Laelia, 122
Lancashire, Ian, 43
Langher, Ullrich, 82, 89
Laroque, François, 8, 227, 255, 258
Lascelles, Mary, 74, 87, 92, 103, 104, 172
Lawrence, Jason, 5, 91, 255
Lea, K. M., 157
Lee, A. C., 87
Lee, Brian S., 237
Leech, Clifford, 242
Lefèvre, Raoul, 62, 63
  Recueil, 62
Leggatt, Alexander, 10, 174
Leonardo, 231
  Treatise on Painting, 231
Lerner, Lawrence S., 154
Les Abusez, 122
Letourneur, Pierre, 59, 68
Lever, James W., 88, 89, 94, 104
Levith, Murray J., 142
Levy Peck, Linda, 174
Lewkenor, Lewis, 146, 147
Lily, William, 115
Livy, 75
Lloyd, Janet, 154
Locatelli, Angela, 154, 155
Lomazzo, Giovanni Paolo, 252
  Trattato della pittura, 252
Lorch, Maristella, 94, 96, 104, 106
Lorraine, Christina of, 203, 206
Lothian, J. M., 44, 92, 103
Loughrey, Bryan, 226
Lucan, 123
Lucas, F. L., 88
Luther, Martin, 4, 16, 73, 74, 87
  On Secular Authority, 73, 87
Lyly, John, 20
Lynch, Stephen J., 70, 154
Lyotard, 68

MacCallum, 19, 25
Machiavelli, Nicolò, 7, 21, 65, 147, 161, 162, 173, 203
  Florentine History, 161
  Principe, 65

Machin, Lewis, 247
Mad Princess, 149
Maguin, Jean-Marie, 237
Maguire, Laurie, 126
Mahar, Cheleen, 43
Mahon, John W., 172
Mallin, Eric, 69
Mantegna, 231, 232
  Martyrdom of St Sebastian, 231, 232
  Minerva Expelling the Vices, 231
Mantuan, 17
  Eclogues, 17
Marcel, Raymond, 193
Maria Magdalena, 199, 200
Marienstras, Richard, 154
Markham, Francis, 42, 44
  Book of Honour, 42
Marlowe, Christopher, 16, 19, 20, 133, 136, 177, 238
  Doctor Faustus, 16
  Hero and Leander, 19
  Jew of Malta, 238
Marowitz, 16
Marrapodi, Michele, 1, 4, 9, 10, 73, 88, 126, 142, 154, 256
Marsden, William, 120, 127
Marston, John, 8, 122, 146, 155, 159, 160, 161, 162, 164, 166, 167, 173, 247, 251
  Certaine Satyres, 173
  Fawn, 160, 165, 166, 167, 168, 173
  Insatiate Countess, 247, 251, 252
  Malcontent, 122, 155, 159, 160, 162, 163, 166, 170, 172, 173, 175
  Sophonisba or the Wonder of Women, 122
Martial, 129
Marx, Karl, 21
Marx, S., 90
Mason Vaughan, Virginia, 155, 156
Mason, H. A., 70
Mati, Piero, 232
McCleod, Randall, 24
McCollum, Linda Carlyle, 44
Melchiori, Giorgio, 8, 90, 239, 249, 252, 257
Merbury, Charles, 161
Michelangelo, 232, 241, 242, 244, 245, 246, 247, 250, 252
  Cristo Redentore, 245, 248, 250
  Cristo Risorto, 246, 247, 252
Middleton, Thomas, 8, 122, 159, 162, 164, 166, 167, 173, 216, 222, 223, 225
  Game at Chess, 216, 222, 226

Phoenix, 159, 160, 162, 166, 168
Michaelmas Term, 122
Miles, Rosalind, 172
Miller, Roy S., 126
Milton, John, 22
   Paradise Lost, 22
Minturno, 112, 113, 117
   Arte Poetica, 113, 117
Miola, Robert S., 2, 3, 9, 10, 13, 25, 253, 254, 255
Mirandula, 18
   Illustrium poetarum flores, 18
Mitchell, Bonner, 173
Mochi, Giovanna, 57
Moi, Toril, 10
Moland, Louis, 69
Molière, 59
Mooney, M., 193
More Smith, G. C., 122
More, Thomas, 19
   Confutation of Tyndale's Answer, 19
Moreau, Jean-Pierre, 238
Morel, Philippe, 237
Moretti, Franco, 163, 173
Moretti, Walter, 88
Morley, Henry, 69
Morsberger, Robert E., 44
Moss, Ann, 117
Mossman, Judith, 215
Moulton, Ian, 154
Muir, Kenneth, 93, 104, 172
Mulryne, J. R., 7, 104, 142, 197, 215, 257, 258
Munday, Anthony, 243
Munro, John, 242
Musa, Mark, 25
Musica humana, 204
Musica mundana, 205
Muzio, 43
   Il duello, 43

Nashe, Thomas, 19, 132, 146
   Unfortunate Traveller, 132
Natura naturans, 232
Neill, Michael, 146, 154, 237
Netto, Jeffrey, 8, 216, 257
New Comedy, 170
Nice, Richard, 23
Norden, John, 26
   Civitatis Londini, 26
North, Thomas, 19, 198, 200, 202, 203, 206, 211

North, Thomas, 58
Norton, H. G., 127
Nova tragedia, 2, 80
Novellino, 110, 117

O'Brian, Edward J., 89
O'Malley, Susan, 154
Onomastic intertextuality, 23
Orgel, Stephen, 208, 215, 234, 238
Ovid, 18, 20
   Metamorphoses, 18

Paccagnella, Ivano, 10
Pafford, J. H. P., 238
Pagano De Divitiis, Gigliola, 155
Painter, William, 76, 104, 111
   Palace of Pleasure, 76, 104, 111-12
Panofsky, E., 193
Paré, Ambroise, 233
Parolin, Peter, 154
Parrott, Andrew, 214
Patey, Caroline, 92, 103
Payne, Susan, 57
Peacham, 23
Peacock, John, 206, 207
Pechter, Edward, 155
Peele, George, 121
   Batte of Alcazar, 121
   Old Wives Tale, 121
Pelling, C. B. R., 214
Pendleton, Thomas A., 172
Penman, Bruce, 116
Pepoli (Pipino), Francesco, 119
Pequigney, Joseph, 144
Peripeteia, 93
Persius, 123
Persons, Robert, 15
   Christian Directory, 15
   First Book of the Christian Exercise, 15
Petowe, Henry, 19
Petrarch, Francesco, 22, 25, 66, 228
   Canzoniere, 22, 66, 228
Petter, Christopher G., 174, 175
Peyré, Yves, 232, 237, 238
Piccolomini, Angelo, 1
Pichot, A., 69
Pinciss, Gerald, M., 89
Pisani, Ugolino, 77
   Philogenia, 77
Plautus, 2, 9, 77, 107, 118, 122, 123
   Captivi, 9
   Menaechmi, 107

Mostellaria, 122, 123-6
Plett, Heinrich F.,10, 13, 24
Plutarch, 3, 20, 45, 48, 50, 54, 57, 118, 197, 200, 201, 202, 203, 209, 211, 212, 236, 255, 257
   Life of Antony, 50, 51, 53, 54, 198, 200
   Life of Brutus, 48, 49, 51, 53, 54, 55
   Life of Caesar, 48, 49, 50, 51, 52, 53
   Lives, 3, 45, 51, 236
   Of Isis and Osiris, 209
Pocock, J. G. A., 155
Polo, Marco, 119, 120
Pomponazzi, 233
Porcelli, Bruno, 88
Porter, Joseph A., 228, 237
Poulsen, Rachel, 154
Praz, Mario, 103
Pressler, Charlotte, 5, 107, 257
Presson, Robert K., 70
Printing intertextuality, 24
Procaccioli, Paolo, 69
Proudfoot, Richard, 81, 89, 174
Pruvost, René, 117
Pugliatti, Paola, 9
Pugliatti, Teresa, 9
Purchas, Samuel, 119, 120, 127
   His Pilgrims, 119, 120, 127
Puttenham, George, 30

Quadri, Marcella, 57
Quintilian, 113

Racine, 59
Ralegh, Walter, 19, 60, 133
Ramusio, G. B., 119, 127
Randolph, Thomas, 122
   Muses Looking-Glass, 122
Raphael, 207, 234
Reception intertextuality, 24
Redmond, Michael J., 6, 7, 10, 158, 174, 256, 257
Reign of Edward the Third, 241, 243, 244, 247, 251, 252, 257
Richards, Kenneth, 153, 157
Richards, Laura, 153, 157
Riche, Barnabe, 92, 93, 104, 110, 114, 115, 117
   Apolonius and Silla, 110, 114
   Riche his Farewell to Militarie Profession, 92, 93, 117
Riddell, James A., 24
Riffaterre, Michael, 24

Robb, N. A., 193
Robortello, Francesco, 1
Rocke, Michael, 143
Rodax, Yvonne, 114, 117
Romano, Giulio, 234, 236
   Posizioni, 234, 236
Romei, Danilo, 70
Rossi, Sebastiano, 205
Rossi, Sergio, 89, 103, 174
Rouillet, Claude, 73
   Philanira, 73
Rowe, Nicholas, 19
Rubinstein, Frankie, 233
Ruggiero, Guido, 135, 143
Rymer, Thomas, 145, 149, 153, 154, 156
   Short View of Tragedy, 154

Sainte-Maure, Benoit de, 62, 63, 70
   Roman de Troye
Salerno, Henry F., 156
Salingar, Leo, 25, 234
Sammut, Alfonso, 106
Sanders, Norman, 105
Santa Ella (Santella), Rodrigo, 119
Saslow, James M., 203, 204, 205, 206, 214
Savage, James E., 69
Saviolo, Vincentio, 33, 34, 35, 36, 37, 38, 39, 40, 41, 44, 256
   Vincentio Saviolo His Practise, 33, 35, 36, 37, 39, 40, 41
Savoia, Dianella, 89, 103, 174
Saxl, F., 193
Scala, Flaminio, 156
   Teatro delle Favole Rappresentative, 156
Scarabelli, Orazio, 204
Scelus, 80
Schleiner, L., 90
Scott Kastan, David, 155
Segre, Cesare, 2, 9, 10, 22, 25, 258
Selleck, Nancy, 154
Sells, Lytton Arthur, 103
Seneca, 18, 123
Serpieri, Alessandro, 2, 3, 10, 45, 126, 255, 257
Shackford, M. Hale, 96, 105
Shaheen, Naseeb, 90, 103
Shakespeare, W., *passim*
   All's Well That Ends Well, 82
   Antony and Cleopatra, 7, 8, 118, 197-215, 227, 230-3, 257, 258
   As You Like It, 17, 37, 96, 105, 133, 222, 226

Coriolanus, 49, 118
Hamlet, 3, 17, 29, 34-5, 37-8, 40, 43, 61, 62, 81, 136, 217, 231
1 Henry IV, 14
2 Henry IV, 17
Henry VIII, 45
Julius Caesar, 7, 19, 47-58, 81, 118, 176, 182-93, 238, 255
King Lear, 15, 61, 182
Love's Labour's Lost, 17, 22, 44
Macbeth, 178
Measure for Measure, 4, 6, 7, 73, 73-90, 92, 93, 94, 96, 97, 104, 158-75, 256
Merchant of Venice, 3, 6, 29-31, 78, 131-44, 147, 154, 182
Merry Wives of Windsor, 157
Midsummer Night's Dream, 21, 141, 217, 228, 233
Much Ado About Nothing, 95
Othello, 4, 5, 6, 92, 93, 94, 96, 98, 99, 100, 101, 102, 104, 105, 145-57, 255, 257
Passionate Pilgrim, 24
Pericles, 240
Rape of Lucrece, 228
Richard II, 133
Richard III, 17
Romeo and Juliet, 8, 22, 35-6, 227, 228-30, 233, 237
Taming of the Shrew, 4, 5, 118, 121, 123, 124, 125, 256
Titus Andronicus, 76, 228, 240
Troilus and Cressida, 4, 59, 60, 62, 64, 65, 66, 68, 81, 256, 257
Tempest, 8, 81, 212, 219, 220-6, 257
Twelfth Night, 3, 5, 31, 32, 38-43, 92, 93, 107, 108, 109, 110, 111, 114, 115, 116, 163, 171, 257
Two Noble Kinsmen, 241
Winter's Tale, 8, 96, 227, 230, 234-7
Shalvi, Alice, 70
Shapiro, James, 140, 144
Sharpham, Edward, 7, 159, 162, 164, 165, 169, 170, 174
 Fleire, 7, 159, 162, 164, 165, 169, 170
Sherbo, Arthur, 154
Sheridan, Alan, 173
Shewring, Margaret, 104, 215
Sidney, Philip, 4, 60
Siegel, Paul N., 69
Silver, George, 32, 33, 34, 38, 43, 44, 256
 Paradoxes of Defence, 32, 33, 34
Simonini, Rinaldo C., 91, 103

Simpson, Evelyn, 214, 215
Simpson, Percy, 214, 215
Sinfield, Alan, 89, 171, 173, 175
Sinklo, John, 122
Sissons,, C. J., 242
Skeat, W. W., 70
Skelton, John, 110
 Magnificence, 110
Smarr, Janet L., 106
Smarr, Janet Levarie, 117
Smart, Stuart, 91, 94, 103, 104
Smith, Gerald A., 173
Smith, Nicholas, 69
Snuggs, Henry L., 117
Snyder, Susan, 155
Sommers, Oskar, 70
Spanmueller (Jacobus Pontanus), 19
 Symbolarum libri XVII Virgilii, 19
Spencer, T. J. B., 200, 214
Spenser, Edmund, 19, 22, 95, 177, 209
 Faerie Queene, 22, 209
 Shepherd's Calendar, 19
Spivack, Bernard, 144
Sprengnether, Madelon, 156
Sprezzatura, 161
Spurgeon, Caroline F. E., 24
St Augustine, 16, 74
 De sermone Domini in monte, 74
St Bernard, 16
Stallybrass, Peter, 155
Still, Judith, 10
Stoker, Whitley, 127
Stow, John, 26
 Survey of London, 26
Strachey, Lytton, 69
Strong, Roy, 203, 214, 215
Stubbes, Philip, 135, 136, 143
 Anatomy of Abuses, 143
Summers, Montague, 69

Taming of a Shrew, 5, 118, 121, 122, 123, 125
Tarlton, Richard, 36
Tasso, Torquato, 61, 102, 106, 198
 Aminta, 22
 Gerusalemme Liberata, 61, 102, 106
Tate, 16
Taylor, Gary, 24, 69, 164, 173, 174, 242
Taylor, Neil, 226
Tennenhouse, Leonard, 172, 174
Terence, 2, 9, 77, 122
 Eunuchus, 9
Thiselton, Alfred Edward, 127

Thomas à Kempis, 16
Thomas, William, 138, 141, 143, 146, 161
    History of Italy, 138, 141, 143
Tillyard, E. M. W., 23
Tolstoy, 60
Tragedia di fin lieto, 80, 82, 92, 94
Tragedy of Gonzago, 61
Trask, Willard R., 258
Tricomi, Albert, 172, 174
Tyndale, 19
Tyndale, William, 76, 88

Ubaldini, Petruccio, 65
Upton, Albert W., 174
Urbano, Pietro, 241

Valla, Lorenzo, 24
Van Mander, Karel, 218, 219, 226
Varholy, Cristine, 154
Vari, Metello, 241
Vasari, 234
Velz, John W., 24
Vickers, Brian, 24
Villari, Susanna, 88
Vince, Ronald W., 116
Virgil, 18, 19, 20, 24
    Aeneid, 99
Vitkus, Daniel J., 154
Vives, Juan Luis, 121, 127
Voltaire, 59, 68
    Lettre sur les Anglais, 59
Voragine, James de, 229
    Golden Legend, 229, 236

Waldman, Guido, 104, 105, 106

Warner, William, 161, 173
    Albion's England, 161, 173
Warton, Thomas, 121, 127
Watson, Curtis Brown, 70
Webster, John, 76, 88, 122, 146, 156
    Appius and Virginia, 76, 88
    Westward Ho!, 156
Wells, Stanley, 24, 69, 242
West, E. J., 103
Whetstone, George, 73, 74, 89, 93, 94, 96, 164, 174
    Heptameron of Civill Discourses, 73, 94
    Promos and Cassandra, 73, 74, 89, 94, 96, 164, 174
Whitington, L., 43
Wilders, John, 214, 237
Wilkes, Chris, 43
Willems, Michèle, 237
Wilson, Jean, 214
Wine, M. L., 173
Withington, Lothrop, 28
Wolfe, John, 24
Wood, Alfred C., 155
Woodward, Jennifer, 215
Worton, Michael, 10
Wright, George T., 143
Wright, Herbert G., 104
Wright, William, 142
Wyatt, Thomas, 22, 25

Yates, Francis A., 193
Young, Carl, 69

Zappia, C., 9
Zwingli, 16

EU authorised representative for GPSR:
Easy Access System Europe, Mustamäe tee 50,
10621 Tallinn, Estonia
gpsr.requests@easproject.com

www.ingramcontent.com/pod-product-compliance
Ingram Content Group UK Ltd.
Pitfield, Milton Keynes, MK11 3LW, UK
UKHW021847140426
5217IPUK00022B/1640